Law Sex And Crime

Law Sex And Crime

BY

Kush Kalra
&
Priyanka Barupal

Foreword by

K K Venugopal

(Senior Advocate)

Vij Books India Pvt Ltd

New Delhi (India)

Published by

Vij Books India Pvt Ltd
2/19, Ansari Road, Darya Ganj
New Delhi - 110002
Phones: 91-11- 43596460, 47340674
Fax: 91-11-47340674
e-mail : vijbooks@rediffmail.com
web : www.vijbooks.com

© 2013, Kush Kalra

First Published   : 2013

ISBN   : 978-93-82652-22-9

Acknowledgements

My special thanks to Bhanu Tanwar (Student of Law, NLU Delhi), Ayushi Gaur (Student of Law, Symbiosis), and Shanya Ruhela (Student of Law, RGNUL) for helping me in research work.

Contents

Acknowledgements   v

Foreword   xi

List of Abbreviations   xiii

Rape   1

1. Depth of Penetration in Rape is Immaterial   9

2. Forcible Sexual Intercourse amounts to Rape   13

3. Semen Stains on Salwar does not Necessarily Mean Rape   16

4. Relaxation in Rape Punishment on Account of Age of Accused   19

5. Gang Rape   22

6. Death sentence converted to imprisonment for rest of life for
    Rape of a Two Year Old Girl   24

7. Partial Penetration is Sufficient to Constitute the Offence of Rape   28

8. Denial of Bail in Case of Rape   31

9. Death Penalty for the offence of Rape   33

10. Rapist degrades the very soul of the helpless female   38

11. Outraging the Modesty of Women   43

12. Attempt to commit rape is lesser offence than that of rape   49

13. No Mercy to Accused in Case of Rape   52

14. Rape and Murder done by Father on His Daughter;
    Not a Fit case for Death Penalty   56

15. Rape and Murder of Two Young Girls, Fit case for Death Penalty   60

16. False Allegation of Rape   68

17. Death Penalty for Rape 73

18. Attempt to Commit Rape not to be treated at par with Rape 81

Prostitution **87**

19. Setting up of Separate Wing in Police for dealing with Immoral Trafficking 90

20. Method to eradicate Prostitution or at least further preventing is to Educate Girls 96

21. Child Prostitution 107

22. Illegitimate sons of a Prostitute would be included within term 'member of family' 113

23. Carrying on trade of Public Prostitution within specified area 116

24. Prostitutes are entitled to live a life of Dignity 119

25. Selling and buying minor for purposes of Prostitution 123

26. Custody of Minor Child Not Given to Prostitute Mother 125

27. Right to Privacy of Unchaste Woman 129

28. Right of Prostitutes to Live with Dignity 132

Sexual Harassment, Pornography, Obscenity & Female Foeticide **135**

29. Annulment of marriage on ground of impotency 142

30. Marriage Promise and Cheating 148

31. Sexual harassment at working place 153

32. Sexual harassment of women at workplace 158

33. Divorce can be granted on ground of cruelty 165

34. Woman be treated with proper respect and Dignity in Society 170

35. Cabaret dances and Obscenity 174

36. Obscenity and Pornography 177

37. Artistic Freedom and Obscenity 182

38. Internet and Pornographic Material 189

39. Publishing Sex oriented material in Newspapers and its ill
effects on Minors 194

40. Abuse and Trafficking 205

41. DNA Test to Determine Paternity 212

**Miscellaneous (Surrogacy, Illegitimate Child, Divorce, Maternity
Leave, Dowry Death, Abortion) 217**

42. Is Surrogate Mother entitled to Maternity Benefits? 228

43. Illegitimate Children Right to Succession in Property 233

44. Identity of Children born from Surrogate Mother 242

45. Guidelines for assisting the Victims of Rape 246

46. Privately viewing obscene film constitutes no offence 252

47. Picture of Woman in the Nude is not per se Obscene 254

48. Showing Blue Films to Young Men will constitute Obscenity 260

49. Vulgar language used in book would not be deemed to be
obscene 264

50. Divorce must be for a reasonable cause 267

51. Irretrievable Breakdown of Marriage 270

52. Sting Operations to Defame Someone 277

53. Female student could not be deprived from her student status
because of her pregnancy 283

54. Mother is Natural Guardian of Minor 288

55. Domestic Violence against Women 292

56. Dowry Death 297

57. Punishment for Adultery 302

58. Compulsory Registration for Marriage — 307

59. Right to Marriage and Right to Privacy — 310

60. De-criminalization of consensual - same - sex acts — 315

61. Unnatural Sex — 333

62. Second marriage during subsistence of first marriage is void — 337

63. Beauty contests not obscene under any law — 342

64. Pregnancies and Abortion — 348

65. Mentally retarded women and Abortion — 354

66. Medical Examination and Right to Privacy — 359

67. Two-finger test violates victim's privacy and dignity — 362

Glossary of Common Legal Terms — 367

Foreword

When Kush Kalra interned in my chambers in January, 2012, I was impressed by his enthusiasm and eagerness to imbibe as much knowledge and information as he could about the theory and practice of Law. His passion for the law, and legal profession was palpable. I am, therefore, not surprised at all that he has written this book and that too on a subject which is of great contemporary relevance in our society today, as, unfortunately, this vice appears to have become endemic. Kush has succinctly and lucidly summarised important judgements on the subject using simple prose and an appealing presentation. This book is a veritable trove of useful material and I am certain that it will be of great utility to layperson and lawyer alike.

New Delhi

14 Jul 2013

K. K. Venugopal

Senior Advocate

Dr. Virendra Kumar,
　　LL.M., S.J.D. (Toronto, Canada)

Tel.: (0172) 2661459(R)
9465217528 (M)
Residence: 1459, Sector 42-B,
Chandigarh 160036
E-mail: vkumar1459_42@yahoo.co.in

Formerly:
Founding Director (Academics),
Chandigarh Judicial Academy;
Professor & Chairman, Department of Laws,
Dean, Faculty of Law; Fellow, Panjab University; &
UGC Emeritus Fellow

June 4, 2013

　　I do admire Kush Kalra for attempting to write a book on *Law, Sex and Crime* at the very threshold of his legal career. A bare perusal of the contents of the book reveals that he painstakingly collected the various judgments of the courts of record impinging upon the realm of criminal law, family law, and constitutional law, and human rights. Through such a maiden venture, involving critical analysis, he has not only equipped himself in one of the major areas of legal practice, but also set an example for very many young entrants showing concretely how to go about in life before 'briefs' start pouring in!

I do hope that the young mind would now intensely explore, how come 'sex', symbolizing the natural instinct of love, turn into an act of 'crime'! This, in turn, him to use 'law' as a powerful instrument to prevent this perversion.

I extend my best wishes to Kush Kalra.

(Virendra Kumar)

Where The Mind Is Without Fear

Where the mind is without fear and the head is held high
Where knowledge is free
Where the world has not been broken up into fragments
By narrow domestic walls
Where words come out from the depth of truth
Where tireless striving stretches its arms towards perfection
Where the clear stream of reason has not lost its way
Into the dreary desert sand of dead habit
Where the mind is led forward by thee
Into ever-widening thought and action
Into that heaven of freedom, my Father, let my country awake

Rabindranath Tagore

List of Abbreviations

AIR	-	All India Reporter
Bom	-	Bombay
D.B.	-	Division Bench
Govt.	-	Government
ILR	-	Indian Law Reporter
IPC	-	Indian Penal Code
Lah	-	Lahore
LJ	-	Law Journal
LR	-	Law Reporter
Mah	-	Maharashtra
M.P.	-	Madhya Pradesh
P.C	-	Privy Council
P&H	-	Punjab and Haryana
Sec	-	Section
SC	-	Supreme Court
SCC	-	Supreme Court Cases
SCR	-	Supreme Court Reporter

Rape

The offence of rape occurs in Chapter XVI of IPC. It is an offence affecting the human body. In that chapter, there is a separate heading for 'Sexual offence', which esSections 375[1], 376, 376A[2], 376B[3], 376C[4], and 376D[5]. `Rape'

---

1 **Section 375 in The Indian Penal Code, 1860**

375. Rape.-- A man is said to commit" rape" who, except in the case hereinafter excepted, has sexual intercourse with a woman under circumstances falling under any of the six following descriptions:- First.- Against her will. Secondly.- Without her consent. Thirdly.- With her consent, when her consent has been obtained by putting her or any person in whom she is interested in fear of death or of hurt. Fourthly.- With her consent, when the man knows that he is not her husband, and that her consent is given because she believes that he is another man to whom she is or believes herself to be lawfully married. Fifthly.- With her consent, when, at the time of giving such consent, by reason of unsoundness of mind or intoxication or the administration by him personally or through another of any stupefying or unwholesome substance, she is unable to understand the nature and consequences of that to which she gives consent. Sixthly.- With or without her consent, when she is under sixteen years of age. Explanation.- Penetration is sufficient to constitute the sexual intercourse necessary to the offence of rape. Exception.- Sexual intercourse by a man with his own wife, the wife not being under fifteen years of age, is not rape.

2 **Section 376A in The Indian Penal Code, 1860**

376A. Intercourse by a man with his wife during separation.-- Whoever has sexual intercourse with his own wife, who is living separately from him under a decree of separation or under any custom or usage without her consent shall be punished with imprisonment of either description for a term which may extend to two years and shall also be liable to fine.

3 **Section 376B in The Indian Penal Code, 1860**

376B. Intercourse by public servant with woman in his custody.-- Whoever, being a public servant, takes advantage of his official position and induces or seduces, any woman, who is in his custody as such public servant or in the custody of a public servant subordinate to him, to have sexual intercourse with him, such sexual intercourse not amounting to the offence of rape, shall be punished with imprisonment of either description for a term which may extend to five years and shall also be liable to fine.

4 **Section 376C in The Indian Penal Code, 1860**

376C. Intercourse by superintendent of jail, remand home, etc.-- Whoever, being the superintendent or manager of a jail, remand home or other place of custody established by or under any law for the time being in force or of a women' s or children' s institution takes advantage of his official position and induces or seduces any female inmate of such jail, remand home, place or institution to have sexual intercourse with him, such sexual intercourse not amounting to the offence of rape, shall be punished with imprisonment of either description for a term which may extend to five years and shall also be liable to fine. Explanation 1.-" Superintendent" in relation to a jail, remand home or other place of custody or a women' s or children' s institution, includes a person holding any other office in such jail, remand home, place or institution by virtue of which he can exercise any authority or control over its inmates. Explanation 2.- The expression" women' s or children' s institution" shall have the same meaning as in Explanation 2 to sub- section (2) of section 376.

5 **Section 376D in The Indian Penal Code, 1860**

376D. Intercourse by any member of the management or staff of a hospital with any woman in that hospital.-- Whoever, being on the management of a hospital or being on the staff of a hospital takes advantage of his position and has sexual intercourse with any woman in that hospital, such sexual intercourse not amounting to the offence of rape, shall be punished with imprisonment of either description for a term which may extend to five years and shall also be liable to fine. Explanation.- The expression" hospital" shall have the same meaning as in Explanation 3 to sub-is defined in Section 375. Sections 375 and 376 have been substantially changed by Criminal Law (Amendment) Act, 1983, and several new sections were introduced by the new Act, i.e. 376A, 376B, 376C and 376D. The fact that sweeping changes were introduced reflects the legislative intent to curb with iron hand, the offence of rape which affects the dignity of a woman. The offence of rape in its simplest term is `the ravishment of a woman, without her consent, by force, fear or fraud', or as `the carnal knowledge of a woman by force against her will'. 'Rape' or `Raptus' is when a man hath carnal knowledge of a woman by force and against her will; or as expressed more fully,' rape is the carnal knowledge of any woman, above the age of particular years, against her will; or of a woman child, under that age, with or against her will'. The essential words in an indictment for rape are rapuit and carnaliter cognovit; but carnaliter cognovit, nor any other circumlocution without the word rapuit, are not sufficient in a legal sense to express rape. In the crime of rape, `carnal knowledge' means the penetration to any the slightest degree of the organ alleged to have been carnally known by the male organ of generation[6]. In `Encyclopedia of Crime and Justice' (Volume 4, page 1356) it is stated "...even slight penetration is sufficient and emission is unnecessary". In Halsbury's Statutes of England and Wales (Fourth Edition) Volume 12, it is stated that even the slightest degree of penetration is sufficient to prove sexual intercourse. It is violation with violence of the private person of a woman-an-outrage by all means. By the very nature of the offence it is an obnoxious act of the highest order. The physical scar may heal up, but the mental scar will always remain. When a woman is ravished, what is inflicted is not merely physical injury but the deep sense of some deathless shame.

What amounts to Rape/Sexual Intercourse?

It has been a consistent view of Supreme Court that even a slightest penetration is sufficient to make out an offence of rape and depth of penetration is immaterial. It is appropriate in this context to reproduce the opinion expressed by Modi in Medical Jurisprudence and Toxicology (Twenty Second Edition) at page 495 which reads thus:

Thus, to constitute the offence of rape, it is not necessary that there should be complete penetration of penis with emission of semen and rupture of hymen. Partial penetration of the penis within the Labia majora or the

---

section (2) of section 376.] Of unnatural offences

6   (Stephen's "Criminal Law" 9th Ed. p.262).

vulva or pudenda with or without emission of semen or even an attempt at penetration is quite sufficient for the purpose of the law. It is therefore quite possible to commit legally, the offence of rape without producing any injury to the genitals or leaving any seminal stains. In such a case, the medical officer should mention the negative facts in his report, but should not give his opinion that no rape had been committed. Rape is crime and not a medical condition. Rape is a legal term and not a diagnosis to be made by the medical officer treating the victim. The only statement that can be made by the medical officer is to the effect whether there is evidence of recent sexual activity. Whether the rape has occurred or not is a **legal conclusion**, not a **medical one**.

Similarly in Parikh's Textbook of Medical Jurisprudence and Toxicology, 'sexual intercourse' has been defined as under: Sexual intercourse.- In law, this term is held to mean the slightest degree of penetration of the vulva by the penis with or without emission of semen. It is therefore quite possible to commit legally the offence of rape without producing any injury to the genitals or leaving any seminal stains.

Name of Rape Victim should not be disclosed:

Section 228A[7] of IPC makes disclosure of identity of victim of certain offences punishable. Printing or publishing name of any matter which may

---

7 Section 228A in The Indian Penal Code, 1860
   228A. [Disclosure of identity of the victim of certain offences, etc.--
   (1) Whoever prints or publishes the name or any matter which may make known the identity of any person against whom an offence under section 376, section 376A, section 376B, section 376C or section 376D is alleged or found to have been committed (hereafter in this section referred to as the victim) shall be punished with imprisonment of either description for a term which may extend to two years and shall also be liable to fine.
   (2) Nothing in sub- section (1) extends to any printing or publication of the name or any matter which may make known the identity of the victim if such printing or publication is-
   (a) by or under the order in writing of the officer- in- charge of the police station or the police officer making the investigation into such offence acting in good faith for the purposes of such investigation; or
   (b) by, or with the authorisation in writing of, the victim; or
   (c) where the victim is dead or minor or of unsound mind, by, or with the authorisation in writing of, the next- of- kin of the victim: Provided that no such authorisation shall be given by the next- of- kin to anybody other than the chairman or the secretary, by whatever name called, of any recognised welfare institution or organisation. Explanation.- For the purposes of this sub- section," recognised welfare institution or organisation" means a social welfare institution or organisation recognised in this behalf by the Central or State Government.
   (3) Whoever prints or publishes any matter in relation to any proceeding before a court with respect to an offence referred to in sub- section (1) without the previous permission of such court shall be punished with imprisonment of either description for a term which may extend to two years and shall also be liable to fine. Explanation.- The printing or publication of the judgment of any High Court or the Supreme Court does not amount to an offence within the meaning of this section.]

make known the identity of any person against whom an offence under Sections 376,376A[8], 376B[9], 376C[10] or 376D[11] is alleged or found to have been committed can be punished. True it is, the restriction, does not relate to printing or publication of judgment by High Court or Supreme Court. But keeping in view the social object of preventing social victimization or ostracism of the victim of a sexual offence for which Section 228A has been enacted, it would be appropriate that in the judgments, be it of Supreme Court, High Court or lower Court, the name of the victim should not be indicated.[12]

---

8 Section 376A in The Indian Penal Code, 1860
376A. Intercourse by a man with his wife during separation.-- Whoever has sexual intercourse with his own wife, who is living separately from him under a decree of separation or under any custom or usage without her consent shall be punished with imprisonment of either description for a term which may extend to two years and shall also be liable to fine.

9 Section 376B in The Indian Penal Code, 1860
376B. Intercourse by public servant with woman in his custody.-- Whoever, being a public servant, takes advantage of his official position and induces or seduces, any woman, who is in his custody as such public servant or in the custody of a public servant subordinate to him, to have sexual intercourse with him, such sexual intercourse not amounting to the offence of rape, shall be punished with imprisonment of either description for a term which may extend to five years and shall also be liable to fine.

10 Section 376C in The Indian Penal Code, 1860
376C. Intercourse by superintendent of jail, remand home, etc.-- Whoever, being the superintendent or manager of a jail, remand home or other place of custody established by or under any law for the time being in force or of a women' s or children' s institution takes advantage of his official position and induces or seduces any female inmate of such jail, remand home, place or institution to have sexual intercourse with him, such sexual intercourse not amounting to the offence of rape, shall be punished with imprisonment of either description for a term which may extend to five years and shall also be liable to fine. Explanation 1.-" Superintendent" in relation to a jail, remand home or other place of custody or a women' s or children' s institution, includes a person holding any other office in such jail, remand home, place or institution by virtue of which he can exercise any authority or control over its inmates. Explanation 2.- The expression" women' s or children' s institution" shall have the same meaning as in Explanation 2 to sub- section (2) of section 376.

11 Section 376D in The Indian Penal Code, 1860
376D. Intercourse by any member of the management or staff of a hospital with any woman in that hospital.-- Whoever, being on the management of a hospital or being on the staff of a hospital takes advantage of his position and has sexual intercourse with any woman in that hospital, such sexual intercourse not amounting to the offence of rape, shall be punished with imprisonment of either description for a term which may extend to five years and shall also be liable to fine. Explanation.- The expression" hospital" shall have the same meaning as in Explanation 3 to sub-section (2) of section 376.] Of unnatural offences

12 See State of Karnataka v. Puttaraja 2003 (8) Supreme 364 and Dinesh alias Buddha v. State of Rajasthan 2006CriLJ1679 .

Directions of Supreme Court for assisting the Victims of Rape[13]:

(1) The complainants of sexual assault cases should be provided with legal representation. It is important to have some one who is well-acquainted with the criminal justice system. The role of the victim's advocate would not only be to explain to the victim the nature of the proceedings, to prepare her for the case and to assist her in the police station and in court but to provide her with guidance as to how she might obtain help of a different nature from other agencies, for example, mind counselling or medical assistance. It is important to secure continuity of assistance by ensuring that the same person who looked after the complainant's interests in the police station represnet her till the end of the case.

(2) Legal assistance will have to be provided at the police station since the victim of sexual assault might very well be in a distressed state upon arrival at the police station, the guidance and support of a lawyer at this stage and whilst she was being questioned would be of great assistance to her.

(3) The police should be under a duty to inform the victim of her right to representation before any questions were asked of her and that the police report should state that the victim was so informed.

(4) A list of advocates willing to act in these cases should be kept at the police station for victims who did not have a particular lawyer in mind or whose own lawyer was unavailable.

(5) The advocate shall be appointed by the court, upon application by the police at the earliest convenient movement, but in order to ensure that victims were questioned without undue delay, advocates would be authorised to act at the police station before leave of the court was sought or obtained.

(6) In all rape trials anonymity of the victims must be maintained, as far as necessary.

(7) It is necessary, having regard to the Directive Principles contained under Article 38(1)[14] of the Constitution of India to set up Criminal Injuries

---

13 Appellants: **Shri Bodhisattwa Gautam Vs.** Respondent: **Miss Subhra Chakraborty**
AIR1996SC922
Hon'ble Judges: and S. Saghir Ahmad, JJ.

14 Article 38(1) in The Constitution Of India 1949
(1) The State shall strive to promote the welfare of the people by securing and protecting as

Compensation Board. Rape victims frequently incur substantial financial loss. Some, for example, are too traumatized to continue in employment.

(8) Compensation for victims shall be awarded by the court on conviction of the offender and by the Criminal Injuries Compensation Board whether or not a conviction has taken place. The Board will take into account pain, suffering and shock as well as loss of earnings due to pregnancy and the expenses of the child but if this occurred as a result of the rape.

Can Death Penalty be awarded to Rapists?

The Constitution Bench of Supreme Court, by a majority, upheld the constitutional validity of death sentence in **Bachan Singh** v. **State of Punjab**[15] . The Court took particular care to say that death sentence shall not normally be awarded for the offence of murder and that it must be confined to the "rarest of rare" cases when the alternative option is foreclosed. In other words, the Constitution Bench did not find death sentence valid in all cases except in the aforesaid cases wherein the lesser sentence would be wholly inadequate. The doctrine of "rarest of rare" confines two aspects and when both the aspects are satisfied only then the death penalty can be imposed. Firstly, the case must clearly fall within the ambit of "rarest of rare" and secondly, when the alternative option is unquestionably foreclosed.

The kind of cases in which protection to life may be withdrawn and there may be the demand for death penalty were enumerated in the following paragraphs:

It may do so "in rarest of rare cases" when its collective conscience is so shocked that it will expect the holders of the judicial power centre to inflict death penalty irrespective of their personal opinion as regards desirability or otherwise of retaining death penalty. The community may entertain such a sentiment when the crime is viewed from the platform of the motive for, or the manner of commission of the crime, or the anti-social or abhorrent nature of the crime, such as for instance:

I. Manner of commission of murder

When the murder is committed in an extremely brutal, grotesque, diabolical, revolting or dastardly manner so as to arouse intense and

---

effectively as it may a social order in which justice, social, economic and political, shall inform all the institutions of the national life

15 (1980) 2 SCC 684.

extreme indignation of the community. For instance,

(i) when the house of the victim is set aflame with the end in view to roast him alive in the house.

(ii) when the victim is subjected to inhuman acts of torture or cruelty in order to bring about his or her death.

(iii) when the body of the victim is cut into pieces or his body is dismembered in a fiendish manner.

II. Motive for commission of murder

When the murder is committed for a motive which evinces total depravity and meanness. For instance when (a) a hired assassin commits murder for the sake of money or reward (b) a cold-blooded murder is committed with a deliberate design in order to inherit property or to gain control over property of a ward or a person under the control of the murderer or vis-à-vis whom the murderer is in a dominating position or in a position of trust, or (c) a murder is committed in the course for betrayal of the motherland.

III. Anti-social or socially abhorrent nature of the crime

(a) When murder of a member of a Scheduled Caste or minority community, etc., is committed not for personal reasons but in circumstances which arouse social wrath. For instance when such a crime is committed in order to terrorize such persons and frighten them into fleeing from a place or in order to deprive them of, or make them surrender, lands or benefits conferred on them with a view to reverse past injustices and in order to restore the social balance.

(b) In cases of "bride burning" and what are known as "dowry deaths" or when murder is committed in order to remarry for the sake of extracting dowry once again or to marry another woman on account of infatuation.

IV. Magnitude of crime

When the crime is enormous in proportion. For instance when multiple murders say of all or almost all the members of a family or a large number of persons of a particular caste, community, or locality, are committed.

V. Personality of victim of murder

When the victim of murder is (a) an innocent child who could not have or has not provided even an excuse, much less a provocation, for murder (b) a helpless woman or a person rendered helpless by old age or infirmity (c) when the victim is a person vis-à-vis whom the murderer is in a position of domination or trust (d) when the victim is a public figure generally loved and respected by the community for the services rendered by him and the murder is committed for political or similar reasons other than personal reasons.

The above principles are generally regarded by Court as the broad guidelines for imposition of death sentence and have been followed by the Court in many subsequent decisions.

1

Depth of Penetration in Rape is Immaterial[1]

Facts in Nutshell:

A minor girl aged about 12 years was subjected to rape[2] by the appellant[3] on 14th October 1988. The appellant was charged and prosecuted[4] for commission of offence under Sections 366[5] and 376[6] of the Indian Penal

---

1   Appellants: **Wahid Khan Vs.** Respondent: **State of Madhya Pradesh**
    AIR2010SC1
    Hon'ble Judges/Coram: J. M. Panchal and Deepak Verma, JJ.

2   **Section 375 in The Indian Penal Code, 1860**
    375. Rape.-- A man is said to commit" rape" who, except in the case hereinafter excepted, has sexual intercourse with a woman under circumstances falling under any of the six following descriptions:- First.- Against her will. Secondly.- Without her consent. Thirdly.- With her consent, when her consent has been obtained by putting her or any person in whom she is interested in fear of death or of hurt. Fourthly.- With her consent, when the man knows that he is not her husband, and that her consent is given because she believes that he is another man to whom she is or believes herself to be lawfully married. Fifthly.- With her consent, when, at the time of giving such consent, by reason of unsoundness of mind or intoxication or the administration by him personally or through another of any stupefying or unwholesome substance, she is unable to understand the nature and consequences of that to which she gives consent. Sixthly.- With or without her consent, when she is under sixteen years of age. Explanation.- Penetration is sufficient to constitute the sexual intercourse necessary to the offence of rape. Exception.- Sexual intercourse by a man with his own wife, the wife not being under fifteen years of age, is not rape.

3   **Meaning of Appellant:** A person who, dissatisfied with the judgment rendered in a lawsuit decided in a lower court or the findings from a proceeding before an Administrative Agency, asks a superior court to review the decision.

4   **Meaning of Prosecute:**
    a. To initiate civil or criminal court action against.
    b. To seek to obtain or enforce by legal action.

5   **Section 366 in The Indian Penal Code, 1860**
    366. Kidnapping, abducting or inducing woman to compel her marriage, etc.-- Whoever kidnaps or abducts any woman with intent that she may be compelled, or knowing it to be likely that she will be compelled, to marry any person against her will, or in order that she may be forced or seduced to illicit intercourse, or knowing it to be likely that she will be forced or seduced to illicit intercourse, shall be punished with imprisonment of either description for a term which may extend to ten years, and shall also be liable to fine; [and whoever, by means of criminal intimidation as defined in this Code or of abuse of authority or any other method of compulsion, induces any woman to go from any place with intent that she may be, or knowing that it is likely that she will be, forced or seduced to illicit intercourse with another person shall also be punishable as aforesaid].

6   **Section 376 in The Indian Penal Code, 1860**
    376. Punishment for rape.--
    (1) Whoever, except in the cases provided for by sub- section (2), commits rape shall be punished with imprisonment of either description for a term which shall not be less than seven years but which may be for life or for a term which may extend to ten years and shall also be liable to fine

Code (for short, `IPC') and the co-accused[7] Sneh Lata was charged under Sections 342[8] and 366, IPC in the Court of III Additional Sessions Judge, Bhopal.

Decision of the Session Judge:

Court acquitted[9] co-accused Sneh Lata of the charges leveled against her, but the appellant was found guilty of commission of offence under Section 376, IPC and was awarded seven years' rigorous imprisonment. Appellant was acquitted of the charge leveled against him under

---

unless the woman raped is his own wife and is not under twelve years of age, in which case, he shall be punished with imprisonment of either description for a term which may extend to two years or with fine or with both:

Provided that the court may, for adequate and special reasons to be mentioned in the judgment, impose a sentence of imprisonment for a term of less than seven years.

(2) Whoever,-

(a) being a police officer commits rape-

(i) within the limits of the police station to which he is appointed; or

(ii) in the premises of any station house whether or not situated in the police station to which he is appointed; or

(iii) on a woman in his custody or in the custody of a police officer subordinate to him; or

(b) being a public servant, takes advantage of his official position and commits rape on a woman in his custody as such public servant or in the custody of a public servant subordinate to him; or

(c) being on the management or on the staff of a jail, remand home or other place of custody established by or under any law for the time being in force or of a women' s or children' s institution takes advantage of his official position and commits rape on any inmate of such jail, remand home, place or institution; or

(d) being on the management or on the staff of a hospital, takes advantage of his official position and commits rape on a woman in that hospital; or

(e) commits rape on a woman knowing her to be pregnant; or

(f) commits rape on a woman when she is under twelve years of age; or

(g) commits gang rape, shall be punished with rigorous imprisonment for a term which shall not be less than ten years but which may be for life and shall also be liable to fine: Provided that the court may, for adequate and special reasons to be mentioned in the judgment, impose a sentence of imprisonment of either description for a term of less than ten years. Explanation 1.- Where a women' s is raped by one or more in a group of persons acting in furtherance of their common intention, each of the persons shall be deemed to have committed gang rape within the meaning of this sub- section. Explanation 2.-" women' s or children' s institution" means an institution, whether called and orphanage or a home for neglected women or children or a widows' home or by any other name, which is established and maintained for the reception and care of women or children. Explanation 3.-" hospital" means the precincts of the hospital and includes the precincts of any institution for the reception and treatment of persons during convalescence or of persons requiring medical attention or rehabilitation.

7   **Meaning of Accused:** A person charged with a criminal offense, or the state of being so charged

8   **Section 342 in The Indian Penal Code, 1860**
    342. Punishment for wrongful confinement.-- Whoever wrongfully confines any person shall be punished with simple imprisonment of either description for a term which may extend to one year, or with fine which may extend to one thousand rupees, or with both.

9   **Meaning of Acquittal:** In the common law tradition, an **acquittal** formally certifies that the accused is free from the charge of an offense, as far as the criminal law is concerned.

Section366, IPC, 1860. Feeling aggrieved by the judgment, appellant preferred Criminal Appeal[10] in the High Court of Madhya Pradesh at Jabalpur. Learned Single Judge, after considering the matter from all angles, came to the conclusion that the findings recorded by the learned Sessions Judge were based on material evidence available on record, thus, proceeded to confirm the findings of guilt as also the punishment awarded to him. Against the judgment of High Court, the criminal appeal by special leave[11] was preferred in Supreme Court.

Arguments of Learned Senior Counsel:

Learned senior counsel appearing for the appellant contended that keeping in mind the medical report of the prosecutrix reflecting her hymen was still in-tact, would be indicative of the fact that no intercourse was at all committed on her. According to him, looking to the totality of the facts and features of the case and the evidence available on record, at best, it would establish a case wherein the appellant could have been convicted only under Section 354[12] of IPC but no case was made out for his conviction under Section 376 thereof.

Arguments of Respondent Counsel:

Learned Counsel appearing for the respondent[13](State) contended that

---

10 **Meaning of Appeal:** In law, an **appeal** is a process for requesting a formal change to an official decision. Very broadly speaking there are appeals on the record and *de novo* appeals. In *de novo* appeals, a new decision maker re-hears the case without any reference to the prior decision maker. In appeals on the record, the decision of the prior decision maker is challenged by arguing that he or she misapplied the law, came to an incorrect factual finding, acted in excess of his jurisdiction, abused his powers, was biased, considered evidence which he should not have considered or failed to consider evidence that he should have considered

11 **Article 136 in The Constitution Of India 1949**
136. Special leave to appeal by the Supreme Court
(1) Notwithstanding anything in this Chapter, the Supreme Court may, in its discretion, grant special leave to appeal from any judgment, decree, determination, sentence or order in any cause or matter passed or made by any court or tribunal in the territory of India
(2) Nothing in clause (1) shall apply to any judgment, determination, sentence or order passed or made by any court or tribunal constituted by or under any law relating to the Armed Forces

12 **Section 354 in The Indian Penal Code, 1860**
354. Assault or criminal force to woman with intent to outrage her modesty.-- Whoever assaults or uses criminal force to any woman, intending to outrage or knowing it to be likely that he will there by outrage her modesty, shall be punished with imprisonment of either description for a term which may extend to two years, or with fine, or with both.

13 **Meaning of Respondent:** A **respondent** is a person who is called upon to issue a response to a communication made by another. In legal usage, this specifically refers to the defendant in a legal proceeding commenced by a petition, or to an appellee, or the opposing party, in an appeal of a decision by an initial fact-finder.

even if full penetration had not been there, slight penetration itself is sufficient and would complete the offence of rape as contemplated under Section 375 of the IPC and thus both the courts were justified in finding appellant guilty under Section 376 of IPC and awarding him punishment accordingly.

What amounts to Rape/Sexual Intercourse?

It has been a consistent view of Supreme Court that even a slightest penetration is sufficient to make out an offence of rape and depth of penetration is immaterial. It is appropriate in this context to reproduce the opinion expressed by Modi in Medical Jurisprudence and Toxicology (Twenty Second Edition) at page 495 which reads thus:

Thus, to constitute the offence of rape, it is not necessary that there should be complete penetration of penis with emission of semen and rupture of hymen. Partial penetration of the penis within the Labia majora or the vulva or pudenda with or without emission of semen or even an attempt at penetration is quite sufficient for the purpose of the law. It is therefore quite possible to commit legally, the offence of rape without producing any injury to the genitals or leaving any seminal stains. In such a case, the medical officer should mention the negative facts in his report, but should not give his opinion that no rape had been committed. Rape is crime and not a medical condition. Rape is a legal term and not a diagnosis to be made by the medical officer treating the victim. The only statement that can be made by the medical officer is to the effect whether there is evidence of recent sexual activity. Whether the rape has occurred or not is a **legal conclusion**, not a **medical one**.

Similarly in Parikh's Textbook of Medical Jurisprudence and Toxicology, 'sexual intercourse' has been defined as under: Sexual intercourse.- In law, this term is held to mean the slightest degree of penetration of the vulva by the penis with or without emission of semen. It is therefore quite possible to commit legally the offence of rape without producing any injury to the genitals or leaving any seminal stains.

Decision of the Supreme Court:

Court held that the act of the appellant certainly constitute an offence of rape.

2

Forcible Sexual Intercourse amounts to Rape[1]

Facts in Nutshell:

Appeal[2], arises from order of conviction[3] and sentence dated 8th of September, 1999 decided by the learned Additional Sessions Judge at Amalner. The Sessions Court convicted the accused[4]/appellant for an offence punishable under Section 376(2)(f)[5] of the Indian Penal Code (the Code, for short) and sentenced him to suffer rigorous imprisonment for life and to pay a fine of Rs. 500/-, in default of fine further rigorous

---

1   Appellants: **Bhawalya @ Bawalal Totaram Vs.** Respondent: **State of Maharashtra** 2004(2)MhLj498

Hon'ble Judges/Coram: B.H. Marlapalle and M.G. Gaikwad, JJ.

2   **Meaning of Appeal:** In law, an **appeal** is a process for requesting a formal change to an official decision. Very broadly speaking there are appeals on the record and de novo appeals. In de novoappeals, a new decision maker re-hears the case without any reference to the prior decision maker. In appeals on the record, the decision of the prior decision maker is challenged by arguing that he or she misapplied the law, came to an incorrect factual finding, acted in excess of his jurisdiction, abused his powers, was biased, considered evidence which he should not have considered or failed to consider evidence that he should have considered.

3   **Meaning of Conviction:** In law, a **conviction** is the verdict that results when a court of law finds a defendant guilty of a crime.

4   **Meaning of Accused:** A person charged with a criminal offense, or the state of being so charged

5   **Section 376 in The Indian Penal Code, 1860**
376. Punishment for rape.--
(2) Whoever,-
(a) being a police officer commits rape-
(i) within the limits of the police station to which he is appointed; or
(ii) in the premises of any station house whether or not situated in the police station to which he is appointed; or
(iii) on a woman in his custody or in the custody of a police officer subordinate to him; or
(b) being a public servant, takes advantage of his official position and commits rape on a woman in his custody as such public servant or in the custody of a public servant subordinate to him; or
(c) being on the management or on the staff of a jail, remand home or other place of custody established by or under any law for the time being in force or of a women' s or children' s institution takes advantage of his official position and commits rape on any inmate of such jail, remand home, place or institution; or
(d) being on the management or on the staff of a hospital, takes advantage of his official position and commits rape on a woman in that hospital; or
(e) commits rape on a woman knowing her to be pregnant; or
(f) commits rape on a woman when she is under twelve years of age; or

imprisonment for one month, whereas he came to be acquitted for the offence punishable under Section 506[6] of the Code.

The prosecution[7] case briefly states that the prosecutrix Rinku d/o Shivaji Patil is the granddaughter (daughter's daughter) of the complainant Santosh s/o Naval Patil, an agriculturist by profession, Suman is the wife of Santosh. The parents of the prosecutrix were residing, at the relevant time, at village Sunwade and it was on 1st February, 1998 that the prosecutrix was lured by the accused with the promise of giving brinjals and chillies. She was taken towards the field of his master Subhash Nago Patil and beneath the Neem tree in the agricultural land of Shri Sudhakar Gulabrao Patil, she was raped by the accused. She sustained bleeding injuries on her vagina and returned to her grandparent's house.

Arguments by Learned Counsel for the Accused:

The Learned counsel for the accused, submitted that there was no evidence to link the injuries suffered by the prosecutrix to the accused and there was no eye-witness. He reiterated that the possibility of the prosecutrix sustaining the alleged injuries, while playing, could not be ruled out, more so when in her cross examination[8] she had admitted that after the incident she had returned home by playing or by acts of playing.

Decision of High Court:

The trial Court rightly recorded its view that the accused had committed a beastly act by forcibly subjecting the minor girl to sexual assault and by luring her with a promise of giving brinjals and chillies from the farm of his master. His intentions and pre-design, as have come on record, were quite eloquent and he committed the heinous crime in a broad-day-light.

---

6 **Section 506 in The Indian Penal Code, 1860**
   506. Punishment for criminal intimidation.-- Whoever commits the offence of criminal intimidation shall be punished with imprisonment of either description for a term which may extend to two years, or with fine, or with both; If threat be to cause death or grievous hurt, etc. If threat be to cause death or grievous hurt, etc.-- and if the threat be to cause death or grievous hurt, or to cause the destruction of any property by fire, or to cause an offence punishable with death or 3[imprisonment for life], of with imprisonment for a term which may extend to seven years, or to impute unchastity to a woman, shall be punished with imprisonment of either description for a term which may extend to seven years, or with fine, or with both.

7 **Meaning of Prosecution:**
   a. the institution and carrying on of legal proceedings against a person.
   b. the officials who institute and conduct such proceedings.

8 **Meaning of Cross-Examination:** In law, **cross-examination** is the interrogation of a witness called by one's opponent.

The trial Court was of the opinion that he did not deserve any leniency and, therefore, awarded sentence of life imprisonment. High Court confirmed the order of Trail Court.

3

Semen Stains on Salwar does not Necessarily Mean Rape[1]

Facts in Nutshell:

Prosecution[2] story: The prosecutrix, and her husband, Dinesh Mishra who was a rickshaw puller by profession, had come to Delhi along with her children. On 28th September, 1995, both the husband and wife had gone to the latter's ex-employer to recover some money that was due to him. When they reached the factory premises they found that Factory Owner was not present but several other persons including the appellant[3], a shop keeper were present. The appellant sent husband out of the factory on the pretext of buying some meat and after some of the workmen who were present had left, he caught hold of the prosecutrix(wife), took her to the first floor of the factory and then committed rape upon her and threatened that in case she reported the matter to anybody she would be dealt with.

Decision of Trial court and High Court:

The appellant, Tameezuddin, was convicted under Section 376[4] of

---

1 Appellants: **Tameezuddin @ Tammu Vs.** Respondent: **State of (NCT) of Delhi** (2009)15SCC566 **Hon'ble Judges/Coram:** H. S. Bedi and Aftab Alam, JJ.

2 **Meaning of Prosecution:**
   a. the institution and carrying on of legal proceedings against a person.
   b. the officials who institute and conduct such proceedings.

3 **Meaning of Appellant:** A person who, dissatisfied with the judgment rendered in a lawsuit decided in a lower court or the findings from a proceeding before an Administrative Agency, asks a superior court to review the decision.

4 **Section 376 in The Indian Penal Code, 1860**
   376. Punishment for rape.--
   (1) Whoever, except in the cases provided for by sub- section (2), commits rape shall be punished with imprisonment of either description for a term which shall not be less than seven years but which may be for life or for a term which may extend to ten years and shall also be liable to fine unless the woman raped is his own wife and is not under twelve years of age, in which case, he shall be punished with imprisonment of either description for a term which may extend to two years or with fine or with both:
   Provided that the court may, for adequate and special reasons to be mentioned in the judgment, impose a sentence of imprisonment for a term of less than seven years.
   (2) Whoever,-
   (a) being a police officer commits rape-

the IPC by the Court of Sessions and sentenced to undergo Rigorous Imprisonment for 84 months and a fine of Rs. 14,000/- and in default of payment of fine to further undergo Rigorous Imprisonment for six months and under Section 506(ii)[5] of the IPC, to a sentence of 36 months and fine and in default of payment of fine, to undergo Rigorous Imprisonment for one month, both the sentences were directed to run concurrently.

The trial Court observed that it would be difficult to believe that any self-respecting woman or her husband would come forward to make a humiliating statement against her honour and that, in such a situation, her statement alleging rape was to be accepted. The trial Court convicted and sentenced the accused. The judgment of the trial Court was affirmed by the High Court in appeal[6]. The matter was referred to Supreme Court

---

(i) within the limits of the police station to which he is appointed; or

(ii) in the premises of any station house whether or not situated in the police station to which he is appointed; or

(iii) on a woman in his custody or in the custody of a police officer subordinate to him; or

(b) being a public servant, takes advantage of his official position and commits rape on a woman in his custody as such public servant or in the custody of a public servant subordinate to him; or

(c) being on the management or on the staff of a jail, remand home or other place of custody established by or under any law for the time being in force or of a women' s or children' s institution takes advantage of his official position and commits rape on any inmate of such jail, remand home, place or institution; or

(d) being on the management or on the staff of a hospital, takes advantage of his official position and commits rape on a woman in that hospital; or

(e) commits rape on a woman knowing her to be pregnant; or

(f) commits rape on a woman when she is under twelve years of age; or

(g) commits gang rape, shall be punished with rigorous imprisonment for a term which shall not be less than ten years but which may be for life and shall also be liable to fine: Provided that the court may, for adequate and special reasons to be mentioned in the judgment, impose a sentence of imprisonment of either description for a term of less than ten years. Explanation 1.- Where a women' s is raped by one or more in a group of persons acting in furtherance of their common intention, each of the persons shall be deemed to have committed gang rape within the meaning of this sub- section. Explanation 2.-" women' s or children' s institution" means an institution, whether called and orphanage or a home for neglected women or children or a widows' home or by any other name, which is established and maintained for the reception and care of women or children. Explanation 3.-" hospital" means the precincts of the hospital and includes the precincts of any institution for the reception and treatment of persons during convalescence or of persons requiring medical attention or rehabilitation.

5   Section 506 in The Indian Penal Code, 1860

506. Punishment for criminal intimidation.-- Whoever commits the offence of criminal intimidation shall be punished with imprisonment of either description for a term which may extend to two years, or with fine, or with both; If threat be to cause death or grievous hurt, etc. If threat be to cause death or grievous hurt, etc.-- and if the threat be to cause death or grievous hurt, or to cause the destruction of any property by fire, or to cause an offence punishable with death or [imprisonment for life], of with imprisonment for a term which may extend to seven years, or to impute unchastity to a woman, shall be punished with imprisonment of either description for a term which may extend to seven years, or with fine, or with both.

6   Meaning of Appeal: In law, an appeal is a process for requesting a formal change to an official decision. Very broadly speaking there are appeals on the record and *de novo* appeals. In *de*

by way of special leave petition[7].

Decision of Supreme Court:

Court held that it is true that in a case of rape the evidence of the prosecutrix[8] must be given predominant consideration, but to hold that this evidence has to be accepted even if the story is improbable and belies logic, would be doing violence to the very principles which govern the appreciation of evidence in a criminal matter. In this background, merely because the Vaginal swabs and the salwar had semen stains thereon Would, at best, be evidence of the commission of **sexual intercourse** but not of **rape.** Court allowed the appeal, set aside the judgments of the trial Court and the High Court and order the appellant's acquittal[9].

---

*novo*appeals, a new decision maker re-hears the case without any reference to the prior decision maker. In appeals on the record, the decision of the prior decision maker is challenged by arguing that he or she misapplied the law, came to an incorrect factual finding, acted in excess of his jurisdiction, abused his powers, was biased, considered evidence which he should not have considered or failed to consider evidence that he should have considered.

7   **Article 136 in The Constitution Of India 1949**
    136. Special leave to appeal by the Supreme Court
    (1) Notwithstanding anything in this Chapter, the Supreme Court may, in its discretion, grant special leave to appeal from any judgment, decree, determination, sentence or order in any cause or matter passed or made by any court or tribunal in the territory of India
    (2) Nothing in clause (1) shall apply to any judgment, determination, sentence or order passed or made by any court or tribunal constituted by or under any law relating to the Armed Forces

8   **Meaning of Prosecutrix:** A female prosecutor.

9   **Meaning of Acquittal:** In the common law tradition, an **acquittal** formally certifies that the accused is free from the charge of an offense, as far as the criminal law is concerned.

4

Relaxation in Rape Punishment on Account of Age of Accused [1]

Facts in Nutshell:

The prosecution[2] case as mentioned in the F.I.R. was that on 27.4.1999, a person selling carrots and salt was roaming around the village. At that time, the victim girl (name not disclosed) aged 10 years was tempted with the carrots and the appellant[3] took her towards the field of Brijendra Singh in village Inguri and committed rape on the girl, who was the niece of the informant Bare Lal.

Decision of the Trail Court:

Appeal[4] has been filed against the, conviction[5] of the appellant Surendra Singh under Section 376[6] I.P.C. to 14 years R.I. and a fine of Rs. 10,000/-

---

1   Appellants: **Surendra Singh S/o Bhimmi Vs.** Respondent: **State of U.P.** 2006CriLJ700
    Hon'ble Judges/Coram: Amar Saran, J.

2   **Meaning of Prosecution:**
    a. the institution and carrying on of legal proceedings against a person.
    b. the officials who institute and conduct such proceedings.

3   **Meaning of Appellant:** A person who, dissatisfied with the judgment rendered in a lawsuit decided in a lower court or the findings from a proceeding before an Administrative Agency, asks a superior court to review the decision.

4   **Meaning of Appeal:** In law, an **appeal** is a process for requesting a formal change to an official decision. Very broadly speaking there are appeals on the record and *de novo* appeals. In *de novo* appeals, a new decision maker re-hears the case without any reference to the prior decision maker. In appeals on the record, the decision of the prior decision maker is challenged by arguing that he or she misapplied the law, came to an incorrect factual finding, acted in excess of his jurisdiction, abused his powers, was biased, considered evidence which he should not have considered or failed to consider evidence that he should have considered.

5   **Meaning of Conviction:** In law, a **conviction** is the verdict that results when a court of law finds a defendant guilty of a crime.

6   **Section 376 in The Indian Penal Code, 1860**
    376. Punishment for rape.--
    (1) Whoever, except in the cases provided for by sub- section (2), commits rape shall be punished with imprisonment of either description for a term which shall not be less than seven years but which may be for life or for a term which may extend to ten years and shall also be liable to fine unless the woman raped is his own wife and is not under twelve years of age, in which case, he shall be punished with imprisonment of either description for a term which may extend to two years or with fine or with both:
    Provided that the court may, for adequate and special reasons to be mentioned in the judgment,

and 5 years R.I. and a fine of Rs. I,000/-under Section 3(2)(v) of the S.C./ S.T. Act[7]. In default of payment of fine under Section376 I PC, three years simple imprisonment was awarded and for non-payment of fine under Section 3(2)(v) of S.C./S.T. Act, one year simple imprisonment was also awarded. The sentences were concurrent.

Section 375, IPC

Explanation to Section 375 I PC clause *sixthly*, which refers to the rape on a girl without her consent when she is under sixteen years of age, penetration is sufficient for constituting the sexual intercourse necessary for making out the offence of rape.

---

impose a sentence of imprisonment for a term of less than seven years.
(2) Whoever,-
(a) being a police officer commits rape-
(i) within the limits of the police station to which he is appointed; or
(ii) in the premises of any station house whether or not situated in the police station to which he is appointed; or
(iii) on a woman in his custody or in the custody of a police officer subordinate to him; or
(b) being a public servant, takes advantage of his official position and commits rape on a woman in his custody as such public servant or in the custody of a public servant subordinate to him; or
(c) being on the management or on the staff of a jail, remand home or other place of custody established by or under any law for the time being in force or of a women' s or children' s institution takes advantage of his official position and commits rape on any inmate of such jail, remand home, place or institution; or
(d) being on the management or on the staff of a hospital, takes advantage of his official position and commits rape on a woman in that hospital; or
(e) commits rape on a woman knowing her to be pregnant; or
(f) commits rape on a woman when she is under twelve years of age; or
(g) commits gang rape, shall be punished with rigorous imprisonment for a term which shall not be less than ten years but which may be for life and shall also be liable to fine: Provided that the court may, for adequate and special reasons to be mentioned in the judgment, impose a sentence of imprisonment of either description for a term of less than ten years. Explanation 1.- Where a women' s is raped by one or more in a group of persons acting in furtherance of their common intention, each of the persons shall be deemed to have committed gang rape within the meaning of this sub- section. Explanation 2.-" women' s or children' s institution" means an institution, whether called and orphanage or a home for neglected women or children or a widows' home or by any other name, which is established and maintained for the reception and care of women or children. Explanation 3.-" hospital" means the precincts of the hospital and includes the precincts of any institution for the reception and treatment of persons during convalescence or of persons requiring medical attention or rehabilitation.

7 **Section 3(2)(v) of the S.C./S.T. Act**
Punishment for offences of atrocities.
(2) Whoever, not being a member of a Scheduled Caste or a Scheduled Tribe,-
(v) commits any offence under the Indian Penal Code (45 of 1860) punishable with imprisonment for a term of ten years or more against a person or property on the ground that such person is a member of a Scheduled Caste or a
Scheduled Tribe or such property belongs to such member, shall be punishable with imprisonment for life and with fine;

Decision of the High Court:

High Court held that there was no error in the judgment of the trial court. However, on the point of sentence, Court held that learned trial judge erred on the side of severity in awarding a sentence of 14 years R.I. and a fine of Rs. 10,000 for the offence and in exceeding the minimum sentence of 10 years prescribed under Section 376(2)(f) I PC, for rape! when the victim[8] is a girl under 12 years. The appellant, who was only 19 years in age as per his statement under Section 313 Cr.P.C.[9] which was recorded. The youthful appellant appears to have been consumed by lust and to have committed this, dastardly crime with a girl of tender years in the heat of passion when he may not have been fully in control of his senses, Under these circumstances Court thought that the sentence awarded to the appellant should be reduced to the legal minimum sentence of 10 years Rigorous Imprisonment in such cases.The fine of Rs. 10,000 is reduced to Rs. 1000. In default of payment of fine the appellant shall undergo 6 months further simple imprisonment. The sentence of 5 years under Section 3(2)(v) S.C./S.T. Act is maintained, but the fine of Rs. 1,000/- awarded against the appellant is set aside. The sentences shall run concurrently.

---

8 **Meaning of Victim:**
   1. One who is harmed or killed by another: *a victim of a mugging.*
   2. A living creature slain and offered as a sacrifice during a religious rite.
   3. One who is harmed by or made to suffer from an act, circumstance, agency, or condition: *victims of war.*
   4. A person who suffers injury, loss, or death as a result of a voluntary undertaking: *You are a victim of your own scheming.*

9 **Section 313, CrPc, 1973**
   313. Power to examine the accused.
   (1) In every inquiry or trial, for the purpose of enabling the accused personally to explain any circumstances appearing in the evidence against him, the Court—
   (a) may at any stage, without previously warning the accused put such questions to him as the Court considers necessary;
   (b) shall after the witnesses for the prosecution have been examined and before he is called on for his defence question him generally on the case:
   Provided that in a summons-case where the Court has dispensed with the personal attendance of the accused, it may also dispense with his examination under clause (b).
   (2) No oath shall be administered to the accused when he is examined under sub-section (1)
   (3) The accused shall not render himself liable to punishment by refusing to answer such question, or by giving false answers to them.
   (4) The answers given by the accused may be taken into consideration in such inquiry or trial, and put in evidence for or against him in any other inquiry into, or trial for, any other offence which such answers may tend to show he had committed.

5

Gang Rape[1]

Facts in Nutshell:

The prosecution[2] case, in short, is as under:

Prosecutrix[3] was returning home along with Shiela Devi, her sister-in-law, after giving fodder to cattle. After they had proceeded few steps from the place, Sohan Singh aged 19 years and his brother Mohan Singh aged about 22 years waylaid them. Mohan Singh confronted prosecutrix whereas Sohan Singh caught hold of Shiela Devi. They threatened them on the point of pistol not to raise any alarm, otherwise they would be met with dire consequences. Mohan Singh got in full grip of prosecutrix and forcibly took her to the nearby maize field. There, he committed offence of rape on the prosecutrix. Subsequently, Sohan Singh also repeated the crime of sexual assault[4] upon her.

Decision of the Trail Court and High Court:

Appellants[5], two in number, were charged and prosecuted for commission of offence under Section 376(2)(g)[6] of the Indian Penal Code (for short,

---

1   Appellants: **Sohan Singh and Anr. Vs.** Respondent: **State of Bihar** 2009(3)ACR3509(SC)
    Hon'ble Judges/Coram: V. S. Sirpurkar and Deepak Verma, JJ

2   **Meaning of Prosecution:**
    a. the institution and carrying on of legal proceedings against a person.
    b. the officials who institute and conduct such proceedings.

3   **Meaning of Prosecutrix:** A female prosecutor.

4   **Meaning of Sexual Assault: Sexual assault** is any involuntary sexual act in which a person is threatened, coerced, or forced to engage against their will, or any sexual touching of a person who has not consented. This includes rape (such as forced vaginal, anal or oral penetration), inappropriate touching, forced kissing, child sexual abuse, or the torture of the victim in a sexual manner.

5   **Meaning of Appellant:** A person who, dissatisfied with the judgment rendered in a lawsuit decided in a lower court or the findings from a proceeding before an Administrative Agency, asks a superior court to review the decision.

6   **Section 376 in The Indian Penal Code, 1860**
    376. Punishment for rape.--
    (2) Whoever,-
    (a) being a police officer commits rape-
    (i) within the limits of the police station to which he is appointed; or
    (ii) in the premises of any station house whether or not situated in the police station to which he is appointed; or

'IPC') for having committed rape on prosecutrix. Additional Sessions Judge, Begusarai in Sessions Trial found them guilty and awarded four years jail sentence to each one of them. The said judgment of the learned Sessions Judge was subject-matter of challenge at the instance of the appellants in the High Court of Patna. The appeal[7] of the accused-appellants has been dismissed and the conviction of the appellants under Section 376(2)(g) of IPC has been upheld and sentence of four years awarded by Trial Judge has also been affirmed. Than the appeal was filed in Supreme Court.

Contentions of Appellants:

It was pleaded by the appellants that they had not committed the rape but they had taken a plea of consensual sex with the prosecutrix which has not been believed by the Trial Court and High Court.

Decision of the Supreme Court:

Court dismissed the appeal of Appellants.

(iii) on a woman in his custody or in the custody of a police officer subordinate to him; or

(b) being a public servant, takes advantage of his official position and commits rape on a woman in his custody as such public servant or in the custody of a public servant subordinate to him; or

(c) being on the management or on the staff of a jail, remand home or other place of custody established by or under any law for the time being in force or of a women' s or children' s institution takes advantage of his official position and commits rape on any inmate of such jail, remand home, place or institution; or

(d) being on the management or on the staff of a hospital, takes advantage of his official position and commits rape on a woman in that hospital; or

(e) commits rape on a woman knowing her to be pregnant; or

(f) commits rape on a woman when she is under twelve years of age; or

(g) commits gang rape, shall be punished with rigorous imprisonment for a term which shall not be less than ten years but which may be for life and shall also be liable to fine: Provided that the court may, for adequate and special reasons to be mentioned in the judgment, impose a sentence of imprisonment of either description for a term of less than ten years. Explanation 1.- Where a women' s is raped by one or more in a group of persons acting in furtherance of their common intention, each of the persons shall be deemed to have committed gang rape within the meaning of this sub- section. Explanation 2.-" women' s or children' s institution" means an institution, whether called and orphanage or a home for neglected women or children or a widows' home or by any other name, which is established and maintained for the reception and care of women or children. Explanation 3.-" hospital" means the precincts of the hospital and includes the precincts of any institution for the reception and treatment of persons during convalescence or of persons requiring medical attention or rehabilitation.

7 **Meaning of Appeal:** In law, an **appeal** is a process for requesting a formal change to an official decision. Very broadly speaking there are appeals on the record and *de novo* appeals. In *de novo* appeals, a new decision maker re-hears the case without any reference to the prior decision maker. In appeals on the record, the decision of the prior decision maker is challenged by arguing that he or she misapplied the law, came to an incorrect factual finding, acted in excess of his jurisdiction, abused his powers, was biased, considered evidence which he should not have considered or failed to consider evidence that he should have considered.

6

Death sentence converted to imprisonment for rest of life for Rape of a Two Year Old Girl[1]

Facts in Nutshell:

Appeals challenge the conviction of the appellant under Sections 302[2], 364[3], 369[4], 376(f)[5], 392[6] and 449[7] of the Indian Penal Code and the award of the **Death sentence** for the offence punishable under

---

1 Appellants: **Sebastian @ Chevithiyan** **Vs.** Respondent: **State of Kerala** (2010)1SCC58
   Hon'ble Judges/Coram: H. S. Bedi and J. M. Panchal, JJ.

2 **Section 302 in The Indian Penal Code, 1860**
   302. Punishment for murder.-- Whoever commits murder shall be punished with death, or 1[imprisonment for life], and shall also be liable to fine.

3 **Section 364 in The Indian Penal Code, 1860**
   364. Kidnapping or abducting in order to murder.-- Whoever kidnaps or abducts any person in order that such person may be murdered or may be so disposed of as to be put in danger of being murdered, shall be punished with [imprisonment for life] or rigorous imprisonment for a term which may extend to ten years, and shall also be liable to fine. Illustrations
   (a) A kidnaps Z from [India], intending or knowing it to be likely that Z may be sacrificed to an idol. A has committed the offence defined in this section.
   (b) A forcibly carries or entices B away from his home in order that B may be murdered. A has committed the offence defined in this section.

4 **Section 369 in The Indian Penal Code, 1860**
   369. Kidnapping or abducting child under ten years with intent to steal from its person.-- Whoever kidnaps or abducts any child under the age of ten years with the intention of taking dishonestly any movable property from the person of such child, shall be punished with imprisonment of either description for a term which may extend to seven years, and shall also be liable to fine.

5 **Section 376 in The Indian Penal Code, 1860**
   376. Punishment for rape.
   (2) Whoever,
   (f) commits rape on a woman when she is under twelve years of age; or

6 **Section 392 in The Indian Penal Code, 1860**
   392. Punishment for robbery.-- Whoever commits robbery shall be punished with rigorous imprisonment for a term which may extend to ten years, and shall also be liable to fine; and, if the robbery be committed on the highway between sunset and sunrise, the imprisonment may be extended to fourteen years.

7 **Section 449 in The Indian Penal Code, 1860**
   449. House- trespass in order to commit offence punishable with death.-- Whoever commits house- trespass in order to the committing of any offence punishable with death, shall be punished with 1[imprisonment for life], or with rigorous imprisonment for a term not exceeding ten years, and shall also be liable to fine.

Section 302 of the I.P.C. and to various terms of imprisonment for the other offences. The facts are as follows:

Father was sleeping in the verandah of his house along with his son Saran, whereas his wife was sleeping inside the house along with their daughter Shemi, aged two years. As a matter of safety, Father used to shut the door of the house from the outside. Husband was told by his wife that Shemi was missing. The couple thereafter made a frantic search for the child in the vicinity and also called out loudly to her. Hearing the noise, the neighbours assembled and joined the search party. An hour later, the naked dead body of the child was found near the bridge across the AVM Canal and it was observed that two gold chains, one from the neck and the other from the waist, were missing. The dead body was brought to the house and the matter was reported to the police. The dead body was also sent for a post-mortem. The Post-mortem revealed that:

*Death was due to combined effects of drawing and blunt injuries sustained around nose and mouth. Injury Nos. 1 to 5 are on **genital area.** Injury Nos. 6 to 9 are also possible by forcible sexual act. The injury Nos. 1 to 36 can be caused by forcibly taking the child and forcible sexual act and inter course and throwing the child in water as well as application of blunt force during these transactions. There is evidence of penetration and emission of semen.* The accused[8] who was seen loitering close by was arrested and sent for a medical examination.

Decision of Trial Court:

The Trial Court awarded the death sentence to the appellant. The Court observed that the appellant had trespassed into the complainant's house and taken the child away and had raped and then killed her.

Decision of Supreme Court:

Court held that evidence that the appellant was a paedophile[9] with extremely violent propensities also stands proved on record in that he had been convicted and sentenced for an offence punishable under Section 354[10] in the year 1998. It is also extremely relevant that the

---

8 **Meaning of Accused:** A person charged with a criminal offense, or the state of being so charged

9 **Meaning of Paedophile:** An adult who is sexually attracted to children

10 **Section 354 in The Indian Penal Code, 1860**
   354. Assault or criminal force to woman with intent to outrage her modesty.-- Whoever assaults or uses criminal force to any woman, intending to outrage or knowing it to be likely that he will there by outrage her modesty, shall be punished with imprisonment of either description for a term

appellant, had, in addition, been tried for the murders of several other children but had been acquitted[11] on the 28th July, 2005 with the benefit of doubt.

Arguments of Learned Counsel for Appellant:

The learned Counsel for the appellant urged that the death sentence in the circumstances was not called for. He has pointed out that the case rested on circumstantial evidence[12] and the death penalty should not ordinarily be awarded in such a case. It has further been emphasised that the appellant was a young man 24 years of age at the time of the incident. Court was of the opinion that in the background of facts, that the death penalty ought to be converted to imprisonment for life but in terms laid down by Supreme Court in *Swamy Shraddananda v. State of Karnataka*[13] as his continuance as a member of an ordered society is uncalled for. The relevant observations from Judgment:

The matter may be looked at from a slightly different angle. The issue of sentencing has two aspects. A sentence may be excessive and unduly harsh or it may be highly disproportionately inadequate. When an appellant comes to this Court carrying a death sentence awarded by the trial court and confirmed by the High Court, this Court may find, as in the present appeal, that the case just falls short of the rarest of the rare category and may feel somewhat reluctant in endorsing the death sentence. But at the same time, having regard to the nature of the crime, the Court may strongly feel that a sentence of life imprisonment subject to remission normally works out to a term of 14 years would be grossly disproportionate and inadequate. What then should the Court do? If the Court's option is limited only to two punishments, one a sentence of imprisonment, for all intents and purposes, of not more than 14 year and the other death, the Court may feel tempted and find itself nudged into endorsing the death penalty. Such a course would indeed be disastrous.

which may extend to two years, or with fine, or with both.

11 **Meaning of Acquittal:** In the common law tradition, an **acquittal** formally certifies that the accused is free from the charge of an offense, as far as the criminal law is concerned.

12 **Meaning of Circumstantial Evidence:** Circumstantial Evidence is also known as indirect evidence. It is distinguished from direct evidence, which, if believed, proves the existence of a particular fact without any inference or presumption required. Circumstantial evidence relates to a series of facts other than the particular fact sought to be proved. The party offering circumstantial evidence argues that this series of facts, by reason and experience, is so closely associated with the fact to be proved that the fact to be proved may be inferred simply from the existence of the circumstantial evidence.

13 (2008) 13 SCC 767

A far more just, reasonable and proper course would be to expand the options and to take over what, as a matter of fact, lawfully belongs to the Court i.e. the vast hiatus between 14 years' imprisonment and death. It needs to be emphasised that the Court would take recourse to the expanded option primarily because in the facts of the case, the sentence of 14 years' imprisonment would amount to no punishment at all.

In the light of the discussions made above we are clearly of the view that there is a good and strong basis for the Court to substitute a death sentence by life imprisonment or by a term in excess of fourteen years and further to direct that the convict must not be released from the prison for the rest of his life or for the actual term as specified in the order, as the case may be.

Court substituted the death sentence given to the appellant by the trial court and confirmed by the High Court by imprisonment for life and directs that he shall not be released from prison till the rest of his life.

7

Partial Penetration is Sufficient to Constitute the Offence of Rape[1]

Ratio Decidendi[2]: *Delay in lodging FIR in case of rape cannot be ground for setting aside conviction[3] of accused if it has been properly explained by prosecution[4]*

Facts in Nutshell:

Appellant[5] was accused[6] of a charge of commission of an offence under Section 376[7] of the Indian Penal Code. He was sentenced to undergo

---

1 Appellants: **Satyapal Vs.** Respondent: **State of Haryana** AIR2009SC2190
   Hon'ble Judges/Coram: S. B. Sinha and Mukundakam Sharma , JJ.

2 **Meaning of Ration Decidendi:** *Ratio decidendi* is a Latin phrase meaning "the reason" or "the rationale for the decision." The *ratio decidendi* is "the point in a case which determines the judgment" or "the principle which the case establishes."

3 **Meaning of Conviction:** In law, a **conviction** is the verdict that results when a court of law finds a defendant guilty of a crime.

4 **Meaning of Prosecution:**
   a. the institution and carrying on of legal proceedings against a person.
   b. the officials who institute and conduct such proceedings.

5 **Meaning of Appellant:** A person who, dissatisfied with the judgment rendered in a lawsuit decided in a lower court or the findings from a proceeding before an Administrative Agency, asks a superior court to review the decision.

6 **Meaning of Accused:** A person charged with a criminal offense, or the state of being so charged

7 **Section 376 in The Indian Penal Code, 1860**
   376. Punishment for rape.--
   (1) Whoever, except in the cases provided for by sub- section (2), commits rape shall be punished with imprisonment of either description for a term which shall not be less than seven years but which may be for life or for a term which may extend to ten years and shall also be liable to fine unless the woman raped is his own wife and is not under twelve years of age, in which case, he shall be punished with imprisonment of either description for a term which may extend to two years or with fine or with both:
   Provided that the court may, for adequate and special reasons to be mentioned in the judgment, impose a sentence of imprisonment for a term of less than seven years.
   (2) Whoever,-
   (a) being a police officer commits rape-
   (i) within the limits of the police station to which he is appointed; or
   (ii) in the premises of any station house whether or not situated in the police station to which he is appointed; or
   (iii) on a woman in his custody or in the custody of a police officer subordinate to him; or

rigorous imprisonment for seven years and to pay fine of Rs. 20,000/-. In default of payment of fine, he was directed to undergo further rigorous imprisonment for two years.

The prosecution case is as under: The prosecutrix[8] was a minor. She was aged about 11 years. Appellant was a co-villager. On 5.02.1993 at about 8.00 a.m., she went to the fields to bring fodder. When she reached near the fields of one Nihala, the appellant came near her and forcibly lifted her. She raised an alarm but the appellant gagged her mouth and started sexually assaulting her. After hearing the voice of her aunt, the appellant left her and ran away.

Decision of Trail Court:

The learned trial Judge found the appellant guilty of commission of the offence under Section 376 of the Indian Penal Code. Aggrieved thereby and dissatisfied therewith, the appellant filed an appeal before the Punjab and Haryana High Court, which was dismissed by reason of the judgment of Trial Court. Appellant approached Supreme Court by way of Appeal.[9]

(b) being a public servant, takes advantage of his official position and commits rape on a woman in his custody as such public servant or in the custody of a public servant subordinate to him; or

(c) being on the management or on the staff of a jail, remand home or other place of custody established by or under any law for the time being in force or of a women' s or children' s institution takes advantage of his official position and commits rape on any inmate of such jail, remand home, place or institution; or

(d) being on the management or on the staff of a hospital, takes advantage of his official position and commits rape on a woman in that hospital; or

(e) commits rape on a woman knowing her to be pregnant; or

(f) commits rape on a woman when she is under twelve years of age; or

(g) commits gang rape, shall be punished with rigorous imprisonment for a term which shall not be less than ten years but which may be for life and shall also be liable to fine: Provided that the court may, for adequate and special reasons to be mentioned in the judgment, impose a sentence of imprisonment of either description for a term of less than ten years. Explanation 1.- Where a women' s is raped by one or more in a group of persons acting in furtherance of their common intention, each of the persons shall be deemed to have committed gang rape within the meaning of this sub- section. Explanation 2.-" women' s or children' s institution" means an institution, whether called and orphanage or a home for neglected women or children or a widows' home or by any other name, which is established and maintained for the reception and care of women or children. Explanation 3.-" hospital" means the precincts of the hospital and includes the precincts of any institution for the reception and treatment of persons during convalescence or of persons requiring medical attention or rehabilitation.

8 **Meaning of Prosecutrix:** A female prosecutor.

9 **Meaning of Appeal:** In law, an **appeal** is a process for requesting a formal change to an official decision. Very broadly speaking there are appeals on the record and *de novo* appeals. In *de novo* appeals, a new decision maker re-hears the case without any reference to the prior decision maker. In appeals on the record, the decision of the prior decision maker is challenged by arguing that he or she misapplied the law, came to an incorrect factual finding, acted in excess of his jurisdiction, abused his powers, was biased, considered evidence which he should not have

Observation of Trail Judge:

Cases of rape, molestations[10] and other offences against the women are quite common and are not unusual.

Judgment of High Court:

The High Court, in its judgment, opined:

Even partial penetration was sufficient to constitute the offence of rape. Absence of hymen is clear indication of the fact that there was penetration. It may be that the penetration was partial or that there was no emission of semen by the appellant.

What constitute the offence of Rape:

In Modi's Medical Jurisprudence, twenty-third edition, at pages 897 and 928, it is stated:

At page 897: To constitute the offence of rape, it is not necessary that there would be complete penetration of the penis with emission of semen and the rupture of hymen. Partial penetration of the penis within the labia majora or the vulva or pudenda with or without emission of semen or even an attempt at penetration is quite sufficient for the purpose of law. It is, therefore, quite possible to commit legally the offence of rape without producing any injury to the genitals or leaving any seminal stains.

At page 928: In small children, the hymen is not usually ruptured, but may become red and congested along with the inflammation and bruising of the labia. If considerable violence is used, there is often laceration of the fourchette and perineum.

Decision of the Supreme Court:

Supreme Court held that for the purpose of satisfaction of the ingredients of rape, it is not necessary that there should be complete penetration[11]. Court dismissed the appeal.

---

considered or failed to consider evidence that he should have considered.

10 **Meaning of Molestation:** The act of subjecting someone to unwanted or improper sexual advances or activity

11 See *Aman Kumar and Anr. v. State of Haryana* 2004CriLJ1399

8

Denial of Bail in Case of Rape[12]

Facts in Nutshell:

This application was filed by the applicant with a prayer that he may be released on bail[13] in case under Section 376 I.P.C.[14] According to

---

12 Appellants: **Sanju alias Sanjeev S/o Sri Jai Singh (In Jail) Vs.** Respondent: **State of U.P.**
   MANU/UP/1094/2005
   Hon'ble Judges/Coram: Ravindra Singh, J.

13 **Meaning of Bail:**
   1. Security, usually a sum of money, exchanged for the release of an arrested person as a guarantee of that person's appearance for trial.
   2. Release from imprisonment provided by the payment of such money.

14 **Section 376 in The Indian Penal Code, 1860**
   376. Punishment for rape.--
   (1) Whoever, except in the cases provided for by sub- section (2), commits rape shall be punished with imprisonment of either description for a term which shall not be less than seven years but which may be for life or for a term which may extend to ten years and shall also be liable to fine unless the woman raped is his own wife and is not under twelve years of age, in which case, he shall be punished with imprisonment of either description for a term which may extend to two years or with fine or with both:
   Provided that the court may, for adequate and special reasons to be mentioned in the judgment, impose a sentence of imprisonment for a term of less than seven years.
   (2) Whoever,-
   (a) being a police officer commits rape-
   (i) within the limits of the police station to which he is appointed; or
   (ii) in the premises of any station house whether or not situated in the police station to which he is appointed; or
   (iii) on a woman in his custody or in the custody of a police officer subordinate to him; or
   (b) being a public servant, takes advantage of his official position and commits rape on a woman in his custody as such public servant or in the custody of a public servant subordinate to him; or
   (c) being on the management or on the staff of a jail, remand home or other place of custody established by or under any law for the time being in force or of a women's or children's institution takes advantage of his official position and commits rape on any inmate of such jail, remand home, place or institution; or
   (d) being on the management or on the staff of a hospital, takes advantage of his official position and commits rape on a woman in that hospital; or
   (e) commits rape on a woman knowing her to be pregnant; or
   (f) commits rape on a woman when she is under twelve years of age; or
   (g) commits gang rape, shall be punished with rigorous imprisonment for a term which shall not be less than ten years but which may be for life and shall also be liable to fine: Provided that the court may, for adequate and special reasons to be mentioned in the judgment, impose a sentence of imprisonment of either description for a term of less than ten years. Explanation 1.- Where a women's is raped by one or more in a group of persons acting in furtherance of their common intention, each of the persons shall be deemed to have committed gang rape within the meaning of this sub- section. Explanation 2.-" women's or children's institution" means an institution, whether called and orphanage or a home for neglected women or children or a widows' home or

prosecution[15] version the prosecutrix[16] Km. Deepa aged about 11 years, the daughter of the first informant was enticed by the applicant at the pretext of providing some money, she was taken in a room of his house, where she was raped by the applicant. The prosecutrix made shrieks . On her shrieks the neighbourer Smt Raj Kumar came at the place of the occurrence and saw the prosecutrix in a unconscious condition and she was lying in a pool of blood. Then she called the mother of the prosecutrix who came there and saw the prosecutrix in the same condition. The accused[17] ran away from the place of the occurrence. The prosecutrix was provided medical aid. Thereafter, the F.I.R. was lodged.

Decision of High Court:

Court held that the applicant is not entitled for bail.

---

by any other name, which is established and maintained for the reception and care of women or children. Explanation 3.-" hospital" means the precincts of the hospital and includes the precincts of any institution for the reception and treatment of persons during convalescence or of persons requiring medical attention or rehabilitation.

15 **Meaning of Prosecution:**
   a. the institution and carrying on of legal proceedings against a person.
   b. the officials who institute and conduct such proceedings.

16 **Meaning of Prosecutrix:** A female prosecutor.

17 **Meaning of Accused:** A person charged with a criminal offense, or the state of being so charged

9

Death Penalty for the offence of Rape[1]

Facts in Nutshell:

Appeal[2] was filed against the judgment and order passed by the Additional Sessions Judge, Bulandshahr, whereby the Appellant[3] was convicted[4] under Section 302, I.P.C.[5] and sentenced to death. The Appellant was also convicted under Section 376(2)(g)[6], I.P.C. and sentenced to twenty years rigorous imprisonment and a fine of Rs. 10,000 under Section 201[7], I.P.C.

---

1   Appellants: **Sanjay Vs.** Respondent: **State of U.P.** 2005(3)ACR2662
    Hon'ble Judges/Coram: Imtiyaz Murtaza and Amar Saran, JJ.

2   **Meaning of Appeal:** In <u>law</u>, an **appeal** is a process for requesting a formal change to an official decision. Very broadly speaking there are appeals on the record and *de novo* appeals. In *de novo*appeals, a new decision maker re-hears the case without any reference to the prior decision maker. In appeals on the record, the decision of the prior decision maker is challenged by arguing that he or she misapplied the law, came to an incorrect factual finding, acted in excess of his jurisdiction, abused his powers, was biased, considered evidence which he should not have considered or failed to consider evidence that he should have considered.

3   **Meaning of Appellant:** A person who, dissatisfied with the judgment rendered in a lawsuit decided in a lower court or the findings from a proceeding before an Administrative Agency, asks a superior court to review the decision.

4   **Meaning of Convicted: S**omeone guilty of an offense or crime, especially by the verdict of a court

5   **Section 302, IPC 1860.**
    Punishment for murder.
    302. Punishment for murder.--Whoever commits murder shall be punished with death, or [imprisonment for life], and shall also be liable to fine.

6   **Section 376 in The Indian Penal Code, 1860**
    376. Punishment for rape.--
    (2) Whoever,-
    (g) commits gang rape, shall be punished with rigorous imprisonment for a term which shall not be less than ten years but which may be for life and shall also be liable to fine: Provided that the court may, for adequate and special reasons to be mentioned in the judgment, impose a sentence of imprisonment of either description for a term of less than ten years. Explanation 1.- Where a women' s is raped by one or more in a group of persons acting in furtherance of their common intention, each of the persons shall be deemed to have committed gang rape within the meaning of this sub- section. Explanation 2.-" women' s or children' s institution" means an institution, whether called and orphanage or a home for neglected women or children or a widows' home or by any other name, which is established and maintained for the reception and care of women or children. Explanation 3.-" hospital" means the precincts of the hospital and includes the precincts of any institution for the reception and treatment of persons during convalescence or of persons requiring medical attention or rehabilitation.

7   **Section 201 in The Indian Penal Code, 1860**
    201. Causing disappearance of evidence of offence, or giving false information to screen offender.--
    Whoever, knowing or having reason to believe that an offence has been committed, causes any

and sentenced to undergo imprisonment for seven years and a fine of Rs. 5,000. In default of payment of fine further imprisonment of two years and one year respectively. The Appellant filed appeal before High Court.

The brief facts of the case as mentioned in the first information report[8] lodged by Dinesh s/o Ram Chandra r/o Jadaul P.S. Khanpur district Bulandshahr are that his maternal cousin Sanjay used to live at his house for the last about 8 months. On 22.2.2004, in the Marriage Hall of Gajendra Singh situated at Bhaipur Doraha seven combined marriages were solemnized. Seven marriage parties had arrived including one of Naresh, in which his daughter aged about 4 years along with her aunt Raj Kumari wife of Ashok Kumar had also gone there, Sanjay had also accompanied them. Sanjay had told her aunt that he is taking away Babita along with him to her home. When Babita did not reach home, he enquired from Sanjay about her whereabouts and he told him that he had left Babita in the Marriage Hall. Since then his daughter is missing. He was thinking that his daughter might have been missing in seven marriage parties. He searched her but could not find. On 28.2.2004, Sanjay was again questioned and then he confessed that he had committed rape and thereafter murdered her and left her in the field of sugarcane.

When Death Penalty can be Awarded:

In *Machhi Singh v. State of Punjab*[9], it was observed that it was only in

---

evidence of the commission of that offence to disappear, with the intention of screening the offender from legal punishment, or with that intention gives any information respecting the offence which he knows or believes to be false, if a capital offence.-- shall, if the offence which he knows or believes to have been committed is punishable with death, be punished with imprisonment of either description for a term which may extend to seven years, and shall also be liable to fine; if punishable with imprisonment for life; if punishable with imprisonment for life.-- and if the offence is punishable with 1[imprisonment for life], or with imprisonment which may extend to ten years, shall be punished with imprisonment of either description for a term which may extend to three years, and shall also be liable to fine; if punishable with less than ten years' imprisonment. if punishable with less than ten years' imprisonment.-- and if the offence is punishable with imprisonment for any term not extending to ten years, shall be punished with imprisonment of the description provided for the offence, for a term which may extend to one-fourth part of the longest term of the imprisonment provided for the offence, or with fine, or with both. Illustration A, knowing that B has murdered Z, assists B to hide the body with the intention of screening B from punishment. A is liable to imprisonment of either description for seven years, and also to fine.

8 **Meaning of F.I.R:** A **First Information Report** (**FIR**) is a written document prepared by police organizations when they receive information about the commission of a cognizable offence. It is generally a complaint lodged with the police by the victim of a cognizable offense or by someone on his on her behalf, but anyone can make such a report either orally or in writing to the police.

9 1983 (3) SCC 413

rarest of rare cases, when the collective conscience of the community is so shocked that it will expect the holders of the judicial power center to inflict death penalty irrespective of their personal opinion as regards desirability or otherwise of retaining death penalty.

A reading of Machhi Singh case (supra) indicates that it would be possible to take the view that the community may entertain such sentiment in the following circumstances ;

(1) When the murder is committed in an extremely brutal, grotesque, diabolical, revolting or dastardly manner so as to arouse intense and extreme indignation of the community.

(2) When the murder is committed for a motive which evinces total depravity and meanness ; e.g., murder by hired assassin for money or reward ; or cold blooded murder for gains of a person vis-a-vis whom the murdered is in a dominating position or in a position of trust ; or the murder is committed in the course for betrayal of the mother land.

(3) When murder of a member of a scheduled caste or minority community, etc. is committed not for personal reasons but in circumstances which arouse social wrath ; or in cases of 'bride burning' or 'dowry death' or when murder is committed in order to remarry for the sake of extracting dowry once again or to marry another woman on account of infatuation.

(4) When the crime is enormous in proportion. For instance when multiple murders, say of all or almost all the members of a family or a large number of persons of a particular caste, community or locality, are committed.

(5) When the victim of murder is an innocent child or a helpless woman or old or infirm person or a person vis-a-vis whom the murderer is in a dominating position, or a public figure generally loved and respected by the community.

Duty of Courts to Protect Injured:

In *Sevaka Perumal v. State of Tamil Nadu*[10] , the Apex Court had observed that Undue sympathy to impose inadequate sentence would do more harm to the justice delivery system to undermine the public confidence in the efficacy of law and society could no longer endure under serious threats. If the Courts do not protect the injured, the injured would then

---

10 (1991) 3 SCC 471

resort to private vengeance. It is, therefore, the duty of every Court to award proper sentence having regard to the nature of the offence and the manner in which it was executed or committed etc.

Crime and Punishment:

The Apex Court in the case of *State of U.P. v. Satish*[11], has held that:

The principle of proportion between crime and punishment is a principle of just desert that serves as the foundation of every criminal sentence that is justifiable. As a principle of criminal justice it is hardly less familiar or less important than the principle that only the guilty ought to be punished. Indeed, the requirement that punishment not be disproportionately great, which is a corollary of just desert, is dictated by the same principle that does not allow punishment of the innocent, for any punishment in excess of what is deserved for the criminal conduct is punishment without guilt.

The criminal law adheres in general to the principle of proportionality in prescribing liability according to the culpability of each kind of criminal conduct. It ordinarily allows some significant discretion to the Judge in arriving at a sentence in each case, presumably to permit sentences that reflect more subtle considerations of culpability that are raised by the special facts of each case. Judges, in essence affirm that punishment ought always to fit the crime; yet in practice sentences are determined largely by other considerations. Sometimes it is the correctional needs of the perpetrator that are offered to justify a sentence. Sometimes the desirability of keeping him out of circulation, and sometimes even the tragic results of his crime. Inevitably these considerations cause a departure from just desert as the basis of punishment and create cases of apparent injustice that are serious and widespread.

Proportion between crime and punishment is a goal respected in principle, and in spite of errant notions, it remains a strong influence in the determination of sentences. Anything less than a penalty greatest severity for serious crime is thought to be a measure of toleration that is unwarranted and unwise. But in fact quite apart from those considerations that make punishment unjustifiable when it is out of proportion to the crime, uniformly disproportionate punishment has some very undesirable practical consequences.

---

11 2005 (1) ARC 648 (SC) : 2005 (1) SCC 311 : JT 2005 (52) SC 153

Decision of High Court:

Court held that Km. Babita was only a four year old helpless child. She was raped and murdered by her own close relative, Appellant's, parents had died and he was given shelter by Dinesh, father of the deceased[12]. He was living in the house of the deceased for the last seven eight months prior to the occurrence. The deceased must have reposed confidence in her as he was her close relative. Even after the occurrence, he did not show any remorse, he remained present throughout with the family members searching deceased in various places. Court held that the Sessions Judge rightly sentenced the Appellant to death and High Court also confirmed the same.

---

12 **Meaning of Deceased:** Someone who is no longer alive

10

Rapist degrades the very soul of the helpless female [1]

Facts in Nutshell:

The prosecutrix[2], a young girl about 18 years of age, was staying with her parents in village Kothi, district Bilaspur, (H.P.). The accused[3], Rajinder@ Raju, resident of village Duhak, district Bilaspur, had taken contract for laying G.I. Pipelines in village Kothi near the residence of the prosecutrix. In that connection, he used to store his material in the house of prosecutrix' parents. On January 16, 1996, prosecutrix had some throat pain. When the accused came to the house of the prosecutrix and came to know that the prosecutrix has been suffering from throat pain, he suggested to the mother of the prosecutrix that his cousin at Ghumarwin was a doctor and if permitted, he could show the prosecutrix to his cousin. The mother of the prosecutrix agreed. The accused took the prosecutrix on his scooter. Instead of taking the prosecutrix to Ghumarwin, he took her to Jablu stating that he had to collect the rent from his tenants. From Jablu, the accused took prosecutrix to Berthin. At Berthin, the accused bought some sweets and told the prosecutrix that he would take her to his house as it was dark. The accused instead of taking her to his house, took the scooter to some kachha road and made her to get down from the scooter. Accused committed the sexual intercourse with her forcibly.

After completion of the investigation[4], a charge-sheet[5] was filed against

---

1 Appellants: **Rajinder @ Raju Vs.** Respondent: **State of H.P.** AIR2009SC3022
   Hon'ble Judges/Coram: V. S. Sirpurkar and R. M. Lodha, JJ.

2 **Meaning of Prosecutrix:** A female prosecutor.

3 **Meaning of Accused:** A person charged with a criminal offense, or the state of being so charged

4 **Meaning of Investigation:** A detailed inquiry or systematic examination.

5   **Meaning of Charge-Sheet:** A document on which a police officer enters details of the charge against a prisoner and the court in which he will appear

the accused under Sections 366[6] and 376[7] IPC and Section 3(XII)[8]of

6 **Section 366 in The Indian Penal Code, 1860**
366. Kidnapping, abducting or inducing woman to compel her marriage, etc.-- Whoever kidnaps or abducts any woman with intent that she may be compelled, or knowing it to be likely that she will be compelled, to marry any person against her will, or in order that she may be forced or seduced to illicit intercourse, or knowing it to be likely that she will be forced or seduced to illicit intercourse, shall be punished with imprisonment of either description for a term which may extend to ten years, and shall also be liable to fine; [and whoever, by means of criminal intimidation as defined in this Code or of abuse of authority or any other method of compulsion, induces any woman to go from any place with intent that she may be, or knowing that it is likely that she will be, forced or seduced to illicit intercourse with another person shall also be punishable as aforesaid].

7 **Section 376 in The Indian Penal Code, 1860**
376. Punishment for rape.--
(1) Whoever, except in the cases provided for by sub- section (2), commits rape shall be punished with imprisonment of either description for a term which shall not be less than seven years but which may be for life or for a term which may extend to ten years and shall also be liable to fine unless the woman raped is his own wife and is not under twelve years of age, in which case, he shall be punished with imprisonment of either description for a term which may extend to two years or with fine or with both:
Provided that the court may, for adequate and special reasons to be mentioned in the judgment, impose a sentence of imprisonment for a term of less than seven years.
(2) Whoever,-
(a) being a police officer commits rape-
(i) within the limits of the police station to which he is appointed; or
(ii) in the premises of any station house whether or not situated in the police station to which he is appointed; or
(iii) on a woman in his custody or in the custody of a police officer subordinate to him; or
(b) being a public servant, takes advantage of his official position and commits rape on a woman in his custody as such public servant or in the custody of a public servant subordinate to him; or
(c) being on the management or on the staff of a jail, remand home or other place of custody established by or under any law for the time being in force or of a women' s or children' s institution takes advantage of his official position and commits rape on any inmate of such jail, remand home, place or institution; or
(d) being on the management or on the staff of a hospital, takes advantage of his official position and commits rape on a woman in that hospital; or
(e) commits rape on a woman knowing her to be pregnant; or
(f) commits rape on a woman when she is under twelve years of age; or
(g) commits gang rape, shall be punished with rigorous imprisonment for a term which shall not be less than ten years but which may be for life and shall also be liable to fine: Provided that the court may, for adequate and special reasons to be mentioned in the judgment, impose a sentence of imprisonment of either description for a term of less than ten years. Explanation 1.- Where a women' s is raped by one or more in a group of persons acting in furtherance of their common intention, each of the persons shall be deemed to have committed gang rape within the meaning of this sub- section. Explanation 2.-" women' s or children' s institution" means an institution, whether called and orphanage or a home for neglected women or children or a widows' home or by any other name, which is established and maintained for the reception and care of women or children. Explanation 3.-" hospital" means the precincts of the hospital and includes the precincts of any institution for the reception and treatment of persons during convalescence or of persons requiring medical attention or rehabilitation.

8 **Section 3(XII) of Scheduled Castes and Scheduled Tribes (Prevention of Atrocities) Act, 1989:**
Section 3(1) Punishment for offences of Atrocities:
3. (1) Whoever, not being a member of a Scheduled Caste or a Scheduled Tribe,-
(xii) being in a position to dominate the will of a woman belonging to a Scheduled Caste or a Scheduled Tribe and uses that position to exploit her sexually to which she would not have

Scheduled Castes and Scheduled Tribes (Prevention of Atrocities) Act, 1989.

Decision of Session Judge:

The Sessions Judge, Bilaspur on consideration of the evidence on record, acquitted the accused of the charge under Section 3(XII) of Scheduled Castes and Scheduled Tribes (Prevention of Atrocities) Act, 1989 but convicted the accused under Sections 366 and 376IPC. The accused was sentenced to rigorous imprisonment for seven years and to pay a fine of Rs. 10,000/- with default stipulation for the graver offence under Section 376 IPC only.

The accused challenged his conviction and sentence before the High Court of Himachal Pradesh. The learned Single Judge dismissed the appeal preferred by the accused. Hence the accused appealed in Supreme Court by special leave[9].

Cases Referred (Rape)

In *State of Rajasthan v. N.K.*[10], Supreme Court held thus:

For the offence of rape as defined in Section 375[11] of the Indian Penal

---

otherwise agreed;

9   **Article 136 in The Constitution Of India 1949**
136. Special leave to appeal by the Supreme Court
(1) Notwithstanding anything in this Chapter, the Supreme Court may, in its discretion, grant special leave to appeal from any judgment, decree, determination, sentence or order in any cause or matter passed or made by any court or tribunal in the territory of India
(2) Nothing in clause (1) shall apply to any judgment, determination, sentence or order passed or made by any court or tribunal constituted by or under any law relating to the Armed Forces

10 2000CriLJ2205

11 **Section 375 in The Indian Penal Code, 1860**
375. Rape-- A man is said to commit" rape" who, except in the case hereinafter excepted, has sexual intercourse with a woman under circumstances falling under any of the six following descriptions:- First.- Against her will. Secondly.- Without her consent. Thirdly.- With her consent, when her consent has been obtained by putting her or any person in whom she is interested in fear of death or of hurt. Fourthly.- With her consent, when the man knows that he is not her husband, and that her consent is given because she believes that he is another man to whom she is or believes herself to be lawfully married. Fifthly.- With her consent, when, at the time of giving such consent, by reason of unsoundness of mind or intoxication or the administration by him personally or through another of any stupefying or unwholesome substance, she is unable to understand the nature and consequences of that to which she gives consent. Sixthly.- With or without her consent, when she is under sixteen years of age. Explanation.- Penetration is sufficient to constitute the sexual intercourse necessary to the offence of rape. Exception.- Sexual intercourse by a man with his own wife, the wife not being under fifteen years of age, is not rape.

Code, the sexual intercourse should have been against the will of the woman or without her consent. Consent is immaterial in certain circumstances covered by clauses thirdly to sixthly, the last one being when the woman is under 16 years of age. Based on these provisions, an argument is usually advanced on behalf of the accused charged with rape that the absence of proof of want of consent where the prosecutrix is not under 16 years of age takes the assault out of the purview of Section 375 of the Indian Penal Code. Certainly consent is no defence if the victim has been proved to be under 16 years of age. If she be of 16 years of age or above, her consent cannot be presumed; an inference as to consent can be drawn if only based on evidence or probabilities of the case. The victim of rape stating on oath that she was forcibly subjected to sexual intercourse or that the act was done without her consent, has to be believed and accepted like any other testimony unless there is material available to draw an inference as to her consent or else the testimony of prosecutrix is such as would be inherently improbable.

Supreme Court, in the case of *Gurmit Singh*[12] , made the following weighty observations in respect of evidence of a victim of sexual assault:

The courts must, while evaluating evidence, remain alive to the fact that in a case of rape, no self- respecting woman would come forward in a court just to make a humiliating statement against her honour such as is involved in the commission of rape on her.

Decision of Supreme Court:

Court held that in the context of Indian Culture, a woman - victim of sexual aggression - would rather suffer silently than to falsely implicate somebody. Any statement of rape is an extremely humiliating experience for a woman and until she is a victim of sex crime, she would not blame anyone but the real culprit. While appreciating the evidence of the prosecutrix, the Courts must always keep in mind that no self-respecting woman would put her honour at stake by falsely alleging commission of rape on her and, therefore, ordinarily a look for corroboration of her testimony is unnecessary and uncalled for. But for high improbability in the prosecution case, the conviction in the case of sex crime may be based on the sole testimony of the prosecutrix.

Court find that the judgment of the High Court affirming the judgment of

---

12 1996CriLJ1728

the trial court convicting the accused under Sections 366 and 376 IPC does not suffer from any legal flaw. The sentence awarded to the appellant does not call for any interference by Supreme Court.

11

Outraging the Modesty of Women[1]

Ratio Decidendi[2]: *In order to constitute the offence under Section 354[3] IPC mere knowledge that the modesty of a woman is likely to be outraged is sufficient without any deliberate intention of having such outrage alone for its object.*

Facts in Nutshell:

The prosecutrix[4] filed a report that on i.e. 25.8.1987 in the morning at about 9.00 or 9.30 a.m. that when she went to the field of Bhinya Raika and was returning back to village Biradhwal, accused Premiya all of a sudden came and caught hold of her. Thereafter, the accused Premiya threw her on the ground, put off his "Paijama", lifted her "Ghaghra" and committed rape on her. When she tried to resist, accused Premiya gave a blow on her eye and threatened to kill her, if she made any sound. The accused[5] was charged for offence punishable under Section 376[6] IPC to

---

1   Appellants: **Premiya @ Prem Prakash Vs.** Respondent: **State of Rajasthan** (2008)10SCC81
   Hon'ble Judges/Coram: Dr. Arijit Pasayat and Mukundakam Sharma , JJ.

2   **Meaning of Ration Decidendi:** *Ratio decidendi* is a Latin phrase meaning "the reason" or "the rationale for the decision." The *ratio decidendi* is "the point in a case which determines the judgment" or "the principle which the case establishes."

3   **Section 354 in The Indian Penal Code, 1860**
   354. Assault or criminal force to woman with intent to outrage her modesty.-- Whoever assaults or uses criminal force to any woman, intending to outrage or knowing it to be likely that he will there by outrage her modesty, shall be punished with imprisonment of either description for a term which may extend to two years, or with fine, or with both.

4   **Meaning of Prosecutrix:** A female prosecutor.

5   **Meaning of Accused:** A person charged with a criminal offense, or the state of being so charged

6   **Section 376 in The Indian Penal Code, 1860**
   376. Punishment for rape.--
   (1) Whoever, except in the cases provided for by sub- section (2), commits rape shall be punished with imprisonment of either description for a term which shall not be less than seven years but which may be for life or for a term which may extend to ten years and shall also be liable to fine unless the woman raped is his own wife and is not under twelve years of age, in which case, he shall be punished with imprisonment of either description for a term which may extend to two years or with fine or with both:
   Provided that the court may, for adequate and special reasons to be mentioned in the judgment, impose a sentence of imprisonment for a term of less than seven years.
   (2) Whoever,-
   (a) being a police officer commits rape-
   (i) within the limits of the police station to which he is appointed; or

which he pleaded not guilty.

Decision of Trail Court and High Court:

Rajasthan High Court at Jodhpur dismissing the appeal[7] filed by the appellant[8] and upholding his conviction[9] for offence punishable under Section 376 of the Indian Penal Code, 1860 (in short the `IPC') and sentence of 7 years imprisonment as was imposed by learned Additional Sessions Judge Hanumangarh. The appellant approached Supreme Court.

(ii) in the premises of any station house whether or not situated in the police station to which he is appointed; or

(iii) on a woman in his custody or in the custody of a police officer subordinate to him; or

(b) being a public servant, takes advantage of his official position and commits rape on a woman in his custody as such public servant or in the custody of a public servant subordinate to him; or

(c) being on the management or on the staff of a jail, remand home or other place of custody established by or under any law for the time being in force or of a women' s or children' s institution takes advantage of his official position and commits rape on any inmate of such jail, remand home, place or institution; or

(d) being on the management or on the staff of a hospital, takes advantage of his official position and commits rape on a woman in that hospital; or

(e) commits rape on a woman knowing her to be pregnant; or

(f) commits rape on a woman when she is under twelve years of age; or

(g) commits gang rape, shall be punished with rigorous imprisonment for a term which shall not be less than ten years but which may be for life and shall also be liable to fine: Provided that the court may, for adequate and special reasons to be mentioned in the judgment, impose a sentence of imprisonment of either description for a term of less than ten years. Explanation 1.- Where a women' s is raped by one or more in a group of persons acting in furtherance of their common intention, each of the persons shall be deemed to have committed gang rape within the meaning of this sub- section. Explanation 2.-" women' s or children' s institution" means an institution, whether called and orphanage or a home for neglected women or children or a widows' home or by any other name, which is established and maintained for the reception and care of women or children. Explanation 3.-" hospital" means the precincts of the hospital and includes the precincts of any institution for the reception and treatment of persons during convalescence or of persons requiring medical attention or rehabilitation.

7   **Meaning of Appeal:** In law, an **appeal** is a process for requesting a formal change to an official decision. Very broadly speaking there are appeals on the record and *de novo* appeals. In *de novo* appeals, a new decision maker re-hears the case without any reference to the prior decision maker. In appeals on the record, the decision of the prior decision maker is challenged by arguing that he or she misapplied the law, came to an incorrect factual finding, acted in excess of his jurisdiction, abused his powers, was biased, considered evidence which he should not have considered or failed to consider evidence that he should have considered.

8   **Meaning of Appellant:** A person who, dissatisfied with the judgment rendered in a lawsuit decided in a lower court or the findings from a proceeding before an Administrative Agency, asks a superior court to review the decision.

9   **Meaning of Conviction:** In law, a **conviction** is the verdict that results when a court of law finds a defendant guilty of a crime.

Name of Rape Victim should not be Disclosed:

Section 228A[10] of IPC makes disclosure of identity of victim of certain offences punishable. Printing or publishing name of any matter which may make known the identity of any person against whom an offence

---

10 **Section 228A in The Indian Penal Code, 1860**
228A. [Disclosure of identity of the victim of certain offences, etc.--
(1) Whoever prints or publishes the name or any matter which may make known the identity of any person against whom an offence under section 376, section 376A, section 376B, section 376C or section 376D is alleged or found to have been committed (hereafter in this section referred to as the victim) shall be punished with imprisonment of either description for a term which may extend to two years and shall also be liable to fine.
(2) Nothing in sub- section (1) extends to any printing or publication of the name or any matter which may make known the identity of the victim if such printing or publication is-
(a) by or under the order in writing of the officer- in- charge of the police station or the police officer making the investigation into such offence acting in good faith for the purposes of such investigation; or
(b) by, or with the authorisation in writing of, the victim; or
(c) where the victim is dead or minor or of unsound mind, by, or with the authorisation in writing of, the next- of- kin of the victim: Provided that no such authorisation shall be given by the next- of- kin to anybody other than the chairman or the secretary, by whatever name called, of any recognised welfare institution or organisation. Explanation.- For the purposes of this sub- section," recognised welfare institution or organisation" means a social welfare institution or organisation recognised in this behalf by the Central or State Government.
(3) Whoever prints or publishes any matter in relation to any proceeding before a court with respect to an offence referred to in sub- section (1) without the previous permission of such court shall be punished with imprisonment of either description for a term which may extend to two years and shall also be liable to fine. Explanation.- The printing or publication of the judgment of any High Court or the Supreme Court does not amount to an offence within the meaning of this section.]

under Sections 376,376A[11], 376B[12], 376C[13] or 376D[14] is alleged or found to have been committed can be punished. True it is, the restriction, does not relate to printing or publication of judgment by High Court or Supreme Court. But keeping in view the social object of preventing social victimization or ostracism of the victim of a sexual offence for which Section 228A has been enacted, it would be appropriate that in the judgments, be it of Supreme Court, High Court or lower Court, the name of the victim should not be indicated.[15]

Offence of Rape:

The offence of rape occurs in Chapter XVI of IPC. It is an offence affecting the human body. In that Chapter, there is a separate heading for `Sexual

---

11 Section 376A in The Indian Penal Code, 1860
376A. Intercourse by a man with his wife during separation.-- Whoever has sexual intercourse with his own wife, who is living separately from him under a decree of separation or under any custom or usage without her consent shall be punished with imprisonment of either description for a term which may extend to two years and shall also be liable to fine.

12 Section 376B in The Indian Penal Code, 1860
376B. Intercourse by public servant with woman in his custody.-- Whoever, being a public servant, takes advantage of his official position and induces or seduces, any woman, who is in his custody as such public servant or in the custody of a public servant subordinate to him, to have sexual intercourse with him, such sexual intercourse not amounting to the offence of rape, shall be punished with imprisonment of either description for a term which may extend to five years and shall also be liable to fine.

13 Section 376C in The Indian Penal Code, 1860
376C. Intercourse by superintendent of jail, remand home, etc.-- Whoever, being the superintendent or manager of a jail, remand home or other place of custody established by or under any law for the time being in force or of a women' s or children' s institution takes advantage of his official position and induces or seduces any female inmate of such jail, remand home, place or institution to have sexual intercourse with him, such sexual intercourse not amounting to the offence of rape, shall be punished with imprisonment of either description for a term which may extend to five years and shall also be liable to fine. Explanation 1.-" Superintendent" in relation to a jail, remand home or other place of custody or a women' s or children' s institution, includes a person holding any other office in such jail, remand home, place or institution by virtue of which he can exercise any authority or control over its inmates. Explanation 2.- The expression" women' s or children' s institution" shall have the same meaning as in Explanation 2 to sub- section (2) of section 376.

14 Section 376D in The Indian Penal Code, 1860
376D. Intercourse by any member of the management or staff of a hospital with any woman in that hospital.-- Whoever, being on the management of a hospital or being on the staff of a hospital takes advantage of his position and has sexual intercourse with any woman in that hospital, such sexual intercourse not amounting to the offence of rape, shall be punished with imprisonment of either description for a term which may extend to five years and shall also be liable to fine. Explanation.- The expression" hospital" shall have the same meaning as in Explanation 3 to sub-section (2) of section 376.] Of unnatural offences

15 See *State of Karnataka v. Puttaraja* 2003 (8) Supreme 364 and *Dinesh alias Buddha v. State of Rajasthan* 2006CriLJ1679 .

offence', which encompasses Sections 375[16], 376, 376A, 376B, 376C, and 376D. `Rape' is defined in Section 375. Sections375 and 376 have been substantially changed by Criminal Law (Amendment) Act, 1983, and several new sections were introduced by the new Act, i.e. 376A, 376B, 376C and 376D. The fact that sweeping changes were introduced reflects the legislative intent to curb with iron hand, the offence of rape which affects the dignity of a woman. The offence of rape in its simplest term is `the ravishment of a woman, without her consent, by force, fear or fraud', or as `the carnal knowledge of a woman by force against her will'. `Rape' or `Raptus' is when a man hath carnal knowledge of a woman by force and against her will (Co. Litt. 123-b); or as expressed more fully,' Rape' is the carnal knowledge of any woman, above the age of particular years, against her will; or of a woman child, under that age, with or against her will' (Hale PC 628). The essential words in an indictment for rape are rapuit and carnaliter cognovit; but carnaliter cognovit, nor any other circumlocution without the word rapuit, are not sufficient in a legal sense to express rape.[17] In the crime of rape, `carnal knowledge' means the penetration to any the slightest degree of the organ alleged to have been carnally known by the male organ of generation[18]. In `Encyclopedia of Crime and Justice'[19] it is stated "...even slight penetration is sufficient and emission is unnecessary". In Halsbury's Statutes of England and Wales (Fourth Edition) Volume 12, it is stated that even the slightest degree of penetration is sufficient to prove sexual intercourse. It is violation with violence of the private person of a woman-an-outrage by all means. By the very nature of the offence it is an obnoxious act of the highest order.

---

16 **Section 375 in The Indian Penal Code, 1860**
    375. Rape.-- A man is said to commit" rape" who, except in the case hereinafter excepted, has sexual intercourse with a woman under circumstances falling under any of the six following descriptions:- First.- Against her will. Secondly.- Without her consent. Thirdly.- With her consent, when her consent has been obtained by putting her or any person in whom she is interested in fear of death or of hurt. Fourthly.- With her consent, when the man knows that he is not her husband, and that her consent is given because she believes that he is another man to whom she is or believes herself to be lawfully married. Fifthly.- With her consent, when, at the time of giving such consent, by reason of unsoundness of mind or intoxication or the administration by him personally or through another of any stupefying or unwholesome substance, she is unable to understand the nature and consequences of that to which she gives consent. Sixthly.- With or without her consent, when she is under sixteen years of age. Explanation.- Penetration is sufficient to constitute the sexual intercourse necessary to the offence of rape. Exception.- Sexual intercourse by a man with his own wife, the wife not being under fifteen years of age, is not rape.

17 1 Hon.6, 1a, 9 Edw. 4, 26 a (Hale PC 628).

18 (Stephen's "Criminal Law" 9th Ed. p.262)

19 (Volume 4, page 1356)

Outraging Modesty of Women:

In order to constitute the offence under Section 354 IPC mere knowledge that the modesty of a woman is likely to be outraged is sufficient without any deliberate intention of having such outrage alone for its object. There is no abstract conception of modesty that can apply to all cases[20]. A careful approach has to be adopted by the court while dealing with a case alleging outrage of modesty. The essential ingredients of the offence under Section 354 IPC are as under:

(i) that the person assaulted must be a woman;

(ii) that the accused must have used criminal force on her; and

(iii) that the criminal force must have been used on the woman intending thereby to outrage her modesty.

Decision of Supreme Court:

Intention is not the sole criterion of the offence punishable under Section 354 IPC, and it can be committed by a person assaulting or using criminal force to any woman, if he knows that by such act the modesty of the woman is likely to be affected. Knowledge and intention are essentially things of the mind and cannot be demonstrated like physical objects. The existence of intention or knowledge has to be culled out from various circumstances in which and upon whom the alleged offence is alleged to have been committed. A victim of molestation and indignation is in the same position as an injured witness and her testimony should receive the same weight. Court held that in the instant case after careful consideration of the evidence, the trial court and the High Court have found the accused guilty. But the offence is Section 354 IPC.

Court altered the conviction of the accused from Section 376 IPC to Section354 IPC.

---

20 . See *State of Punjab* v. *Major Singh,* 1967CriLJ1

12

Attempt to commit rape is lesser offence than that of rape[1]

Ratio Decidendi[2]: *"If an accused is charged of a major offence but is not found guilty thereunder, he can be convicted of minor offence, if the facts established indicate that such minor offence has been committed."*

Facts in Nutshell:

Prosecutrix[3] was a working woman and was working in Battery Company at Vardhman Nagar. According to the allegations made in the First Information Report filed by her, she met the accused[4]-appellant at Boudha Vihar situated at Seminary Hills. At the said meeting, the accused-appellant told her that he was in need of maid servant and she will be paid Rs. 400/- with meals and residence facility. Thereafter, the accused - appellant invited her to attend the Paritrana Path (Puja). However, the function of Puja was postponed. The accused-appellant asked the complainant (lady) to sleep in kitchen room along with their children. Further allegation made out in the FIR was that in night the complainant found that somebody was touching her head and hence she gave jerk to the hand. When she again felt that somebody was touching her body she got up. She found that the accused-appellant was sitting near her bed whereupon she shouted. Immediately, the accused-appellant gagged her mouth and lifted the petticoat and removed the underwear of the prosecutrix and committed sexual intercourse.

---

1 Appellants: **Pandharinath Vs.** Respondent: **State of Maharashtra** AIR2010SC1453
  Hon'ble Judges/Coram: Mukundakam Sharma and B. S. Chauhan, JJ.

2 **Meaning of Ration Decidendi:** *Ratio decidendi* is a Latin phrase meaning "the reason" or "the rationale for the decision." The *ratio decidendi* is "the point in a case which determines the judgment" or "the principle which the case establishes."

3 **Meaning of Prosecutrix:** A female prosecutor.

4 **Meaning of Accused:** A person charged with a criminal offense, or the state of being so charged

Decision of the Trail Court and High Court:

The trial court, after convicting[5] the appellant under Section 376[6] IPC sentenced him to suffer rigorous imprisonment for five years and to pay a fine of Rs. 1,000/- in default to suffer further rigorous imprisonment for six months. The said sentence was, however, altered by the High Court by awarding a sentence to undergo rigorous imprisonment for the period of one year and to pay a fine of Rs. 1,000/- and in default to undergo further rigorous imprisonment for a period of six months. The High Court by its Judgment held the appellant guilty under Section 511[7] of

---

5 **Meaning of Conviction:** In law, a **conviction** is the verdict that results when a court of law finds a defendant guilty of a crime.

6 **Section 376 in The Indian Penal Code, 1860**
376. Punishment for rape.--
(1) Whoever, except in the cases provided for by sub- section (2), commits rape shall be punished with imprisonment of either description for a term which shall not be less than seven years but which may be for life or for a term which may extend to ten years and shall also be liable to fine unless the woman raped is his own wife and is not under twelve years of age, in which case, he shall be punished with imprisonment of either description for a term which may extend to two years or with fine or with both:
Provided that the court may, for adequate and special reasons to be mentioned in the judgment, impose a sentence of imprisonment for a term of less than seven years.
(2) Whoever,-
(a) being a police officer commits rape-
(i) within the limits of the police station to which he is appointed; or
(ii) in the premises of any station house whether or not situated in the police station to which he is appointed; or
(iii) on a woman in his custody or in the custody of a police officer subordinate to him; or
(b) being a public servant, takes advantage of his official position and commits rape on a woman in his custody as such public servant or in the custody of a public servant subordinate to him; or
(c) being on the management or on the staff of a jail, remand home or other place of custody established by or under any law for the time being in force or of a women' s or children' s institution takes advantage of his official position and commits rape on any inmate of such jail, remand home, place or institution; or
(d) being on the management or on the staff of a hospital, takes advantage of his official position and commits rape on a woman in that hospital; or
(e) commits rape on a woman knowing her to be pregnant; or
(f) commits rape on a woman when she is under twelve years of age; or
(g) commits gang rape, shall be punished with rigorous imprisonment for a term which shall not be less than ten years but which may be for life and shall also be liable to fine: Provided that the court may, for adequate and special reasons to be mentioned in the judgment, impose a sentence of imprisonment of either description for a term of less than ten years. Explanation 1.- Where a women' s is raped by one or more in a group of persons acting in furtherance of their common intention, each of the persons shall be deemed to have committed gang rape within the meaning of this sub- section. Explanation 2.-" women' s or children' s institution" means an institution, whether called and orphanage or a home for neglected women or children or a widows' home or by any other name, which is established and maintained for the reception and care of women or children. Explanation 3.-" hospital" means the precincts of the hospital and includes the precincts of any institution for the reception and treatment of persons during convalescence or of persons requiring medical attention or rehabilitation.

7 **Section 511 in The Indian Penal Code, 1860**

the IPC for the offence of attempt to commit rape and sentenced him to rigorous imprisonment for one year and to pay a fine of Rs. 1,000/-. Being aggrieved by the aforesaid judgment and order of conviction and sentence, the accused-appellant filed the appeal in Supreme Court by way of special leave[8].

The trial court was of the view that the appellant is liable to convicted under Section 376 IPC. The High Court, however, held the appellant guilty of the offence under Section 376 IPC read with Section 511 of the IPC. It is well settled legal position that if an accused is charged of a major offence but is not found guilty thereunder, he can be convicted of minor offence, if the facts established indicate that such minor offence has been committed[9].

Decision of Supreme Court:

Court held that section 376 IPC was not applicable but a lesser offence under 376 read with 511 IPC is made out, the court was not prevented from taking recourse to and punishing the accused for the commission of such lesser offence. The attempt to commit rape was a lesser offence than that of rape, and there is no bar of converting the act of the accused from Section 376 to 511.

---

511. Punishment for attempting to commit offences punishable with imprisonment for life or other imprisonment.-- Whoever attempts to commit an offence punishable by this Code with 1[imprisonment for life] or imprisonment, or to cause such an offence to be committed, and in such attempt does any act towards the commission of the offence, shall, where no express provision is made by this Code for the punishment of such attempt, be punished with 2[imprisonment o f any description provided for the offence, for a term which may extend to one- half of the imprisonment for life or, as the case may be, one- half of the longest term of imprisonment provided for that offence], or with such fine as is provided for the offence, or with both. Illustrations

(a) A makes an attempt to steal some jewels by breaking open a box, and finds after so opening the box, that there is no jewel in it. He has done an act towards the commission of theft, and therefore is guilty under this section.

(b) A makes an attempt to pick the pocket of Z by thrusting his hand into Z' s pocket. A fails in the attempt in consequence of Z' s having nothing in his pocket. A is guilty under this section.

8   Article 136 in The Constitution Of India 1949

136. Special leave to appeal by the Supreme Court

(1) Notwithstanding anything in this Chapter, the Supreme Court may, in its discretion, grant special leave to appeal from any judgment, decree, determination, sentence or order in any cause or matter passed or made by any court or tribunal in the territory of India

(2) Nothing in clause (1) shall apply to any judgment, determination, sentence or order passed or made by any court or tribunal constituted by or under any law relating to the Armed Forces

9   State of Maharashtra v. Rajendra Jawanmal Gandhi (1997)8SCC386

13

No Mercy to Accused in Case of Rape[1]

Facts in Nutshell:

Prosecutrix[2] lodged report at police station Khajuraho to that effect that she was in the field of Hannu Gadariya at Bhusaur. The said field was taken on share basis by her husband, in which gram and wheat were sown. As usual, she had gone to the field for guarding. One hut was situated there, in which she lives and cooks and eats food at that place. At the said time she was alone in the hut. Her husband had gone to village Rajnagar. Accused[3] Motilal Gadariya who was resident of same village, came there and enquired from her about her husband Barelal. She told him that he had gone to Rajnagar, and he went away. She started sweeping with broom, inside the hut. After some time, Motilal forcibly entered her hut and knocked her down on the floor. He pulled up her saree and committed sexual intercourse. She kept shouting to break free, but there was no body. Then he ran away.

Decision of High Court:

Appellant[4] Challenged in the appeal[5] the judgment of a learned Single Judge of the Madhya Pradesh High Court at Jabalpur upholding the conviction[6] of

---

1 Appellants: **Moti Lal Vs.** Respondent: **State of M.P.** (2008)11SCC20
   Hon'ble Judges/Coram: Dr. Arijit Pasayat and P. Sathasivam , JJ.

2 **Meaning of Prosecutrix:** A female prosecutor.

3 **Meaning of Accused:** A person charged with a criminal offense, or the state of being so charged

4 **Meaning of Appellant:** A person who, dissatisfied with the judgment rendered in a lawsuit decided in a lower court or the findings from a proceeding before an Administrative Agency, asks a superior court to review the decision.

5 **Meaning of Appeal:** In law, an **appeal** is a process for requesting a formal change to an official decision. Very broadly speaking there are appeals on the record and de novo appeals. In de novoappeals, a new decision maker re-hears the case without any reference to the prior decision maker. In appeals on the record, the decision of the prior decision maker is challenged by arguing that he or she misapplied the law, came to an incorrect factual finding, acted in excess of his jurisdiction, abused his powers, was biased, considered evidence which he should not have considered or failed to consider evidence that he should have considered.

6 **Meaning of Conviction:** In law, a **conviction** is the verdict that results when a court of law finds a defendant guilty of a crime.

the appellant for offence punishable under Sections 450[7] and 376(1)[8] of the Indian Penal Code, 1860 (in short the `IPC') and sentence of five years and seven years rigorous imprisonment respectively and fine of Rs. 2,000/- and 1,000/- respectively. Appellant (hereinafter also referred to as an `accused') was charged for commission of offences punishable under Sections 450 and 376(1)IPC and 3(1)(xii)[9] of the Scheduled Castes and Scheduled Tribes Prevention of Atrocities Act, 1989, (in short the `Act').

A woman or a girl who is raped is not an accomplice[10].

A girl or a woman in the tradition bound non-permissive society of India would be extremely reluctant even to admit that any incident which is likely to reflect on her chastity had ever occurred. She would be conscious of the danger of being ostracized by the society and when in the face of these factors the crime is brought to light, there is inbuilt assurance that the charge is genuine rather than fabricated. Just as a witness who has sustained an injury, which is not shown or believed to be self-inflicted, is the best witness in the sense that he is least likely to exculpate the real offender, the evidence of a victim of sex offence is entitled to great weight, absence of corroboration notwithstanding. A woman or a girl

---

7   Section 450 in The Indian Penal Code, 1860
    450. House- trespass in order to commit offence punishable with imprisonment for life.-- Whoever commits house- trespass in order to the committing of any offence punishable with 1[imprisonment for life], shall be punished with imprisonment of either description for a term not exceeding ten years, and shall also be liable to fine.

8   Section 376 in The Indian Penal Code, 1860
    376. Punishment for rape.--
    (1) Whoever, except in the cases provided for by sub- section (2), commits rape shall be punished with imprisonment of either description for a term which shall not be less than seven years but which may be for life or for a term which may extend to ten years and shall also be liable to fine unless the woman raped is his own wife and is not under twelve years of age, in which case, he shall be punished with imprisonment of either description for a term which may extend to two years or with fine or with both:
    Provided that the court may, for adequate and special reasons to be mentioned in the judgment, impose a sentence of imprisonment for a term of less than seven years.

9   Section 3(XII) of Scheduled Castes and Scheduled Tribes (Prevention of Atrocities) Act, 1989:
    Section 3(1) Punishment for offences of Atrocities:
    3. (1) Whoever, not being a member of a Scheduled Caste or a Scheduled Tribe,-
    (xii) being in a position to dominate the will of a woman belonging to a Scheduled Caste or a Scheduled Tribe and uses that position to exploit her sexually to which she would not have otherwise agreed

10 Meaning of Accomplice: At law, an accomplice is a person who actively participates in the commission of a crime, even though they take no part in the actual criminal offense. For example, in a bank robbery, the person who points the gun at the teller and asks for the money is guilty of armed robbery. However, anyone else directly involved in the commission of the crime, such as the lookout or the getaway car driver, is an accomplice, even though in the absence of an underlying offense keeping a lookout or driving a car would not be an offense.

who is raped is not an accomplice.

It is settled law that the victim of sexual assault is not treated as accomplice and as such, her evidence does not require corroboration[11] from any other evidence including the evidence of a doctor. In a given case even if the doctor who examined the victim does not find sign of rape, it is no ground to disbelieve the sole testimony of the prosecutrix. In normal course a victim of sexual assault does not like to disclose such offence even before her family members much less before public or before the police. The Indian women has tendency to conceal such offence because it involves her prestige as well as prestige of her family. Only in few cases, the victim girl or the family members has courage to go before the police station and lodge a case.

Of late, crime against women in general and rape in particular is on the increase. It is an irony that while we are celebrating women's rights in all spheres, we show little or no concern for her honour. It is a sad reflection on the attitude of indifference of the society towards the violation of human dignity of the victims of sex crimes. We must remember that a rapist not only violates the victim's privacy and personal integrity, but inevitably causes serious psychological as well as physical harm in the process. Rape is not merely a physical assault -- it is often destructive of the whole personality of the victim. A murderer destroys the physical body of his victim, a rapist degrades the very soul of the helpless female. The Court, therefore, shoulders a great responsibility while trying an accused on charges of rape. They must deal with such cases with utmost sensitivity. The Courts should examine the broader probabilities of a case and not get swayed by minor contradictions or insignificant discrepancies in the statement of the prosecutrix, which are not of a fatal nature, to throw out an otherwise reliable prosecution case. If evidence of the prosecutrix inspires confidence, it must be relied upon without seeking corroboration of her statement in material particulars. If for some reason the Court finds it difficult to place implicit reliance on her testimony, it may look for evidence which may lend assurance to her testimony, short of corroboration required in the case of an accomplice[12]. A prosecutrix of a sex-offence cannot be put on par with an accomplice. She is in fact a victim of the crime.

---

11 **Meaning of Corroboration:** Confirmation that some fact or statement is true through the use of documentary evidence

12 *State of Punjab v.Gurmeet Singh,* 1996CriLJ1728 .

Decision of Supreme Court:

Court held that the measure of punishment in a case of rape cannot depend upon the social status of the victim or the accused. It must depend upon the conduct of the accused, the state and age of the sexually assaulted female and the gravity of the criminal act. Crimes of violence upon women need to be severely dealt with. The socio-economic status, religion, race, caste or creed of the accused or the victim are irrelevant considerations in sentencing policy. Protection of society and deterring the criminal is the avowed object of law and that is required to be achieved by imposing an appropriate sentence. The sentencing Courts are expected to consider all relevant facts and circumstances bearing on the question of sentence and proceed to impose a sentence commensurate with the gravity of the offence. Courts must hear the loud cry for justice by the society in cases of the heinous crime of rape on innocent helpless girls of tender years, married women and respond by imposition of proper sentence. Public abhorrence of the crime needs reflection through imposition of appropriate sentence by the Court. There are no extenuating or mitigating circumstances available on the record which may justify imposition of any sentence less than the prescribed minimum. To show mercy in the case of such a heinous crime would be a travesty of justice and the plea for leniency is wholly misplaced.

14

Rape and Murder done by Father on His Daughter; Not a Fit case for Death Penalty[1]

Ratio Decidendi[2]: "No Accused shall be awarded death penalty unless case falls within category of rarest of rare."

Facts in Nutshell:

Appeals[3] were filed against the common final judgment and order passed by the High Court of Punjab and Haryana at Chandigarh whereby the High Court accepted the murder reference and confirmed the death sentence imposed on the Appellant[4] by the Sessions Judge, Ludhiana and dismissed the appeal filed by him.

According to the prosecution[5], on 08.01.2006, the Appellant-accused[6] had committed murder of his wife and daughter in the background of inimical relationship between them on account of criminal cases registered against him by his wife for committing **rape on his minor**

---

1 Appellants: **Mohinder Singh Vs.** Respondent: **State of Punjab** 2013(2)SCALE24
   Hon'ble Judges/Coram: P. Sathasivam and Fakkir Mohamed Ibrahim Kalifulla, JJ.

2 **Meaning of Ration Decidendi:** *Ratio decidendi* is a Latin phrase meaning "the reason" or "the rationale for the decision." The *ratio decidendi* is "the point in a case which determines the judgment" or "the principle which the case establishes."

3 **Meaning of Appeal:** In law, an **appeal** is a process for requesting a formal change to an official decision. Very broadly speaking there are appeals on the record and *de novo* appeals. In *de novo* appeals, a new decision maker re-hears the case without any reference to the prior decision maker. In appeals on the record, the decision of the prior decision maker is challenged by arguing that he or she misapplied the law, came to an incorrect factual finding, acted in excess of his jurisdiction, abused his powers, was biased, considered evidence which he should not have considered or failed to consider evidence that he should have considered.

4 **Meaning of Appellant:** A person who, dissatisfied with the judgment rendered in a lawsuit decided in a lower court or the findings from a proceeding before an Administrative Agency, asks a superior court to review the decision.

5 **Meaning of Prosecution:**
   a. the institution and carrying on of legal proceedings against a person.
   b. the officials who institute and conduct such proceedings.

6 **Meaning of Accused:** A person charged with a criminal offense, or the state of being so charged

daughter, for which he was sentenced to rigorous imprisonment for 12 years, and for attacking her after release on parole[7] for which an FIR was registered against him.

Decision of the Session Judge and High Court:

The Sessions Judge, Ludhiana convicted[8] the Appellant Under Section 302[9] of Indian Penal Code and sentenced him to death. Against the said order, the Appellant preferred an appeal before the High Court and the State filed a reference Under Section 366[10] of the Code of Criminal Procedure, 1973 (in short 'the Code') for confirmation of death sentence. By a common impugned order the High Court while accepting the murder reference confirmed the death reference imposed by the trial Court and dismissed the appeal filed by the Appellant-accused. Aggrieved by the said judgment, the Appellant preferred appeal by way of special leave[11] before Supreme Court.

When Death Sentence can be awarded:

In *Panchhi and Ors.* v. *State of U.P.*[12], Supreme Court held that brutality is not the sole criterion of determining whether a case falls under the "rarest of rare" categories, thereby justifying the commutation of a death sentence to life imprisonment. Court observed:

---

7 **Meaning of Parole:**
   a. Early release of a prisoner who is then subject to continued monitoring as well as compliance with certain terms and conditions for a specified period.
   b. The duration of such conditional release.

8 **Meaning of Convicted:** Someone guilty of an offense or crime, especially by the verdict of a court

9 **Section 302, IPC 1860.**
   Punishment for murder.
   302. Punishment for murder.--Whoever commits murder shall be punished with death, or [imprisonment for life], and shall also be liable to fine.

10 **Section 366 in The Code Of Criminal Procedure, 1973**
   366. Sentence of death to be submitted by Court of session for confirmation.
   (1) When the Court of Session passes a sentence of death, the proceedings shall be submitted to the High Court, and the sentence shall not be executed unless it is confirmed by the High Court.
   (2) The Court passing the sentence shall commit the convicted person to jail custody under a warrant.

11 **Article 136 in The Constitution Of India 1949**
   136. Special leave to appeal by the Supreme Court
   (1) Notwithstanding anything in this Chapter, the Supreme Court may, in its discretion, grant special leave to appeal from any judgment, decree, determination, sentence or order in any cause or matter passed or made by any court or tribunal in the territory of India
   (2) Nothing in clause (1) shall apply to any judgment, determination, sentence or order passed or made by any court or tribunal constituted by or under any law relating to the Armed Forces

12 (1998) 7 SCC 177

No doubt brutality looms large in the murders in this case particularly of the old and also the tender age child. It may be that the manner in which a murder was perpetrated may be a ground but not the sole criterion for judging whether the case is one of the "rarest of rare cases" as indicated in Bachan Singh's case.

The Constitution Bench of Supreme Court, by a majority, upheld the constitutional validity of death sentence in **Bachan Singh** v. **State of Punjab**[13] . The Court took particular care to say that death sentence shall not normally be awarded for the offence of murder and that it must be confined to the "rarest of rare" cases when the alternative option is foreclosed. In other words, the Constitution Bench did not find death sentence valid in all cases except in the aforesaid cases wherein the lesser sentence would be wholly inadequate. The doctrine of "rarest of rare" confines two aspects and when both the aspects are satisfied only then the death penalty can be imposed. Firstly, the case must clearly fall within the ambit of "rarest of rare" and secondly, when the alternative option is unquestionably foreclosed. **Bachan Singh** v. **State of Punjab**[14] suggested selection of death punishment as the penalty of last resort when, alternative punishment of life imprisonment will be futile and serves no purpose.

In life sentence, there is a possibility of achieving deterrence, rehabilitation and retribution in different degrees. But the same does not hold true for the death penalty. It is unique in its absolute rejection of the potential of convict to rehabilitate and reform. It extinguishes life and thereby terminates the being, therefore, puts an end anything to do with the life. This is the big difference between two punishments. Thus, before imposing death penalty, it is imperative to consider the same.

It is well settled law that awarding of life sentence is a rule and death is an exception. The application of the "rarest of rare" case principle is dependant upon and differs from case to case. Life imprisonment cannot be equivalent to imprisonment for 14 years or 20 years or even 30 years, rather it always means the whole natural life. Supreme Court has always clarified that the punishment of a fixed term of imprisonment so awarded would be subject to any order passed in exercise of clemency powers of the President of India or the Governor of the State, as the case may be.

---

13 (1980) 2 SCC 684.

14 (1980) 2 SCC 684

Principles that are required to be borne in mind in case of Death Penalty:

(1) The 'rarest of rare' case comes when a convict would be a menace and threat to the harmonious and peaceful coexistence of the society. The crime may be heinous or brutal but may not be in the category of "the rarest of the rare case". There must be no reason to believe that the accused cannot be reformed or rehabilitated and that he is likely to continue criminal acts of violence as would constitute a continuing threat to the society.

(2) Life sentence is the rule and the death penalty is the exception. The condition of providing special reasons for awarding death penalty is not to be construed linguistically but it is to satisfy the basic features of a reasoning supporting and making award of death penalty unquestionable.

(3) The circumstances and the manner of committing the crime should be such that it pricks the judicial conscience of the Court to the extent that the only and inevitable conclusion should be awarding of death penalty.

(4) When the case falls under the category of 'rarest of rare' case penalty of death is clearly called for and any leniency shown in the matter of sentence would not only be misplaced but will certainly give rise to and foster a feeling of private revenge among the people leading to destabilization of the society.

Decision of the Supreme Court:

Court held that the present case was not a case where death penalty should be imposed. The Appellant-accused, therefore, instead of being awarded death penalty, was sentenced to undergo rigorous imprisonment for life, meaning thereby, the end of his life.

15

Rape and Murder of Two Young Girls, Fit case for Death Penalty[1]

Facts in Nutshell:

Two young girls who had not even seen ten summers in life were the victims of the sexual assault[2] and animal lust of the accused appellant[3]. They were not only raped but were murdered by the accused appellant. This was not the first occasion when the appellant was convicted[4] for rape of minor girls.

Decision of the Trial Court and High Court:

Death sentence awarded by learned Sessions Judge, Satara having been affirmed in appeal[5] and in the reference made under Section 366[6] of the Code of Criminal Procedure, 1973 (in short the `Code') by a Division Bench of the Bombay High Court, appeal was filed in Supreme Court. Appellant[7]

---

1   Appellants: **Mohan Anna Chavan Vs.** Respondent: **State of Maharashtra** 2008(3)ACR2885(SC) **Hon'ble Judges/Coram:** Dr. Arijit Pasayat, P. Sathasivam and Mukundakam Sharma , JJ.

2   **Meaning of Sexual Assault: Sexual assault** is any involuntary sexual act in which a person is threatened, coerced, or forced to engage against their will, or any sexual touching of a person who has not consented. This includes rape (such as forced vaginal, anal or oral penetration), inappropriate touching, forced kissing, child sexual abuse, or the torture of the victim in a sexual manner.

3   **Meaning of Appellant:** A person who, dissatisfied with the judgment rendered in a lawsuit decided in a lower court or the findings from a proceeding before an Administrative Agency, asks a superior court to review the decision.

4   **Meaning of Convicted:** Someone guilty of an offense or crime, especially by the verdict of a court

5   **Meaning of Appeal:** In law, an **appeal** is a process for requesting a formal change to an official decision. Very broadly speaking there are appeals on the record and *de novo* appeals. In *de novo* appeals, a new decision maker re-hears the case without any reference to the prior decision maker. In appeals on the record, the decision of the prior decision maker is challenged by arguing that he or she misapplied the law, came to an incorrect factual finding, acted in excess of his jurisdiction, abused his powers, was biased, considered evidence which he should not have considered or failed to consider evidence that he should have considered.

6   **Section 366 in The Code Of Criminal Procedure, 1973**
366. Sentence of death to be submitted by Court of session for confirmation.
(1) When the Court of Session passes a sentence of death, the proceedings shall be submitted to the High Court, and the sentence shall not be executed unless it is confirmed by the High Court.
(2) The Court passing the sentence shall commit the convicted person to jail custody under a warrant.

7   **Meaning of Appellant:** A person who, dissatisfied with the judgment rendered in a lawsuit

as convicted sections 363[8], 376[9], 302[10] and 201[11] of the Indian Penal Code,

decided in a lower court or the findings from a proceeding before an Administrative Agency, asks a superior court to review the decision.

8 **Section 363 in The Indian Penal Code, 1860**
363. Punishment for kidnapping.-- Whoever kidnaps any person from 1[India] or from lawful guardianship, shall be punished with imprisonment of either description for a term which may extend to seven years, and shall also be liable to fine.

9 **Section 376 in The Indian Penal Code, 1860**
376. Punishment for rape.--
(1) Whoever, except in the cases provided for by sub- section (2), commits rape shall be punished with imprisonment of either description for a term which shall not be less than seven years but which may be for life or for a term which may extend to ten years and shall also be liable to fine unless the woman raped is his own wife and is not under twelve years of age, in which case, he shall be punished with imprisonment of either description for a term which may extend to two years or with fine or with both:
Provided that the court may, for adequate and special reasons to be mentioned in the judgment, impose a sentence of imprisonment for a term of less than seven years.
(2) Whoever,-
(a) being a police officer commits rape-
(i) within the limits of the police station to which he is appointed; or
(ii) in the premises of any station house whether or not situated in the police station to which he is appointed; or
(iii) on a woman in his custody or in the custody of a police officer subordinate to him; or
(b) being a public servant, takes advantage of his official position and commits rape on a woman in his custody as such public servant or in the custody of a public servant subordinate to him; or
(c) being on the management or on the staff of a jail, remand home or other place of custody established by or under any law for the time being in force or of a women' s or children' s institution takes advantage of his official position and commits rape on any inmate of such jail, remand home, place or institution; or
(d) being on the management or on the staff of a hospital, takes advantage of his official position and commits rape on a woman in that hospital; or
(e) commits rape on a woman knowing her to be pregnant; or
(f) commits rape on a woman when she is under twelve years of age; or
(g) commits gang rape, shall be punished with rigorous imprisonment for a term which shall not be less than ten years but which may be for life and shall also be liable to fine: Provided that the court may, for adequate and special reasons to be mentioned in the judgment, impose a sentence of imprisonment of either description for a term of less than ten years. Explanation 1.- Where a women' s is raped by one or more in a group of persons acting in furtherance of their common intention, each of the persons shall be deemed to have committed gang rape within the meaning of this sub- section. Explanation 2.-" women' s or children' s institution" means an institution, whether called and orphanage or a home for neglected women or children or a widows' home or by any other name, which is established and maintained for the reception and care of women or children. Explanation 3.-" hospital" means the precincts of the hospital and includes the precincts of any institution for the reception and treatment of persons during convalescence or of persons requiring medical attention or rehabilitation.

10 **Section 302, IPC 1860.**
Punishment for murder.
302. Punishment for murder.--Whoever commits murder shall be punished with death, or [imprisonment for life], and shall also be liable to fine.

11 **Section 201 in The Indian Penal Code, 1860**
201. Causing disappearance of evidence of offence, or giving false information to screen offender.-- Whoever, knowing or having reason to believe that an offence has been committed, causes any evidence of the commission of that offence to disappear, with the intention of screening the

1860 (in short the `IPC').

Rape:

The offence of rape occurs in Chpater XVI of IPC. It is an offence affecting the human body. In that chapter, there is a separate heading for 'Sexual offence', which encompasses Sections 375[12], 376, 376A[13], 376B[14], 376C[15],

---

offender from legal punishment, or with that intention gives any information respecting the offence which he knows or believes to be false, if a capital offence; if a capital offence.-- shall, if the offence which he knows or believes to have been committed is punishable with death, be punished with imprisonment of either description for a term which may extend to seven years, and shall also be liable to fine; if punishable with imprisonment for life; if punishable with imprisonment for life.-- and if the offence is punishable with 1[imprisonment for life], or with imprisonment which may extend to ten years, shall be punished with imprisonment of either description for a term which may extend to three years, and shall also be liable to fine; if punishable with less than ten years' imprisonment. if punishable with less than ten years' imprisonment.-- and if the offence is punishable with imprisonment for any term not extending to ten years, shall be punished with imprisonment of the description provided for the offence, for a term which may extend to one-fourth part of the longest term of the imprisonment provided for the offence, or with fine, or with both. Illustration A, knowing that B has murdered Z, assists B to hide the body with the intention of screening B from punishment. A is liable to imprisonment of either description for seven years, and also to fine.

12 **Section 375 in The Indian Penal Code, 1860**
375. Rape.-- A man is said to commit" rape" who, except in the case hereinafter excepted, has sexual intercourse with a woman under circumstances falling under any of the six following descriptions:- First.- Against her will. Secondly.- Without her consent. Thirdly.- With her consent, when her consent has been obtained by putting her or any person in whom she is interested in fear of death or of hurt. Fourthly.- With her consent, when the man knows that he is not her husband, and that her consent is given because she believes that he is another man to whom she is or believes herself to be lawfully married. Fifthly.- With her consent, when, at the time of giving such consent, by reason of unsoundness of mind or intoxication or the administration by him personally or through another of any stupefying or unwholesome substance, she is unable to understand the nature and consequences of that to which she gives consent. Sixthly.- With or without her consent, when she is under sixteen years of age. Explanation.- Penetration is sufficient to constitute the sexual intercourse necessary to the offence of rape. Exception.- Sexual intercourse by a man with his own wife, the wife not being under fifteen years of age, is not rape.

13 **Section 376A in The Indian Penal Code, 1860**
376A. Intercourse by a man with his wife during separation.-- Whoever has sexual intercourse with his own wife, who is living separately from him under a decree of separation or under any custom or usage without her consent shall be punished with imprisonment of either description for a term which may extend to two years and shall also be liable to fine.

14 **Section 376B in The Indian Penal Code, 1860**
376B. Intercourse by public servant with woman in his custody.-- Whoever, being a public servant, takes advantage of his official position and induces or seduces, any woman, who is in his custody as such public servant or in the custody of a public servant subordinate to him, to have sexual intercourse with him, such sexual intercourse not amounting to the offence of rape, shall be punished with imprisonment of either description for a term which may extend to five years and shall also be liable to fine.

15 **Section 376C in The Indian Penal Code, 1860**
376C. Intercourse by superintendent of jail, remand home, etc.-- Whoever, being the superintendent or manager of a jail, remand home or other place of custody established by or

and 376D[16]. 'Rape' is defined in Section 375. Sections375 and 376 have been substantially changed by Criminal Law (Amendment) Act, 1983, and several new sections were introduced by the new Act, i.e. 376A, 376B, 376C and 376D. The fact that sweeping changes were introduced reflects the legislative intent to curb with iron hand, the offence of rape which affects the dignity of a woman. The offence of rape in its simplest term is 'the ravishment of a woman, without her consent, by force, fear or fraud', or as 'the carnal knowledge of a woman by force against her will'. 'Rape' or 'Raptus' is when a man hath carnal knowledge of a woman by force and against her will; or as expressed more fully,' rape is the carnal knowledge of any woman, above the age of particular years, against her will; or of a woman child, under that age, with or against her will'. The essential words in an indictment for rape are rapuit and carnaliter cognovit; but carnaliter cognovit, nor any other circumlocution without the word rapuit, are not sufficient in a legal sense to express rape. In the crime of rape, 'carnal knowledge' means the penetration to any the slightest degree of the organ alleged to have been carnally known by the male organ of generation[17]. In 'Encyclopedia of Crime and Justice' (Volume 4, page 1356) it is stated "...even slight penetration is sufficient and emission is unnecessary". In Halsbury's Statutes of England and Wales (Fourth Edition) Volume 12, it is stated that even the slightest degree of penetration is sufficient to prove sexual intercourse. It is violation with violence of the private person of a woman-an-outrage by all means. By the very nature of the offence it is an obnoxious act of the highest order. The physical scar may heal up, but the mental scar will always remain.

---

under any law for the time being in force or of a women' s or children' s institution takes advantage of his official position and induces or seduces any female inmate of such jail, remand home, place or institution to have sexual intercourse with him, such sexual intercourse not amounting to the offence of rape, shall be punished with imprisonment of either description for a term which may extend to five years and shall also be liable to fine. Explanation 1.-" Superintendent" in relation to a jail, remand home or other place of custody or a women' s or children' s institution, includes a person holding any other office in such jail, remand home, place or institution by virtue of which he can exercise any authority or control over its inmates. Explanation 2.- The expression" women' s or children' s institution" shall have the same meaning as in Explanation 2 to sub- section (2) of section 376.

16 **Section 376D in The Indian Penal Code, 1860**
376D. Intercourse by any member of the management or staff of a hospital with any woman in that hospital.-- Whoever, being on the management of a hospital or being on the staff of a hospital takes advantage of his position and has sexual intercourse with any woman in that hospital, such sexual intercourse not amounting to the offence of rape, shall be punished with imprisonment of either description for a term which may extend to five years and shall also be liable to fine. Explanation.- The expression" hospital" shall have the same meaning as in Explanation 3 to sub-section (2) of section 376.] Of unnatural offences

17 (Stephen's "Criminal Law" 9th Ed. p.262).

When a woman is ravished, what is inflicted is not merely physical injury but the deep sense of some deathless shame.

Crime and Punishment:

Undue sympathy to impose inadequate sentence would do more harm to the justice system to undermine the public confidence in the efficacy of law and society could not long endure under such serious threats. It is, therefore, the duty of every court to award proper sentence having regard to the nature of the offence and the manner in which it was executed or committed etc. This position was illuminatingly stated by Supreme Court in Sevaka Perumal etc. v. State of Tamil Naidu[18]

The criminal law adheres in general to the principle of proportionality in prescribing liability according to the culpability of each kind of criminal conduct. It ordinarily allows some significant discretion to the Judge in arriving at a sentence in each case, presumably to permit sentences that reflect more subtle considerations of culpability that are raised by the special facts of each case. Judges in essence affirm that punishment ought always to fit the crime; yet in practice sentences are determined largely by other considerations. Sometimes it is the correctional needs of the perpetrator that are offered to justify a sentence. Sometimes the desirability of keeping him out of circulation, and sometimes even the tragic results of his crime. Inevitably these considerations cause a departure from just desert as the basis of punishment and create cases of apparent injustice that are serious and widespread.

Proportion between crime and punishment is a goal respected in principle, and in spite of errant notions, it remains a strong influence in the determination of sentences. The practice of punishing all serious crimes with equal severity is now unknown in civilized societies, but such a radical departure from the principle of proportionality has disappeared from the law only in recent times. Even now for a single grave infraction drastic sentences are imposed. Anything less than a penalty of greatest severity for any serious crime is thought then to be a measure of toleration that is unwarranted and unwise. But in fact, quite apart from those considerations that make punishment unjustifiable when it is out of proportion to the crime, uniformly disproportionate punishment has some very undesirable practical consequences.

---

18 1991CriLJ1845 .

Death Penalty (Cases Referred):

In *Jashubha Bharatsinh Gohil v. State of Gujarat*[19], it has been held by Supreme Court that in the matter of death sentence, the Courts are required to answer new challenges and mould the sentencing system to meet these challenges. The object should be to protect the society and to deter the criminal in achieving the avowed object to law by imposing appropriate sentence. It is expected that the Courts would operate the sentencing system so as to impose such sentence which reflects the conscience of the society and the sentencing process has to be stern where it should be. Even though the principles were indicated in the background of death sentence and life sentence, the logic applies to all cases where appropriate sentence is the issue.

Imposition of sentence without considering its effect on the social order in many cases may be in reality a futile exercise. The social impact of the crime, e.g. where it relates to offences against women, dacoity, kidnapping, misappropriation of public money, treason and other offences involving moral turpitude or moral delinquency which have great impact on social order, and public interest, cannot be lost sight of and per se require exemplary treatment. Any liberal attitude by imposing meager sentences or taking too sympathetic view merely on account of lapse of time in respect of such offences will be result-wise counter productive in the long run and against societal interest which needs to be cared for and strengthened by string of deterrence inbuilt in the sentencing system.

In *Dhananjoy Chatterjee v. State of W.B.*[20] , Supreme Court has observed that shockingly large number of criminals go unpunished thereby increasingly, encouraging the criminals and in the ultimate making justice suffer by weakening the system's creditability. The imposition of appropriate punishment is the manner in which the Court responds to the society's cry for justice against the criminal. Justice demands that Courts should impose punishment befitting the crime so that the Courts reflect public abhorrence of the crime. The Court must not only keep in view the rights of the criminal but also the rights of the victim of the crime and the society at large while considering the imposition of appropriate punishment.

---

19 [1994]3SCR471
20 [1994]1SCR37

In *Bachan Singh v. State of Punjab*[21] following propositions emerges:

(i) The extreme penalty of death need not be inflicted except in gravest cases of extreme culpability.

(ii) Before opting for the death penalty the circumstances of the `offender' also require to be taken into consideration along with the circumstances of the `crime'.

(iii) Life imprisonment is the rule and death sentence is an exception. In other words death sentence must be imposed only when life imprisonment appears to be an altogether inadequate punishment having regard to the relevant circumstances of the crime, and provided, and only provided, the option to impose sentence of imprisonment for life cannot be conscientiously exercised having regard to the nature and circumstances of the crime and all the relevant circumstances.

(iv) A balance sheet of aggravating and mitigating circumstances has to be drawn up and in doing so the mitigating circumstances have to be accorded full weightage and a just balance has to be struck between the aggravating and the mitigating circumstances before the option is exercised.

When the collective conscience of the community is so shocked, that it will expect the holders of the judicial power centre to inflict death penalty irrespective of their personal opinion as regards desirability or otherwise of retaining death penalty, the same can be awarded. The community may entertain such sentiment in the following circumstances:

(1) When the murder is committed in an extremely brutal, grotesque, diabolical, revolting, or dastardly manner so as to arouse intense and extreme indignation of the community.

(2) When the murder is committed for a motive which evinces total depravity and meanness; e.g. murder by hired assassin for money or reward; or cold-blooded murder for gains of a person vis-`-vis whom the murderer is in a dominating position or in a position of trust; or murder is committed in the course for betrayal of the motherland.

(3) When murder of a member of a Scheduled Caste or minority community, etc. is committed not for personal reasons but in

---

21 1980CriLJ636

circumstances which arouse social wrath; or in cases of `bride burning' or `dowry deaths' or when murder is committed in order to remarry for the sake of extracting dowry once again or to marry another woman on account of infatuation.

(4) When the crime is enormous in proportion. For instance when multiple murders, say of all or almost all the members of a family or a large number of persons of a particular caste, community, or locality, are committed.

(5) When the victim of murder is an innocent child, or a helpless woman or old or infirm person or a person vis-`-vis whom the murderer is in a dominating position, or a public figure generally loved and respected by the community.

Decision of the Supreme Court:

Court held that the judgment of the High Court, confirming the conviction[22] and sentence imposed by the trial court, do not warrant any interference. Court dismissed the appeal.

---

22 **Meaning of Conviction:** In law, a **conviction** is the verdict that results when a court of law finds a defendant guilty of a crime.

16

False Allegation of Rape[1]

Ratio Decidendi[2]: *The purpose of enacting Section 344[3] Cr.PC, appears to be further arm the Court with a weapon to deal with more flagrant cases and not to take away the weapon already in its possession.*

Facts in Nutshell:

Petitioner[4] lodged a report against two persons at Police Station to the effect that on 28.1.1993 between 6.00 to 7.00 a.m. she was waylaid by them who dragged her and committed rape on her, one after another. She claimed to have narrated the incident to her father and uncle and, thereafter lodged the report at the police station. On the basis of the

---

1   Appellants: **Mahila Vinod Kumari Vs.** Respondent: **State of Madhya Pradesh** AIR2008SC2965
    Hon'ble Judges/Coram: Dr. Arijit Pasayat and P. Sathasivam , JJ.

2   **Meaning of Ration Decidendi:** *Ratio decidendi* is a Latin phrase meaning "the reason" or "the rationale for the decision." The *ratio decidendi* is "the point in a case which determines the judgment" or "the principle which the case establishes."

3   **Section 344, CrPc, 1973:**
    344. Summary procedure for trial for giving false evidence.
    (1) If, at the time of delivery of any judgment or final order disposing of any judicial proceeding, a Court of Session or Magistrate of the first class expresses an opinion to the effect that any witness appearing in such proceeding had knowingly or wilfully given false evidence or had fabricated false evidence with the intention that such evidence should be used in such proceeding, it or he may, if satisfied that it is necessary and expedient in the interest of justice that the witness should be tried summarily for giving or fabricating, as the case may be, false
    evidence, take cognizance of the offence and may, after giving the offender a reasonable opportunity of showing cause why he should not be punished for such offence, try such offender summarily and sentence him to imprisonment for a term which may extend to three months, or to fine which may extend to five hundred rupees, or with both.
    (2) In every such case the Court shall follow, as nearly as may be practicable, the procedure prescribed for summary trials.
    (3) Nothing in this section shall affect the power of the Court to make a complaint under section 340 for the offence, where it does not choose to proceed under this section.
    (4) Where, after any action is initiated under sub-section (1), it is made to appear to the Court of Session or Magistrate of the first class that an appeal or an application for revision has been preferred or filed against the judgment or order in which the opinion referred to in that subsection has been expressed, it or he shall stay further proceedings of the trial until the disposal of the appeal or the application for revision, as the case may be, and thereupon the further proceedings of the trial shall abide by the results of the appeal or application for revision.

4   **Meaning of Petitioner:** A person who presents a petition (**Meaning of Petition:** A formal written application requesting a court for a specific judicial action)

~ 68 ~

report, matter was investigated. The accused[5] persons were arrested. The accused persons faced trial for alleged commission of offence punishable under Section 376 (2)(g)[6] of the Indian Penal Code, 1860 (in short `the IPC').

Decision of Trail Court and High Court:

The Trial Court found that the petitioner had tendered false evidence and had fabricated[7] evidence against the accused persons with the intention that such evidence shall be used in the proceedings, and, therefore, directed cognizance in terms of Section 344 of the Code of Criminal Procedure, 1973 (in short `the Code') to be taken against the petitioner. A show-cause notice was issued and the case was registered against the petitioner who filed reply to the effect that being an illiterate lady, she had committed the mistake and may be excused. The Trial Court found that the petitioner admitted her guilt that she had lodged false report of rape against the accused[8]. She was, accordingly, sentenced to undergo *three months' simple imprisonment*. Aggrieved by the order, the petitioner filed an appeal before the Madhya Pradesh High Court, which was dismissed. Stand before the High Court was that being an illiterate lady, she does not understand law and the particulars of the offence were not explained to her.

---

5   **Meaning of Accused:** A person charged with a criminal offense, or the state of being so charged

6   **Section 376 in The Indian Penal Code, 1860**
    376. Punishment for rape.--
    (2) Whoever,--
    (g) commits gang rape, shall be punished with rigorous imprisonment for a term which shall not be less than ten years but which may be for life and shall also be liable to fine: Provided that the court may, for adequate and special reasons to be mentioned in the judgment, impose a sentence of imprisonment of either description for a term of less than ten years. Explanation 1.- Where a women' s is raped by one or more in a group of persons acting in furtherance of their common intention, each of the persons shall be deemed to have committed gang rape within the meaning of this sub- section. Explanation 2.-" women' s or children' s institution" means an institution, whether called and orphanage or a home for neglected women or children or a widows' home or by any other name, which is established and maintained for the reception and care of women or children. Explanation 3.-" hospital" means the precincts of the hospital and includes the precincts of any institution for the reception and treatment of persons during convalescence or of persons requiring medical attention or rehabilitation.

7   **Meaning of Fabricated:**
    1. To make; create.
    2. To construct by combining or assembling diverse

8   **Meaning of Accused:** A person charged with a criminal offense, or the state of being so charged

Purpose of Enacting Section 344 CrPc, 1973

The purpose of enacting Section 344, Cr.P.C. corresponding to Section 479-A of the Code of Criminal Procedure, 1898 (hereinafter referred to as 'the Old Code') appears to be further arm the Court with a weapon to deal with more flagrant cases and not to take away the weapon already in its possession. The object of the legislature underlying enactment of the provision is that the evil of perjury[9] and fabrication of evidence has to be eradicated and can be better achieved now as it is open to the courts to take recourse to Section 340(1)[10] (corresponding to Section 476 of the Old Code) in cases in which they are failed to take action under Section 344 Cr.P.C.

This section introduces an additional alternative procedure to punish perjury by the very Court before which it is committed in place of old Section 479 A which did not have the desired effect to eradicate the evils of perjury. The salient features of this new provision are:

(1) Special powers have been conferred on two specified Courts, namely Court of Session and Magistrate of the First Class, to take cognizance of an offence of perjury committed by a witness in a proceeding before it instead of filing a complaint before a Magistrate and try and punish the offender by following the procedure of summary trials. *For summary trial, see Ch. 21.*

(2) This power is to be exercised after having the matter considered by the Court only at the time of delivery of the judgment or final

---

9 **Meaning of Perjury: Perjury**, also known as **forswearing**, is the willful act of swearing a false oath or of falsifying an affirmation to tell the truth, whether spoken or in writing, concerning matters material to a judicial proceeding.

10 **Section 340(1), CrPc, 1973:**
340. Procedure in cases mentioned in section 195.
(1) When upon an application made to it in this behalf or otherwise any Court is of opinion that it is expedient in the interest of justice that an inquiry should be made into any offence referred to in clause (b) of sub-section (1) of section 195, which appears to have been committed in or in relation to a proceeding in that Court or, as the case may be, in respect of a document produced or given in evidence in a proceeding in that Court, such Court may, after such preliminary inquiry, if any, as it thinks necessary,—
(a) record a finding to that effect;
(b) make a complaint thereof in writing;
(c) send it to a Magistrate of the first class having jurisdiction;
(d) take sufficient security for the appearance for the accused before such Magistrate, or if the alleged offence is non-bailable and the Court thinks it necessary so to do send the accused in custody to such Magistrate; and
(e) bind over any person to appear and give evidence before such Magistrate

order.

(3) The offender shall be given a reasonable opportunity of showing cause before he is punished.

(4) The maximum sentence that may be imposed is 3 month's imprisonment or a fine up to Rs. 500 or both.

(5) The order of the Court is appealable (vide Section 351[11]).

(6) The procedure in this section is an alternative to one under Sections340-343. The Court has been given an option to proceed to punish summarily under this section or to resort to ordinary procedure by way of complaint under Section 340 so that, as for instance, where the Court is of opinion that perjury committed is likely to raise complicated questions or deserves more severe punishment than that permitted under this section or the case is otherwise of such a nature or for some reasons considered to be such that the case should be disposed of under the ordinary procedure which would be more appropriate, the Court may chose to do so [vide Sub-section (3)].

(7) Further proceedings of any trial initiated under this section shall be stayed and thus, any sentence imposed shall also not be executed until the disposal of an appeal or revision against the judgment or order in the main proceedings in which the witness gave perjured evidence or fabricated false evidence [vide Sub-section (4)].

---

11 Section 351, CrPc, 1973:
351. Appeals from convictions under sections 344, 345, 349 and 350.
(1) Any person sentenced by any Court other than a High Court under section 344, section 345, section 349 or section 350 may, notwithstanding anything contained in this Code appeal to the Court to which decrees or orders made in such Court are ordinarily appealable.
(2) The provisions of Chapter XXIX shall, so far as they are applicable, apply to appeals under this section, and the Appellate Court may alter or reverse the finding, or reduce or reverse the sentence appealed against.
(3) An appeal from such conviction by a Court of small causes shall lie to the Court of Session for the sessions division within which such Court is situate.
(4) An appeal from such conviction by any Registrar of Sub-Registrar deemed to be a civil Court by virtue of a direction issued under section 347 shall lie to the Court of Session for the sessions division within which the office of such Registrar of Sub-Registrar is situate.

Decision of the Supreme Court:

Court dismissed the Special Leave Petition[12] of Petitioner.

---

12 **Article 136 in The Constitution Of India 1949**
   136. Special leave to appeal by the Supreme Court
   (1) Notwithstanding anything in this Chapter, the Supreme Court may, in its discretion, grant special leave to appeal from any judgment, decree, determination, sentence or order in any cause or matter passed or made by any court or tribunal in the territory of India
   (2) Nothing in clause (1) shall apply to any judgment, determination, sentence or order passed or made by any court or tribunal constituted by or under any law relating to the Armed Forces

17

Death Penalty for Rape[1]

Ratio Decidendi[2]: *While deciding the question as to whether the extreme penalty of death sentence is to be awarded, a balance sheet of aggravating and mitigating circumstances has to be drawn up.*

Facts in Nutshell:

The victim was an unfortunate teenaged girl of about 5 years. There was "Devi Jagran" at the house of Chandrasen in village Basai Khurd in the eventful night. A number of persons of the locality had assembled there. The informant- Naresh Kumar alongwith his brother Vishal and niece Vaishali had also gone there. Around 9 P.M. the accused[3] Bantu-a neighbour of the informant reached there. After exhibiting playful and friendly gestures with Girl with whom he was familiar before because of neighborhood, enticed her away on the pretext of giving her a balloon. Several persons including Naresh Kumar and Nand Kishore saw him going away with the girl from the place of "Devi Jagran". When Girl did not return for a long time, a frantic search was made to trace her out by the members of the family. Around 9.30 PM they reached near the field of one Dharma in which grown up Dhaincha plants were there. With the help of torches they saw that the accused Bantu was thrusting a stem/stick of Dhaincha in the vagina of Vaishali having thrown her down. An alarm was raised, by them and Bantu was caught red handed in completely naked state. Vaishali was lying on the ground unconscious with a part of stem of Dhaincha inserted in her vagina. She was bleeding profusely. She had other injuries also on her person and was not responding at all.

---

1 Appellants: **Bantu Vs.** Respondent: **The State of U.P.** (2008)11SCC113
   Hon'ble Judges/Coram: Dr. Arijit Pasayat and Mukundakam Sharma , JJ.

2 **Meaning of Ration Decidendi:** *Ratio decidendi* is a Latin phrase meaning "the reason" or "the rationale for the decision." The *ratio decidendi* is "the point in a case which determines the judgment" or "the principle which the case establishes."

3 **Meaning of Accused:** A person charged with a criminal offense, or the state of being so charged

Decision of the Trial Court and High Court:

Death sentence awarded by learned Special Judge /Additional Sessions Judge, Agra having been confirmed by the Allahabad High Court in appeal[4] and in the reference made under Section 366[5] of the Code of Criminal Procedure, 1973 (in short the `code') appeal was filed in Supreme Court. The appellant[6] was convicted for offences punishable

---

4   **Meaning of Appeal:** In law, an **appeal** is a process for requesting a formal change to an official decision. Very broadly speaking there are appeals on the record and *de novo* appeals. In *de novo* appeals, a new decision maker re-hears the case without any reference to the prior decision maker. In appeals on the record, the decision of the prior decision maker is challenged by arguing that he or she misapplied the law, came to an incorrect factual finding, acted in excess of his jurisdiction, abused his powers, was biased, considered evidence which he should not have considered or failed to consider evidence that he should have considered.

5   **Section 366 in The Code Of Criminal Procedure, 1973**
     366. Sentence of death to be submitted by Court of session for confirmation.
     (1) When the Court of Session passes a sentence of death, the proceedings shall be submitted to the High Court, and the sentence shall not be executed unless it is confirmed by the High Court
     (2) The Court passing the sentence shall commit the convicted person to jail custody under a warrant.

6   **Meaning of Appellant:** A person who, dissatisfied with the judgment rendered in a lawsuit decided in a lower court or the findings from a proceeding before an Administrative Agency, asks a superior court to review the decision.

under Sections 364[7], 376[8] and 302[9] of the Indian Penal Code, 1860 (in short the `IPC'). The girl who had not seen six summers in life was the

---

7 **Section 364 in The Indian Penal Code, 1860**

364. Kidnapping or abducting in order to murder.-- Whoever kidnaps or abducts any person in order that such person may be murdered or may be so disposed of as to be put in danger of being murdered, shall be punished with 1[imprisonment for life] or rigorous imprisonment for a term which may extend to ten years, and shall also be liable to fine. Illustrations

(a) A kidnaps Z from 2[India], intending or knowing it to be likely that Z may be sacrificed to an idol. A has committed the offence defined in this section.

(b) A forcibly carries or entices B away from his home in order that B may be murdered. A has committed the offence defined in this section.

8 **Section 376 in The Indian Penal Code, 1860**

376. Punishment for rape.--

(1) Whoever, except in the cases provided for by sub- section (2), commits rape shall be punished with imprisonment of either description for a term which shall not be less than seven years but which may be for life or for a term which may extend to ten years and shall also be liable to fine unless the woman raped is his own wife and is not under twelve years of age, in which case, he shall be punished with imprisonment of either description for a term which may extend to two years or with fine or with both:

Provided that the court may, for adequate and special reasons to be mentioned in the judgment, impose a sentence of imprisonment for a term of less than seven years.

(2) Whoever,-

(a) being a police officer commits rape-

(i) within the limits of the police station to which he is appointed; or

(ii) in the premises of any station house whether or not situated in the police station to which he is appointed; or

(iii) on a woman in his custody or in the custody of a police officer subordinate to him; or

(b) being a public servant, takes advantage of his official position and commits rape on a woman in his custody as such public servant or in the custody of a public servant subordinate to him; or

(c) being on the management or on the staff of a jail, remand home or other place of custody established by or under any law for the time being in force or of a women' s or children' s institution takes advantage of his official position and commits rape on any inmate of such jail, remand home, place or institution; or

(d) being on the management or on the staff of a hospital, takes advantage of his official position and commits rape on a woman in that hospital; or

(e) commits rape on a woman knowing her to be pregnant; or

(f) commits rape on a woman when she is under twelve years of age; or

(g) commits gang rape, shall be punished with rigorous imprisonment for a term which shall not be less than ten years but which may be for life and shall also be liable to fine: Provided that the court may, for adequate and special reasons to be mentioned in the judgment, impose a sentence of imprisonment of either description for a term of less than ten years. Explanation 1.- Where a women' s is raped by one or more in a group of persons acting in furtherance of their common intention, each of the persons shall be deemed to have committed gang rape within the meaning of this sub- section. Explanation 2.-" women' s or children' s institution" means an institution, whether called and orphanage or a home for neglected women or children or a widows' home or by any other name, which is established and maintained for the reception and care of women or children. Explanation 3.-" hospital" means the precincts of the hospital and includes the precincts of any institution for the reception and treatment of persons during convalescence or of persons requiring medical attention or rehabilitation.

9 **Section 302, IPC 1860.**
Punishment for murder.
302. Punishment for murder.--Whoever commits murder shall be punished with death, or [imprisonment for life], and shall also be liable to fine.

victim of sexual assault and animal lust of the accused appellant. She was not only raped but was murdered by the accused appellant.

Rape:

The offence of rape occurs in Chapter XVI of IPC. It is an offence affecting the human body. In that Chapter, there is a separate heading for `Sexual offence', which encompasses

Sections 375[10], 376, 376A[11], 376B[12], 376C[13], and 376D[14]. `Rape' is defined

---

10 **Section 375 in The Indian Penal Code, 1860**
375. Rape.-- A man is said to commit" rape" who, except in the case hereinafter excepted, has sexual intercourse with a woman under circumstances falling under any of the six following descriptions:- First.- Against her will. Secondly.- Without her consent. Thirdly.- With her consent, when her consent has been obtained by putting her or any person in whom she is interested in fear of death or of hurt. Fourthly.- With her consent, when the man knows that he is not her husband, and that her consent is given because she believes that he is another man to whom she is or believes herself to be lawfully married. Fifthly.- With her consent, when, at the time of giving such consent, by reason of unsoundness of mind or intoxication or the administration by him personally or through another of any stupefying or unwholesome substance, she is unable to understand the nature and consequences of that to which she gives consent. Sixthly.- With or without her consent, when she is under sixteen years of age. Explanation.- Penetration is sufficient to constitute the sexual intercourse necessary to the offence of rape. Exception.- Sexual intercourse by a man with his own wife, the wife not being under fifteen years of age, is not rape.

11 **Section 376A in The Indian Penal Code, 1860**
376A. Intercourse by a man with his wife during separation.-- Whoever has sexual intercourse with his own wife, who is living separately from him under a decree of separation or under any custom or usage without her consent shall be punished with imprisonment of either description for a term which may extend to two years and shall also be liable to fine.

12 **Section 376B in The Indian Penal Code, 1860**
376B. Intercourse by public servant with woman in his custody.-- Whoever, being a public servant, takes advantage of his official position and induces or seduces, any woman, who is in his custody as such public servant or in the custody of a public servant subordinate to him, to have sexual intercourse with him, such sexual intercourse not amounting to the offence of rape, shall be punished with imprisonment of either description for a term which may extend to five years and shall also be liable to fine.

13 **Section 376C in The Indian Penal Code, 1860**
376C. Intercourse by superintendent of jail, remand home, etc.-- Whoever, being the superintendent or manager of a jail, remand home or other place of custody established by or under any law for the time being in force or of a women' s or children' s institution takes advantage of his official position and induces or seduces any female inmate of such jail, remand home, place or institution to have sexual intercourse with him, such sexual intercourse not amounting to the offence of rape, shall be punished with imprisonment of either description for a term which may extend to five years and shall also be liable to fine. Explanation 1.-" Superintendent" in relation to a jail, remand home or other place of custody or a women' s or children' s institution, includes a person holding any other office in such jail, remand home, place or institution by virtue of which he can exercise any authority or control over its inmates. Explanation 2.- The expression" women' s or children' s institution" shall have the same meaning as in Explanation 2 to sub- section (2) of section 376.

14 **Section 376D in The Indian Penal Code, 1860**
376D. Intercourse by any member of the management or staff of a hospital with any woman in

in Section 375. Sections375 and 376 have been substantially changed by Criminal Law (Amendment) Act, 1983, and several new sections were introduced by the new Act, i.e. 376-A, 376-B, 376-C and 376-D. The fact that sweeping changes were introduced reflects the legislative intent to curb with iron hand, the offence of rape which affects the dignity of a woman. The offence of rape in its simplest term is 'the ravishment of a woman, without her consent, by force, fear or fraud', or as 'the carnal knowledge of a woman by force against her will'. 'Rape' or 'Raptus' is when a man hath carnal knowledge of a woman by force and against her will ; or as expressed more fully,' rape is the carnal knowledge of any woman, above the age of particular years, against her will; or of a woman child, under that age, with or against her will' . The essential words in an indictment for rape are rapuit and carnaliter cognovit; but carnaliter cognovit, nor any other circumlocution without the word rapuit, are not sufficient in a legal sense to express rape. In the crime of rape, 'carnal knowledge' means the penetration to any the slightest degree of the organ alleged to have been carnally known by the male organ of generation[15]. In Encyclopedia of Crime and Justice' (Volume 4, page 1356) it is stated "...even slight penetration is sufficient and emission is unnecessary". In Halsbury's Statutes of England and Wales (Fourth Edition) Volume 12, it is stated that even the slightest degree of penetration is sufficient to prove sexual intercourse. It is violation with violence of the private person of a woman-an-outrage by all means. By the very nature of the offence it is an obnoxious act of the highest order. The physical scar may heal up, but the mental scar will always remain. When a woman is ravished, what is inflicted is not merely physical injury but the deep sense of some deathless shame.

The law regulates a social interests, arbitrates conflicting claims and demands. Security of persons and property of the people is an essential function of the State. It could be achieved through instrumentality of criminal law. Undoubtedly, there is a cross cultural conflict where living law must find answer to the new challenges and the courts are required to mould the sentencing system to meet the challenges. The contagion of lawlessness would undermine social order and lay it in ruins. Protection

---

that hospital.-- Whoever, being on the management of a hospital or being on the staff of a hospital takes advantage of his position and has sexual intercourse with any woman in that hospital, such sexual intercourse not amounting to the offence of rape, shall be punished with imprisonment of either description for a term which may extend to five years and shall also be liable to fine. Explanation.- The expression" hospital" shall have the same meaning as in Explanation 3 to sub-section (2) of section 376.] Of unnatural offences

15 (Stephen's "Criminal Law" 9th Ed. p.262).

of society and stamping out criminal proclivity must be the object of law which must be achieved by imposing appropriate sentence. Therefore, law as a corner-stone of the edifice of "order" should meet the challenges confronting the society. Friedman in his "Law in Changing Society" stated that, "State of criminal law continues to be as it should be a decisive reflection of social consciousness of society". Therefore, in operating the sentencing system, law should adopt the corrective machinery or the deterrence based on factual matrix. By deft modulation sentencing process be stern where it should be, and tempered with mercy where it warrants to be. The facts and given circumstances in each case, the nature of the crime, the manner in which it was planned and committed, the motive for commission of the crime, the conduct of the accused, the nature of weapons used and all other attending circumstances are relevant facts which would enter into the area of consideration. For instance a murder committed due to deep seated mutual and personal rivalry may not call for penalty of death. But an organised crime or mass murders of innocent people would call for imposition of death sentence as deterrence. In Mahesh v. State of M.P.[16], Supreme Court while refusing to reduce the death sentence observed thus:

It will be a mockery of justice to permit the accused to escape the extreme penalty of law when faced with such evidence and such cruel acts. To give the lesser punishment for the accused would be to render the justicing system of the country suspect. The common man will lose faith in courts. In such cases, he understands and appreciates the language of deterrence more than the reformative jargon.

Therefore, undue sympathy to impose inadequate sentence would do more harm to the justice system to undermine the public confidence in the efficacy of law and society could not long endure under such serious threats. It is, therefore, the duty of every court to award proper sentence having regard to the nature of the offence and the manner in which it was executed or committed etc.[17]

In Ravji v. State of Rajasthan[18] it has been held that it is the nature and gravity of the crime but not the criminal, which are germane for consideration of appropriate punishment in a criminal trial. The Court will be failing in its duty if appropriate punishment is not awarded for a

---

16 1987CriLJ1073

17 *Sevaka Perumal etc. v. State of Tamil Naidu* , 1991CriLJ1845 .

18 AIR1996SC787

crime which has been committed not only against the individual victim but also against the society to which the criminal and victim belong. The punishment to be awarded for a crime must not be irrelevant but it should conform to and be consistent with the atrocity and brutality with which the crime has been perpetrated, the enormity of the crime warranting public abhorrence and it should "respond to the society's cry for justice against the criminal". If for extremely heinous crime of murder perpetrated in a very brutal manner without any provocation, most deterrent punishment is not given, the case of deterrent punishment will lose its relevance.

When Death Penalty can be awarded:

In *Bachan Singh v. State of Punjab*[19] Constitution Bench of Supreme Court at para 132 summed up the position as follows: (SCC p.729)

(i) The extreme penalty of death need not be inflicted except in gravest cases of extreme culpability.

(ii) Before opting for the death penalty the circumstances of the `offender' also require to be taken into consideration along with the circumstances of the `crime'.

(iii) Life imprisonment is the rule and death sentence is an exception. In other words death sentence must be imposed only when life imprisonment appears to be an altogether inadequate punishment having regard to the relevant circumstances of the crime, and provided, and only provided, the option to impose sentence of imprisonment for life cannot be conscientiously exercised having regard to the nature and circumstances of the crime and all the relevant circumstances.

(iv) A balance sheet of aggravating and mitigating circumstances has to be drawn up and in doing so the mitigating circumstances have to be accorded full weightage and a just balance has to be struck between the aggravating and the mitigating circumstances before the option is exercised.

The community may entertain such sentiment in the following circumstances:

(1) When the murder is committed in an extremely brutal, grotesque,

---

19 1980CriLJ636

diabolical, revolting, or dastardly manner so as to arouse intense and extreme indignation of the community.

(2) When the murder is committed for a motive which evinces total depravity and meanness; e.g. murder by hired assassin for money or reward; or cold-blooded murder for gains of a person vis-a`-vis whom the murderer is in a dominating position or in a position of trust; or murder is committed in the course for betrayal of the motherland.

(3) When murder of a member of a Scheduled Caste or minority community, etc. is committed not for personal reasons but in circumstances which arouse social wrath; or in cases of `bride burning' or `dowry deaths' or when murder is committed in order to remarry for the sake of extracting dowry once again or to marry another woman on account of infatuation.

(4) When the crime is enormous in proportion. For instance when multiple murders, say of all or almost all the members of a family or a large number of persons of a particular caste, community, or locality, are committed.

(5) When the victim of murder is an innocent child, or a helpless woman or old or infirm person or a person vis-`-vis whom the murderer is in a dominating position, or a public figure generally loved and respected by the community.

Decision of the Supreme Court:

Court held that the case falls in the rarest of rare category. The depraved acts of the accused call for only one sentence that is death sentence.

18

Attempt to Commit Rape not to be treated at par with Rape[1]

Ratio Decidendi[2]: *"If an attempt to commit the rape is clearly established then the offender[3] has to be penalized under Section 511[4] and not under Section 376[5] of IPC."*

---

1 Appellants: **Arjun Singh Vs.** Respondent: **State of H.P.** AIR2009SC1568
   Hon'ble Judges/Coram: Dr. Arijit Pasayat and Asok Kumar Ganguly, JJ.

2 **Meaning of Ration Decidendi:** *Ratio decidendi* is a Latin phrase meaning "the reason" or "the rationale for the decision." The *ratio decidendi* is "the point in a case which determines the judgment" or "the principle which the case establishes."

3 **Meaning of Offender:** One that offends, especially one that breaks a public law

4 **Section 511 in The Indian Penal Code, 1860**
   511. Punishment for attempting to commit offences punishable with imprisonment for life or other imprisonment.-- Whoever attempts to commit an offence punishable by this Code with 1[imprisonment for life] or imprisonment, or to cause such an offence to be committed, and in such attempt does any act towards the commission of the offence, shall, where no express provision is made by this Code for the punishment of such attempt, be punished with 2[imprisonment o f any description provided for the offence, for a term which may extend to one- half of the imprisonment for life or, as the case may be, one- half of the longest term of imprisonment provided for that offence], or with such fine as is provided for the offence, or with both. Illustrations
   (a) A makes an attempt to steal some jewels by breaking open a box, and finds after so opening the box, that there is no jewel in it. He has done an act towards the commission of theft, and therefore is guilty under this section.
   (b) A makes an attempt to pick the pocket of Z by thrusting his hand into Z' s pocket. A fails in the attempt in consequence of Z' s having nothing in his pocket. A is guilty under this section.

5 **Section 376 in The Indian Penal Code, 1860**
   376. Punishment for rape.--
   (1) Whoever, except in the cases provided for by sub- section (2), commits rape shall be punished with imprisonment of either description for a term which shall not be less than seven years but which may be for life or for a term which may extend to ten years and shall also be liable to fine unless the woman raped is his own wife and is not under twelve years of age, in which case, he shall be punished with imprisonment of either description for a term which may extend to two years or with fine or with both:
   Provided that the court may, for adequate and special reasons to be mentioned in the judgment, impose a sentence of imprisonment for a term of less than seven years.
   (2) Whoever,-
   (a) being a police officer commits rape-
   (i) within the limits of the police station to which he is appointed; or
   (ii) in the premises of any station house whether or not situated in the police station to which he is appointed; or
   (iii) on a woman in his custody or in the custody of a police officer subordinate to him; or
   (b) being a public servant, takes advantage of his official position and commits rape on a woman in his custody as such public servant or in the custody of a public servant subordinate to him; or
   (c) being on the management or on the staff of a jail, remand home or other place of custody

Facts in Nutshell:

Victim boarded the bus to Shimla from Solan. When the bus reached near petrol pump (HIMFED) situated near Nav Bahar towards Chotta Shimla, all the passengers got down, except the prosecutrix and accused-appellant[6] Arjun Singh. Accused Arjun Singh committed forcible sexual intercourse with the prosecutrix[7] against her will and without her consent. The victim was kidnapped by the accused who was minor at the time of kidnapping. The accused[8] had induced the prosecutrix that he would marry her after reaching Nalagarh. The FIR was registered.

The trial Court held that the age of the victim was less than 16. It was also submitted by the accused persons that no rape has been committed. This plea also was rejected by the trial court. Accordingly the trial court while holding the appellant guilty, acquitted[9] co-accused. Appeal before the High Court was dismissed.

---

established by or under any law for the time being in force or of a women' s or children' s institution takes advantage of his official position and commits rape on any inmate of such jail, remand home, place or institution; or

(d) being on the management or on the staff of a hospital, takes advantage of his official position and commits rape on a woman in that hospital; or

(e) commits rape on a woman knowing her to be pregnant; or

(f) commits rape on a woman when she is under twelve years of age; or

(g) commits gang rape, shall be punished with rigorous imprisonment for a term which shall not be less than ten years but which may be for life and shall also be liable to fine: Provided that the court may, for adequate and special reasons to be mentioned in the judgment, impose a sentence of imprisonment of either description for a term of less than ten years. Explanation 1.- Where a women' s is raped by one or more in a group of persons acting in furtherance of their common intention, each of the persons shall be deemed to have committed gang rape within the meaning of this sub- section. Explanation 2.-" women' s or children' s institution" means an institution, whether called and orphanage or a home for neglected women or children or a widows' home or by any other name, which is established and maintained for the reception and care of women or children. Explanation 3.-" hospital" means the precincts of the hospital and includes the precincts of any institution for the reception and treatment of persons during convalescence or of persons requiring medical attention or rehabilitation.

6 **Meaning of Appellant:** A person who, dissatisfied with the judgment rendered in a lawsuit decided in a lower court or the findings from a proceeding before an Administrative Agency, asks a superior court to review the decision.

7 **Meaning of Prosecutrix:** A female prosecutor.

8 **Meaning of Accused:** A person charged with a criminal offense, or the state of being so charged

9 **Meaning of Acquittal:** In the common law tradition, an **acquittal** formally certifies that the accused is free from the charge of an offense, as far as the criminal law is concerned.

Decision of the Trail Court and High Court:

Challenge in appeal[10] is to the judgment of a learned Single Judge of the Himachal Pradesh High Court upholding the conviction[11] of the appellant[12] for offences punishable under Sections 376, 511, 363[13] and 366[14] as well as Section 109[15] of the Indian Penal Code, 1860 (in short the IPC). He was sentenced to undergo rigorous imprisonment for 7 years, 3 years, 4 years, 5 years and 7 years for the aforesaid offences along with fine with default

10 **Meaning of Appeal:** In law, an **appeal** is a process for requesting a formal change to an official decision. Very broadly speaking there are appeals on the record and *de novo* appeals. In *de novo* appeals, a new decision maker re-hears the case without any reference to the prior decision maker. In appeals on the record, the decision of the prior decision maker is challenged by arguing that he or she misapplied the law, came to an incorrect factual finding, acted in excess of his jurisdiction, abused his powers, was biased, considered evidence which he should not have considered or failed to consider evidence that he should have considered.

11 **Meaning of Conviction:** In law, a **conviction** is the verdict that results when a court of law finds a defendant guilty of a crime.

12 **Meaning of Appellant:** A person who, dissatisfied with the judgment rendered in a lawsuit decided in a lower court or the findings from a proceeding before an Administrative Agency, asks a superior court to review the decision.

13 **Section 363 in The Indian Penal Code, 1860**
363. Punishment for kidnapping.-- Whoever kidnaps any person from 1[India] or from lawful guardianship, shall be punished with imprisonment of either description for a term which may extend to seven years, and shall also be liable to fine.

14 **Section 366 in The Indian Penal Code, 1860**
366. Kidnapping, abducting or inducing woman to compel her marriage, etc.-- Whoever kidnaps or abducts any woman with intent that she may be compelled, or knowing it to be likely that she will be compelled, to marry any person against her will, or in order that she may be forced or seduced to illicit intercourse, or knowing it to be likely that she will be forced or seduced to illicit intercourse, shall be punished with imprisonment of either description for a term which may extend to ten years, and shall also be liable to fine; [and whoever, by means of criminal intimidation as defined in this Code or of abuse of authority or any other method of compulsion, induces any woman to go from any place with intent that she may be, or knowing that it is likely that she will be, forced or seduced to illicit intercourse with another person shall also be punishable as aforesaid].

15 **Section 109 in The Indian Penal Code, 1860**
109. Punishment of abetment if the act abetted is committed in consequence and where no express provision is made for its punishment.-- Whoever abets any offence shall, if the act abetted is committed in consequence of the abetment, and no express provision is made by this Code for the punishment of such abetment, be punished with the punishment provided for the offence. Explanation.- An act or offence is said to be committed in consequence of abetment, when it is committed in consequence of the instigation, or in pursuance of the conspiracy, or with the aid which constitutes the abetment. Illustrations
(a) A offers a bribe to B, a public servant, as a reward for showing A some favour in the exercise of B' s official functions. B accepts the bribe. A has abetted the offence defined in section 161.
(b) A instigates B to give false evidence. B, in consequence of the instigation, commits that offence. A is guilty of abetting that offence, and is liable to the same punishment as B.
(c) A and B conspire to poison Z. A, in pursuance of the conspiracy, procures the poison and delivers it to B in order that he may administer it to Z. B, in pursuance of the conspiracy, administers the poison to Z in A' s absence and thereby causes Z' s death. Here B is guilty of murder. A is guilty of abetting that offence by conspiracy, and is liable to the punishment for murder.

stipulation.

Proof of Age of Person:

In *State of Chhattisgarh v. Lekhram*[16] it was held that the register maintained in a school is admissible evidence to prove the date of birth of the person concerned in terms of Section 35[17] of the Indian Evidence Act, 1872 (in short 'Evidence Act'). It may be true that in the entry of the school register is not conclusive but it has evidentiary value.

Rape:

The offence of rape occurs in Chapter XVI of IPC. It is an offence affecting the human body. In that Chapter, there is a separate heading for 'Sexual

---

16 2006CriLJ2139

17 **Section 35 in The Indian Evidence Act, 1872**
    35. Relevancy of entry in public record made in performance of duty.- An entry in any public or other official book, register or record, stating a fact in issue or relevant fact, and made by a public servant in the discharge of his official duty, or by any other person in performance of a duty specially enjoined by the law of the country in which such book, register or record is kept, is itself a relevant fact.

offence', which encompasses Sections 375[18], 376, 376A[19], 376B[20], 376C[21], and 376D[22]. 'Rape' is defined in Section 375. Sections 375 and376 have been substantially changed by Criminal Law (Amendment) Act, 1983, and several new sections were introduced by the new Act,

18 **Section 375 in The Indian Penal Code, 1860**
375. Rape.-- A man is said to commit" rape" who, except in the case hereinafter excepted, has sexual intercourse with a woman under circumstances falling under any of the six following descriptions:- First.- Against her will. Secondly.- Without her consent. Thirdly.- With her consent, when her consent has been obtained by putting her or any person in whom she is interested in fear of death or of hurt. Fourthly.- With her consent, when the man knows that he is not her husband, and that her consent is given because she believes that he is another man to whom she is or believes herself to be lawfully married. Fifthly.- With her consent, when, at the time of giving such consent, by reason of unsoundness of mind or intoxication or the administration by him personally or through another of any stupefying or unwholesome substance, she is unable to understand the nature and consequences of that to which she gives consent. Sixthly.- With or without her consent, when she is under sixteen years of age. Explanation.- Penetration is sufficient to constitute the sexual intercourse necessary to the offence of rape. Exception.- Sexual intercourse by a man with his own wife, the wife not being under fifteen years of age, is not rape.

19 **Section 376A in The Indian Penal Code, 1860**
376A. Intercourse by a man with his wife during separation.-- Whoever has sexual intercourse with his own wife, who is living separately from him under a decree of separation or under any custom or usage without her consent shall be punished with imprisonment of either description for a term which may extend to two years and shall also be liable to fine.

20 **Section 376B in The Indian Penal Code, 1860**
376B. Intercourse by public servant with woman in his custody.-- Whoever, being a public servant, takes advantage of his official position and induces or seduces, any woman, who is in his custody as such public servant or in the custody of a public servant subordinate to him, to have sexual intercourse with him, such sexual intercourse not amounting to the offence of rape, shall be punished with imprisonment of either description for a term which may extend to five years and shall also be liable to fine.

21 **Section 376C in The Indian Penal Code, 1860**
376C. Intercourse by superintendent of jail, remand home, etc.-- Whoever, being the superintendent or manager of a jail, remand home or other place of custody established by or under any law for the time being in force or of a women' s or children' s institution takes advantage of his official position and induces or seduces any female inmate of such jail, remand home, place or institution to have sexual intercourse with him, such sexual intercourse not amounting to the offence of rape, shall be punished with imprisonment of either description for a term which may extend to five years and shall also be liable to fine. Explanation 1.-" Superintendent" in relation to a jail, remand home or other place of custody or a women' s or children' s institution, includes a person holding any other office in such jail, remand home, place or institution by virtue of which he can exercise any authority or control over its inmates. Explanation 2.- The expression" women' s or children' s institution" shall have the same meaning as in Explanation 2 to sub- section (2) of section 376.

22 **Section 376D in The Indian Penal Code, 1860**
376D. Intercourse by any member of the management or staff of a hospital with any woman in that hospital.-- Whoever, being on the management of a hospital or being on the staff of a hospital takes advantage of his position and has sexual intercourse with any woman in that hospital, such sexual intercourse not amounting to the offence of rape, shall be punished with imprisonment of either description for a term which may extend to five years and shall also be liable to fine. Explanation.- The expression" hospital" shall have the same meaning as in Explanation 3 to sub-section (2) of section 376.] Of unnatural offences

i.e. 376A, 376B, 376C and 376D. The fact that sweeping changes were introduced reflects the legislative intent to curb with iron hand, the offence of rape which affects the dignity of a woman. The offence of rape in its simplest term is 'the ravishment of a woman, without her consent, by force, fear or fraud', or as 'the carnal knowledge of a woman by force against her will'. 'Rape' or 'Raptus' is when a man hath carnal knowledge of a woman by force and against her will ; or as expressed more fully,' rape is the carnal knowledge of any woman, above the age of particular years, against her will; or of a woman child, under that age, with or against her will' . The essential words in an indictment for rape are rapuit and carnaliter cognovit; but carnaliter cognovit, nor any other circumlocution without the word rapuit, are not sufficient in a legal sense to express rape[23]. In the crime of rape, 'carnal knowledge' means the penetration to any the slightest degree of the organ alleged to have been carnally known by the male organ of generation[24]. In 'Encyclopedia of Crime and Justice' (Volume 4, page 1356) it is stated "......even slight penetration is sufficient and emission is unnecessary". In Halsbury's Statutes of England and Wales (Fourth Edition) Volume 12, it is stated that even the slightest degree of penetration is sufficient to prove sexual intercourse. It is violation with violence of the private person of a woman-an-outrage by all means. By the very nature of the offence it is an obnoxious act of the highest order.

Decision of the Supreme Court:

Court held that though the rape does not appear to have been committed but the attempt to commit the rape was clearly established. That being so the conviction for offence punishable under Section 376 IPC was not made out but the offence punishable under Section-511 IPC was clearly made out. Court uphold the conviction[25] of the appellant for the offences punishable under Sections 365, 366 and 511 IPC with the corresponding sentence as imposed by the trial court and sustained by the High Court. The convictions in terms of Sections 109 and 376 IPC were set aside by Supreme Court.

---

23 1 Hon.6, la, 9 Edw. 4, 26 a (Hale PC 628)

24 (Stephen's "Criminal Law" 9th Ed. p.262)

25 **Meaning of Conviction:** In law, a **conviction** is the verdict that results when a court of law finds a defendant guilty of a crime.

Prostitution

No denying the fact that prostitution always remains as a running sore in the body of civilization and destroys all moral values. The causes and evil effects of prostitution manning the society are so notorious and frightful that none can gainsay it. This malignity is daily and hourly threatening the community at large slowly but steadily making its way onwards leaving a track marked with broken hopes. Therefore, the necessity for appropriate and drastic action to eradicate this evil has become apparent but its successful consummation ultimately rests with the public at large.

It is highly deplorable and heart-rending to note that many poverty stricken children and girls in the prime of youth are taken to 'flesh market' and forcibly pushed into the 'flesh trade' which is being carried on in utter violation of all cannons of morality, decency and dignity of humankind. There cannot be two opinions indeed there is none that this obnoxious and abominable crime committed with all kinds of unthinkable vulgarity should be eradicated at all levels by drastic steps.

The immoral Traffic (Prevention) Act, 1956:

The immoral Traffic (Prevention) Act, 1956 was enacted to provide, in pursuance of the International Convention signed at New York on 9th May, 1950, for the prevention of immoral traffic. Government of India in the year 1950 ratified an International Convention for suppression of traffic in persons and of the exploitation of the prostitution of others. The principal object of the Act is to prevent commercialization of the vice and trafficking among women and girls. As Krishna Iyer Judge has observed in Chita J. *Vaswani v. State of W.B.*[1] no nation, with all its boasts, and all its hopes, can ever morally be clean till all its women are really free. Free to live without sale of their young flesh to lascivious wealth or commercializing their luscious figures. India, to redeem this 'gender justice' and to proscribe prostitution whereby rich men buy poor women through houses of vice, has salved its social conscience by enacting the Act.

The scope of the Immoral Traffic (Prevention) Act, 1956 is very vast. Section (3) of the Act provides for punishment for keeping a brothel

---

1   1976CriLJ1

or allowing a premises to be used as a brothel. "Brothel" is defined in Section 2(a) as including a house, room, or place or any portion of any house, room or place, which is used for the purpose of prostitution for the gain of another person or for the mutual gain of two or more prostitutes. "Prostitute" is defined in Section 2(e) as meaning a female who offers her body, for promiscuous sexual intercourse for hire whether in money or in kind. Section 2(f) defines "prostitution" means the sexual exploitation or abuse of persons for commercial purpose and the expression "prostitute" shall be construed accordingly.

Moreover, the amendment in the law in 1986 has amended the definition of "prostitution" (i.e. the act of a female offering her body for promiscuous sexual intercourse for hire whether in money or in kind, or whether offered immediately or otherwise) and replaced it by the following new definition "prostitution" means the sexual exploitation or abuse of persons (male or female) for commercial purposes, and the expression "prostitute" will be construed accordingly.

The only situations for which a prostitute can be punished are:

(1) Where prostitution is carried on in premises which are within a distance of 200 yards of any place of public religious worship, educational institution, hotel, hospital, nursing home or such other public place of any kind as may be notified in this behalf by the Commissioner of Police or District Magistrate.

(2) Where a prostitute makes positive attempts to seduce or solicit persons for purposes of prostitution.

Prostitutes are entitled to live a life of Dignity:

Women become prostitutes not because they enjoy prostitution but due to poverty. The level of poverty in this country is appalling. Almost 50% of our people are living below the poverty line in horrible conditions, e.g., without employment, proper food, housing, medical care, education, etc. In Rajasthan, people were eating Rotts made of grass. In Orissa people were eating mango kernels, and in Tamil Nadu women are selling one of their kidneys to feed their families. Starvation deaths have been reported in Rajasthan, Orissa, M. P., etc. and it is no wonder that to escape from this abject poverty, a large number of women are compelled to sell their bodies to earn some money to fill their stomachs. Ordinarily, no woman will surrender her body to a man voluntarily unless she respects and loves him. Prostitutes are normally not bad women and they are wrongly regarded as women of vice by society. In fact, in the novels and stories of the great Bengali writer Sharad Chandra Chattopadhyaya many prostitutes are shown to be women of high character, e.g., Rajya Laxmi in Sharad Chandra's famous novel 'Shri Kant,' and Chandramukhi in 'Devdas'. Similarly in the great novel "Crime and Punishment" by the famous Russian writer Dostoyevsky, we come across the character of Sofia Marmaledov who was compelled to become a prostitute due to poverty, although she was depicted as a young woman of high character who earns for her family members who would otherwise starve. In the famous poem 'Chakle' by the great Urdu writer Sahir Ludhiyanvi, the plight of prostitutes in India has been vividly depicted, and this poem has been sung (with some modifications) in the Hindi Film 'Pyasa'. Hence, the approach of society towards the prostitutes must change, and sympathy must be shown towards them as it must be realized that they are not necessarily women of bad character but have been driven to the profession due to acute poverty in their family. In *Chinnamma Sivadas v. State (Delhi Administration)*[2], the Supreme Court held that the State Government should evolve a scheme in which women rescued from brothels and deserted women lodged in protective homes must be able to live with human dignity and find gainful employment after discharge.

Prostitutes are also entitled to live a life of dignity which is part of Article 21[3] of the Constitution as interpreted by the Supreme Court. People including the police must have a sympathetic approach towards them and should not harass them, rather they should have sympathy towards them, and attempt should be made to rehabilitate them in society. The State Government must formulate a scheme for rehabilitation of prostitutes in society and this is only possible if these women are given technical skills so that they can earn their bread by these skills instead of doing so by selling their bodies for filling their stomachs.

---

2   1982 Cr App R 264

3   **Article 21 in The Constitution Of India 1949**
    21. Protection of life and personal liberty No person shall be deprived of his life or personal liberty except according to procedure established by law

19

Setting up of Separate Wing in Police for dealing with Immoral Trafficking[1]

Facts in Nutshell:

Court initiated suomoto[2] proceedings in the matter in following terms:

For a couple of preceding days, painful reports regarding inducement[3], and blackmail of teen-aged girls to lure and coerce them into immoral physical submission have appeared in press. What makes the reports alarming were allegations that some persons highly placed in different spheres were directly involved therein. Pushing innocent minor girls in flesh trade[4] is an extremely treacherous act. The present case covers some broad areas: firstly protection and rehabilitation of the victims and secondly remedial measures to prevent such immoral acts in future.

Immoral Traffic Act, 1956

The immoral Traffic (Prevention) Act, 1956 was enacted to provide, in pursuance of the International Convention signed at New York on 9th May, 1950, for the prevention of immoral traffic. Government of India in the year 1950 ratified an International Convention for suppression of traffic in persons and of the exploitation of the prostitution of others. The principal object of the Act is to prevent commercialization of the vice and trafficking among women and girls. As Krishna Iyer J. has observed in Chita J. *Vaswani v. State of W.B.*[5] no nation, with all its boasts, and

---

1   Appellants: **Suomoto Proceedings in Flesh Trade Vs.** Respondent: **State and Ors.**
    2008(1)JKJ161
    Hon'ble Judges: Hakim Imtiyaz Hussain and Bashir. A. Kirmani, JJ.

2   **Meaning of SuoMoto:** Suo motu, meaning "on its own motion," is a Latin legal term, approximately equivalent to the English term sua sponte. It is used, for example, where a government agency acts on its own cognizance, as in "the Commission took suo motu control over the matter.

3   **Meaning of Inducement:** Something that helps bring about an action or a desired result

4   **Meaning of Flesh Trade:** Selling humans or their different body parts in exchange of remuneration is called Flesh Trade.

5   1976CriLJ1

all its hopes, can ever morally be clean till all its women are really free. Free to live without sale of their young flesh to lascivious wealth or commercializing their luscious figures. India, to redeem this 'gender justice' and to proscribe prostitution whereby rich men buy poor women through houses of vice, has salved its social conscience by enacting the Act.

The scope of the Immoral Traffic (Prevention) Act, 1956 is very vast. Section (3)[6] of the Act provides for punishment for keeping a brothel or allowing a premises to be used as a brothel. Section 3(1) provides for the conviction and punishment of a person who keeps or manages or acts or assists in the keeping or management of a brothel. Sub-section (2) of that section provides for the conviction and punishment of a person who being (a) a tenant, lessee or occupier or person in charge of any premises, uses or knowingly allows any other person to use, such premises or any part thereof as a brothel, (b) the owner, lessor or landlord of any premises or the agent of such owner, lessor or landlord, lets the premises or any part

---

6 **Section 3of Immoral Traffic (Prevention) Act, 1956:**
3. Punishment for keeping a brothel or allowing premises to be used as a brothel. (1) Any person who keeps or manages, or acts or assists in the keeping or management of, a brothel shall be punishable on first conviction with rigorous imprisonment for a term of not less than one year and not more than three years and also with fine which may extend to two thousand rupees and in the event of a second or subsequent conviction, with rigorous imprisonment for a term of not less than two years and not more than five years and also with fine which may extend to two thousand rupees.
(2) Any person who-
being the tenant, lessee, occupier or person in charge of any premises, uses, or knowingly allows any other person to use, such premises or any part thereof as a brothel, or
being the owner, lessor or landlord of any premises or the agent of such owner, lessor or landlord, lets the same or any part thereof with the knowledge that the same or any part thereof is intended to be used as a brothel, or is wilfully a party to the use of such premises or any part thereof as a brothel, shall be punishable on first conviction with imprisonment for a term which may extend to two years and with fine which may extend to two thousand rupees and in the event of a second or subsequent conviction, with rigorous imprisonment for a term which may extend to five years and also with fine.
[1][(2A) For the purposes of sub-section (2) it shall be presumed until the contrary is proved, that any person referred to in clause(a) or clause(b) of that sub-section, is knowingly allowing the premises or any part thereof to be used as a brothel or, as the case maybe, has knowledge that the premises or any part thereof are being used as a brothel, if, -
a report is published in a newspaper having circulation in the area in which such person resides to the effect that the premises or any part thereof have been found to be used for prostitution as a result of a search made under this Act; or
a copy of the list of all things found during the search referred to in clause (a) is given to such person].
(3) Notwithstanding anything contained in any other law for the time being in force, on conviction of any person referred to in clause (a) or clause (b) of sub-section (2) of any offence under that sub-section in respect of any premises or any part thereof, any lease or agreement under which such premises have been leased out or are held or occupied at the time of the commission of the offence, shall become void and inoperative with effect from the date of the said conviction.

thereof with the knowledge that the same or any part thereof is intended to he used as a brothel or is willfully a party to the use of such premises or any part thereof, as a brothel. "Brothel" is defined in Section 2(a) as including a house, room, or place or any portion of any house, room or place, which is used for the purpose of prostitution for the gain of another person or for the mutual gain of two or more prostitutes. "Prostitute" is defined in Section 2(e) as meaning a female who offers her body, for promiscuous sexual intercourse for hire whether in money or in kind.

Section 7[7] provides for the punishment of prostitution in or in the

---

7 **Section 7 of Immoral Traffic (Prevention) Act, 1956:**
Prostitution in or in the vicinity of public places. [(1) Any [person], who carries on prostitution and the person with whom such prostitution is carried on, in any premises,-
which are within the area or areas, notified under sub-section (3), or
which are within a distance of two hundred metres of any place of public religious worship, educational institution, hostel, hospital, nursing home or such other public place of any kind as may be notified in this behalf by the Commissioner of Police or Magistrate in the manner prescribed,
shall be punishable with imprisonment for a term which may extend to three months].
[(1A) Where an offence committed under sub-section (1) is in respect of a child or minor, the person committing the offence shall be punishable with imprisonment of either description for a term which shall not be less than seven years but which may be for life or for a term which may extend to ten years and shall also be liable to fine: Provided that the court may, for adequate and special reasons to be mentioned in the judgement impose a sentence of imprisonment for a term of less than seven years].
(2) Any person who-
being the keeper of any public place knowingly permits prostitution for purposes of their trade to resort to or remain in such place; or
being the tenant, lessee, occupier or person in charge of any premises referred to in sub-section (1) knowingly permits the same or any part thereof to be used for prostitution; or
being the owner, lessor or landlord, of any premises referred to in sub-section (1) or the agent of such owner, lessor or landlord, lets the same or any part thereof may be used for prostitution, or is wilfully a party to such use,
shall be punishable on first conviction with imprisonment for a term which may extend to three months or with fine which may extend to two hundred rupees, or with both, and in the event of a second or subsequent conviction with imprisonment for a term which may extend to six months and also with fine [2][which may extend to two hundred rupees, and if the public place or premises happen to be a hotel, the license for carrying on the business of such hotel under any law for the time being in force shall also be liable to be suspended for a period of not less than three months but which may extend to one year:
Provided that if an offence committed under this sub-section is in respect of a child or minor in a hotel, such license shall also be liable to be cancelled.
Explanation.- For the purposes of this sub-section, "Hotel" shall have the meaning as in clause (6) of Section 2 of the Hotel-Receipts Tax Act, 1980 (54 of 1980)].
[(3) The State Government may, having regard to the kinds of persons frequenting any area or areas in the State, the nature and the density of population therein and other relevant considerations, by notification in the Official Gazette, direct that prostitution shall not be carried on in such area or areas as may be specified in the notification.
(4) Where a notification is issued under sub-section (3) in respect of any area or areas, the State Government shall define the limits of such area or areas in the notification with reasonable certainty.
(5) No such notification shall be issued so as to have effect from a date earlier than the expiry of a

vicinity of public places. Public place is defined in Section 2(h) as meaning any place intended for use by or accessible to the public and includes any public conveyance. Section 18 is very important and gives powers to the Magistrates to attach any house, room, place which is being run or used as a brothel by any person, or is being used by prostitutes for carrying on their trade.

Sections 3 and 7 provide for the punishment of persons guilty of the offences mentioned therein. Any contravention of the provisions mentioned therein amounts to a cognizable[8], offence in view of Section 14[9], whereas a proceeding under Section 18[10] is in no sense

---

period of ninety days after the date on which it is issued.

8 **Meaning of Cognizable:**
Section 2(C) of CrPc, 1973
(c) "cognizable offence" means an offence for which, and "cognizable case" means a case in which, a police officer may, in accordance with the First Schedule or under and other law for the time being in force, arrest without warrant.

9 **Section 14of Immoral Traffic (Prevention) Act, 1956:**
Offences to be cognizable. - Notwithstanding anything contained in [the Code of Criminal Procedure, 1973 (2 of 1974)] any offence punishable under this Act shall be deemed to be a cognizable offence within the meaning of that Code:
Provided that, notwithstanding anything contained in that Code,-
arrest without warrant may be made only by special police officer or under his direction or guidance, or subject to his prior approval;
when the special police officer requires any officer subordinate to him to arrest without warrant otherwise than in his presence any person for an offence under this Act, he shall give that subordinate officer an order in writing, specifying the person to be arrested and the offence for which the arrest is being made; and the latter officer before arresting the person shall inform him of the substance of the order and, on being required by such person, show him the order;
any police officer not below the rank of [2][sub-inspector] specially authorised by the special police officer may, if he has reason to believe that on account of delay involved in obtaining the order of the special police officer, any valuable evidence relating to any offence under this Act is likely to be destroyed or concealed, or the person who has committed or is suspected to have committed the offence is likely to escape, or if the name and address of such a person is unknown or there is reason to suspect that a false name or address has been given, arrest the person concerned without such order, but in such a case he shall report, as soon as may be, to the special police officer the arrest and the circumstances in which the arrest was made.

10 **Section 18 of Immoral Traffic (Prevention) Act, 1956:**
Closure of brothel and eviction of offenders from the premises.- (1) A magistrate may, on receipt of information from the police or otherwise, that any house , room, place or any portion thereof within a distance of [3][two hundred meters] of any public place referred to in sub-section (1) of section 7, is being run or used as a brothel by any person or is being used by prostitutes for carrying on their trade, issue notice on the owner, lessor or landlord of such house, room, place, portion or the agent of the owner, lessor or landlord or on tenant, lessee, occupier of, or any other person in charge of such house, room, place, or portion, to show cause within seven days of the receipt of the notice why the same should not be attached for improper uses thereof; and if, after hearing the person concerned, the magistrate is satisfied that the house, room, place or portion is being used as a brothel or for carrying on prostitution, then the magistrate may pass orders - directing eviction of the occupier within seven days of the passing of the order from the house, room, place or portion;

a prosecution. It is a preventive measure. It is intended to minimise the chance of a brothel being run or prostitution being carried on in premises near about public places.

It is clear from the various provisions that the Act is a complete code with respect to what is to be done under it. It deals with the suppression of immoral traffic in women and girls, a matter which has to be tackled with effectively. The Act creates new offences and provides for the forum before which they would be tried. Necessary provisions of the Code of Criminal procedure have been adopted fully or with modifications. Thus due provisions have been made not only lo punish the accused but' also to prevent immoral trafficking and exploitation of woman. Though the Act applies to the State also but the State Government has not taken the Act seriously and has not paid due attention to implement various provisions of the Act. Even the rules have not been framed under the Act.. If the provisions of the Act are strictly enforced and the functionaries under the Act are made responsible for implementation of the Act, it is likely to check menace of immoral trafficking in the State.

---

directing that before letting it out during the period of one year [1][, or in a case where a child or minor has been found in such house, room, place or portion during a search under section 15, during the period of three years,] immediately after the passing of the order, the owner, lessor or landlord or the agent of the owner, lessor or landlord shall obtain the previous approval of the magistrate : Provided that, if the magistrate finds that the owner, lessor or landlord as well as the agent of the owner, lessor or landlord, was innocent of the improper user of the house, room, place or portion, he may cause the same, to be restored to the owner, lessor or landlord, or the agent of the owner, lessor or landlord, with a direction that the house, room, place or portion shall not be leased out, or otherwise given possession of, to or for the benefit of the person who was allowing the improper user therein. (2) A court convicting a person of any offence under section 3 or section 7 may pass orders under sub-section (1), without further notice such person to show cause as required in that sub-section. (3) Orders passed by the magistrate or court under sub-section (1) or sub-section (2) shall not be subject to appeal and shall not be stayed or set aside by the order of any court, civil or criminal and the said orders shall cease to have validity after the [2][expiry of one year or three years , as the case may be] : Provided that where a conviction under section 3 or section 7 is set aside on appeal on the ground that such house, room, place or any portion thereof is not being run or used as a brothel or is not being used by prostitutes for carrying on their trade, any order passed by the trial court under sub-section (1) shall also be set aside. (4) Notwithstanding anything contained in any other law for the time being in force, when a magistrate passes an order under sub-section (1), or a court passes an order under sub-section (2), any lease or agreement under which the house, room, place or portion is occupied at the time shall become void and inoperative. (5) When an owner, lessor or landlord, or the agent of such owner, lessor or landlord fails to comply with a direction given under clause (b) of sub-section (1) he shall be punishable with fine which may extend to five hundred rupees or when he fails to comply with a direction under the proviso to that sub-section, he shall be deemed to have committed an offence under clause (b) of sub-section (2) of section 3 or clause (c) of sub-section (2) of section 7, as the case may be, and punished accordingly.

Directions of High Court:

Court held that due protection be given by the State to the victims who approach the authorities for the purpose. State shall also take steps for rehabilitation of any such victim who needs the assistance of the government in this behalf. For this it will be appropriate for the Government to constitute a committee of senior officers including an officer from the Social Welfare Department to examine such cases if any and work out proper ways to rehabilitate such girls.

State shall pay due attention to fully enforce the provisions of the Act. Functionaries under the act be made responsible for strict implementation of the Act. It will be proper to constitute a high level committee to suggest ways and means to make the Act effective.

It would perhaps be in fitness of things that Government seriously examines **setting up of a separate wing in police for dealing with anti-social offences like immoral trafficking and drug abuse** etc. which generally support each others. The department of Social Welfare could be saddled with responsibility for dignified rehabilitation of exploited girls pushed into immoral life through a mix of lure and greed. To top these arrangement, stringent administrative measures are required to be prescribed against any person from officialdom whether in uniform or civics found to be involved in these anti social crimes either by commission or omission. By assuring all these measures, the Government, would only be discharging its constitutional duties that a responsible Government is always charged with.

Integral to what has been said above is the fact that society at large has to wake up to the situation. All those who claim to hold the reins of society have a heavy obligation cast on them to ponder over the situation, feel its agony and act. The common citizenry, if they wish to live a dignified and respectable life shall have to do a lot of self accounting and soul searching and question themselves as to how, why and for what their daughters have become vulnerable to being lured, enticed or coerced into sale of their flesh. A society, that does not subject itself to account; does not put interrogatories to itself; does not take itself to task, is doomed to die, die morally, mentally, and spiritually and get reduced to a herd of shameless creatures, shorn of all dignity, crawling in dirt and crumbling in filth, till mother earth gets rid of their worthless weight. The choice is simple and straight, but certainly not difficult to make. Made however, it has to be, before it ceases to be there.

20

Method to eradicate Prostitution or at least further preventing is to Educate Girls[1]

Ratio Decidendi[2]: *"Court shall passed detention[3] order if detenue indulging in activity in connection with immoral traffic."*

Facts in Nutshell:

Pramod Bhagwan Nayak, petitioner[4] original detenu[5], filed habeas corpus[6] petition[7] challenging the order passed by the Police Commissioner.

The grounds of detention revealed the activities carried on by the detenu fall within 'immoral traffic" as defined in Section 2(g)[8] of the P.A.S.A. Act. The grounds of detention further revealed that the detenu was an immoral traffic offender. He was carrying on such activity by taking on rent Flats at Belgiam Square, Surat. The petitioner was engaged in the activity of immoral traffic by bringing girls and women from other cities to Surat and by supplying them to various customers in consideration of

---

1　Appellants: **Pramod Bhagwan Nayak Vs.** Respondent: **State of Gujarat** (2007)1GLR796
　Hon'ble Judges: K.M. Mehta, J.

2　**Meaning of Ration Decidendi:** *Ratio decidendi* is a Latin phrase meaning "the reason" or "the rationale for the decision." The *ratio decidendi* is "the point in a case which determines the judgment" or "the principle which the case establishes."

3　**Meaning of Detention:** Detention is the process when a state, government or citizen lawfully holds a person by removing their freedom of liberty at that time. This can be due to (pending) criminal charges being raised against the individual as part of a prosecution or to protect a person or property.

4　**Meaning of Petitioner:** A person who presents a petition (**Meaning of Petition:** A formal written application requesting a court for a specific judicial action)

5　**Meaning of Detenu:** A person held in custody; a detainee.

6　**Meaning of Habeas Corpus:** A writ of *habeas corpus* is a writ (legal action) that requires a person under arrest to be brought before a judge or into court. The principle of habeas corpus ensures that a prisoner can be released from unlawful detention—that is, detention lacking sufficient cause or evidence.

7　**Meaning of Petition:** A formal message requesting something that is submitted to an authority

8　Section 2(g) of the P.A.S.A. Act provides that "immoral traffic offender" which means a person who habitually commits or abets the commission of any offence under the Suppression of Immoral Traffic in Women and Girls Act, 1956 (104 of 1956).

money and also providing rooms for the said purpose, he was running the business of prostitution and also earning his livelihood from the said income. It was also alleged in the grounds that he was giving threats to the people who are coming in his way in such anti-social activities and also beating them in public, and therefore, are not coming forward to file any complaint against the detenu in public. Thus, it has been alleged that the activities are directly causing or are likely to cause harm, danger to life, property and public health. It has been further alleged in the ground that immoral trafficking is resulting in spreading sexual disease including dangerous diseases like H.I.V. AIDS etc., and there is no need of any documentary evidence to prove that such activity is dangerous to public health particularly when there is sufficient material on record of the case to show that the detenu was involved in the anti-social activities of running brothel or involved in the offences of immoral trafficking.

Article 23 of Constitution:

Article 23 of Constitution of India which provides prohibition of traffic in human beings and forced labour.

(1) Traffic in human beings and beggar and other similar forms of forced labour are prohibited and any contravention of this provision shall be an offence punishable in accordance with law.

(2) Nothing in this Article shall prevent the State from imposing compulsory service for public purposes and in imposing such service the State shall not make any discrimination on grounds only of religion, race, caste or class or any of them.

Immoral Traffic (Prevention) Act, 1956

Section 2 of the said Act provides definitions which are important. Section 2(a) of the said Act defines "brothel". "Brothel" includes any house, room or place which is used for purposes of sexual exploitation or abuse for the gain of another person or the mutual gain of two or more prostitutes. Thus, where a single person practices prostitution for his or her own livelihood without another prostitute or some other person being involved in the maintenance of such premises, his or her residence will not amount to "brothel".

Section 2(f) defines "prostitution" means the sexual exploitation or abuse of persons for commercial purpose and the expression "prostitute" shall be construed accordingly.

Moreover, the amendment in the law in 1986 has amended the definition of "prostitution" (i.e. the act of a female offering her body for promiscuous sexual intercourse for hire whether in money or in kind, or whether offered immediately or otherwise) and replaced it by the following new definition "prostitution" means the sexual exploitation or abuse of persons (male or female) for commercial purposes, and the expression "prostitute" will be construed accordingly.

Section 2(g) provides "protective home". Section 2(h) provides "public place". Section 3 provides punishment for keeping a brothel or allowing premises to be used as brothel. Section 4 of the said Act provides punishment for living on the earning of prostitution. Section 5 of the said Act provides procuring, inducing or taking person for the sake of prostitution. Section 6 of the said Act provides detaining a person in premises where prostitution is carried on. Section 7 of the Act provides prostitution in or in the vicinity of public places. Section 8 of the Act providing seducing or soliciting for purpose of prostitution. Section 9 of the Act provides seduction of a person in custody. Section 18 of the Act provides closure of brothels and eviction of offenders from the premises. Section 19 of the Act provides application for being kept in a protective home or provided care and protection by Court. Section 20 provides removal of prostitute from any place.

Questions over Prostitution:

There has been a considerable acrimonious[9] debate over the Question: Is prostitution a form of exploitation to be abolished or an occupation to be regulated? The question is no longer about morality : Is prostitution a vice and there involved evil or lacking in morals? There are basically two camps, those seeking to eradicate prostitution and those who view the women involved as sex workers.

Prostitution and Violation of Right to Life:

Prostitution in the modern times is not confined to street-walking and its forms are diversified into various kinds, such as prostitution services, including date clubs, various kinds of services in adult entertainment, business facilities, meet and mate on the internet etc. Pornography acts

---

9 **Meaning of acrimonious:** Characterized by bitterness or sharpness of manner, speech, temper, etc.

as an arm of prostitution and often women coerced into pornography are coerced into prostitution.

Economic crisis, natural diseases, political unrest and conflict situations make women and children more vulnerable and easy prey to sex traffickers and recruits. The term "sex worker" does not dignify the women involved though it may dignify the pimps, procurers and traffickers who can call themselves "managers", "supervisors" and "organisers". Prostitution for women is considered not merely temporal activity, but rather a heavily stigmatized social status which in most societies remains fixed on them regardless of any improvement in behaviour. In a study of street prostitutes in Toronto, approximately 90% of women contacted indicated that they wished to stop working on the streets at some point of time, but felt unable or unclear about how to even begin the process[10]. Often women who themselves view sex service as a temporary and part-time engagement are forced by legal and social labelling to remain prostitutes and to bear that status in all the walks of their life. Prostitutes epitomise social illegitimacy and are designated as a fair game for police scrutiny and social attack. If prostitutes by circumstances regulated by commercial interests of the middlemen and organizers cannot leave, they remain as sexual slaves. Women in prostitution usually begin their career due to poverty and are kept indebted and poor by pimps and other middlemen who control their earnings and movements making them a legal non-person in a biased society. Article 23[11] of the Constitution of India prohibits traffic in human beings, beggar and other similar form of forced labour. The victim of prostitution is the prostitute herself who is placed in a slave-like condition and subjected to virtually unlimited authority of others in the trade for rendering distinctly personal service. Through, contrived and manipulated indebtedness to which she gets subjected, she is unable to ward off the shackles of poverty and inch towards a dignified living. Servitude results from indebtedness and poverty. The victims of the vice of prostitution believe that they have no viable alternative but

---

10 (See : Prostitution and Civil Rights by Catharine A. MacKinnon, Michigan Journal of Gender & Law, 1993, Volume : 13-31)

11 Article 23 in The Constitution Of India 1949
    23. Prohibition of traffic in human beings and forced labour
    (1) Traffic in human beings and begar and other similar forms of forced labour are prohibited and any contravention of this provision shall be an offence punishable in accordance with law
    (2) Nothing in this article shall prevent the State from imposing compulsory service for public purpose, and in imposing such service the State shall not make any discrimination on grounds only of religion, race, caste or class or any of them

to continue in the field of their exploitation for survival. Poverty and indebtedness make exit from prostitution impossible for such women. This condition of involuntary servitude of most of the women and girls in prostitution, where their distinctly personal services are bought and sold as chattel, would justify the Court and other constitutional authorities in viewing prostitution as a form of modern slavery and its perpetrators, pimps and traffickers as exploitation of the victim prostitutes in violation of their right against exploitation guaranteed by Article 23.

Our Constitution values human dignity which inheres in various aspects of what it means to be a human being. One of these aspects is the fundamental dignity of human body which is not simply organic. The very nature of commodifying the human body devalues the respect that the Constitution regards as inherent in the human body by guaranteeing fundamental right against exploitation under Article 23 and by issuing directives under Articles 39(e)[12] and 46[13] that the State should strive towards securing that, health and strength of men and women are not abused and citizens are not forced to enter avocations unsuited to their age or strength and to promote with special care the educational and economic interests of the weaker sections of the people and protect them from social injustice and all forms of exploitations.

The most potent rejoinder against recognition of the degrading practice of prostitution, which undermines womanhood itself, comes from Article 51A(e)[14] of the Constitution, which ordains that it shall be the duty of every citizen of India to renounce practices derogatory to the dignity of women. The fact that prostitution is a practice derogatory to the dignity of women is universally recognized and is clearly reflected from

---

12 **Article 39 in The Constitution Of India 1949**
39. Certain principles of policy to be followed by the State: The State shall, in particular, direct its policy towards securing
(e) that the health and strength of workers, men and women, and the tender age of children are not abused and that citizens are not forced by economic necessity to enter avocations unsuited to their age or strength;

13 **Article 46 in The Constitution Of India 1949**
46. Promotion of educational and economic interests of Scheduled Castes, Scheduled Tribes and other weaker sections The State shall promote with special care the educational and economic interests of the weaker sections of the people, and, in particular, of the Scheduled Castes and the Scheduled Tribes, and shall protect them from social injustice and all forms of exploitation

14 **Article 51A in The Constitution Of India 1949**
51A. Fundamental duties It shall be the duty of every citizen of India
(e) to promote harmony and the spirit of common brotherhood amongst all the people of India transcending religious, linguistic and regional or sectional diversities; to renounce practices derogatory to the dignity of women;

the "Convention for the Suppression of the Traffic in Persons and of the Exploitation of the Prostitution of Others", to which India was a signatory having signed it on 9-5-1950 and which was ratified on 9-5-1953. The Convention was approved by the General Assembly of the United Nations in its Resolution 317(IV) of 2 December, 1949. The preamble of the Convention records that:

> ...prostitution and the accompanying evil of the traffic in persons for the purpose of prostitution are incompatible with the dignity and worth of the human person and endanger the welfare of the individual, the family and the community...

The parties to the Convention agreed under Article 1 to punish any person who, to gratify the passions of another, procures, entices or leads away, for purposes of prostitution, another person, even with the consent of that person, or exploits the prostitution of "another person", even with the consent of that person. The "Convention on the Elimination of all Forms of Discrimination Against Women of 1979" provided in Article 6 that State Parties shall take all appropriate measures, including legislation, to suppress all forms of traffic in women and exploitation of prostitution of women. The General Assembly of the United Nations passed a Resolution on 16-12-1983[15] in its meeting No. 100 reaffirming the objectives of the United Nations Decade for Women : Equality, Development and Peace, bearing in mind, "the essential role of women in the welfare of the family and the development of society" and "considering that prostitution and the accompanying evil of the traffic in persons for the purpose of prostitution are incompatible with the dignity and worth of the human person and endanger the welfare of the individual, the family and the community", urged the Members States "to take all appropriate humane measures, including legislation, to combat prostitution, exploitation of the prostitution of others and all forms of traffic in persons and to provide special protection to victims of prostitution through measures including education, social guarantees and employment opportunities for those victims with a view to their rehabilitation".

To recognize prostitution as a legitimate means of livelihood would be an open invitation to trafficking in women and girls is one of the most corrosive forms of violation of human rights. It results in gradual total destruction of a women's personal identity, and her right to live as a free human being in a civilized society. The victim is subjected to violence,

---

15 (A/RES/38/107)

total humiliation and violation of personal integrity. The victim of such devastating violence may also end up with life-threatening H.I.V./A.I.D.S./ S.T.D. or a lifetime of trauma, drug addiction or personality disintegration. It is a denial of the right to liberty and security of person, the right to freedom from torture, violence, cruelty or degrading treatment, the right to a home and a family, the right to health care-everything that makes for a life with dignity. Trafficking has been rightly referred to as a modern form of slavery"[16].

The restriction on personal liberty by Section 7[17] is in the interests of general public and is imposed by law enacted by the Parliament in the background of the Convention for Suppression of the Traffic in Persons and of the Exploitation of Prostitution of Others signed and ratified by India, and the deprivation of liberty to carry on prostitution in public places is as per the procedure established by law. Therefore, there is no violation of the fundamental right to life and personal liberty of persons guaranteed by Article 21[18] of the Constitution.

Prostitution[19] - The Consequent Harms - Prostitution has been denunciated in almost all societies for various reasons; the most fundamental reason being that it offends the elementary norms of decency and culture and involves human debasement of the lowest order. It has been condemned as an evil, albeit inevitable, by social reformers, religious thinkers and philosophers alike, illegitimate sex is considered to be a great sin under all the religious systems and it should be too evident that the lowest level of illegitimate sexual conduct is reached in prostitution. 'What can be called more sordid, more void of modesty, more full of shame than prostitutes, brothels and every other evil of this kind? Yet remove prostitutes from human affairs, and you will pollute all things with lust; set them among honest matrons, and you will dishonour all things with disgrace and turpitude', commented St. Augustine on prostitution. Thomas Aquinas expressed the same idea in the following words:

Prostitution is like the filth in the sea, or a sewer in the palace. Take away

---

16 (See : Consultation Paper on "Trafficking in Women and Girls" by Justice Sujata Manohar for the Expert Group Meeting on "Trafficking in Women and Girls" 18-22 November, 2002 Glen Cove, New York, USA)."

17 Section 7 of the Act provides prostitution in or in the vicinity of public places

18 **Article 21 in The Constitution Of India 1949**
  21. Protection of life and personal liberty No person shall be deprived of his life or personal liberty except according to procedure established by law

19 Criminology, 5th Edition, Page 457, Observation on Page No. 461

the sewer, and you will fill the palace with pollution; and likewise with the filth (in the sea). Take away prostitutes from the world, and you will fill it with sodomy'.

Further combating prostitution on page 463 the learned author has observe thus:

In India the main legislation dealing with the problem is the Suppression of Immoral Traffic Act, 1956 (to be referred hereafter as S.I.T.A.). The Act does not prohibit prostitution as such but seeks to remove some of the conditions which promote prostitution. The provisions are directed mainly towards those who either organize prostitution by running brothels or induct women into the sex trade.

Cases Referred:

The Hon'ble Supreme Court in the case of *Vishal Jeet v. Union of India and Ors. States and Union Territories*[20] has observed in Para 11 as under:

With the growing danger in society to healthy and decent living with morality, the world public opinion congregated at New York in a convention for suppression of traffic in persons for exploitation for immoral purposes. Pursuant to the signing of that convention on May 9, 1950, our Parliament has passed an act called "Suppression of Immoral Traffic in Women and Girls Act, 1956" which is now changed as "the Immoral Traffic (Prevention) Act, 1956" to which certain drastic amendments are introduced by the Amendment Acts XLVI of 1978 and XLIV of 1986. This Act aims at suppressing the evils of prostitution in women and girls and achieving a public purpose viz., to rescue the fallen women and girls and to stamp out the evils of prostitution and also to provide an opportunity to these fallen victims so that they could become decent members of the society. Besides the above Act, there are various provisions in the Indian Penal Code such as Sections 366A[21] (dealing with procuration of minor girl), 366B[22] (dealing with offence of importation of girl from foreign

---

20 1990CriLJ1469

21 **Section 366 A, IPC, 1860**
   366A. Procuration of minor girl
   Whoever, by any means whatsoever, induces any minor girl under the age of eighteen years to go from any place or to do any act with intent that such girl may be, or knowing that it is likely that she will be, forced or seduced to illicit intercourse with another person shall be punishable with imprisonment which may extend to ten years, and shall also be liable to fine.

22 **Section 366 B, IPC, 1860**
   366B. Importation of girl from foreign country

country), 372[23] (dealing with selling of minor for purposes of prostitution etc.) and 373[24] (dealing with the offence of buying minor for purposes of prostitution etc.) The Juvenile Justice Act, 1986 which provides for the care, protection, treatment, development and rehabilitation of neglected or delinquent juveniles contains a specific provision namely Section 13 of Act, 1986 which empowers a police officer or any other person or organisation authorised by the State Government in this behalf to take charge of any neglected juveniles and bring them before the Board constituted under this Act which Board under Section 15 of Act, 1986 has to hold an enquiry and make such orders in relation to the neglected juveniles as it may deem fit.

In in the same Judgment on Para 32 of the judgment, the Hon'ble Court has given directions thus:

(1) State Government to see that strict vigilance is maintained in the areas where sex workers normally operate and to rescue the child sex workers. Further, adequate steps should be taken to see that those who indulge in trafficking of women should be suitably punished. For this purpose, appropriate directions should be issued to the investigating agencies to take immediate steps. Sometimes, it is noticed that a Police Officer who detects this type of activity does not take immediate action on the ground that such duty is assigned to some other Officer. In Courts view, this was not the proper approach because all Police Officers are bound to prevent

---

Whoever imports into [161][India] from any country outside India [or from the State of Jammu and Kashmir] any girl under the age of twenty-one years with intent that she may be, or knowing it to be likely that she will be, forced or seduced to illicit intercourse with another person, [***] shall be punishable with imprisonment which may extend to ten years and shall also be liable to fine.]

23 **Section 372, IPC, 1860**
Selling minor for purposes of prostitution, etc
Whoever sells, lets to hire, or otherwise disposes of any [person under the age of eighteen years with intent that such person shall at any age be employed or used for the purpose of prostitution or illicit intercourse with any person or for any unlawful and immoral purpose, or knowing it to be likely that such person will at any age be] employed or used for any such purpose, shall be punished with imprisonment of either description for a term which may extend to ten years, and shall be liable to fine.

24 **Section 373, IPC, 1860**
Buying minor for purposes of prostitution, etc
Whoever buys, hires or otherwise obtains possession of any [person under the age of eighteen years with intent that such person shall at any age be employed or used for the purpose of prostitution or illicit intercourse with any person or for any unlawful and immoral purpose, of knowing it to be likely that such person will at any age be] employed or used for any purpose, shall be punished with imprisonment of either description for a term which may extend to ten years, and shall also be liable to fine.

or take immediate action in those case where cognizable offences[25] are committed. It is true that they may not investigate those cases but can certainly report them to the proper officer and during such time take preventive measures. Section 107 of the Indian Penal Code provides that "a person abets the doing of a thing who intentionally aids by act of illegal omission, the doing of that thing".

(2) It is high time that the State Government should take serious steps:

(a) to prevent forcible pushing of women and young girls into prostitution;

(b) to prevent trafficking in women i.e. buying and selling of young girls.

These girls may be victims of kidnapping; they may be victims of various deprivations; they may be victims of circumstances beyond their control. For this purpose, regular raids, should be carried out in the area where sex workers operate. On numerous occasions it is reported in newspapers that persons from social organisations who dare to rescue these girls are manhandled, beaten or threatened. To prevent such situation, for the time-being the **Government must have a Squad of Police Officers who can take immediate action.**

(3) To set up homes for rehabilitation of rescued sex workers including children so as to enable these rescued sex workers to acquire alternative skills in order to enable them to have alternative source of employment. It is also to be noted that when the girls were rescued, it was difficult for the State authorities to provide residential accommodation to them. The State was not having any infrastructure to meet such a situation.

In a civilised State, it is the duty of the State to take preventive measures to eradicate **child prostitution** without giving room for any complaint of culpable indifference. One should not forget that these rescued girls are also fellow human beings who require some support and treatment for getting out of the immoral activities.

(4) Regularly carry out A.I.D.S. awareness programme in the areas where sex workers normally operate[26].

---

25 **Meaning of Cognizable:**
   Section 2 (C) CrPc, 1973
   (c) "cognizable offence" means an offence for which, and "cognizable case" means a case in which, a police officer may, in accordance with the First Schedule or under any other law for the time being in force, arrest without warrant;

26 (Quoted from the Book "Women and the Law - II" by Christine Chorine, Mihir Desai, Colin Gonsalves Women rights published page 827).

The only situations for which a prostitute can be punished are:

(1) Where prostitution is carried on in premises which are within a distance of 200 yards of any place of public religious worship, educational institution, hotel, hospital, nursing home or such other public place of any kind as may be notified in this behalf by the Commissioner of Police or District Magistrate.

(2) Where a prostitute makes positive attempts to seduce or solicit persons for purposes of prostitution.

Decision of the High Court:

Court held that it is no doubt true that prostitution is a very old profession which is carrying on since ages and though the Government and other agencies were trying to make effort to eradicate the same, they have not been fully successful. Court suggested another method to eradicate prostitution or at least further preventing is to educate girls and women up to 12th Standard or up to the age of 18 years and the Government may make the same free or reasonably so cheap so all girls can take education irrespective of their financial position. If the girls are educated and studied, further opportunity can be given by the State Government to earn their own livelihood. It is well known that no women or girls join the profession at their own sweet will or volition. They have to do it under severe compulsion as there is no other alternative to them. If education and employment opportunity is provided to them, girls will not automatically fall into the trap of this profession.

Another advantage is that if the females are educated they will understand family planning and that may also solve problem of population which is also a very important question which the Government faces.

21

Child Prostitution[1]

Facts in Nutshell:

The writ petition[2] under Article 32[3] of the Constitution of India at the instance of an Advocate was filed by way of a Public Interest Litigation[4] seeking issuance of certain directions, directing the Central Bureau of Investigation (1) to institute an enquiry against those police officers under whose jurisdiction Red Light areas as well Devadasi[5] and Jogin traditions are flourishing and to take necessary action against such erring police

---

1   Appellants: **Vishal Jeet Vs.** Respondent: **Union of India and others** AIR1990SC1412
    Hon'ble Judges: S. Ratnavel Pandian and K. Jayachandra Reddy, JJ.

2   **Meaning of Writ Petition:** Under the Indian legal system, jurisdiction to issue 'prerogative writs' is given to the Supreme Court, and to the High Courts of Judicature of all Indian states. Parts of the law relating to writs are set forth in the Constitution of India. The Supreme Court, the highest in the country, may issue writs under Article 32 of the Constitution for enforcement of Fundamental Rights and under Articles 139 for enforcement of rights other than Fundamental Rights, while High Courts, the superior courts of the States, may issue writs under Articles 226. 'Writ' is eminently designed by the makers of the Constitution, and in the same way it is developed very widely and efficiently by the courts in India. The Constitution broadly provides for five kinds of "prerogative" writs, namely, Habeas Corpus, Certiorari, Mandamus, Quo Warranto and Prohibition.

3   **Article 32 in The Constitution Of India 1949**
    32. Remedies for enforcement of rights conferred by this Part
    (1) The right to move the Supreme Court by appropriate proceedings for the enforcement of the rights conferred by this Part is guaranteed
    (2) The Supreme Court shall have power to issue directions or orders or writs, including writs in the nature of habeas corpus, mandamus, prohibition, quo warranto and certiorari, whichever may be appropriate, for the enforcement of any of the rights conferred by this Part
    (3) Without prejudice to the powers conferred on the Supreme Court by clause (1) and (2), Parliament may by law empower any other court to exercise within the local limits of its jurisdiction all or any of the powers exercisable by the Supreme Court under clause (2)
    (4) The right guaranteed by this article shall not be suspended except as otherwise provided for by this Constitution

4   **Meaning of Public Interest Litigation:**
    Public-interest litigation is litigation for the protection of the public interest. PIL may be introduced in a court of law by the court itself (*suo motu*), rather than the aggrieved party or another third party. For the exercise of the court's jurisdiction, it is unnecessary for the victim of the violation of his or her rights to personally approach the court. In PIL, the right to file suit is given to a member of the public by the courts through judicial activism.

5   **Meaning of Devadasi:** In Hinduism, a **devadasi** (Sanskrit: *servant of deva or devi* (god)) is a girl "married" to a deity and dedicated to worship and service of the deity or a temple for the rest of her life. Originally, in addition to taking care of the temple and performing rituals, these women learned and practiced Sadir (Bharatanatya), Odissi and other classical Indian artistic traditions and enjoyed a high social status as dance and music were essential part of temple worship.

officers and law breakers; (2) to bring all the inmates of the red light areas and also those who are engaged in 'flesh trade' to protective homes of the respective States and to provide them with proper medical aid, shelter, education and training in various disciplines of life so as to enable them to choose a more dignified way of life and (3) to bring the children of those prostitutes and other children found begging in streets and also the girls pushed into 'flesh trade' to protective homes and then to rehabilitate them.

Many unfortunate teen-aged female children (hereinafter refer red to as 'the children') and girls in full bloom are being sold in various parts of the country, for paltry sum even by their parents finding themselves unable to maintain their children on account of acute poverty and unbearable miseries and hoping that their children would be engaged only in household duties or manual labour. But those who are acting as pimps or brokers in the 'flesh trade' and brothel keepers who hunt for these teenaged children and young girls to make money either purchase or kidnap them by deceitful means and unjustly and forcibly inveigle them into 'flesh trade'. Once these unfortunate victims are taken to the dens of prostitutes and sold to brothel keepers, they are shockingly and brutally treated and confined in complete seclusion in a tiny claustrophobic room for several days without food until they succumb to the vicious desires of the brothel keepers and enter into the unethical and squalid business of prostitution. These victims though unwilling to lead this obnoxious way of life have no other way except to surrender themselves retreating into silence and submitting their bodies to all the dirty customers including even sexagenarians with plastic smile.

Prostitution:

No denying the fact that prostitution always remains as a running sore in the body of civilisation and destroys all moral values. The causes and evil effects of prostitution manning the society are so notorious and frightful that none can gainsay it. This malignity is daily and hourly threatening the community at large slowly but steadily making its way onwards leaving a track marked with broken hopes. Therefore, the necessity for appropriate and drastic action to eradicate this evil has become apparent but its successful consummation[6] ultimately rests with the public at large.

---

6 **Meaning of Consummation: Consummation** or **consummation of a marriage,** in many traditions and statutes of civil or religious law, is the first (or first officially credited) act of sexual intercourse between two people, either following their marriage to each other or after a prolonged sexual attraction. Its legal significance arises from theories of marriage as having the

It is highly deplorable and heart-rending to note that many poverty stricken children and girls in the prime of youth are taken to 'flesh market' and forcibly pushed into the 'flesh trade' which is being carried on in utter violation of all cannons of morality, decency and dignity of humankind. There cannot be two opinions indeed there is none that this obnoxious and abominable crime committed with all kinds of unthinkable vulgarity should be eradicated at all levels by drastic steps.

Article 23 of Indian Constitution:[7]

Article 23 which relates to Fundamental Rights in Part III of the Constitution[8] and which has been put under the caption 'Right against exploitation' prohibits 'traffic in human beings and begar and other similar forms of labour' and provides that any contravention of Article 23(1) shall be an offence punishable in accordance with law. The expression 'traffic in human beings' is evidently a very wide expression including the prohibition of traffic in women for immoral or other purposes. Article 35(a)(ii)[9] of the Constitution reads that notwithstanding anything in this

purpose of producing legally recognized descendants of the partners, or of providing sanction to their sexual acts together, or both, and amounts to treating a marriage*ceremony* as falling short of *completing* the creation of the state of being married. Thus in some Western traditions, a marriage is not considered a binding contract until and unless it has been consummated.

7 **Article 23 in The Constitution Of India 1949**
23. Prohibition of traffic in human beings and forced labour
(1) Traffic in human beings and begar and other similar forms of forced labour are prohibited and any contravention of this provision shall be an offence punishable in accordance with law
(2) Nothing in this article shall prevent the State from imposing compulsory service for public purpose, and in imposing such service the State shall not make any discrimination on grounds only of religion, race, caste or class or any of them

8 **Part III of Indian Constitution:**
'Part III – Fundamental Rights' is a charter of rights contained in the Constitution of India. It guarantees civil liberties such that all Indians can lead their lives in peace and harmony as citizens of India. These include individual rights common to most liberal democracies, such asequality before law, freedom of speech and expression, and peaceful assembly, freedom to practice religion, and the right to constitutional remedies for the protection of civil rights by means of writs such as habeas corpus. Violation of these rights result in punishments as prescribed in the Indian Penal Code or other special laws, subject to discretion of the judiciary. The Fundamental Rights are defined as basichuman freedoms which every Indian citizen has the right to enjoy for a proper and harmonious development of personality. These rights universally apply to all citizens, irrespective of race, place of birth, religion, caste, creed, colour or gender. Aliens (persons who are not citizens) are also considered in matters like equality before law. They are enforceable by the courts, subject to certain restrictions. The Rights have their origins in many sources, including England's Bill of Rights, the United States Bill of Rights and France's Declaration of the Rights of Man.

9 **Article 35 in The Constitution Of India 1949**
35. Legislation to give effect to the provisions of this Part Notwithstanding anything in this Constitution,
(a) Parliament shall have, and the Legislature of a State shall not have, power to make laws
(i) with respect to any of the matters which under clause (3) of Article 16, clause (3) of Article 32,

Constitution, Parliament shall have, and the legislature of a State shall not have, power to make laws for prescribing punishment for those acts which are declared to be offences under this part. The power of legislation, under this article, is given to the Parliament exclusively, for, otherwise the laws relating to fundamental rights would not have been uniform throughout the country. The power is specifically denied to the state legislatures. In implementation of the principles underlying Article 23(1)[10] the Suppression of Immoral Traffic in Women & Girls Act, 1956 (SITA for short) has been enacted under Article 35 with the object of inhibiting or abolishing the immoral traffic in women and girls.

"The Immoral Traffic (Prevention) Act, 1956" and IPC

"Suppression of Immoral Traffic in Women and Girls Act, 1956 which is now changed as "The Immoral Traffic (Prevention) Act, 1956" to which certain drastic amendments are introduced by the Amendment Acts of 46 of 1978 and 44 of 1986. This Act dims at suppressing the evils of prostitution in women and girls and achieving a public purpose viz. to rescue the fallen women and girls and to stamp out the evils of prostitution and also to provide all opportunity to these fallen victims so that they could become decent members of the society. Besides the above Act, there are various provisions in the Indian Penal Code such as Sections 366-A[11] (dealing with precaution of minor girl), 366-B[12] (dealing with offence of importation of girl from foreign country), 372[13] (dealing

---

Article 33 and Article 34 may be provided for by law made by Parliament; and
(ii) for prescribing punishment for those acts which are declared to be offences under this Part; and Parliament shall, as soon as may be after the commencement of this Constitution, make laws for prescribing punishment for the acts referred to in sub clause (ii);

10 **Article 23 (1): Power to make rules:** The State Government may, by notification in the Official Gazette, make rules for carrying out the purposes of this Act.

11 **Section 366 A IPC, 1860**
Procuration of minor girl.
366A. Procuration of minor girl.--Whoever, by any means whatsoever, induces any minor girl under the age of eighteen years to go from any place or to do any act with intent that such girl may be, or knowing that it is likely that she will be, forced or seduced to illicit intercourse with another person shall be punishable with imprisonment which may extend to ten years, and shall also be liable to fine.

12 **Section 366 B IPC, 1860**
Importation of girl from foreign country.
366B. Importation of girl from foreign country.--Whoever imports into [India] from any country outside India [or from the State of Jammu and Kashmir] any girl under the age of twenty-one years with intent that she may be, or knowing it to be likely that she will be, forced or seduced to illicit intercourse with another person, shall be punishable with imprisonment which may extend to ten years, and shall also be liable to fine.]

13 **Section 372 in The Indian Penal Code, 1860**

with selling of minor for purposes of prostitution etc.) and 373[14] (dealing with the offence of buying minor for purposes of prostitution etc.).

Importance of Children in Society:

Bhagwati, J. in *Lakshmi Kant Pandey v. Union of India*[15] while emphasizing the importance of children has expressed his view thus:

It is obvious that in a civilized society the importance of child welfare cannot be over-emphasized, because the welfare of the entire community, its growth and development, depend on the health and well-being of its children. Children are a 'supremely important national asset' and the future well-being of the nation depends on how its children grow and develop.

Directions of Supreme Court with regard to Child Rehabilitation:

1. All the State Governments and the Governments of Union Territories should direct their concerned law enforcing authorities to take appropriate and speedy action under the existing laws in eradicating child prostitution without giving room for any complaint of remissness or

---

372. Selling minor for purposes of prostitution, etc.-- Whoever sells, lets to hire, or otherwise disposes of any 2[person under the age of eighteen years with intent that such person shall at any age be employed or used for the purpose of prostitution or illicit intercourse with any person or for any unlawful and immoral purpose, or knowing it to be likely that such person will at any age be] employed or used for any such purpose, shall be punished with imprisonment of either description for a term which may extend to ten years, and shall also be liable to fine. 3[Explanation I.- When a female under the age of eighteen years is sold, let for hire, or otherwise disposed of to a prostitute or to any person who keeps or manages a brothel, the person so disposing of such female shall, until the contrary is proved, be presumed to have disposed of her with the intent that she shall be used for the purpose of prostitution. Explanation II.- For the purposes of this section" illicit intercourse" means sexual intercourse between persons not united by marriage, or by any union or tie which though not amounting to a marriage, is recognised by the personal law or custom of the community to which they belong or, where they belong to different communities, of both such communities, as constituting between them a quasi- marital relation.]

14 **Section 373 in The Indian Penal Code, 1860**
373. Buying minor for purposes of prostitution, etc.-- Whoever buys, hires or otherwise obtains possession of any [person under the age of eighteen years with intent that such person shall at any age be employed or used for the purpose of prostitution or illicit intercourse with any person or for any unlawful and immoral purpose, or knowing it to be likely that such person will at any age be] employed or used for any such purpose, shall be punished with imprisonment of either description for a term which may extend to ten years, and shall also be liable to fine. [Explanation I.- Any prostitute or any person keeping or managing a brothel, who buys, hires or otherwise obtains possession of a female under the age of eighteen years shall, until the contrary is proved, be presumed to have obtained possession of such female with the intent that she shall be used for the purpose of prostitution. Explanation II.-" Illicit intercourse" has the same meaning as in section 372.]

15 [1984]2SCR795

culpable indifference.

2. The State Governments and the Governments of Union Territories should set up a separate Advisory Committee within their respective zones consisting of the secretary of the Social Welfare Department or Board, the Secretary of the Law Department, sociologists, criminologists, members of the women's organisations, members of Indian Council of Child Welfare and Indian Council of Social Welfare as well the members of various voluntary social organisations and associations etc., the main objects of the Advisory Committee being to make suggestions of:

(a) the measures to be taken in eradicating the child prostitution, and

(b) the social welfare programmes to be implemented for the care, protection, treatment, development and rehabilitation of the young fallen victims namely the children and girls rescued either from the brothel houses or from the vices of prostitution.

3. All the State Governments and the Governments of Union Territories should take steps in providing adequate and rehabilitative homes manned by well-qualified trained social workers, psychiatrists and doctOrs.

4. The Union Government should set up a committee of its own in the line, Court have suggested under direction No. (2) the main object of which is to evolve welfare programmes to be implemented on the national level for the care, protection, rehabilitation etc. etc. of the young fallen victims namely the children and girls and to make suggestions of amendments to the existing laws or for enactment of any new law, if so warranted for the prevention of sexual exploitation of children.

5. The Central Government and the Governments of States and Union Territories should devise a machinery of its own for ensuring the proper implementation of the suggestions that would be made by the respective committees.

6. The Advisory Committee can also go deep into devadasi system and Jogin tradition and give their valuable advice and suggestions as to what best the Government could do in that regard.

22

Illegitimate[1] sons of a Prostitute would be included within term 'member of family'[2]

Facts in Nutshell:

The landlord-plaintiff-appellant[3] was admittedly a bedini (country Prostitute) by caste and profession. She owns the suit house having purchased the same from one Ram Singh under the registered deed of sale[4] dated 21-12-1974. The tenant-defendant[5]-respondent has been holding the house at a monthly rent of Rs. 22/- since 3-5-1973 from the ex-landlord under a written rent note. The case of the plaintiff[6] was that she bona fide needs the suit accommodation for the residence of herself and her two sons, namely, Pooran Singh and Anoop Singh, both studying in College and Higher Secondary School respectively. It was also alleged that she wanted to reconstruct the house which could not be done unless the premises were vacated. The defendant in his written statement denied the case of the plaintiff and' submitted that the plaintiff was in possession of other alternative accommodation, hence her need was not genuine and that the requirement of illegitimate sons could not be considered.

---

1 **Meaning of Illegitimate:**
   1. Against the law; illegal.
   2. Born out of wedlock.

2 Appellants: **Sushila Devi d/o Ramsingh Vs.** Respondent: **Maharajsingh Devisingh**
   1990(35)MPLJ445
   Hon'ble Judges: R.C. Lahoti, J.

3 **Meaning of Appellant:** A person who, dissatisfied with the judgment rendered in a lawsuit decided in a lower court or the findings from a proceeding before an Administrative Agency, asks a superior court to review the decision.

4 **Meaning of Sale Deed:** It is an instrument in writing which transfers the ownership of the property or properties in exchange for a price paid/consideration. This is a document that requires to be registered compulsorily.

5 **Meaning of Defendant:** The party against which an action is brought.

6 **Meaning of Plaintiff:** The party that institutes a suit in a court.

Decision of the Trial Court:

The trial Court decreed[7] the suit. On appeal[8], the decree has been reversed by holding that the plaintiff was a country-prostitute and her sons were illegitimate, whose requirement bore no relevance under the law. The Lower Appellate Court relied on a decision of the Supreme Court in *Guljar Singh v. Motasingh*[9] in holding that the illegitimate sons could not be considered to be 'members of the family' of the landlord.

Question before the High Court:

Whether the Lower Appellate Court has rightly constructed the meaning of the term 'member of the family' so as to exclude illegitimate sons of a bedini - country prostitute?

Family:

In *Baldev Sahai Bangia v. R. C. Bhasin*[10] , their Lordships held that a conspectus of the connotation of the term family emerging from a reference to several dictionaries clearly shows that "the word 'family' has to be given not a restricted but a wider meaning". Therein Webster's Third New International Dictionary was cited with approval which defined 'family' as including *all persons related by blood or marriage.*

In *Muhammad and Ors. v. Sinnanalu Ammo*, the Kerala High Court held that the expression 'family'' was elastic and that its ambit had to be determined in all the circumstances of the case having regard to the habits, ideas and socio-economic milieu of the parties.

Decision of the High Court:

Court held that in so far as a prostitute is concerned, marriages are not

---

7 **Meaning of Decree:**
   1. An authoritative order having the force of law.
   2. The judgment of a court of equity, admiralty, probate, or divorce.

8 **Meaning of Appeal:** In law, an **appeal** is a process for requesting a formal change to an official decision. Very broadly speaking there are appeals on the record and *de novo* appeals. In *de novo* appeals, a new decision maker re-hears the case without any reference to the prior decision maker. In appeals on the record, the decision of the prior decision maker is challenged by arguing that he or she misapplied the law, came to an incorrect factual finding, acted in excess of his jurisdiction, abused his powers, was biased, considered evidence which he should not have considered or failed to consider evidence that he should have considered.

9 AIR 1965 SC 608

10 AIR 1982 SC 1091

commonly performed in the very nature of the profession led by her, and her illegitimate children must be held to be members of her family as related to her by blood.

Illegitimate offspring of a prostitute is recognised by personal law also. Though prostitution, according to the Hindu Law, entails degradation and loss of caste, it does not sever the tie which connects the prostitute to her kindred (child) by blood. The sons of a dancing woman, though by different fathers, are entitled to succeed to each other[11].

---

11 (see Hindu Law by Mulla, 15th Edn., 1986, para 164, pp. 213-214)

23

Carrying on trade of
Public Prostitution within specified area[1]

Facts in Nutshell:

Appeal[2] by four women whose application under Article 226[3] of the Constitution was dismissed by a learned single Judge of Allahabad High

---

1   Appellants: **Smt. Sona Bai and Ors. Vs.** Respondent: **Municipality of Agra**
    AIR1956All736
    Hon'ble Judges: Agarwala and Beg, JJ.

2   **Meaning of Appeal:** In law, an **appeal** is a process for requesting a formal change to an official decision. Very broadly speaking there are appeals on the record and *de novo* appeals. In *de novo* appeals, a new decision maker re-hears the case without any reference to the prior decision maker. In appeals on the record, the decision of the prior decision maker is challenged by arguing that he or she misapplied the law, came to an incorrect factual finding, acted in excess of his jurisdiction, abused his powers, was biased, considered evidence which he should not have considered or failed to consider evidence that he should have considered.

3   **Article 226 in The Constitution Of India 1949**
    226. Power of High Courts to issue certain writs
    (1) Notwithstanding anything in Article 32 every High Court shall have powers, throughout the territories in relation to which it exercise jurisdiction, to issue to any person or authority, including in appropriate cases, any Government, within those territories directions, orders or writs, including writs in the nature of habeas corpus, mandamus, prohibitions, quo warranto and certiorari, or any of them, for the enforcement of any of the rights conferred by Part III and for any other purpose
    (2) The power conferred by clause (1) to issue directions, orders or writs to any Government, authority or person may also be exercised by any High Court exercising jurisdiction in relation to the territories within which the cause of action, wholly or in part, arises for the exercise of such power, notwithstanding that the seat of such Government or authority or the residence of such person is not within those territories
    (3) Where any party against whom an interim order, whether by way of injunction or stay or in any other manner, is made on, or in any proceedings relating to, a petition under clause (1), without
    (a) furnishing to such party copies of such petition and all documents in support of the plea for such interim order; and
    (b) giving such party an opportunity of being heard, makes an application to the High Court for the vacation of such order and furnishes a copy of such application to the party in whose favour such order has been made or the counsel of such party, the High Court shall dispose of the application within a period of two weeks from the date on which it is received or from the date on which the copy of such application is so furnished, whichever is later, or where the High Court is closed on the last day of that period, before the expiry of the next day afterwards on which the High Court is open; and if the application is not so disposed of, the interim order shall, on the expiry of that period, or, as the case may be, the expiry of the aid next day, stand vacated
    (4) The power conferred on a High Court by this article shall not be in derogation of the power conferred on the Supreme court by clause (2) of Article 32

Court. Appellants[4] complained that the Municipal Board, Agra was enforcing a byelaw which it had made in 1948 and under which the Municipal Board could direct that a public prostitute may not reside within a specified area of the city of Agra. Under that byelaw the mohallas where the public prostitutes were not to reside were specified and then it was provided that no person shall let or otherwise dispose of any house or building to public prostitutes or for a brothel[5] within the area or in the streets so specified.

The byelaw further provided for a penalty of Rs. 50/- for breach of the provisions of the aforesaid byelaw and when the breach was continuing breach, for a further fine of Rs. 5/- for every day after the date of first conviction[6] during which the offender[7] was proved to have persisted in the offence.

The Executive Officer of the Municipal Board, Agra, issued notices to the appellants to remove themselves from the locality which fell within the purview of the byelaw, on failing which further legal action would be taken against them.

Decision of Learned Single Judge:

In the application the applicants had urged that they were not public prostitutes, but were singing and dancing girls. The learned single Judge observed that as, according to their allegation, they were not public prostitutes, the byelaw did not apply to them at all, and that, therefore, they had no locus standi[8] to challenge the byelaw in the Court.

Arguments of Learned Counsel for Appellants:

Learned counsel for the appellants contended that the byelaw was ultra vires[9] on two grounds : firstly, it imposes an unreasonable restriction

---

4   **Meaning of Appellant:** A person who, dissatisfied with the judgment rendered in a lawsuit decided in a lower court or the findings from a proceeding before an Administrative Agency, asks a superior court to review the decision.

5   **Meaning of Brothel:** A house or other place where men pay to have sexual intercourse with prostitutes

6   **Meaning of Conviction:** In law, a **conviction** is the verdict that results when a court of law finds a defendant guilty of a crime.

7   **Meaning of Offender:** One that offends, especially one that breaks a public law

8   **Meaning of Locus Standi:** The right of a party to appear and be heard before a court

9   **Meaning of Ultra Vires:** *Ultra vires* is a Latin phrase meaning literally "beyond the powers",

upon the right to carry on a trade which is guaranteed under Article19(1)(g)[10] of the Constitution.

Decision of High Court:

Court held that the restriction on carrying on trade of public prostitution within a specified area of the Municipality is eminently a reasonable one. In the interests of the health and morals of the persons of a particular locality the Municipal Board may properly direct that public prostitutes may not carry on their trade in that locality.

---

although its standard legal translation and substitute is "beyond power". If an act requires legal authority and it is done with such authority, it is characterised in law as *intra vires* (literally "within the powers"; standard legal translation and substitute, "within power"). If it is done without such authority, it is *ultra vires*. Acts that are *intra vires* may equivalently be termed "valid" and those that are *ultra vires* "invalid".

10 **Article 19 in The Constitution Of India 1949**
  19. Protection of certain rights regarding freedom of speech etc
  (1) All citizens shall have the right
  (g) to practise any profession, or to carry on any occupation, trade or business

24

Prostitutes are entitled to live a life of Dignity[1]

Facts in Nutshell:

Writ petition[2] was filed for a mandamus[3] directing the respondents[4] and their subordinates and other officers not to evict the petitioners[5] from their residences and not to harass them. Petitioners were doing the profession of singing and dancing for the last several years and have nothing to do with prostitution nor have they violated the Immoral Traffic (Prevention) Act, 1956. It was alleged that the police authorities and so-called social workers started harassing everybody in the red-light area on the basis of the allegations that they were indulging in the vice of prostitution.

1   Appellants: **Radha and Ors. Vs.** Respondent: **State of U.P. and Ors.**
    2003 1 AWC455
    Hon'ble Judges: M. Katju and Rakesh Tiwari, JJ.

2   **Meaning of Writ Petition:** Under the Indian legal system, jurisdiction to issue 'prerogative writs' is given to the Supreme Court, and to the High Courts of Judicature of all Indian states. Parts of the law relating to writs are set forth in the Constitution of India. The Supreme Court, the highest in the country, may issue writs under Article 32 of the Constitution for enforcement of Fundamental Rights and under Articles 139 for enforcement of rights other than Fundamental Rights, while High Courts, the superior courts of the States, may issue writs under Articles 226. 'Writ' is eminently designed by the makers of the Constitution, and in the same way it is developed very widely and efficiently by the courts in India. The Constitution broadly provides for five kinds of "prerogative" writs, namely, Habeas Corpus, Certiorari, Mandamus, Quo Warranto and Prohibition.

3   **Meaning of Mandamus: Mandamus** is a judicial remedy — in the form of an order from a superior court, to any government subordinate court, corporation, or public authority — to do (or forbear from doing) some specific act which that body is obliged under law to do (or refrain from doing) — and which is in the nature of public duty, and in certain cases one of a statutory duty. It cannot be issued to compel an authority to do something against statutory provision. For example, it cannot be used to force a lower court to reject or authorize applications that have been made, but if the court refuses to rule one way or the other then a mandamus can be used to order the court to rule on the applications.

4   **Meaning of Respondent:** A **respondent** is a person who is called upon to issue a response to a communication made by another. In legal usage, this specifically refers to the defendant in a legal proceeding commenced by a petition, or to an appellee, or the opposing party, in an appeal of a decision by an initial fact-finder.

5   **Meaning of Petitioner:** A person who presents a petition (**Meaning of Petition:** A formal written application requesting a court for a specific judicial action)

Question before the Court:

Whether Prostitutes can be evicted from their residences and can be harassed merely because they are prostitutes.

Prostitution:

It may be mentioned that prostitution itself is no offence except in the manner mentioned in Sections7[6] and 8[7] of the Immoral Traffic

---

6 **Section 7 of Immoral Traffic Act, 1956: Prostitution in or in the vicinity of public places.** [(1) Any [person], who carries on prostitution and the person with whom such prostitution is carried on, in any premises,-which are within the area or areas, notified under sub-section (3), or which are within a distance of two hundred metres of any place of public religious worship, educational institution, hostel, hospital, nursing home or such other public place of any kind as may be notified in this behalf by the Commissioner of Police or Magistrate in the manner prescribed, shall be punishable with imprisonment for a term which may extend to three months].

[(1A) Where an offence committed under sub-section (1) is in respect of a child or minor, the person committing the offence shall be punishable with imprisonment of either description for a term which shall not be less than seven years but which may be for life or for a term which may extend to ten years and shall also be liable to fine: Provided that the court may, for adequate and special reasons to be mentioned in the judgement impose a sentence of imprisonment for a term of less than seven years].

(2) Any person who-

being the keeper of any public place knowingly permits prostitution for purposes of their trade to resort to or remain in such place; or

being the tenant, lessee, occupier or person in charge of any premises referred to in sub-section (1) knowingly permits the same or any part thereof to be used for prostitution; or

being the owner, lessor or landlord, of any premises referred to in sub-section (1) or the agent of such owner, lessor or landlord, lets the same or any part thereof may be used for prostitution, or is wilfully a party to such use,

shall be punishable on first conviction with imprisonment for a term which may extend to three months or with fine which may extend to two hundred rupees, or with both, and in the event of a second or subsequent conviction with imprisonment for a term which may extend to six months and also with fine [which may extend to two hundred rupees, and if the public place or premises happen to be a hotel, the license for carrying on the business of such hotel under any law for the time being in force shall also be liable to be suspended for a period of not less than three months but which may extend to one year:

Provided that if an offence committed under this sub-section is in respect of a child or minor in a hotel, such license shall also be liable to be cancelled.

7 **Section 8 of Immoral Traffic Act, 1956: Seducing or soliciting for purpose of prostitution.** - Whoever, in any public place or within sight of, and in such manner as to be seen or heard from, any public place, whether from within any building or house or not -

by words, gestures, wilful exposure of her person (whether by sitting by a window or on the balcony of a building or house or in any other way), or otherwise tempts or endeavours to tempt, or attracts or endeavours to attract the attention of, any person for the purpose of prostitution; or solicits or molests any person, or loiters or acts in such manner as to cause obstruction or annoyance to persons residing nearby or passing by such public place or to offend against public decency, for the purpose of prostitution,

shall be punishable on first conviction, with imprisonment for a term which may extend to six months, or with fine which may extend to five hundred rupees, or with both, and in the event of a second or subsequent conviction, with imprisonment for a term which may extend to five hundred rupees, and also with fine which may extend to five hundred rupees :

(Prevention) Act, 1956[8]. Women become prostitutes not because they enjoy prostitution but due to poverty. The level of poverty in this country is appalling. Almost 50% of our people are living below the poverty line in horrible conditions, e.g., without employment, proper food, housing, medical care, education, etc. In Rajasthan, people were eating Rotis made of grass. In Orissa people were eating mango kernels, and in Tamil Nadu women are selling one of their kidneys to feed their families. Starvation deaths have been reported in Rajasthan, Orissa, M. P., etc. and it is no wonder that to escape from this abject poverty, a large number of women are compelled to sell their bodies to earn some money to fill their stomachs. Ordinarily, no woman will surrender her body to a man voluntarily unless she respects and loves him. Prostitutes are normally not bad women and they are wrongly regarded as women of vice by society. In fact, in the novels and stories of the great Bengali writer Sharad Chandra Chattopadhyaya many prostitutes are shown to be women of high character, e.g., Rajya Laxmi in Sharad Chandra's famous novel 'Shri Kant,' and Chandramukhi in 'Devdas'. Similarly in the great novel "Crime and Punishment" by the famous Russian writer Dostoyevsky, we come across the character of Sofia Marmaledov who was compelled to become a prostitute due to poverty, although she was depicted as a young woman of high character who earns for her family members who would otherwise starve. In the famous poem 'Chakle' by the great Urdu writer Sahir Ludhiyanvi, the plight of prostitutes in India has been vividly depicted, and this poem has been sung (with some modifications) in the Hindi Film 'Pyasa'. Hence, the approach of society towards the prostitutes must change, and sympathy must be shown towards them as it must be realized that they are not necessarily women of bad character but have been driven to the profession due to acute poverty in their family.

Prostitutes are entitled to live a Life of Dignity:

Prostitutes are also entitled to live a life of dignity which is part of Article 21[9] of the Constitution as interpreted by the Supreme Court. People including the police must have a sympathetic approach towards them and should not harass them, rather they should have sympathy

---

[Provided that where an offence under this section is committed by a man he shall be punishable with imprisonment for a period of not less than seven days but which may extend to three months

8 See *T. Jacob v. State of Kerala*, AIR 1971 Ker 166.

9 **Article 21 in The Constitution Of India 1949**
   21. Protection of life and personal liberty No person shall be deprived of his life or personal liberty except according to procedure established by law

towards them, and attempt should be made to rehabilitate them in society. The State Government must formulate a scheme for rehabilitation of prostitutes in society and this is only possible if these women are given technical skills so that they can earn their bread by these skills instead of doing so by selling their bodies for filling their stomachs.

In *Chinnamma Sivadas v. State (Delhi Administration)*[10], the Supreme Court held that the State Government should evolve a scheme in which women rescued from brothels and deserted women lodged in protective homes must be able to live with human dignity and find gainful employment after discharge.

Decision of the High Court:

Court held that the prostitutes are also entitled to live a life of dignity and directed the State Government of Uttar Pradesh that a scheme should be framed whereby in every city in the State of U. P., the prostitutes are given some technical training so that they can earn their bread through such technical skills.

---

10 1982 Cr App R 264

25

Selling and buying minor for purposes of Prostitution[1]

Ratio Decidendi[2]: *"Court shall impose deterrent sentence on accused for offence committed for immoral purpose."*

Facts in Nutshell:

Hanumanthappa, father of the victim, lodged a complaint alleging that his daughter Shilpa, aged 13 years (studying in 6th standard) was kidnapped by the appellants from his house and they had taken her to Bombay with an intention to force her to have illicit intercourse and thereafter, had sold the victim to Shanta at Bombay for Rs. 5000/- for the purpose of prostitution and for immoral purposes.

Decision of the High Court:

Appeals[3] were directed against the judgment and final order by the High Court of Karnataka whereby the High Court allowed the appeals filed by the State of Karnataka (respondent) and convicted[4] the appellants[5]

---

1   Appellants: **Manjappa Vs.** Respondent: **State of Karnataka**
    (2010)9SCC334
    Hon'ble Judges: P. Sathasivam and Anil R. Dave, JJ.

2   **Meaning of Ration Decidendi:** *Ratio decidendi* is a Latin phrase meaning "the reason" or "the rationale for the decision." The *ratio decidendi* is "the point in a case which determines the judgment" or "the principle which the case establishes."

3   **Meaning of Appeal:** In law, an **appeal** is a process for requesting a formal change to an official decision. Very broadly speaking there are appeals on the record and *de novo* appeals. In *de novo* appeals, a new decision maker re-hears the case without any reference to the prior decision maker. In appeals on the record, the decision of the prior decision maker is challenged by arguing that he or she misapplied the law, came to an incorrect factual finding, acted in excess of his jurisdiction, abused his powers, was biased, considered evidence which he should not have considered or failed to consider evidence that he should have considered.

4   **Meaning of Convicted:** Someone guilty of an offense or crime, especially by the verdict of a court

5   **Meaning of Appellant:** A person who, dissatisfied with the judgment rendered in a lawsuit decided in a lower court or the findings from a proceeding before an Administrative Agency, asks a superior court to review the decision.

for the offences punishable under Sections 366A[6], 372[7], 373[8] read with Section 34[9] I.P.C. and sentenced them to undergo imprisonment for a period of seven years with a fine of Rs. 50,000/- each, in default, to undergo simple imprisonment for two years.

Decision of the Supreme Court:

Court held that it was not a fit case for reduction of sentence. In a case of this nature, it is just and proper that a deterrent sentence is to be imposed on the accused[10].

---

6 **Section 366 A, IPC, 1860**
   366A. Procuration of minor girl
   Whoever, by any means whatsoever, induces any minor girl under the age of eighteen years to go from any place or to do any act with intent that such girl may be, or knowing that it is likely that she will be, forced or seduced to illicit intercourse with another person shall be punishable with imprisonment which may extend to ten years, and shall also be liable to fine.

7 **Section 372, IPC, 1860**
   Selling minor for purposes of prostitution, etc
   Whoever sells, lets to hire, or otherwise disposes of any [person under the age of eighteen years with intent that such person shall at any age be employed or used for the purpose of prostitution or illicit intercourse with any person or for any unlawful and immoral purpose, or knowing it to be likely that such person will at any age be] employed or used for any such purpose, shall be punished with imprisonment of either description for a term which may extend to ten years, and shall be liable to fine.

8   **Section 373, IPC, 1860**
   Buying minor for purposes of prostitution, etc
   Whoever buys, hires or otherwise obtains possession of any [person under the age of eighteen years with intent that such person shall at any age be employed or used for the purpose of prostitution or illicit intercourse with any person or for any unlawful and immoral purpose, of knowing it to be likely that such person will at any age be] employed or used for any purpose, shall be punished with imprisonment of either description for a term which may extend to ten years, and shall also be liable to fine.

9 **Section 34 in The Indian Penal Code, 1860**
   34. [Acts done by several persons in furtherance of common intention.-- When a criminal act is done by several persons in furtherance of the common intention of all, each of such persons is liable for that act in the same manner as if it were done by him alone.]

10 **Meaning of Accused:** A person charged with a criminal offense, or the state of being so charged

26

Custody of Minor Child Not Given to Prostitute Mother[1]

Facts in Nutshell:

The brief facts are that the respondent[2]/applicant filed an application under Section 7[3] of the Guardians and Wards Act, 1890 before the court saying that he was working in Mumbai (Maharashtra), where he came in contact with the appellant[4]/opposite party and later on they fell in love and ultimately, they entered into a marital relation. Since then they started living in the house of the respondent[5]/applicant and ultimately in their wedlock one daughter was born in a nursing home. But the parents of appellant/opposite parry the demand of money etc. was raised for construction of house, which was fulfilled by the respondent/applicant, but even thereafter several demands were also made. On 18th March, 2006 the appellant/opposite party alongwith newly born daughter went to her parental home saying that she will go to 'Vaishno

---

1 Appellants: **Smt. Mamta Singh and Anr. Vs.** Respondent: **Sri Kamal Kant Gautam** 2009 3 AWC2713 **Hon'ble Judges:** Amitava Lala and Shishir Kumar, JJ.

2 **Meaning of Respondent:** A **respondent** is a person who is called upon to issue a response to a communication made by another. In legal usage, this specifically refers to the defendant in a legal proceeding commenced by a petition, or to an appellee, or the opposing party, in an appeal of a decision by an initial fact-finder.

3 **Section 7 in The Guardians And Wards Act, 1890**
7. Power of the Court to make order as to guardianship.-
(1) Where the Court is satisfied that it is for the welfare of a minor that an order should be made--
(a) appointing a guardian of his person or property, or both, or
(b) declaring a person to be such a guardian, the Court may make an order accordingly.
(2) An order under this section shall imply the removal of any guardian who has not been appointed by will or other instrument or appointed or declared by the Court.
(3) Where a guardian has been appointed by will or other instrument or appointed or declared by the Court, an order under this section appointing or declaring another person to be guardian in his stead shall not be made until the powers of the guardian appointed or declared as aforesaid have ceased under the provisions of this Act.

4 **Meaning of Appellant:** A person who, dissatisfied with the judgment rendered in a lawsuit decided in a lower court or the findings from a proceeding before an Administrative Agency, asks a superior court to review the decision.

5 **Meaning of Respondent:** A **respondent** is a person who is called upon to issue a response to a communication made by another. In legal usage, this specifically refers to the defendant in a legal proceeding commenced by a petition, or to an appellee, or the opposing party, in an appeal of a decision by an initial fact-finder.

Devi' for 'darshan'. However, the respondent/applicant after coming to know the fact that the appellant/opposite party alongwith newly born daughter is in fact residing at her parental house at Agra, he went there, where he found that the appellant/opposite party belongs to "Bediya" community and the activities like prostitution, etc. are their occupation. The respondent/ applicant felt sorrow and he requested the appellant/ opposite party to handover his wife (the appellant) and daughter to him when she raised a demand for a sum of Rs. 25,00,000 and misbehaved with him. However, the appellant/opposite party once again has indulged herself in the occupation of prostitution for quite some time. It was stated by the respondent/applicant before the court that if his daughter remains in such a society, it will cause adverse effect on her personality. In such circumstances, by filing application the respondent/ applicant sought relief to get back the custody of his daughter in his favour.

The appellants/opposite parties filed their written statement and admitted that they belong to "Bedtya" community and their occupation was dancing and singing from the ancient time. They have also stated that the appellant/opposite party was a bar dancer in Mumbai and she came in contact with the respondent/applicant so many times and thereafter she also went for outing with him. The respondent/ applicant after taking the appellant/ opposite party to a temple put "Sindoor" (vermilion) in her "Mating" and photographs were taken, but the appellant/opposite party never lived with him and continued with her work of Bar dancer. Thereafter, the appellant/opposite party went to Kolkata, where she came in contact with many youths, who did intercourse with her and the child was born out of such relationship with any one of them.

Decision of Trail Court:

The Trail court held with a strong presumption that it is settled law that marriage may be void but the birth of child never becomes void. A person, who does not belong to community of "Bediya" would obviously hesitate in keeping her daughter in "Bediya" community and such hesitation will arise only when he will have full confidence about the birth of daughter in their wedlock. Trail Court reached to a conclusion that the application filed by the respondent/applicant (wife) deserves to be allowed and accordingly, allowed the same with costs and the appellant/ opposite (husband) party was directed to give custody of the child to the respondent/applicant within a period of one month. Being aggrieved by and/or dissatisfied with such order, this appeal[6] was preferred by the appellants/opposite parties before High Court.

D.N.A. (deoxyribonucleic acid): D.N.A. determines the particular structure and functions of every cell and is responsible for characteristics being passed on from parents to their children. Earlier outlook with regard to D.N.A. evidence in matrimonial cases appears to be orthodox in nature. Law courts were of the opinion that compelling one to go for forensic test, like, D.N.A. will hit personal liberty of an individual as per Article 21[7] of the Constitution of India. But after a three Judges' Bench judgment of the Supreme Court in *Sharda v. Dharmpal*[8] there is a sea change to get an appropriate co-ordination between the science and the law. The three Judges' Bench of the Supreme Court precisely held as follows:

(1) A matrimonial court has the power to order a person to undergo medical test.

(2) Passing of such an order by the Court would not be in violation of the right to personal liberty under Article 21 of the Indian Constitution.

(3) However, the Court should exercise such a power if the applicant has a strong prima facie case and there is sufficient material before the Court. If despite the order of the Court, the respondent refuses to submit himself to medical examination, the Court will be entitled to draw an adverse inference against him.

Personal liberty as prescribed under Article 21 of the Constitution of India cannot be confined to one when personal liberty of two others inclusive of a minor child is at stake. They have their right to know their parental and birth right and if in spite of having scientific mechanism available for the purpose, it is refused, the same will lead to illegality. Law is to be moved forward to meet the necessity of the modern society taking

---

6 **Meaning of Appeal:** In law, an **appeal** is a process for requesting a formal change to an official decision. Very broadly speaking there are appeals on the record and *de novo* appeals. In *de novo* appeals, a new decision maker re-hears the case without any reference to the prior decision maker. In appeals on the record, the decision of the prior decision maker is challenged by arguing that he or she misapplied the law, came to an incorrect factual finding, acted in excess of his jurisdiction, abused his powers, was biased, considered evidence which he should not have considered or failed to consider evidence that he should have considered.

7 **Article 21 in The Constitution Of India 1949**
21. Protection of life and personal liberty No person shall be deprived of his life or personal liberty except according to procedure established by law

8 2003 (4) SCC 493 : 2003 (2) AWC 1534 (SC)

advantage of scientific mechanism without shutting eyes. It is not only a question of predominance effect of welfare of the child but it leans in favour of an innocent child from being bastardised.

Decision of the High Court:

Court held that child was born in their wedlock and, therefore, the paramount consideration is welfare of the child and it is correct to say that the child's welfare cannot be protected if she is given in such a society, to which her mother belongs. If her mother separates herself from such society and lives with the respondent/ applicant permanently, that will be for the benefit of the family as well as for the child but court cannot compel them. As far as Child was concerned, she will be definitely given in the custody of her father (respondent/applicant), who besides being financially sound was well educated and lives in a reputed society and he is able to protect the welfare of the child.

In *Sumedha Nagpal v. State of Delhi and Ors.*[9], court held that the lap of the mother is the natural cradle where the safety and welfare of the child can be assured and there is no substitute for the same, but still the Court has to bear in mind the welfare of the minor child and not decide such a question merely based upon the rights of the parties under the law.

---

9   2000 (9) SCC 745

27

Right to Privacy of Unchaste Woman[1]

Facts in Nutshell:

The respondent[2] Madhukar Narayan Mardikar, was serving as a Police Inspector. On 13th November, 1965 he allegedly visited the hutment of one Banubi w/o Babu Sheikh in uniform and demanded to have sexual intercourse with her. On her refusing he tried to have her by force. She resisted his attempt and raised a hue and cry. Her husband and neighbours collected outside the hutment. The respondent directed that the woman be taken to the Police Station as she had abused him. She was taken on foot to the Police Station by Head Constable.

The Inspector-General of Police on an examination of the report prima facie concurred with the findings recorded by the Inquiry Officer and directed notice to issue to the respondent(Police officer) to show cause why he should not be dismissed from service. The respondent filed a detailed reply to the second show cause notice. After taking the same into consideration the Inspector-General of Police ordered his dismissal. The respondent filed an appeal against the said order of dismissal which was partly allowed. It was held that having regard to the length of service, put in by the respondent, the punishment of dismissal from service should be replaced by removal from service. It was also stated that if the respondent so desired he could apply for compassionate pension. Feeling aggrieved by this order the respondent approached the High Court of Bombay, Nagpur Bench, Nagpur, with a Writ Petition[3] under

---

1 Appellants: **State of Maharashtra and another Vs.** Respondent: **Madhukar Narayan Mardikar** AIR1991SC207
Hon'ble Judges: K. Jagannatha Shetty and A. M. Ahmadii, JJ.

2 **Meaning of Respondent:** A **respondent** is a person who is called upon to issue a response to a communication made by another. In legal usage, this specifically refers to the defendant in a legal proceeding commenced by a petition, or to an appellee, or the opposing party, in an appeal of a decision by an initial fact-finder.

3 **Meaning of Writ Petition:** Under the Indian legal system, jurisdiction to issue 'prerogative writs' is given to the Supreme Court, and to the High Courts of Judicature of all Indian states. Parts of the law relating to writs are set forth in the Constitution of India. The Supreme Court, the highest in the country, may issue writs under Article 32 of the Constitution for enforcement of Fundamental Rights and under Articles 139 for enforcement of rights other than Fundamental Rights, while High Courts, the superior courts of the States, may issue writs under Articles 226. 'Writ' is eminently designed by the makers of the Constitution, and in the same way it is developed very widely and

Articles 226[4]/227[5] of the Constitution. The Division Bench of the High Court quashed[6] the impugned order of removal on the ground that the respondent was denied a reasonable opportunity to meet the charges levelled against him as the department had failed to supply him with copies of certain important documents having a bearing on the charges

---

efficiently by the courts in India. The Constitution broadly provides for five kinds of "prerogative" writs, namely, Habeas Corpus, Certiorari, Mandamus, Quo Warranto and Prohibition.

4 **Article 226 in The Constitution Of India 1949**
226. Power of High Courts to issue certain writs
(1) Notwithstanding anything in Article 32 every High Court shall have powers, throughout the territories in relation to which it exercise jurisdiction, to issue to any person or authority, including in appropriate cases, any Government, within those territories directions, orders or writs, including writs in the nature of habeas corpus, mandamus, prohibitions, quo warranto and certiorari, or any of them, for the enforcement of any of the rights conferred by Part III and for any other purpose
(2) The power conferred by clause (1) to issue directions, orders or writs to any Government, authority or person may also be exercised by any High Court exercising jurisdiction in relation to the territories within which the cause of action, wholly or in part, arises for the exercise of such power, notwithstanding that the seat of such Government or authority or the residence of such person is not within those territories
(3) Where any party against whom an interim order, whether by way of injunction or stay or in any other manner, is made on, or in any proceedings relating to, a petition under clause (1), without
(a) furnishing to such party copies of such petition and all documents in support of the plea for such interim order; and
(b) giving such party an opportunity of being heard, makes an application to the High Court for the vacation of such order and furnishes a copy of such application to the party in whose favour such order has been made or the counsel of such party, the High Court shall dispose of the application within a period of two weeks from the date on which it is received or from the date on which the copy of such application is so furnished, whichever is later, or where the High Court is closed on the last day of that period, before the expiry of the next day afterwards on which the High Court is open; and if the application is not so disposed of, the interim order shall, on the expiry of that period, or, as the case may be, the expiry of the aid next day, stand vacated
(4) The power conferred on a High Court by this article shall not be in derogation of the power conferred on the Supreme court by clause (2) of Article 32

5 **Article 227 in The Constitution Of India 1949**
227. Power of superintendence over all courts by the High Court
(1) Every High Court shall have superintendence over all courts and tribunals throughout the territories interrelation to which it exercises jurisdiction
(2) Without prejudice to the generality of the foregoing provisions, the High Court may
(a) call for returns from such courts;
(b) make and issue general rules and prescribe forms for regulating the practice and proceedings of such courts; and
(c) prescribe forms in which books, entries and accounts shall be kept by the officers of any such courts
(3) The High Court may also settle tables of fees to be allowed to the sheriff and all clerks and officers of such courts and to attorneys, advocates and pleaders practising therein: Provided that any rules made, forms prescribed or tables settled under clause (2) or clause (3) shall not be inconsistent with the provision of any law for the time being in force, and shall require the previous approval of the Governor
(4) Nothing in this article shall be deemed to confer on a High Court powers of superintendence over any court or tribunal constituted by or under any law relating to the Armed Forces

6 **Meaning of Quashed:** To set aside or annul, especially by judicial action.

levelled against him. The State of Maharashtra feeling aggrieved by the said order approached Supreme Court by way of Special Leave under Article 136[7] of the Constitution.

High Court Observation (Unchaste Woman):

The High Court Observed that since Banubi was an unchaste woman[8] it would be extremely unsafe to allow the fortune and career of a Government Official to be put in jeopardy upon the uncorroborated[9] version of such a woman who makes no secret of her illicit intimacy with another person.

Decision of Supreme Court:

Court set aside the order of the High Court and restore the order of removal from service passed by the appellate authority and directed that it be given effect to in accordance with law. Court observed : *"Even a woman of easy virtue is entitled to privacy and no one can invade her privacy as and when he likes. So also it is not open to any and every person to violate her person as and when he wishes. She is entitled to protect her person if there is an attempt to violate it against her wish. She is equally entitled to the protection of law. Therefore, merely because she is a woman of easy virtue, her evidence cannot be thrown overboard"*.

---

7   **Article 136 in The Constitution Of India 1949**
    136. Special leave to appeal by the Supreme Court
    (1) Notwithstanding anything in this Chapter, the Supreme Court may, in its discretion, grant special leave to appeal from any judgment, decree, determination, sentence or order in any cause or matter passed or made by any court or tribunal in the territory of India
    (2) Nothing in clause (1) shall apply to any judgment, determination, sentence or order passed or made by any court or tribunal constituted by or under any law relating to the Armed Forces

8   **Meaning of Unchaste Woman:** An unchaste woman is one who is not morally pure or innocent, or someone who has experienced sex. Prostitutes, for example, would be considered as unchaste women.

9   **Meaning of Uncorroborated:** Lacking confirmation or evidence

28

Right of Prostitutes to Live with Dignity[1]

Ratio Decidendi[2]: "Sex workers are also human beings, hence, entitled to life of dignity under Article 21 of the Constitution of India[3]"

Sex Workers and Right to Live with Dignity:

Sex workers are also human beings and no one has a right to assault or murder them. A person becomes a prostitute not because she enjoys it but because of poverty. Society must have sympathy towards the sex workers and must not look down upon them. They are also entitled to a life of dignity in view of Article 21 of the Constitution.

In the novels and stories of the great Bengali writer Sharat Chandra Chattopadhyaya, many prostitutes have been shown to be women of very high character, e.g., Rajyalakshmi in 'Shrikant', Chandramukhi in 'Devdas', etc. The plight of prostitutes has been depicted by the great Urdu poet Sahil Ludhianvi in his poem 'Chakle' which has been sung in the Hindi film Pyasa "Jineh Naaz Hai Hind Par wo kahan hain" (simplified version of the verse 'Sana Khwan-e-taqdees-e-Mashrik Kahan Hain'). We may also refer to the character Sonya Marmelodova in Dostoyevsky's famous novel 'Crime and Punishment'. Sonya is depicted as a girl who sacrifices her body to earn some bread for her impoverished family. Reference may also be made to Amrapali, who was a contemporary of Lord Buddha.

Observation of Supreme Court:

Central and the State Governments through Social Welfare Boards should

---

1 Appellants: **Budhadev Karmaskar Vs.** Respondent: **State of West Bengal**
   2011(3)ACR3003(SC)
   Hon'ble Judges: Markandey Katju and Gyan Sudha Misra, JJ.

2 **Meaning of Ration Decidendi:** *Ratio decidendi* is a Latin phrase meaning "the reason" or "the rationale for the decision." The *ratio decidendi* is "the point in a case which determines the judgment" or "the principle which the case establishes."

3 **Article 21 in The Constitution Of India 1949**
   21. Protection of life and personal liberty No person shall be deprived of his life or personal liberty except according to procedure established by law

prepare schemes for rehabilitation all over the country for physically and sexually abused women commonly known as prostitutes as Court was of the view that the prostitutes also have a right to live with dignity under Article 21 of the Constitution of India since they are also human beings and their problems also need to be addressed.

A woman is compelled to indulge in prostitution not for pleasure but because of abject poverty. If such a woman is granted opportunity to avail some technical or vocational training, she would be able to earn her livelihood by such vocational training and skill instead of by selling her body.

Hence, direction was given to the Central and the State Governments to prepare schemes for giving technical/vocational training to sex workers and sexually abused women in all cities in India. The schemes should mention in detail who will give the technical/vocational training and in what manner they can be rehabilitated and settled by offering them employment. For instance, if a technical training is for some craft like sewing garments, etc. then some arrangements should also be made for providing a market for such garments, otherwise they will remain unsold and unused, and consequently the woman will not be able to feed herself.

Sex workers are also human beings and hence they are entitled to a life of dignity. The word 'life' in Article 21 of the Constitution means a life of dignity and not just an animal life. Court was of the opinion that sex workers obviously cannot lead a life of dignity as long as they remain sex workers.

Sex among human beings is different from sex among animals. Sex in humans has a cultural aspect to it also, and is not just a physical act. A sex worker who has to surrender her body to a man for money obviously is not leading a life of dignity. Ordinarily, no woman will willingly surrender her body to a man unless she loves and respects him. A sex worker is obviously not surrendering her body to a man because she loves and respect him, but just for sheer survival. As Nancy says in Charles Dicken's novel 'Oliver Twist', "you adapt or you die". Apart from that, sex workers are always in danger of getting sexually transmitted diseases (STD), and they are often abused and beaten by the proprietors of the brothel and others who give them a pittance out of her earnings. A woman becomes a sex worker not because she enjoys it but due to abject poverty. One estimate suggests that there are 3 million sex workers in India, many even from Nepal, Bangaldesh, and even the former Soviet Union. This is due to massive poverty in the country, and abroad.

Sex workers are not bad persons, but they are unfortunate girls who have been forced to go into this flesh trade due to terrible poverty. Hence society should not look down upon the sex workers but should have sympathy with them. In fact, in the novels of the great Bengali writer Sharat Chandra Chattopadhayay it has been shown that many of the sex workers were women of very high character, e.g. Rajyalakshmi, Chandramukhi, etc. and the same has been shown in the novels of many European writers. The Russian writer Dostoyevsky's novel 'Crime & Punishment' has shown Sonia Marmeladova as a woman of high character who became a sex worker to feed her starving family. Similarly, in Charles Dicken's novel 'Oliver Twist', the sex worker Nancy is shown to be a girl of high character who sacrifices her life to save Oliver. In Victor Hugo's famous novel 'Les Miserables', Fantine sacrifices her hair and teeth to provide for her daughter Cosette. Martha in 'David Copperfield' is also depicted as a woman of noble heart.

If sex workers are given proper technical training they will be able to come out of sex work and instead earn their livelihood through their technical skills instead of by selling their bodies. That will enable them to live a life of dignity.

Court was of the opinion that the States should not only come out with schemes indicating therein rehabilitation of the sex workers but they should also demonstrate their commitment to the cause by coming out with some concrete results at least in phases.

Sexual Harassment, Pornography, Obscenity & Female Foeticide

Sexual harassment:

Sexual harassment includes such unwelcome sexually determined behaviour as physical contacts and advances, sexually coloured remarks, showing pornography and sexual demands, whether by words or actions. Such conduct can be humiliating and may constitute a health and safety problem; it is discriminatory when the woman has reasonable grounds to believe that her objection would disadvantage her in connection with her employment, including recruiting or promotion, or when it creates a hostile working environment. Effective complaints procedures and remedies, including compensation, should be provided.

Against the growing social menace of Sexual harassment of women at the work place, a three Judge Bench of Supreme Court by a rather innovative judicial law making process issued certain guidelines in *Vishaka v. State of Rajasthan*[1], after taking note of the fact that the present civil and penal laws in the country do not adequately provide for specific protection of woman from sexual harassment at places of work and that enactment of such a legislation would take a considerable time. In Vishaka's case (supra), a definition of sexual harassment was suggested. Verma, J., (as the former Chief Justice then was), speaking for the three-Judge Bench opined:

Definition:

For this purpose, sexual harassment includes such unwelcome sexually determined behavior (whether directly or by implication) as:

(a) physical contact and advance;

(b) a demand or request for sexual favours;

(c) sexually-colored remarks;

(d) showing pornography;

---

1 AIR1997SC3011

(e) any other unwelcome physical, verbal or non-verbal conduct of sexual nature.

Where any of these acts in committed in circumstances whereunder the victim of such conduct has a reasonable apprehension that in relation to the victim's employment or work whether she is drawing salary, or honorarium or voluntary, whether in Government, public or private enterprise such conduct can be humiliating and may constitute a health and safety problem. It is discriminatory for instance when the woman has reasonable grounds to believe that her objection would disadvantage her in connection with her employment or work including recruiting or promotion or when it creates a hostile work environment. Adverse consequences might be visited if the victim does not consent to the conduct in question or raises any objection thereto.

An analysis of the above definition, shows that sexual harassment is a form of sex discrimination projected through unwelcome sexual advances, request for sexual favours and other verbal or physical conduct with sexual overtones, whether directly or by implication, particularly when submission to or rejection of such a conduct by the female employee was capable of being used for effecting the employment of the female employee and unreasonably interfering with her work performance and had the effect of creating an intimidating or hostile working environment for her.

There is no gainsaying that each incident of sexual harassment, at the place of work, results in violation of the Fundamental Right to Gender Equality and the Right to Life and Liberty - the two most precious Fundamental Rights guaranteed by the Constitution of India. As early as in 1993 at the 1LO Seminar held at Manila, it was recognized that sexual harassment of woman at the work place was a form of 'gender discrimination against woman'. The contents of the fundamental rights guaranteed in our Constitution are of sufficient amplitude to encompass all facets of gender equality, including prevention of sexual harassment and abuse and the courts are under a constitutional obligation to protect and preserve those fundamental rights. That sexual harassment of a female at the place of work is incompatible with the dignity and honour of a female and needs to be eliminated and that there can be no compromise with such violations, admits of no debate. The message of international instruments such as the Convention on the Elimination of All Forms of Discrimination Against Woman, 1979 ("CEDAW") and the Beijing Declaration which directs all State parties to take appropriate measures to prevent discrimination of all forms against women beside taking steps to protect the honour and dignity of women is loud and clear. The International Covenant on Economic, Social and Cultural Rights contains several provisions particularly important for woman. Article 7 recognises her right to fair conditions of work and reflects that women shall not be subjected to sexual harassment at the place of work which may vitiate working environment. These international instruments cast an obligation on the Indian State to gender sensitive its laws and the Courts are under an obligation to see that the message of the international instruments is not allowed to be drowned. This Court has in numerous cases emphasised that while discussing constitutional requirements, court and counsel must never forget the core principle embodied in the International Conventions and Instruments and as far as possible give effect to the principles contained in those international instruments. The Courts are under an obligation to give due regard to International Conventions and Norms for construing domestic laws more so when there is no inconsistency between them and there is a void in domestic law[2].

Meaning of Obscene:

Webster's Third New International Dictionary at page 1557 defines 'obscene' as what is repulsive by reason of malignance, hypocrisy, cynicism, irresponsibility, gross disregard of moral or ethical principals. In *Ranjit D. Udeshi v. State of Maharashtra[3]*, it was laid down that in a prosecution under Section 292 IPC the question whether the book was obscene or not does not altogether depend on oral evidence of a writer and art critic because the offending novel and the portions which are the subject of the charge must be judged of by the court. It was held that the word 'obscene' means what is offensive to modesty or decency which gives rise to emotions of lewdness, filthiness and repulsiveness. It was also held that there is some difference between the obscenity and pornography as the latter denotes writings, pictures etc. only intended to arouse sexual desire while the former may include writing etc. not intended to do so but which have that tendency and both, of course, offend against public decency and morals but pornography is obscenity in a more aggravated form. It was observed that merely treating with sex and nudity in art and literature cannot be regarded as evidence of obscenity without something more. It was further held that the test of obscenity, as

---

2 *Vishaka and Ors. v. State of Rajasthan and Ors.*, AIR1997SC3011

3 1965CriLJ8

applied in India, is this : whether the tendency of the matter charged as obscenity is to deprave and corrupt those whose minds are open to such immoral influences and into whose hands a publication of this sort may fall. If it is quite certain that the book would suggest to the minds of the young of either sex, or even to persons of more advanced years, thoughts of a most impure and libidinous character, the book would be treated as obscene. It was also emphasized that an overall view of the obscene matter in the setting of the whole work would, of course, be necessary but the obscene matter also must be considered by itself and separately to find out whether it is so gross and its obscenity so decided that it is likely to deprave and corrupt those whose minds are open to influences of this sort and into whose hands the book is likely to fall.

In *Samaresh Bose v. Amal Mitra*[4]. In this judgment it was held that in judging the question of obscenity the Judge in the first place should try to place himself in the position of the author and from the view point of the author the Judge should try to understand what is it that the author seeks to convey and what the author conveys has any literary and artistic value and thereafter the Judge should place himself in the position of a reader of every age group in whose hands the book is likely to fall and should try to appreciate what kind of possible influence the book is likely to have on the minds of the readers. It was also held in this very judgment that a novel written by a well known writer of novels and stories, by which the author intends to expose various evils and ills pervading the society and to oppose with particular emphasis the problems which ail and afflict the society in spheres, cannot be said to be obscene merely because slang and unconventional words have been used in the book in which there have been emphasis on sex and discretion of female bodies and there are the narrations of feelings, thoughts and actions in vulgar language. It was also observed that some portions of the books may appear to be vulgar and readers of cultured and refined taste may feel shocked and disgusted and equally in some portions, the words used and description given may not appear to be in proper taste and in some places there may have been an exhibition of bad taste leaving it to the readers of experience but certainly not sufficient to bring home to the adolescents any suggestion which is depraving or lascivious.

Obscenity and Pornography:

There is difference between obscenity, and pornography. The latter

---

4   1986CriLJ24

denotes writings, pictures etc. intended to arouse sexual desire. While obscenity includes writings etc. not intended to do so but which have that tendency. Both offend public decency and morals. Pornography is obscenity in a more aggravated form. Among all the creatures of nature human beings are the most refined ones. Male species of all types of animals and birds are considered more beautiful than their respective females. But in literature, ladies are described as beautiful. A pretty damsel is beautiful to behold. A thing of beauty is a joy for ever. Are the bodies of females obscene? A brazenly nude body may evoke a feeling of disgust and revolution. If nudity is properly covered, human body whether of male or female cannot be regarded as objects of obscenity without something more. That something more is to be found in the facial expression or pose in which it is photographed. The photograph of a female body, cannot be considered as obscene or as an indecent representation of woman, if the above mentioned something more is absent.

Decline in Female Child Sex Ratio:

2011 Census of India, published by the Office of the Registrar General and Census Commissioner of India, would show a decline in female child sex ratio in many States of India from 2001-2011. The Annual Report on Registration of Births and Deaths - 2009, published by the Chief Registrar of NCT of Delhi would also indicate a sharp decline in the female sex ratio in almost all the Districts. Mushrooming of various Sonography Centres, Genetic Clinics, Genetic Counselling Centres, Genetic Laboratories, Ultrasonic Clinics, Imaging Centres in almost all parts of the country calls for more vigil and attention by the authorities under the Act. But, unfortunately, their functioning was not being properly monitored or supervised by the authorities under the Act or to find out whether they are misusing the pre-natal diagnostic techniques for determination of sex of foetus leading to foeticide[5].

In *Centre for Enquiry into Health and Allied Themes (CEHAT) and Ors. v. Union of India and Ors.*[6] , the two-Judge Bench commenced the judgment stating that the practice of female infanticide still prevails despite the fact that the gentle touch of a daughter and her voice has a soothing effect on the parents. The Court also commented on the immoral and unethical part of it as well as on the involvement of the qualified and unqualified doctors

---

5   **Meaning of Foeticide:** The killing of a fetus; especially illegal abortion.

6   (2001) 5 SCC 577

or compounders to abort the foetus of a girl child. Female foeticide has its roots in the social thinking which is fundamentally based on certain erroneous notions, ego-centric traditions, pervert perception of societal norms, and obsession with ideas which are totally individualistic sans the collective good. All involved in female foeticide deliberately forget to realize that when the foetus of a girl child is destroyed, a woman of future is crucified. To put it differently, the present generation invites the sufferings on its own and also sows the seeds of suffering for the future generation, as in the ultimate eventuate, the sex ratio gets affected and leads to manifold social problems.

When a female foeticide takes place, every woman who mothers the child must remember that she is killing her own child despite being a mother. That is what abortion would mean in social terms. Abortion of a female child in its conceptual eventuality leads to killing of a woman. Law prohibits it; scriptures forbid it; philosophy condemns it; ethics deprecate it, morality decries it and social science abhors it. Henrik Ibsen emphasized on the individualism of woman.

In **Madhu Kishwar v. State of Bihar** [8] the Court had stated that Indian women have suffered and are suffering discrimination in silence. Self-sacrifice and self-denial are their nobility and fortitude and yet they have been subjected to all inequities, indignities, inequality and discrimination. The way women had suffered has been aptly reflected by an author who has spoken with quite a speck of sensibility: -

Dowry is an intractable disease for women, a bed of arrows for annihilating self-respect, but without the boon of wishful death.

Awareness on Female Foeticide:

The authorities of the Government, the Non-Governmental Organisations and other volunteers are required to remember that there has to be awareness camps which are really effective. The people involved with the same must take it up as a service, a crusade. They must understand and accept that it is an art as well as a science and not simple arithmetic. It cannot take the colour of a routine speech. The awareness camps should not be founded on the theory of Euclidian geometry[7]. It must engulf

---

7 **Meaning of Euclidian Geometry:**
  Euclidean geometry is a mathematical system attributed to the Alexandrian Greek mathematician Euclid, which he described in his textbook on geometry: the *Elements*. Euclid's method consists in assuming a small set of intuitively appealing axioms, and deducing many other propositions (theorems) from these.

the concept of social vigilance with an analytical mind and radiate into the marrows of the society. If awareness campaigns are not appositely conducted, the needed guidance for the people would be without meaning and things shall fall apart and everyone would try to take shelter in cynical escapism. It is difficult to precisely state how an awareness camp is to be conducted. It will depend upon what kind and strata of people are being addressed to. The persons involved in such awareness campaign are required to equip themselves with constitutional concepts, culture, philosophy, religion, scriptural commands and injunctions, the mandate of the law as engrafted under the Act and above all the development of modern science. It needs no special emphasis to state that in awareness camps while the deterrent facets of law are required to be accentuated upon, simultaneously the desirability of law to be followed with spiritual obeisance, regard being had to the purpose of the Act, has to be stressed upon. It should be clearly spelt out that female foeticide is the worst type of dehumanisation of the human race.

29

Annulment of marriage on ground of impotency[1]

Facts in Nutshell:

The wife appealed[2] in High Court. Her prayer to declare her marriage with the respondent[3] nullity on the ground of impotency of the respondent was declined by the learned single judge. She was however, granted a decree[4] of judicial separation[5] on the ground of cruelty.

The marriage between the parties was solemnized 'at Delhi under the Indian Christian Marriage Act, 1872 (short hereinafter referred to as 'the Act'). The wife. professes the Christian religion and comes from Meghalaya. The Railway Traffic Service through a competitive examination. She Came to Delhi to join her duties and was residing at the Railway Rest House, New Delhi. There she met respondent and developed Friendship and got married. It was alleged that the parties could not marry in the Church as the husband was not a Christian and

---

1   Appellants: **Jordan Diengdoh Vs.** Respondent: **Swaranjeet Singh Chopra**
    AIR1984Delhi45
    Hon'ble Judges/Coram: D.K. Kapur and D.P. Wadhwa, JJ.

2   **Meaning of Appeal:** In law, an **appeal** is a process for requesting a formal change to an official decision. Very broadly speaking there are appeals on the record and *de novo* appeals. In *de novo* appeals, a new decision maker re-hears the case without any reference to the prior decision maker. In appeals on the record, the decision of the prior decision maker is challenged by arguing that he or she misapplied the law, came to an incorrect factual finding, acted in excess of his jurisdiction, abused his powers, was biased, considered evidence which he should not have considered or failed to consider evidence that he should have considered.

3   **Meaning of Respondent:** A **respondent** is a person who is called upon to issue a response to a communication made by another. In legal usage, this specifically refers to the defendant in a legal proceeding commenced by a petition, or to an appellee, or the opposing party, in an appeal of a decision by an initial fact-finder.

4   **Meaning of Decree:**
    1. An authoritative order having the force of law.
    2. The judgment of a court of equity, admiralty, probate, or divorce.

5   **Meaning of Judicial Separation:** A court decree requiring a man and wife to cease cohabiting but not dissolving the marriage

they, therefore, decided to have a civil marriage[6]. Though the parties got married under the Act, the wife claimed that she was always under the mistaken belief that the marriage was performed under the Special Marriage Act, 1954. Wife alleged that certain mandatory requirements for the solemnization of the marriage under the Act were not complied with which make the marriage, under the Act, as null and void[7]. In short, she said, there was no marriage under the Act, and the parties are not husband and wife. Wife also claimed that 'the respondent (husband) was impotent at the time of the marriage and continues to be so at the time of institution of the suit'.

The appellant[8] (wife) has averred that on the wedding night she discovered that the respondent-husband was suffering from premature ejaculation[9] and that he was unable in give Tier any in mind and body and that, Therefore, the respondent was impotent and that this impotency of the husband prevented her from having any orgasm[10] during coitus. She further stated that she expected that in due course of time the respondent's ability and technique would improve and she would get satisfactory orgasm but that the respondent continued to ejaculate prematurely leaving her in a state of vascular congestion leaving her physically tense, dissatisfied, mentally disturbed and physically unwell'. All this led to deterioration in her physical health and well-being.

---

6 **Meaning of Civil Marriage: Civil marriage** is a marriage performed, recorded, and recognized by a government official

7 **Meaning of Void:**
   1. without contents; empty
   2. Not legally binding

8 **Meaning of Appellant:** A person who, dissatisfied with the judgment rendered in a lawsuit decided in a lower court or the findings from a proceeding before an Administrative Agency, asks a superior court to review the decision.

9 **Meaning of Ejaculation:** Ejaculate is the ejecting of semen from the penis, and is usually accompanied by orgasm. It is usually the result of sexual stimulation. Rarely, it is due to prostatic disease. Ejaculation may occur spontaneously during sleep (a nocturnal emission)

10 **Meaning of Orgasm: Orgasm** is the sudden discharge of accumulated sexual tension during the sexual response cycle, resulting in rhythmic muscular contractions in the pelvicregion characterized by sexual pleasure. Experienced by males and females, orgasms are controlled by the involuntary or autonomic nervous system.

Petition has been filed under Ss. 18[11], 19[12] and 22[13] of the Indian Divorce Act, 1869. Under S. 18, any husband or wife may present a petition praying that his or her marriage may be declared null and void. S. 19 gives the grounds on which such a decree can be passed. S. 22 deals with a decree of judicial separation on grounds like adultery, cruelty or desertion. No decree of nullity can, therefore, be granted unless there exists any one of the grounds stated in S. 19.

Impotency:

The concept of impotency is not the same as understood by a common man and woman and by medical men. A man is potent if he can achieve erection and penetration in a natural way. This view has been taken by the courts and no contrary view has been brought. A marriage is said to be consummated when there is first act of sexual intercourse after marriage. In other words, consummation is to engage in the first act of sexual intercourse after marriage.

Judgments Referred:

In *Nijhawan v. Nijhawan*[14] , the wife had stated in her petition[15] that her husband was not getting proper erection and got discharged before he could perform the act and that after getting some treatment he got somewhat better and the wife got pregnant 'although there was no normal

---

11 **Section 18 in The Indian Divorce Act, 1869**
   18. Petition for decree of nullity.- Any husband or wife may present a petition to the District Court or to the High Court, praying that his or her marriage may be declared null and void.

12 **Section 19 in The Indian Divorce Act, 1869**
   19. Grounds of decree.- Such decree may be made on any of the following grounds:-
   (1) that the respondent was impotent at the time of the marriage and at the time of the institution of the suit;
   (2) that the parties are within the prohibited degrees of consanguinity (whether natural or legal) or affinity;
   (3) that either party was a lunatic or idiot at the time of the marriage;
   (4) that the former husband or wife of either party was living at the time of the marriage, and the marriage with such former husband or wife was then in force. Nothing in this section shall affect the jurisdiction of the High Court to make decrees of nullity of marriage on the ground that the consent of either party was obtained by force or fraud.

13 **Section 22 in The Indian Divorce Act, 1869**
   22. Bar to decree for divorce a mensa et toro; but judicial separation obtainable by husband or wife.- No decree shall hereafter be made for a divorce a mensa et toro, but the husband or wife may obtain a decree of judicial separation, on the ground of adultery, or cruelty, or desertion without reasonable excuse for two years or upwards, and such decree shall have the effect of a divorce a mensa et toro under the existing law, and such other legal effect as hereinafter mentioned.

14 AIR1973Delhi200

15 **Meaning of Petition:** A formal message requesting something that is submitted to an authority

and complete sexual intercourse between the parties as there was some penetration'. A son was born to the parties. It was thus alleged that the husband was sexually weak and debilitated so much so that he was unable to perform normal sexual intercourse with the wife. In her statement, the wife had stated that the husband was not performing the act of coitus[16] and that he used to get discharged before he could get his organ in contact with her organ and that after some time she noticed some improvement in the husband in as much as instead of getting discharged at the very beginning of his sexual advances he could retain it for a minute or two but he would get discharged before coming to her and all that the husband was able to do was to rub his organ on her organ and get discharged in the mouth of the vagina without any penetration and that this was how she got conceived. Thus, it was alleged that though the husband was getting erection of his organ the difficulty was that he used to get discharged before being able to penetrate the organ. The court accepted the evidence of the wife that the husband was sexually weak. The court thereafter considered the question as to whether the sexual weakness of the husband could result in a finding of impotency. Court held that it would be somewhat hazardous to coming to a conclusion that the respondent is impotent. The court, Therefore, returned no finding of impotency of the husband. This was a case under S. 12(1)(a)[17] of the Hindu Marriage Act "or annulling the marriage on the ground of impotency, and the language of this section before its amendment in 1976 was the same as that of S. 19(1) of the Indian Divorce Act. This is what the court observed :-

"In order to attract Section 12(1)(a) it has to be positively proved that the respondent was impotent at all material times i.e. right from the time of the marriage till the institution of the petition. This requirement is so strict that even if it could be shown that the marriage was consummated just once during this period, a decree of nullity cannot be .granted. The burden of proving that the respondent was impotent at all material times is on the petitioner".

---

16 **Meaning of Coitus: Sexual intercourse,** or **copulation** or **coitus,** is the insertion and thrusting of a male's penis into a female's vagina for the purposes of sexual pleasure or reproduction

17 **Section 12(1) in The Hindu Marriage Act, 1955**
(1) Any marriage solemnized, whether before or after the commencement of this Act, shall be voidable and may be annulled by a decree of nullity on any of the following grounds, namely:-
(a) [that the marriage has not been consummated owing to the importance of the respondent;]

In *Diovijay Singh v. Pratap Kumari*[18] the Supreme Court held that a party was impotent if his or her mental or physical condition made consummation of the marriage a practical impossibility.

In *Ved Parkash Sachdeva v. Smt. Mohani Sachdeva* [2], the husband was unable to produce erection and Therefore, could not consummate the marriage in spite of various attempts made by him V. D. Misra J., held that the incapacity to accomplish the act of sexual intercourse was called impotency. "By sexual intercourse is meant not an incipient, partial or imperfect, but a normal and complete coitus", it was observed.

In *K. Balavendram v. S. Harry*[19], the wife had contended that the husband's male organ was so abnormally big as to render sexual intercourse with her impracticable and it proved to be positively dangerous to the life of the wife, and that on several occasions when the husband attempted to have intercourse with her, the wife evinced great aversion to the act and also suffered great pain on each occasion with the result that she had to push the husband away or jump out of bed. She stated that in the circumstances, the marriage was never consummated and that consummation of the marriage was impossible. It was contended that it was a case of incurable impotence of the husband towards the wife and that the marriage should be declared null and void on the ground of impotency under Section 19(1)[20] of the Divorce Act 1869. The husband though denied the allegations but failed to subject himself to any medical examination. The court observed as follows:-

"In the present case, the evidence leaves us in no doubt that the marriage cannot be consummated in the ordinary and normal way on account of the abnormal size of the respondent's (husband's) organ. According to the petitioner's (wife's) evidence which must be accepted, ordinary and complete intercourse is physically impossible. It must be held therefore

---

18 [1970]1SCR559

19 AIR1954Mad316

20 **Section 19 in The Indian Divorce Act, 1869**
19. Grounds of decree.- Such decree may be made on any of the following grounds:-
(1) that the respondent was impotent at the time of the marriage and at the time of the institution of the suit;
(2) that the parties are within the prohibited degrees of consanguinity (whether natural or legal) or affinity;
(3) that either party was a lunatic or idiot at the time of the marriage;
(4) that the former husband or wife of either party was living at the time of the marriage, and the marriage with such former husband or wife was then in force. Nothing in this section shall affect the jurisdiction of the High Court to make decrees of nullity of marriage on the ground that the consent of either party was obtained by force or fraud.

that the respondent was impotent so far as the petitioner was concerned both at the time of the marriage and at the time of the institution of the suit".

Decision of Delhi High Court:

Court held that 'ordinary and complete', 'complete and natural' or 'full and complete' intercourse cannot be extended to mean more than erection and penetration which should be complete and natural. To pronounce the impotency of the husband the court is not concerned with the techniques employed by the husband for sexual intercourse. It cannot, therefore, be said that the respondent-husband in present case was impotent within the meaning of S. 19(1) of the Indian Divorce Act.

30

Marriage Promise and Cheating[1]

Facts in Nutshell:

The accused[2] appellant Bipul Medhi was convicted[3] under Section 417[4], IPC and sentenced to rigorous 'imprisonment for six months and to pay fine of Rs, 1,000 in default further imprisonment for two months.

The prosecution[5] allegation, in brief, was that accused Bipul Medhi developed some intimacy and friendship with Sewali Kalita and the affair continued for two-and-half years. The accused, thereafter, promised to marry Sewali and believing on the said plea, Sewali allowed the accused to have cohabitation with her and as of such cohabitation, she became pregnant. The victim also alleged rape, whereupon the accused was tried for commission of offence under Section 493[6]/376[7] IPC. On conclusion

---

1   Appellants: **Bipul Medhi Vs.** Respondent: **State of Assam**
    2008CriLJ1099
    Hon'ble Judges/Coram: P.G. Agarwal and Iqbal Ahmed Ansari, JJ.

2   **Meaning of Accused:** A person charged with a criminal offense, or the state of being so charged.

3   **Meaning of Convicted: S**omeone guilty of an offense or crime, especially by the verdict of a court

4   **Section 417 in The Indian Penal Code, 1860**
    417. Punishment for cheating.- Whoever cheats shall be punished with imprisonment of either description for a term which may extend to one year, or with fine, or with both.

5   **Meaning of Prosecution:**
    a. the institution and carrying on of legal proceedings against a person.
    b. the officials who institute and conduct such proceedings.

6   **Section 493 in The Indian Penal Code, 1860**
    493. Cohabitation caused by a man deceitfully inducing a belief of lawful marriage.-- Every man who by deceit causes any woman who is not lawfully married to him to believe that she is lawfully married to him and to cohabit or have sexual intercourse with him in that belief, shall be punished with imprisonment of either description for a term which may extend to ten years, and shall also be liable to fine.

7   **Section 376 in The Indian Penal Code, 1860**
    376. Punishment for rape.--
    (1) Whoever, except in the cases provided for by sub- section (2), commits rape shall be punished with imprisonment of either description for a term which shall not be less than seven years but which may be for life or for a term which may extend to ten years and shall also be liable to fine unless the woman raped is his own wife and is not under twelve years of age, in which case, he shall be punished with imprisonment of either description for a term which may extend to two years or with fine or with both:

of the, trial, the learned trial court convicted the accused-appellant as aforesaid. Reference was made to High Court.

Cheating:

In the case of *Joleswar Kalita v. State of Assam*[8], the question raised was that the prosecutrix could not have surrendered to the petitioner, if she was not deceived and as the prosecutrix had suffered damage or harm in body, mind and reputation due to deception, the offence of cheating under Section 415[9], IPC is made out hon'ble Sangma, J, declined to

---

Provided that the court may, for adequate and special reasons to be mentioned in the judgment, impose a sentence of imprisonment for a term of less than seven years.

(2) Whoever,-

(a) being a police officer commits rape-

(i) within the limits of the police station to which he is appointed; or

(ii) in the premises of any station house whether or not situated in the police station to which he is appointed; or

(iii) on a woman in his custody or in the custody of a police officer subordinate to him; or

(b) being a public servant, takes advantage of his official position and commits rape on a woman in his custody as such public servant or in the custody of a public servant subordinate to him; or

(c) being on the management or on the staff of a jail, remand home or other place of custody established by or under any law for the time being in force or of a women's or children's institution takes advantage of his official position and commits rape on any inmate of such jail, remand home, place or institution; or

(d) being on the management or on the staff of a hospital, takes advantage of his official position and commits rape on a woman in that hospital; or

(e) commits rape on a woman knowing her to be pregnant; or

(f) commits rape on a woman when she is under twelve years of age; or

(g) commits gang rape, shall be punished with rigorous imprisonment for a term which shall not be less than ten years but which may be for life and shall also be liable to fine: Provided that the court may, for adequate and special reasons to be mentioned in the judgment, impose a sentence of imprisonment of either description for a term of less than ten years. Explanation 1.- Where a women's is raped by one or more in a group of persons acting in furtherance of their common intention, each of the persons shall be deemed to have committed gang rape within the meaning of this sub- section. Explanation 2.-" women's or children's institution" means an institution, whether called and orphanage or a home for neglected women or children or a widows' home or by any other name, which is established and maintained for the reception and care of women or children. Explanation 3.-" hospital" means the precincts of the hospital and includes the precincts of any institution for the reception and treatment of persons during convalescence or of persons requiring medical attention or rehabilitation.

8 MANU/GJ/0078/1987

9 **Section 415 in The Indian Penal Code, 1860**

415. Cheating.-- Whoever, by deceiving any person, fraudulently or dishonestly induces the person so deceived to deliver any property to any person, or to consent that any person shall retain any property, or intentionally induces the person so deceived to do or omit to do anything which he would not do or omit if he were not so deceived, and which act or omission causes or is likely to cause damage or harm to that person in body, mind, reputation or property, is said to" cheat". Explanation.- A dishonest concealment of facts is a deception within the meaning of this section. Illustrations

(a) A, by falsely pretending to be in the Civil Service, intentionally deceives Z, and thus dishonestly induces Z to let him have on credit goods for which he does not mean to pay. A cheats.

accept, the above submission and held that the petitioner could not be convicted for cheating under the penal law and it was held as follows:

Section 415/417, IPC come under Chapter XVII - Offenses against property. Therefore, in order to bring the case even under the later part of the section, deception must be in relation to property. The expression 'to do' or 'omit to do any thing in Section 415 apply to a person who is deceived in relation to property though the property may or may not be delivered. It does not apply to the case of the woman who is made to surrender her chastity to a man who deceived her.

The facts in *Moni Gogoi v. Smti. Sarumani Hazarika*[10] were also more or less identical and the accused promised the complainant that he would marry her and on that understanding, he requested her to have sexual intercourse with the complainant, who became pregnant and gave birth to a child. The accused deserted the complainant and refused to marry her. The learned Single Judge (hon'ble S.D. Roy, J, as his lordship then was) set aside the order of conviction[11] and acquitted[12] the accused.

(b) A, by putting a counterfeit mark on an article, intentionally deceives Z into a belief that this article was made by a certain celebrated manufacturer, and thus dishonestly induces Z to buy and pay for the article. A cheats.

(c) A, by exhibiting to Z a false sample of an article intentionally deceives Z into believing that the article corresponds with the sample, and thereby dishonestly induces Z to buy and pay for the article. A cheats.

(d) A, by tendering in payment for an article a bill on a house with which A keeps no money, and by which A expects that the bill will be dishonoured, intentionally deceives Z, and thereby dishonestly induces Z to deliver the article, intending not to pay for it. A cheats

(e) A, by pledging as diamond articles which he knows are not diamonds, intentionally deceives Z, and thereby dishonestly induces Z to lend money. A cheats.

(f) A Intentionally deceives Z into a belief that A means to repay any money that Z may lend to him and thereby dishonestly induces Z to lend him money, A not intending to repay it. A cheats.

(g) A intentionally deceives Z into a belief that A means to deliver to Z a certain quantity of indigo plant which he does not intend to deliver, and thereby dishonestly induces Z to advance money upon the faith of such delivery. A cheats; but if A, at the time of obtaining the money, intends to deliver the indigo plant, and afterwards breaks his contract and does not deliver it, he does not cheat, but is liable only to a civil action for breach of contract.

(h) A intentionally deceives Z into a belief that A has performed A's part of a contract made with Z, which he has not performed, and thereby dishonestly induces Z to pay money. A cheats.

(i) A sells and conveys an estate to B. A, knowing that in consequence of such sale he has no right to the property, sells or mortgages the same to Z, without disclosing the fact of the previous sale and conveyance to B, and receives the purchase or mortgage money from Z. A cheats.

10 MANU/GJ/0224/1992

11 **Meaning of Conviction:** In law, a **conviction** is the verdict that results when a court of law finds a defendant guilty of a crime.

12 **Meaning of Acquittal:** In the common law tradition, an **acquittal** formally certifies that the accused is free from the charge of an offense, as far as the criminal law is concerned.

Consent:

The Indian Penal Code does not define "consent" in positive terms. There is, however, a negative definition of the word "consent" in Section 90 of the Indian Penal Code, which lays down as to what cannot be regarded as "consent" under the Indian Penal Code. The relevant provisions of Section 90, IPC reads as follows:

Consent known to be given under fear or misconception - A consent is not such a consent as is intended by section of this Code, if the consent is given by a person under fear of injury, or under a misconnection of fact, and if the person doing the act knows, or has reason to believe, that the consent was given in consequence of such fear or misconception; or

Consent of insane person - If the consent is given by a person, who, from unsoundness of mind, or intoxication, is unable to understand the nature and consequence of that to which he gives his consent; or

Consent of child - Unless the contrary appears from the context, if the consent is given by a person who is under twelve years of age.

In Black's Law Dictionary, the word 'consent' has been defined as follows:

Consent. - Agreement, approval, or permission as to some act, or purpose, esp. given voluntarily by a competent person. Consent is an affirmative defence to assault, battery, and related torts, as well as such torts on defamation, invasion of privacy, conversion, and trespass-consent, vb.- consensual, adj.

Decision of High Court:

Court held that When an accused makes a false promise to marry, which he never intends to carry out, and induces thereby the victim, so deceived, to have with him sexual act, which the victim would not have indulged in or permitted, had she not been induced by such deception and, when such act of having sexual intercourse by her with the accused causes, or is likely to cause, damage or harm to her body, mind or reputation, the act of the accused would amount to cheating. Thus, when a woman is induced to part with her chastity or virginity, which is the most valued possession of hers, the person, who so induces the woman by making false representation, would be liable for punishment under Section 417,

IPC if the victim's having sexual intercourse, with such a person, causes or is likely to cause harm to her body, mind or reputation, for, in such a case, unless so deceived, the victim would, not have permitted sexual act by the accused. To put it differently, had such a victim not been deceived, she would not have permitted sexual act or would have refrained from allowing such sexual act and, clearly in such a cas, but for her permitting such sexual act, she would not have suffered harm to her body, mind or reputation.

31

Sexual harassment at working place[1]

Questions before the Court:

Does an action of the superior against a female employee which is against moral sanctions and does not withstand test of decency and modesty not amount to Sexual harassment? Is physical contact with the female employee an essential ingredient of such a charge? Does the allegation that the superior 'tried to molest' a female employee at the "place of work", not constitute an act unbecoming of good conduct and behavior expected from the superior?

Facts in Nutshell:

The respondent[2] was working as a Private Secretary to the Chairman a of the Apparel Export Promotion Council, (the appellant[3]). It was alleged that on 12.8.1988, he tried to molest a woman employee of the Council, Miss X who was at the relevant, time working as a Clerk-cum-Typist. She was not competent or trained to take dictations. The respondent, however insisted that she go with him to the [Business center at Taj Palace Hotel for taking dictation from the Chairman and type out the matter. Under the pressure of the respondent, she went to take the dictation from the Chairman. While Miss X was waiting for the Director in the room, the respondent tried to sit too dose to her and despite her objection did not give up his objectionable behavior. She later on took dictation from the Director. The respondent told her to type it at the Business center of the Taj Palace Hotel, which is located in the Basement of the Hotel. He offered to help her so that her typing was not found fault with by the Director. He volunteered to show her the Business center for getting the matter

---

1   Appellants: **Apparel Export Promotion Council Vs.** Respondent: **A.K. Chopra**
    AIR1999SC625
    Hon'ble Judges/Coram: Dr. A. S. Anand , CJI., V. N. Khare , J.

2   **Meaning of Respondent:** A **respondent** is a person who is called upon to issue a response to a communication made by another. In legal usage, this specifically refers to the defendant in a legal proceeding commenced by a petition, or to an appellee, or the opposing party, in an appeal of a decision by an initial fact-finder.

3   **Meaning of Appellant:** A person who, dissatisfied with the judgment rendered in a lawsuit decided in a lower court or the findings from a proceeding before an Administrative Agency, asks a superior court to review the decision.

typed and taking advantage of the isolated place, again tried to sit close to her and touch her despite her objections. The draft typed matter was corrected by Director (Finance) who asked Miss X to retype the same. The respondent again went her to the Business center and repeated his overtures. Miss X told the respondent that she would "leave the place if he continued to behave like that". The respondent did not stop. Though he went out from the Business center for a while, he again came back and resumed his objectionable acts. According to Miss X, the respondent had tried to molest her physically in the lift also while coming to the basement but she saved herself by pressing the emergency button, which made the door of the lift to open. She succeeded in meeting Director and narrated the whole incident to him orally submitted a written complaint also. The respondent was placed under suspension.

Aggrieved, by an order of removal from service, the respondent filed a departmental appeal before the Staff Committee of the appellant. The Division Bench of High Court agreed with the findings recorded by the learned Single Judge that the respondent had "tried" to molest and that he had not "actually molested" Miss X and that he had "not managed" to make the slightest physical contact with the lady and went on to hold that such an act of the respondent was not a sufficient ground for his dismissal from service. Aggrieved by the judgment of the Division Bench, the employer (appellant) filed appeal by special leave[4] in Supreme Court.

Sexual Harassment at Workplace:

Against the growing social menace of Sexual harassment of women at the work place, a three Judge Bench of Supreme Court by a rather innovative judicial law making process issued certain guidelines in *Vishaka v. State of Rajasthan*[5], after taking note of the fact that the present civil and penal laws in the country do not adequately provide for specific protection of woman from sexual harassment at places of work and that enactment of such a legislation would take a considerable time. In Vishaka's case (supra), a definition of sexual harassment was suggested. Verma, J., (as

---

4 **Article 136 in The Constitution Of India 1949**
   136. Special leave to appeal by the Supreme Court
   (1) Notwithstanding anything in this Chapter, the Supreme Court may, in its discretion, grant special leave to appeal from any judgment, decree, determination, sentence or order in any cause or matter passed or made by any court or tribunal in the territory of India
   (2) Nothing in clause (1) shall apply to any judgment, determination, sentence or order passed or made by any court or tribunal constituted by or under any law relating to the Armed Forces

5 AIR1997SC3011

the former Chief Justice then was), speaking for the three-Judge Bench opined:

Definition:

For this purpose, sexual harassment includes such unwelcome sexually determined behavior (whether directly or by implication) as:

(a) physical contact and advance;

(b) a demand or request for sexual favours;

(c) sexually-colored remarks;

(d) showing pornography;

(e) any other unwelcome physical, verbal or non-verbal conduct of sexual nature.

Where any of these acts in committed in circumstances where under the victim of such conduct has a reasonable apprehension that in relation to the victim's employment or work whether she is drawing salary, or honorarium or voluntary, whether in Government, public or private enterprise such conduct can be humiliating and may constitute a health and safety problem. It is discriminatory for instance when the woman has reasonable grounds to believe that her objection would disadvantage her in connection with her employment or work including recruiting or promotion or when it creates a hostile work environment. Adverse consequences might be visited if the victim does not consent to the conduct in question or raises any objection thereto.

An analysis of the above definition, shows that sexual harassment is a form of sex discrimination projected through unwelcome sexual advances, request for sexual favours and other verbal or physical conduct with sexual overtones, whether directly or by implication, particularly when submission to or rejection of such a conduct by the female employee was capable of being used for effecting the employment of the female employee and unreasonably interfering with her work performance and had the effect of creating an intimidating or hostile working environment for her.

There is no gainsaying that each incident of sexual harassment, at the place of work, results in violation of the Fundamental Right to Gender Equality and the Right to Life and Liberty - the two most precious Fundamental Rights guaranteed by the Constitution of India. As early as in 1993 at the 1LO Seminar held at Manila, it was recognized that sexual harassment of woman at the work place was a form of 'gender discrimination against woman'. The contents of the fundamental rights guaranteed in our Constitution are of sufficient amplitude to encompass all facets of gender equality, including prevention of sexual harassment and abuse and the courts are under a constitutional obligation to protect and preserve those fundamental rights. That sexual harassment of a female at the place of work is incompatible with the dignity and honour of a female and needs to be eliminated and that there can be no compromise with such violations, admits of no debate. The message of international instruments such as the Convention on the Elimination of All Forms of Discrimination Against Woman, 1979 ("CEDAW") and the Beijing Declaration which directs all State parties to take appropriate measures to prevent discrimination of all forms against women beside taking steps to protect the honour and dignity of women is loud and clear. The International Covenant on Economic, Social and Cultural Rights contains several provisions particularly important for woman. Article 7 recognises her right to fair conditions of work and reflects that women shall not be subjected to sexual harassment at the place of work which may vitiate working environment. These international instruments cast an obligation on the Indian State to gender sensitive its laws and the Courts are under an obligation to see that the message of the international instruments is not allowed to be drowned. This Court has in numerous cases emphasised that while discussing constitutional requirements, court and counsel must never forget the core principle embodied in the International Conventions and Instruments and as far as possible give effect to the principles contained in those international instruments. The Courts are under an obligation to give due regard to International Conventions and Norms for construing domestic laws more so when there is no inconsistency between them and there is a void in domestic law[6].

Decision of the Supreme Court:

Court held that the High Court overlooked the ground realities and ignored the fact that the conduct of the respondent against his junior female employee, Miss X, was wholly against moral sanctions, decency and was offensive to her modesty. Reduction of punishment in a case like this is bound to have demoralizing effect on the women employees and is

---

6   *Vishaka and Ors. v. State of Rajasthan and Ors.*, AIR1997SC3011

a retrograde step. There was no justification for the High Court to interfere with the punishment imposed by the departmental authorities. The act of the respondent was unbecoming of good conduct and behavior expected from a superior officer and undoubtedly amounted to sexual harassment of Miss X and the punishment imposed by the appellant, was, thus, commensurate with the gravity of his objectionable behavior and did not warrant any interference by the High Court in exercise of its power of judicial review[7].

---

7 **Meaning of Judicial Review:** The power of Judiciary to review and determine validity of a law or an order may be described as the power of "Judicial Review." It means that the constitution is the Supreme law of the land and any law in consistent there with is void. The term refers to "the power of a court to inquire whether a law executive order or other official action conflicts with the written constitution and if the court concludes that it does, to declare it unconstitutional and void."

32

Sexual harassment of women at workplace[1]

Facts in Nutshell: This writ petition[2] have been filed for the enforcement of the fundamental rights[3] of working women under

---

1 Appellants: **Vishaka and others** Vs. Respondent: **State of Rajasthan and Others**
   AIR1997SC3011
   Hon'ble Judges: J. S. Verma, C.J.I., Sujata V. Manohar and B. N. Kirpal, JJ.

2 A writ petition is a right endowed by the law for a person to seek speedy trial before an appellate court after a trial court's judgment on his case. The petitioner seeks to rush his case to prevent irreparable harm.

3 The six fundamental rights recognized by the constitution are:
   1) Right to equality, including equality before law, prohibition of discrimination on grounds of religion, race, caste, sex or place of birth, and equality of opportunity in matters of employment, abolition of untouchability and abolition of titles.
   2) Right to freedom which includes speech and expression, assembly, association or union or cooperatives, movement, residence, and right to practice any profession or occupation (some of these rights are subject to security of the State, friendly relations with foreign countries, public order, decency or morality), right to life and liberty, right to education, protection in respect to conviction in offences and protection against arrest and detention in certain cases.
   3) Right against exploitation, prohibiting all forms of forced labour, child labour and traffic in human beings;
   4) Right to freedom of religion, including freedom of conscience and free profession, practice, and propagation of religion, freedom to manage religious affairs, freedom from certain taxes and freedom from religious instructions in certain educational institutes.
   5) Cultural and Educational rights preserving Right of any section of citizens to conserve their culture, language or script, and right of minorities to establish and administer educational institutions of their choice.
   6) Right to constitutional remedies for enforcement of Fundamental Rights. Fundamental rights for Indians have also been aimed at overturning the inequalities of pre-independence social practices. Specifically, they have also been used to abolish untouchability and hence prohibit discrimination on the grounds of religion, race, caste, sex, or place of birth. They also forbid trafficking of human beings and forced labour. They also protect cultural and educational rights of ethnic and religious minorities by allowing them to preserve their languages and also establish and administer their own education institutions.
   Right to property was originally a fundamental right, but is now a legal right.

Articles 14[4] 19[5] and 21[6] of the Constitution of India. With the increasing awareness and emphasis on gender justice, there is increase in the effort to guard against such violations; and the resentment towards incidents of sexual harassment is also increasing. The petition has been brought as a class action by certain social activists and NGOs with the aim of focussing attention towards societal aberration, and assisting in finding suitable methods for realisation of the true concept of 'gender equality'; and to prevent sexual harassment of working women in all work places through judicial process, to fill the vacuum in existing legislation.

The cause for the filing of the writ petition was an incident of alleged brutal gang rape of a social worker in a village of Rajasthan. The incident reveals the hazards to which a working woman may be exposed and the depravity to which sexual harassment can degenerate; and the urgency for safeguards by an alternative mechanism in the absence of legislative measures. The fundamental right to carry on any occupation, trade or profession[7] depends on the availability of a "safe" working environment. Right to life means life with dignity.

Beijing Statement of Principles of the Independence of the Judiciary in the LAWASIA region

The obligation of Court under Article 32 of the Constitution[8] for the

---

4   Article 14 in The Constitution Of India 1949
    14. Equality before law The State shall not deny to any person equality before the law or the equal protection of the laws within the territory of India Prohibition of discrimination on grounds of religion, race, caste, sex or place of birth

5   Article 19 in Constitution of India
    Protection of certain rights regarding freedom of speech etc
    (1) All citizens shall have the right
    (a) to freedom of speech and expression;
    (b) to assemble peaceably and without arms;
    (c) to form associations or unions;
    (d) to move freely throughout the territory of India;
    (e) to reside and settle in any part of the territory of India; and
    (f) omitted
    (g) to practise any profession, or to carry on any occupation, trade or business

6   Article 21 in The Constitution Of India
    Protection of life and personal liberty No person shall be deprived of his life or personal liberty except according to procedure established by law

7   Article 19(1) (g) of the Constitution of India
    Article 19(1)(g) --To practise any profession, or to carry on any occupation, trade or business

8   Article 32. Remedies for enforcement of rights conferred by this Part
    (1) The right to move the Supreme Court by appropriate proceedings for the enforcement of the rights conferred by this Part is guaranteed
    (2) The Supreme Court shall have power to issue directions or orders or writs, including writs in the

enforcement of the fundamental rights in the absence of legislation must be viewed along with the role of judiciary envisaged in the Beijing Statement of Principles of the Independence of the Judiciary in the LAWASIA region. These principles were accepted by the Chief Justices of the Asia and the Pacific at Beijing in 1995 as those representing the minimum standards necessary to be observed in order to maintain the independence and effective functioning of the judiciary. The objectives of the judiciary mentioned in the Beijing Statement are:

Objectives of the Judiciary:

The objectives and functions of the judiciary include the following:

(a) to ensure that all persons are able to live securely under the Rule of Law;

(b) to promote, within the proper limits of the judicial function, the observance and the attainment of human rights; and

(c) to administer the law impartially among persons and between persons and the State.

Sexual harassment

Sexual harassment includes such unwelcome sexually determined behavior as physical contacts and advances, sexually coloured remarks, showing pornography and sexual demands, whether by words or actions. Such conduct can be humiliating and may constitute a health and safety problem; it is discriminatory when the woman has reasonable grounds to believe that her objection would disadvantage her in connection with her employment, including recruiting or promotion, or when it creates a hostile working environment. Effective complaints procedures and remedies, including compensation, should be provided.

---

nature of habeas corpus, mandamus, prohibition, quo warranto and certiorari, whichever may be appropriate, for the enforcement of any of the rights conferred by this Part

(3) Without prejudice to the powers conferred on the Supreme Court by clause (1) and (2), Parliament may by law empower any other court to exercise within the local limits of its jurisdiction all or any of the powers exercisable by the Supreme Court under clause (2)

(4) The right guaranteed by this article shall not be suspended except as otherwise provided for by this Constitution

Guidelines/Directions of the Court

It is necessary and expedient for employers in work places as well as other responsible persons or institutions to observe certain guidelines to ensure the prevention of sexual harassment of women:

1. Duty of the Employer or other responsible persons in work places and other institutions:

It shall be the duty of the employer or other responsible persons in work places or other institutions to prevent or deter the commission of acts of sexual harassment and to provide the procedures for the resolution, settlement or prosecution of acts of sexual harassment by taking all steps required.

2. Definition:

For this purpose, sexual harassment includes such unwelcome sexually determined behavior (whether directly or by implication) as:

a) physical contact and advances;

b) a demand or request for sexual favours;

c) sexually coloured remarks;

d) showing pornography;

e) any other unwelcome physical, verbal or non-verbal conduct of sexual nature.

Where any of these acts is committed in circumstances whereunder the victim of such conduct has a reasonable apprehension that in relation to the victim's employment or work whether she is drawing salary, or honorarium or voluntary, whether in Government, public or private enterprise such conduct can be humiliating and may constitute a health and safety problem. It is discriminatory for instance when the woman has reasonable grounds to believe that her objection would disadvantage her in connection with her employment or work including recruiting or promotion or when it creates a hostile work environment. Adverse consequences might be visited if the victim does not consent to the conduct in question or raises any objection thereto.

3. Preventive Steps:

All employers or persons in charge of work place whether in the public or private sector should take appropriate steps to prevent sexual harassment. Without prejudice to the generality of this obligation they should take the following steps:

(a) Express prohibition of sexual harassment as defined above at the work place should be notified, published and circulated in appropriate ways.

(b) The Rules/Regulations of Government and Public Sector bodies relating to conduct and discipline should include rules/regulations prohibiting sexual harassment and provide for appropriate penalties in such rules against the offender.

(c) As regards private employers steps should be taken to include the aforesaid prohibitions in the. standing orders under the Industrial Employment (Standing Orders) Act, 1946.

(d) Appropriate work conditions should be provided in respect of work, leisure, health and hygiene to further ensure that there is no hostile environment towards women at work places and no employee woman should have reasonable grounds to believe that she is disadvantaged in connection with her employment.

4. Criminal Proceedings:

Where such conduct amounts to a specific offence under the Indian Penal Code or under any other law, the employer shall initiate appropriate action in accordance with law by making a complaint with the appropriate authority.

In particular, it should ensure that victims, or witnesses are not victimized or discriminated against while dealing with complaints of sexual harassment. The victims of sexual harassment should have the option to seek transfer of the perpetrator or their own transfer.

5. Disciplinary Action:

Where such conduct amounts to misconduct in employment as defined by the relevant service rules, appropriate disciplinary action should be initiated by the employer in accordance with those rules.

6. Complaint Mechanism:

Whether or not such conduct constitutes an offence under law or a breach of the service rules, an appropriate complaint mechanism should be created in the employer's organization for redress of the complaint made by the victim. Such complaint mechanism should ensure time bound treatment of complaints.

7. Complaints Committee:

The complaint mechanism, referred to in (6) above, should be adequate to provide, where necessary, a Complaints Committee, a special counselor or other support service, including the maintenance of confidentiality.

The Complaints Committee should be headed by a woman and not less than half of its member should be women. Further, to prevent the possibility of any undue pressure or influence from senior levels, such Complaints Committee should involve a third party, either NGO or other body who is familiar with the issue of sexual harassment.

The Complaints Committee must make an annual report to the Government department concerned of the complaints and action taken by them.

The employers and person in charge will also report on the compliance with the aforesaid guidelines including on the reports of the Complaints Committee to the Government department.

8. Workers' Initiative:

Employees should be allowed to raise issues of sexual harassment at workers' meeting and in other appropriate forum and it should be affirmatively discussed in Employer-Employee Meetings.

9. Awareness:

Awareness of the rights of female employees in this regard should be created in particular by prominently notifying the guidelines (and appropriate legislation when enacted on the subject) in a suitable manner.

10. Third Party Harassment:

Where sexual harassment occurs as a result of an act or omission by any third party or outsider, the employer and person in charge will take all steps necessary and reasonable to assist the affected person in terms of support and preventive action.

Court also held that the guidelines shall be observed by Private employers as well. The directions would be binding and enforceable in law until suitable legislation is enacted to occupy the field.

33

Divorce can be granted on ground of cruelty[1]

Ratio Decidendi[2]: "Decree of divorce can be granted on ground of cruelty."

Facts in Nutshell:

Appellant[3] being aggrieved by the judgment and decree[4] passed in Civil Suit by IIIrd Additional District Judge (Fast Track Court) dismissing the suit of the appellant, filed first appeal[5] under Section 28[6] of the Hindu

---

1 Appellants: **Amita Pathak Vs.** Respondent: **S. Shiv Prasad**
  I(2012)DMC350
  Hon'ble Judges/Coram: K.K. Lahoti & Vimla Jain, JJ.

2 **Meaning of Ration Decidendi:** *Ratio decidendi* is a Latin phrase meaning "the reason" or "the rationale for the decision." The *ratio decidendi* is "the point in a case which determines the judgment" or "the principle which the case establishes."

3 **Meaning of Appellant:** A person who, dissatisfied with the judgment rendered in a lawsuit decided in a lower court or the findings from a proceeding before an Administrative Agency, asks a superior court to review the decision.

4 **Meaning of Decree:**
  1. An authoritative order having the force of law.
  2. The judgment of a court of equity, admiralty, probate, or divorce.

5 **Meaning of Appeal:** In law, an **appeal** is a process for requesting a formal change to an official decision. Very broadly speaking there are appeals on the record and *de novo* appeals. In *de novo* appeals, a new decision maker re-hears the case without any reference to the prior decision maker. In appeals on the record, the decision of the prior decision maker is challenged by arguing that he or she misapplied the law, came to an incorrect factual finding, acted in excess of his jurisdiction, abused his powers, was biased, considered evidence which he should not have considered or failed to consider evidence that he should have considered.

6 **Section 28 in The Hindu Marriage Act, 1955**
  28. Appeals from decrees and orders.
  (1) All decrees made by the court in any proceeding under this Act shall, subject to the provisions of sub- section (3), be appealable as decrees of the court made in the exercise of its original civil jurisdiction, and every such appeal shall lie to the court to which appeals ordinarily lie from the decisions of the court given in the exercise of its original civil jurisdiction.
  (2) Orders made by the court in any proceeding under this Act under section 25 or section 26 shall, subject to the provisions of sub- section (3), be appealable if they are not interim orders, and every such appeal shall lie to the court to which appeals ordinarily lie from the decisions of the court given in exercise of its original civil jurisdiction.
  (3) There shall be no appeal under this section on the subject of costs only.
  (4) Every- appeal under this section shall be preferred within a period of thirty days from the date of the decree or order.

Marriage Act, 1955 (hereinafter referred to as the Act). Brief facts of the case are that the marriage of appellant Smt. Amita Pathak was solemnized with respondent S. Shiv Prasad as per Hindu rites, religion and out of their wedlock, no child was born. Initially the appellant and respondent[7] were living together in a joint family in Kerala but after a period of near-about two months, due to some stress, the appellant and respondent started living separately with the consent of their family members. Thereafter, the respondent started misbehaving, abusing, insulting and beating the appellant. He had badly tortured the appellant physically and mentally for two months. When appellant had asked the respondent that why he was behaving in such a manner then respondent told her that he had no proper source of income, therefore, she should get Rupees four or five lakh in dowry from her parents. If she fails, he would continue such bad behaviour. The appellant informed about the demand to her parents and her parents had arranged some money and gave to respondent. The respondent again started insulting and beating the appellant. Consequently, the appellant lodged a report at Police Station, Kottayam . The Police had warned the respondent. The respondent asked the appellant to give her ornaments amounting to Rs. 5,00,000 for keeping them in a bank locker and started beating the appellant.

The appellant also alleged that she did not have any physical or sexual relationship with the respondent after the marriage. He did not perform sexual intercourse with her. He had illicit relationship with other ladies. His first wife had committed suicide. The respondent was facing a charge punishable under Section 302[8] of IPC for murder of his first wife. The respondent had also threatened the appellant that he would commit suicide and falsely implicate her entire family. Being dissatisfied with the respondent, the appellant filed suit[9] under Section 13[10] of the Hindu

---

7   **Meaning of Respondent:** A **respondent** is a person who is called upon to issue a response to a communication made by another. In legal usage, this specifically refers to the defendant in a legal proceeding commenced by a petition, or to an appellee, or the opposing party, in an appeal of a decision by an initial fact-finder.

8   **Section 302, IPC 1860.**
    Punishment for murder.
    302. Punishment for murder.--Whoever commits murder shall be punished with death, or [imprisonment for life], and shall also be liable to fine.

9   **Meaning of Suit:**
    Generic term for any filing of a complaint (or petition) asking for legal redress by judicial action, often called a "lawsuit." In common parlance a suit asking for a court order for action rather than a money judgment is often called a "petition," but technically it is a "suit in equity."

10 **Section 13 in The Hindu Marriage Act, 1955**
    13. Divorce.

Marriage Act for seeking divorce against the respondent on the ground of cruelty and that both of them were living separately and there was no possibility of amicable settlement between them in future.

Decision of the Trail Court:

The Trial Court found that no case for divorce was made out and dismissed the petition. Being aggrieved by the judgment and decree[11] appeal was preferred in High Court.

Cruelty is a Ground for Divorce:

Cruelty is a ground of divorce under Section 13(1)(a) of the Hindu Marriage Act.

In *Dastane v. Dastane* [12], the Supreme Court has observed thus:

That where an allegation of cruelty is made, the inquiry in any case covered by that provision had to be whether the conduct charged as cruelty is of such a character as to cause in the mind of the petitioner[13] a reasonable

---

(1) Any marriage solemnized, whether before or after the commencement of this Act, may, on a petition presented by either the
husband or the wife, be dissolved by a decree of divorce on the ground that the other party-
(i) 1[has, after the solemnization of the marriage, had voluntary, sexual intercourse with any person other than his or her spouse; or
(ia) has, after the solemnization of the marriage, treated the petitioner with cruelty; or
(ib) has deserted the petitioner for a continuous period of not less than two years immediately preceding the presentation of the petition; or]
(ii) has ceased to be a Hindu by conversion to another religion; or
(iii) [has been incurably of unsound mind, or has been suffering continuously or intermittently from mental disorder of such a kind and to such an extent that the petitioner cannot reasonably be expected to live with the respondent. Explanation.- In this clause,-
(a) the expression" mental disorder" means mental illness, arrested or incomplete development of mind, psychopathic disorder or any other disorder or disability of mind and includes schizophrenia;
(b) the expression" psychopathic disorder" means a persistent disorder or disability of mind (whether or not including sub- normality of intelligence) which results in abnormally aggressive or seriously irresponsible conduct on the part of the other party, and whether or not it require or is susceptible to medical treatment; or]
(iv) has [been suffering from a virulent and incurable from of leprosy; or
(v) has [been suffering from venereal disease in a communicable from; or
(vi) has renounced the world by entering any religious order; or
(vii) has not been heard of as being alive for a period of seven years or more by those persons who would naturally have heard of it, had that party been alive.

11 **Meaning of Decree:**
   1. An authoritative order having the force of law.
   2. The judgment of a court of equity, admiralty, probate, or divorce.

12 II (1981) DMC 293 (SC) : AIR 1975 SC 1534

13 **Meaning of Petitioner**: A person who presents a petition (**Meaning of Petition**: A formal written application requesting a court for a specific judicial action)

apprehension that it will be harmful or injurious for the petitioner to live with the respondent. It was also pointed out that it was not necessary, as under the English Law, that the cruelty must be of such a character as to cause danger to life, limb or health, or as to give rise to a reasonable apprehension of such a danger though, of course, harm or injury to health, reputation, the working character or the like would be an important consideration in determining whether the conduct of the respondent amounts to cruelty or not. What was required was that the petitioner must prove that the respondent has treated the petitioner with such cruelty as to cause a reasonable apprehension in the mind of the petitioner that it will be harmful or injurious for the petitioner to live with the respondent.

It has been stated in the case of *Vinita Saxena v. Pankaj Pander*[14] , that non-consummation of marriage by itself constitutes mental cruelty and good ground to grant divorce.

Court also observed in *Rita Nijhawan v. Balkishan Nijhawan*[15] :

Matrimonial harmony, cohabitation and discharge of marital obligation by one spouse towards other is one of the most essential feature to keep matrimonial bond alive between the parties. When one of the spouses has totally withdrawn from the society of other as also either refusing to cohabit and/or denying to discharge his/her matrimonial obligation towards the other, it will be clear case of cruelty on the part of such spouse to whom such acts are attributable. Where the spouses are of normal physical and mental health, number of persistent refusal or inability of the sexual act would amount to cruelty. The marriage without vigorous sexual activity is an anathema. Denial of sexual activity in marriage has an extremely unfavourable influence on a wife's or husband's mind and body and leads to deprivation and frustration. There is nothing more fatal to a marriage than disappointment in sexual intercourse. To force a husband to such sexless life, which inevitably damages the physical as well as mental health is nothing, but cruelty?

In *Smt. Shakuntala Kumari v. Om Prakash Ghai*[16], it has been held thus:

A normal and healthy sexual relationship is one of the basic ingredients of a happy and harmonious marriage. If this is not possible due to ill-

14 AIR 2006 SC 1662
15 AIR 1973 Delhi 200
16 AIR 1981 Delhi 53

health on the part of one of the spouses, it may or may not amount to cruelty depending on the circumstances of the case. But willful denial of sexual relationship by a spouse when the other spouse is anxious for it would amount to mental cruelty, especially when the parties are young and newly married.

In *Smt. Maya v. Brij Nath* [17], while dealing with the concept of cruelty in the Hindu Marriage Act, the Court observed as under:

Cruelty has not been defined in the Act. But it is now well settled that the conduct should be grave and weighty so as to make cohabitation virtually unendurable. It must be more serious than the ordinary wear and tear of marriage. The cumulative conduct taking into consideration the circumstances and the background of the parties has to be examined to reach a conclusion whether the act amounts to cruelty. The petitioner in a divorce petition has to prove that he was treated with cruelty. The burden of proving the cruelty lies on him.

Decision of the High Court:

Court held that the respondent had not have any sexual intercourse with the appellant. This amounts to mental cruelty, apart from this there is ample evidence that the respondent treated the appellant with cruelty, therefore, the appellant successfully proved the ground of cruelty. On the basis of such ground she is entitled for a decree of divorce. The judgment and decree passed by the Trial Court was set aside.

---

17 AIR 1982 De 240

34

Woman be treated with proper respect and Dignity in Society[1]

Ratio Decidendi[2]: "Actions shall be taken in place, where woman are not treated with proper respect and dignity in society."

Facts in Nutshell:

Indian society's discrimination towards female child still exists due to various reasons which has its roots in the social behaviour and prejudices against the female child and, due to the evils of the dowry system, still prevailing in the society, in spite of its prohibition under the Dowry Prohibition Act. The decline in the female child ratio all over the country leads to an irresistible conclusion that the practice of eliminating female foetus by the use of pre-natal diagnostic techniques is widely prevalent in this country. Complaints are many, where at least few of the medical professionals do perform Sex Selective Abortion having full knowledge that the sole reason for abortion is because it is a female foetus. The provisions of the Medical Termination of Pregnancy Act, 1971 are also being consciously violated and misused.

The Parliament wanted to prevent the same and enacted the Pre-Conception and Pre-Natal Diagnostic Techniques (Prohibition on Sex-Selection) Act, 1994 (for short 'the Act') which has its roots in Article 15(2)[3] of the Constitution of India. The Act is a welfare legislation.

---

1   Appellants: **Voluntary Health Association of Punjab Vs.** Respondent: **Union of India (UOI) and Ors.**
2013(3)SCALE195
Hon'ble Judges/Coram: Dipak Misra and K.S. Panicker Radhakrishnan, JJ.

2   **Meaning of Ration Decidendi:** *Ratio decidendi* is a Latin phrase meaning "the reason" or "the rationale for the decision." The *ratio decidendi* is "the point in a case which determines the judgment" or "the principle which the case establishes."

3   **Article 15 in The Constitution Of India 1949**
15. Prohibition of discrimination on grounds of religion, race, caste, sex or place of birth
(1) The State shall not discriminate against any citizen on grounds only of religion, race, caste, sex, place of birth or any of them
(2) No citizen shall, on grounds only of religion, race, caste, sex, place of birth or any of them, be subject to any disability, liability, restriction or condition with regard to

The Parliament was fully conscious of the fact that the increasing imbalance between men and women leads to increased crime against women, trafficking, sexual assault, polygamy etc. Unfortunately, facts reveal that perpetrators of the crime also belong to the educated middle class and often they do not perceive the gravity of the crime.

Supreme Court, as early as, in 2001 in *Centre for Enquiry into Health and Allied Themes v. Union of India[4]* had noticed the misuse of the Act and gave various directions for its proper implementation.

Decline in Female Child Sex:

2011 Census of India, published by the Office of the Registrar General and Census Commissioner of India, would show a decline in female child sex ratio in many States of India from 2001-2011. The Annual Report on Registration of Births and Deaths - 2009, published by the Chief Registrar of NCT of Delhi would also indicate a sharp decline in the female sex ratio in almost all the Districts. Mushrooming of various Sonography Centres, Genetic Clinics, Genetic Counselling Centres, Genetic Laboratories, Ultrasonic Clinics, Imaging Centres in almost all parts of the country calls for more vigil and attention by the authorities under the Act. But, unfortunately, their functioning was not being properly monitored or supervised by the authorities under the Act or to find out whether they are misusing the pre-natal diagnostic techniques for determination of sex of foetus leading to foeticide[5].

In *Centre for Enquiry into Health and Allied Themes (CEHAT) and Ors. v. Union of India and Ors.[6]* , the two-Judge Bench commenced the judgment stating that the practice of female infanticide still prevails despite the fact that the gentle touch of a daughter and her voice has a soothing effect on the parents. The Court also commented on the immoral and unethical part of it as well as on the involvement of the qualified and unqualified doctors or compounders to abort the foetus of a girl child. Female foeticide has its roots in the social thinking which is fundamentally based on certain erroneous notions, ego-centric traditions, pervert perception of societal norms, and obsession with ideas which are totally individualistic sans

---

(a) access to shops, public restaurants, hotels and palaces of public entertainment; or
(b) the use of wells, tanks, bathing ghats, roads and places of public resort maintained wholly or partly out of State funds or dedicated to the use of the general public

4   (2001) 5 SCC 577

5   **Meaning of Foeticide:** The killing of a fetus; especially illegal abortion.

6   (2001) 5 SCC 577

the collective good. All involved in female foeticide deliberately forget to realize that when the foetus of a girl child is destroyed, a woman of future is crucified. To put it differently, the present generation invites the sufferings on its own and also sows the seeds of suffering for the future generation, as in the ultimate eventuate, the sex ratio gets affected and leads to manifold social problems.

When a female foeticide takes place, every woman who mothers the child must remember that she is killing her own child despite being a mother. That is what abortion would mean in social terms. Abortion of a female child in its conceptual eventuality leads to killing of a woman. Law prohibits it; scriptures forbid it; philosophy condemns it; ethics deprecate it, morality decries it and social science abhors it. Henrik Ibsen emphasized on the individualism of woman.

In **Madhu Kishwar v. State of Bihar** [7] the Court had stated that Indian women have suffered and are suffering discrimination in silence. Self-sacrifice and self-denial are their nobility and fortitude and yet they have been subjected to all inequities, indignities, inequality and discrimination. The way women had suffered has been aptly reflected by an author who has spoken with quite a speck of sensibility: -

Dowry is an intractable disease for women, a bed of arrows for annihilating self-respect, but without the boon of wishful death.

Awareness on Female Foeticide:

The authorities of the Government, the Non-Governmental Organisations and other volunteers are required to remember that there has to be awareness camps which are really effective. The people involved with the same must take it up as a service, a crusade. They must understand and accept that it is an art as well as a science and not simple arithmetic. It cannot take the colour of a routine speech. The awareness camps should not be founded on the theory of Euclidian geometry[8]. It must engulf the concept of social vigilance with an analytical mind and radiate into the marrows of the society. If awareness campaigns are not appositely conducted, the needed guidance for the people would be without

---

7   AIR 1996 SC 1864

8   **Meaning of Euclidian Geometry:**
    Euclidean geometry is a mathematical system attributed to the Alexandrian Greek mathematician Euclid, which he described in his textbook on geometry: the *Elements*. Euclid's method consists in assuming a small set of intuitively appealing axioms, and deducing many other propositions (theorems) from these.

meaning and things shall fall apart and everyone would try to take shelter in cynical escapism. It is difficult to precisely state how an awareness camp is to be conducted. It will depend upon what kind and strata of people are being addressed to. The persons involved in such awareness campaign are required to equip themselves with constitutional concepts, culture, philosophy, religion, scriptural commands and injunctions, the mandate of the law as engrafted under the Act and above all the development of modern science. It needs no special emphasis to state that in awareness camps while the deterrent facets of law are required to be accentuated upon, simultaneously the desirability of law to be followed with spiritual obeisance, regard being had to the purpose of the Act, has to be stressed upon. It should be clearly spelt out that female foeticide is the worst type of dehumanisation of the human race.

35

Cabaret dances and Obscenity[1]

Facts in Nutshell:

The petitioner[2] was being prosecuted[3] under S. 294[4] I. P. C. upon the allegation that on September 20, 1979, the petitioner along with three other women was performing cabaret dances in Delhi. They were wearing nothing except under wears and brassieres and were vibrating the various parts of their body. This was considered obscene because such type of dances injuriously affect the character of the people. The proprietor of the Restaurant and all the four women dancers have been summoned[5] by the learned Metropolitan Magistrate by his order which the petitioner challenged in petition.

Question before the Court:

The short question was whether such types of semi-nude dances are covered by S. 294 I. P. C. According to that section, "Whoever to the annoyance of others (a) does any obscene act in any public place, or (b) sings, recites or utters any obscene song, ballad or words, in or near any public place, shall be punished with imprisonment of either description for a term A which may extend to three months, or with fine, or with both."

---

1   Appellants: **Sadhna Vs.** Respondent: **State**
    (1982)ILR Delhi339
    Hon'ble Judges/Coram: M.L. Jain, J.

2   **Meaning of Petitioner:** A person who presents a Petition. (**Meaning of Petition:** A formal message requesting something that is submitted to an authority)

3   **Meaning of Prosecute:**
    a. To initiate civil or criminal court action against.
    b. To seek to obtain or enforce by legal action.

4   **Section 294 in The Indian Penal Code, 1860**
    294. [Obscene acts and songs.-- Whoever, to the annoyance of others,
    (a) does any obscene act in any public place, or
    (b) sings, recites or utters any obscene song, ballad or words, in or near any public place, shall be punished with imprisonment of either description for a term which may extend to three months, or with fine, or with both.]

5   **Meaning of Summoned:** To order to appear in court by the issuance of a summons.

Obscenity:

According to *Ranjit D.. Udeshi v. The State of Maharashtra*[6], the test of obscenity is whether the tendency of the matter charged as obscenity is to deprave and corrupt those whose minds are open to immoral influences, but the test of obscenity must agree with the freedom of speech and expression guaranteed under our Constitution. Therefore, sex and nudity in art and literature cannot be regarded as evidence of obscenity without something more. In *Chandrakant Kalyandas Kakodhit v. The State of Maharashtra and others*[7], it was observed that it is a duty of the court to consider the obscene matter by taking an overall view. The concept of obscenity would differ from country to country depending on the standards of morals of contemporary society. What is considered as a piece of literature in, France may be obscene in England and what is considered in both countries as not harmful to public order and morals, may be obscene in our country.

In Chandrakant (supra), the Supreme Court observed that the standards of contemporary society in India are also fast changing. The adults and adolescents have available to them a large number of classics, novels, stories and pieces of literature which have a content of sex, love and romance. In the field of art and cinema also the adolescent is shown situations which even a quarter of century ago would be considered derogatory to public morality, but having regard to changed conditions, are more taken for granted without in any way tending to debase or debauch the mind.

In *State of Maharashtra v. Joyce Zee alias Temiko*[8], the dancers entered smoking on the heads of the customers, danced for some time and then invited, them to remove their clothes fill they were left in panties, They went round the tables', Swished their backs and breasts against the customers, pushed their nipples in the mouths of some and imitated sexual acts. And yet the High Court of Bombay held that no offence under S. 294 was made out. The learned Judge observed that if the State wants to prohibit such cabaret, shows as wrongful exploitation of sex or as socially harmful or indecent, it may enact some special legislation.

---

6   1965 (2) Cri.L. J. 8

7   1970CriLJ1273

8   (1975) 77 B. R. L. J. 218

Decision of the High Court:

Court held that where cabaret shows are prominently advertised people book their seats often in advance and pay excessively to attend those shows for hours with hundreds like them, it would not be possible to convict a cabaret dancer merely because a section of the people not attending such shows equate them, perhaps rightly, with pornography, and feel annoyed and disturbed at the level of entertainment made accessible so openly. Cabarets are shown all over the world and unless there is a special legislation to ban them, it will be a misuse of S. 294 I. P. C., to punish the entertainers and organizers of such shows.

36

Obscenity and Pornography[1]

Facts in Nutshell:

Petitioner[2] approached High Court and seeks to quash[3] the complaint filed by the police against him for offence Under Sections 3[4], 4[5] and 6[6] of the Indecent Representation of Women (Prohibition) Act, 1986, hereinafter referred to as 'the Act' and Section 292-A[7], IPC.

---

1 Appellants: **P.K. Somanath Vs.** Respondent: **State of Kerala and Ors.**
   1990CriLJ542
   Hon'ble Judges/Coram: K. Sreedharan, J.

2 **Meaning of Petitioner:** A person who presents a Petition. (**Meaning of Petition:** A formal message requesting something that is submitted to an authority)

3 **Meaning of Quash:** To annul or set aside. In law, a motion to quash asks the judge for an order setting aside or nullifying an action, such as "quashing" service of a summons when the wrong person was served.

4 **Section 3: Prohibition of advertisements containing indecent representation of women** - No person shall publish, or cause to be published, or arrange or take part in the publication or exhibition of, any advertisement which contains indecent representation of women in any form.

5 **Section 4: Prohibition of publication or sending by post of books, pamphlets, etc. containing indecent representation of women**- No person shall produce or cause to be produced, sell, let to hire, distribute, circulate or send by post any book, pamphlet, paper, slide, film, writing, drawing, painting, photograph, representation or figure which contains indecent representation of women in any

6 **Section 6: Penalty** - Any person who contravenes the provisions of section 3 or section 4 shall be punishable on first conviction with imprisonment of either description for a term which may extend to two years, and with fine which may extend to two thousand rupees, and in the event of a second or subsequent conviction with imprisonment for terms of not less than six months but which may extend to five years and also with a fine not less than ten thousand rupees but which may extend to one lakh rupees.

7 **Indian Penal Code, 1860**
   292A. Printing, etc., of grossly indecent or scurrilous matter or matter intended for blackmail
   Whoever,-
   (a) prints or causes to be printed in any newspaper, periodical or circular, or exhibits or causes to be exhibited, to public view or distributes or causes to be distributed or in any manner puts into circulation any picture or any printed or written document which is grossly indecent, or in scurrilous or intended for blackmail; or
   (b) sells or lets for hire, or for purposes of sale or hire makes, produces or has in his possession, any picture or any printed or written document which is grossly indecent or is scurrilous or intended for blackmail; or
   (c) conveys any picture or any printed or written document which is grossly indecent or is scurrilous or intended for blackmail knowing or having reason to believe that such picture or document will be printed, sold, let for hire distributed or publicly exhibited or in any manner put into circulation; or

Petitioner, the Printer and Publisher of a Cinema Magazine by name, 'Love'. The issue of that magazine dated 15-11-1988 contained photographs which depicted as indecent representation of women. On getting information of that publication, Sub Inspector of Police searched the premises of accused and seized two issues of the magazine, 'Love'. It was alleged that the petitioner committed the offences mentioned earlier in publishing that issue of 'Love'.

Question before the Court:

The question that arises for consideration was whether the publication was obscene Under Section 292-A, IPC or whether it contains indecent representation of women as coming within the purview of the Act.

Obscenity:

The word 'obscene' has not been defined in the Indian Penal Code or in the Act. Courts were deciding the question as to whether a publication is obscene or not, by resorting to the test laid down by Cockburn, C.J., in famous Hicklin's case[8] . The test of obscenity in the learned Judge's words is "I think the test of obscenity is this, whether the tendency of the matter charged as obscenity is to deprave and corrupt those whose minds are open to such immoral influences, and into whose hands a publication of this sort may fall x x x x x it is quite certain that it would suggest to the minds, of the young of either sex, or even to persons of more advanced years, thoughts of a most impure and libidinous character."

(d) takes part in, or receives profits from, any business in the course of which he knows or has reason to believe that any such newspaper, periodical, circular, picture or other printed or written document is printed, exhibited, distributed, circulated, sold. let for hire, made, produced, kept, conveyed or purchased.. or

(e) advertises or makes known by any means whatsoever that any person is engaged or is ready to engage in any Act which is an offence under this section, or that any such newspaper, periodical, circular, picture or other printed or written document which is grossly indecent or is scurrilous or intended for blackmail, can be procured from or through any person; or

(f) offers or attempts to do any act which is an offence under this section [shall be punished with imprisonment of either description for a term which may extend to two years, or with fine, or with both]:

Provided that for a second or any subsequent offence under this section, he shall be punished with imprisonment of either description for a term which shall not be less than six months [and not more than two years].

8   (1868-3 QB 360)

In *Ranjit. D. Udeshi v. State of Maharashtra*[9] Hidayathullah, J., (as he then was) speaking for the Constitution Bench observed (Para 21):

"The Court must, therefore, apply itself to consider each work at a time. This should not, of course, be done in the spirit of the lady who charged Dr. Johnson with putting improper words in his Dictionary and was rebuked by him. "Madam, you must have been looking for them". To adopt such an attitude towards Art and Literature would make the Courts a Board of Censors. An overall view of the obscene matter in setting of the whole work would, of course, be necessary, but the obscene matter must be considered by itself and separately to find out whether it is so gross and its obscenity so decided that it is likely to deprave and corrupt those whose minds are open to influences of this sort and into whose hands the book is likely to fall. In this connection the interests of our contemporary society and particularly the influence of the book etc. On it must not be overlooked. A number of considerations may here enter which it is not necessary to enumerate, but we must draw attention to one fact. Today our National and Regional Languages are strengthening themselves by new literary standards after a deadening period under the impact of English. Emulation by our writers of an obscene book under the aegis of this Court's determination is likely to pervert our entire literature because obscenity pays and true art finds little popular support. Only an obscurant will deny the need for such caution. This consideration marches with all law and precedent on this subject and so considered we can only say that where obscenity and art are mixed, art must be so preponderating as to throw the obscenity into a shadow or the obscenity so trivial and insignificant that it can have no effect and may be overlooked. In other words, treating with sex in a manner offensive to public decency and morality (and these are the words of our fundamental Law), judged of by our National standards and considered likely to pander to lascivious, prurient or sexually precocious minds, must determine the result. We need not attempt to bowdlerize all literature and thus rob speech and expression of freedom. A balance should be maintained between freedom of speech and expression and public decency and morality but when the latter is substantially transgressed the former must give way."

The verdict as to whether the book or article or photographs printed therein, considered as a whole, panders to the prurient and is obscene must be judged by the Court[10]. For considering that question, it is not

9   AIR 1965 SC 881 : (1965 (2) Cri LJ 8)

10   *C. K. v. State of Maharashtra* AIR 1970 SC 1390 : (1970 Cri LJ 1273).

necessary for court to examine or compare the publication with reference to any other magazines, books or story. The court is to adjudicate on it, on the basis of well established notions of decency and morality.

As observed by the Supreme Court, the concept of obscenity would differ from country to country depending on the standards of morals and contemporary society. What is considered as a piece of literature in a foreign country may be obscene in our country. Even standards of contemporary society in India are fast changing. The adults and adolescents have available to them a large number of classics, novels, stories and pieces of literature which contain sex, love and romance. If reference to sex by itself is considered as obscene no book can be sold except which are purely religious. In the field of cinema the adolescents are shown situations which even a quarter of a century ago would have been considered derogatory to public morality. Having regard to the changed conditions more such scenes are taken for granted without in any way tending to debase or debauch the mind. What the courts have to see is whether a class into whose hands the book falls suffer in their moral outlook or became depraved by reading it or might have impure and lacherous thoughts aroused in their minds[11].

In judging the question of obscenity the judge should place himself in the position of a reader of every age group in whose hands the book is likely to fall and should try to appreciate what kind of possible influence the book is likely to create in the minds of readers. He should apply his judicial mind dispassionately to decide whether the publication in question can be said to be obscene within the meaning of Section 292 IPC by an objective assessment of the whole book. In *Samaresh Bose v. Amal Mitra*[12] , their Lordships of the Supreme Court stated (para 34):

"A vulgar writing is not necessarily obscene. Vulgarity arouses a feeling of disgust and revulsion and also boredom but does not have the effect of depraving, debasing and corrupting the morals of any reader of the novel, whereas obscenity has the tendency to deprave and corrupt those whose minds are open to such immoral influences."

Their Lordships went on to state (para 34):

"If a reference to sex by itself in any novel is considered to be obscene and not fit to be read by adolescents, adolescents will not be in a position

---

11 *Chandrakant v. State of Maharashtra*, AIR 1970 SC 1390 : (1970 Cri LJ 1273).

12 MANU/SC/0102/1985

to read any novel and will have to read books which are purely religious".

Obscenity and Pornography:

There is difference between obscenity, and pornography. The latter denotes writings, pictures etc. intended to arouse sexual desire. While obscenity includes writings etc. not intended to do so but which have that tendency. Both offend public decency and morals. Pornography is obscenity in a more aggravated form. Among all the creatures of nature human beings are the most refined ones. Male species of all types of animals and birds are considered more beautiful than their respective females. But in literature, ladies are described as beautiful. A pretty damsel is beautiful to behold. A thing of beauty is a joy for ever. Are the bodies of females obscene? A brazenly nude body may evoke a feeling of disgust and revolution. If nudity is properly covered, human body whether of male or female cannot be regarded as objects of obscenity without something more. That something more is to be found in the facial expression or pose in which it is photographed. The photograph of a female body, cannot be considered as obscene or as an indecent representation of woman, if the above mentioned something more is absent.

Decision of the High Court:

Court held that the magazine contained photograph of a lady as its centre-spread. Lower portion of one of her thighs and cleavage are exposed. Facial expression is not at all provocative. The lady has properly covered her nudity. This photograph has not got the effect of arousing sexual feelings in an ordinary human being. Nor has it got the effect of depraving or corrupting the minds of those who are open to influence and into whose hands the magazine is likely to fall. The impugned publication contains photographs of ladies on pages 11, 14, 15, 22 and 23. In those photographs the models are seen with dress which can be described as an apology for a dress. The pose, facial expression and lay out are certainly objectionable and provocative. Those pictures, prima facie, come within the mischief of the provisions contained in the Act. Therefore Court held the impugned publication offended the provisions of the Act.

37

Artistic Freedom and Obscenity[1]

Facts in Nutshell:

Petitions[2] challenge the summoning[3] orders against the petitioner[4] arise from such a contemporary painting celebrating **nudity** made by an accomplished painter/petitioner. The said painting depicts India in an abstract and graphical representation of a woman in **nude** with her hair flowing in the form of Himalayas displaying her agony. It was stated that the said painting was sold to a private collector in the year 2004 and that the petitioner did not deal with the same in any manner whatsoever after sale. Subsequently in the year 2006, the said painting entitled "Bharat Mata" was advertised as part of an on-line auction for charity for Kashmir earthquake victims organized by a non-governmental organisation with which the petitioner claimed to have no involvement. It was stated that the petitioner at no point in time had given a title to the said painting. The advertisement of the said painting led to large scale protests for which the petitioner also had to tender an apology.

Art and Nudity:

Pablo Picasso, a renowned artist said, "Art is never chaste. It ought to be forbidden to ignorant innocents, never allowed into contact with those not sufficiently prepared. Yes, art is dangerous. Where it is chaste, it is not art." Art, to every artist, is a vehicle for personal expression. An aesthetic work of art has the vigour to connect to an individual sensory, emotionally, mentally and spiritually. With a 5000-year-old culture, Indian Art has been rich in its tapestry of ancient heritage right from the medieval times to the contemporary art adorned today with each painting having a story to narrate.

---

1 Appellants: **Maqbool Fida Husain Vs.** Respondent: **Raj Kumar Pandey**
   2008CriLJ4107
   Hon'ble Judges/Coram: Sanjay Kishan Kaul, J.

2 **Meaning of Petition:** A formal written application requesting a court for a specific judicial action

3 **Meaning of Summon:** To order to appear in court by the issuance of a summons

4 **Meaning of Petitioner:** A person who presents a Petition. (**Meaning of Petition:** A formal message requesting something that is submitted to an authority)

Ancient Indian art has been never devoid of eroticism where sex worship and graphical representation of the union between man and woman has been a recurring feature. The sculpture on the earliest temples of 'Mithuna' image or the erotic couple in Bhubeneshwar, Konarak and Puri in Orissa (150-1250 AD); Khajuraho in Madhya Pradesh (900-1050 AD); Limbojimata temple at Delmel, Mehsana (10th Century AD); Kupgallu Hill, Bellary, Madras; and Nilkantha temple at Sunak near Baroda to name a few. These and many other figures are taken as cult figures in which rituals related to Kanya and Kumari worship for progeny gained deep roots in early century A.D. Even the very concept of 'Lingam' of the God Shiva resting in the centre of the Yoni, is in a way representation of the act of creation, the union of Prakriti and Purusua. The ultimate essence of a work of ancient Indian erotic art has been religious in character and can be enunciated as a state of heightened delight or ananda, the kind of bliss that can be experienced only by the spirit.

Today Indian art is confidently coming of age. Every form of stylistic expression in the visual arts, from naturalism to abstract expressionism derives its power from the artist's emotional connection to his perceptual reality. The Nude in contemporary art, a perennial art subject, considered to be the greatest challenges in art has still not lost its charm and focuses on how the human form has been re-interpreted by the emerging and influential artists today. The paintbrush has become a powerful tool of expression as the pen is for some, and has thus occasionally come under the line of fire for having crossed the 'Lakshman Rekha' and for plunging into the forbidden, which is called 'obscene', 'vulgar', 'depraving', 'prurient' and 'immoral'. No doubt this form of art is a reflection of a very alluring concept of beauty and there is certainly something more to it than pearly 'flesh' but what needs to be determined is which art falls under the latter category.

India has embraced different eras and civilizations which have given her a colour of mystery and transformed into her glorious past adapting various cultures and art forms. In the Mughal period too one may see murals and miniatures depicting mating couples. That has been the beauty of our land. Art and authority have never had a difficult relationship until recently. In fact, art and artists used to be patronized by various kings and the elite class. It is very unfortunate that the works of many artists today who have tried to play around with nudity have come under scrutiny and have had to face the music which has definitely made the artists to think twice before exhibiting their work of art. Therefore, looking at a piece of art from the painters' perspective becomes very important especially in the context of nudes. What needs to be seen is that the work is not sensational for the sake of being so and hence needs to be understood before any objections are raised. The courts have been grappling with the problem of balancing the individuals' right to speech and expression and the frontiers of exercising that right. The aim has been to arrive at a decision that would protect the "quality of life" without making "closed mind" a principal feature of an open society or an unwilling recipient of information the arbiter to veto or restrict freedom of speech and expression.

Obscenity:

The general law of obscenity in India can be found in Section 292[5] of the

---

5 **Section 292 in The Indian Penal Code, 1860**
292. [Sale, etc., of obscene books, etc.-- [(1) For the purposes of sub- section (2), a book, pamphlet, paper, writing, drawing, painting representation, figure or any other object, shall be deemed to be obscene if it is lascivious or appeals to the prurient interest or if its effect, or (where it comprises two or more distinct items) the effect of any one of its items, is, if taken as a whole, such as to tend to deprave and corrupt persons who are likely, having regard to all relevant circumstances, to read, see or hear the matter contained or embodied in it.]
(2) 3[ ] Whoever-
(a) sells, lets to hire, distributes, publicly exhibits or in any manner puts into circulation, or for purposes of sale, hire, distribution, public exhibition or circulation, makes, reduces or has in his possession any obscene book, pamphlet, paper, drawing, painting, representation or figure or any other obscene object whatsoever, or
(b) imports, exports or conveys any obscene object for any of the purposes aforesaid, or knowing or having reason to believe that such object will be sold, let to hire, distributed or publicly exhibited or in any manner put into circulation, or
(c) takes part in or receives profits from any business in the course of which he knows or has reason to believe that any such obscene objects are, for any of the purposes aforesaid, made, produced, purchased, kept, imported, exported, conveyed, publicly exhibited or in any manner put into circulation, or
(d) advertises or makes known by any means whatsoever that any person is engaged or is ready to engage in any act which is an offence under this section, or that any such obscene object can be procured from or through any person, or
(e) offers or attempts to do any act which is an offence under this section, shall be punished 1[on first conviction with imprisonment of either description for a term which may extend to two years, and with fine which may extend to two thousand rupees, and, in the event of a second or subsequent conviction, with imprisonment of either description for a term which may extend to five years, and also with fine which may extend to five thousand rupees]. [Exception- This section does not extend to-
(a) any book, pamphlet, paper, writing, drawing, painting, representation or figure-
(i) the publication of which is proved to be justified as being for the public good on the ground that such book, pamphlet, paper, writing, drawing, painting, representation or figure is in the interest of science, literature, art or learning or other objects of general concern, or
(ii) which is kept or used bona fide for religious purposes;
(b) any representation sculptured, engraved, painted or otherwise represented on or in-
(i) any ancient monument within the meaning of the Ancient Monuments and Archaeological Sites and Remains Act, 1958 (24 of 1958), or

Indian Penal Code, 1860. Section 292 IPC was enacted by the Obscene Publications Act to give effect to Article I of the International Convention for suppression of or traffic in obscene publications to which India is a signatory. By Act 36 of 1969, Section 292 was amended to give more precise meaning to the word 'obscene' as used in the section in addition to creating an exception for publication of matter which is proved to be justified as being for the public good, being in the interest of science, literature, art or learning or other objects of general concern. Prior to its amendment, Section 292 contained no definition of obscenity. The amendment also literally does not provide for a definition of 'obscenity' inasmuch as it introduces a deeming provision.

On a bare reading of Sub-section (1) of Section 292 it is obvious that a book etc. shall be deemed to be obscene (i) if it is lascivious; (ii) it appeals to the prurient interest, and (iii) it tends to deprave and corrupt persons who are likely to read, see or hear the matter alleged to be obscene. It is only once the impugned matter is found to be obscene that the question of whether the impugned matter falls within any of the exceptions contained in the section would arise.

Section 67 of the Information Technology Act, 2000 relevant for the subject under discussion reads as follows:

67. Publishing of information which is obscene in electronic form.-- Whoever publishes or transmits or causes to be published in the electronic form, any material which is lascivious or appeals to the prurient interest or if its effect is such as to tend to deprave and corrupt persons who are likely, having regard to all relevant circumstances, to read, see or hear the matter contained or embodied in it, shall be punished on first conviction with imprisonment of either description for a term which may extend to five years and with fine which may extend to one lakh rupees and in the event of a second or subsequent conviction with imprisonment of either description for a term which may extend to ten years and also with fine which may extend to two lakh rupees.

Thus Section 67 is the first statutory provisions dealing with obscenity on the Internet. It must be noted that the both under the Indian Penal Code, 1860 and the Information Technology Act, 2000 the test to determine obscenity is similar. Therefore, it is necessary to understand the broad parameters of the law laid down by the courts in India, in order to

(ii) any temple, or on any car used for the conveyance of idols, or kept or used for any religious purpose.]

determine "obscenity".

The Indian Penal Code on obscenity has grown out of the English Law and while interpreting the meaning of "obscenity" the Supreme Court in *Ranjit D. Udeshi v. State of Maharashtra*[6] uniformly adopted the test laid down by the English Court in Hicklins case[7] wherein it was held that the word "obscene" in the section is not limited to writings, pictures etc. intended to arouse sexual desire. At the same time, the mere treating with sex and nudity in art and literature is not per se evidence of obscenity. It was emphasized that the work as a whole must be considered, the obscene matter must be considered by itself and separately to find out whether it is so gross and its obscenity so decided that it is likely to deprave and corrupt those whose minds are open to influences of this sort. Where art and obscenity are mixed, art must so preponderate as to throw the obscenity out into the shadow or the obscenity so trivial and insignificant that it can have no effect and may be overlooked. The Courts explained that the Hicklin's test does not emphasize merely on stray words, as the words are "matters charged" and to that extent it must be held to secundum subjectum materiam, that is to say, applicable to the matter there considered. Thus, the court must apply itself to consider each work at a time.

It was further observed that there exists a distinction between "obscenity" and "pornography", while later consists of pictures, writings etc. which are intended to arouse sexual feelings whereas the former consists of writings etc. which though are not intended to arouse sexual feelings but definitely has that tendency.

In *Shri Chandrakant Kalyandas Kakodkar v. The State of Maharashtra* [8] which case relates to articles and pictures in the magazine being alleged to be obscene and calculated to corrupt and deprave the minds of the reader, the courts reiterated the ratio as was laid down in Ranjit Udeshi's case (supra) and held that the concept of obscenity would differ from country to country depending on the contemporary standards of the society. But to insist that the standard should always be for the writer to see that the adolescent ought not to be brought into contact with

---

6   1965CriLJ8

7   The Hicklin's rule allowed a publication to be judged for obscenity based on isolated passages of a work considered out of context and judged by their apparent influence on most susceptible readers, such as children or weak-minded adults.

8   1970CriLJ1273

sex or that if they read any references to sex in what is written whether that is the dominant theme or not, they would be affected, would be to require authors to write books only for the adolescent and not for the adults. It was held that with the standards of contemporary society in india fast changing, the adults and adolescents have available to them a large number of pieces of literature which have a content of sex, love and romance and if a reference to sex by itself is considered obscene, no books could be sold except those which are purely religious. Thus, what one has to see is whether a class, not an isolated case, into whose hands the book, article or story falls suffer in their moral outlook or become depraved by reading it or might have impure and lecherous thought aroused in their minds.

In *Samaresh Bose v. Amal Mitra*[9] the courts while distinguishing between vulgarity and obscenity held that "vulgarity" may arouse a feeling of revulsion, disgust and even boredom but unlike "pornography" or "obscenity" do not have the tendency to corrupt or deprave the minds of a person. In addition to the above, the court observed that for the purposes of judging obscenity, firstly the judge must place himself in the position of the author in order to appreciate what the author really wishes to convey, and thereafter he must place himself in the position of the reader of every age group in whose hands the book is likely to fall and then arrive at a dispassionate conclusion.

The court in *Sada Nand and Ors. v. State (Delhi Administration)*[10] laid down the test to the affect that the pictures of a nude/semi-nude woman cannot per se be called obscene unless the same are suggestive of deprave mind and are designed to excite sexual passion in the persons who are likely to look at them or see them. This will depend on the particular posture and the background in which a nude semi-nude woman is shown.

Contemporary standards:

In judging as to whether a particular work is obscene, regard must be had to contemporary mores and national standards. While the Supreme Court of India held Lady Chatterley's Lover to be obscene, in England the jury in the case of *R v. Penguin Books, Ltd.*[11] acquitted[12] the publishers

---

9 1986CriLJ24

10 (1986) 2 Delhi 81

11 (1961) Cri L.R. 176

12 **Meaning of Acquittal:** In the common law tradition, an **acquittal** formally certifies that the

finding that the publication did not fall foul of the obscenity test. This was heralded as a turning point in the fight for literary freedom in UK. "Community mores and standards" played a part in the Indian Supreme Court taking a different view from the English jury. Judging the work as a whole. A holistic view must thus be taken apart from a closer scrutiny of the impugned subject to come to a conclusion whether the same is grossly obscene and likely to deprave and corrupt.

Decision of the High Court:

Court held that it may be said that education broadens the horizons of the people and means to acquire knowledge to enhance one's ability to reason and make a sound judgment. However, when one is instructed to only view things in a certain manner, regardless of truth and facts, this is actually a form of programming - not education. There are very few people with a gift to think out of the box and seize opportunities and therefore such peoples' thoughts should not be curtailed by the age old moral sanctions of a particular section in the society having oblique or collateral motives who express their dissent at the every drop of a hat. The society instead should be engaged in more meaningful activities which would go to show the importance of education over plain literacy. The summoning orders and warrants[13] of arrest issued against the petitioner in the complaint cases were quashed.

---

accused is free from the charge of an offense, as far as the criminal law is concerned.

13 **Meaning of Warrant:** A judicial writ authorizing an officer to make a search, seizure, or arrest or to execute a judgment.

38

Internet and Pornographic Material[1]

Facts in Nutshell:

An Internet website carried a listing which offered for sale a video clip, shot on a mobile phone, of two children of a school in Delhi indulging in an explicitly sexual act. The petitioner[2], who was the Managing Director (MD) of the company that owned the website at the relevant point in time, asks   Court to annul his criminal prosecution[3] for the offences of making available for sale and causing to be published an obscene product within the meaning of Section 292[4] Indian Penal Code (IPC) and

---

1   Appellants: **Avnish Bajaj Vs.** Respondent: **State**
    2008(105)DRJ721
    Hon'ble Judges/Coram: S. Muralidhar, J.

2   **Meaning of Petitioner:** A person who presents a Petition. (**Meaning of Petition:** A formal message requesting something that is submitted to an authority)

3   **Meaning of Prosecution:**
    a. the institution and carrying on of legal proceedings against a person.
    b. the officials who institute and conduct such proceedings.

4   **Section 292 in The Indian Penal Code, 1860**
    292. [Sale, etc., of obscene books, etc.-- [(1) For the purposes of sub- section (2), a book, pamphlet, paper, writing, drawing, painting representation, figure or any other object, shall be deemed to be obscene if it is lascivious or appeals to the prurient interest or if its effect, or (where it comprises two or more distinct items) the effect of any one of its items, is, if taken as a whole, such as to tend to deprave and corrupt persons who are likely, having regard to all relevant circumstances, to read, see or hear the matter contained or embodied in it.]
    (2) 3[ ] Whoever-
    (a) sells, lets to hire, distributes, publicly exhibits or in any manner puts into circulation, or for purposes of sale, hire, distribution, public exhibition or circulation, makes, reduces or has in his possession any obscene book, pamphlet, paper, drawing, painting, representation or figure or any other obscene object whatsoever, or
    (b) imports, exports or conveys any obscene object for any of the purposes aforesaid, or knowing or having reason to believe that such object will be sold, let to hire, distributed or publicly exhibited or in any manner put into circulation, or
    (c) takes part in or receives profits from any business in the course of which he knows or has reason to believe that any such obscene objects are, for any of the purposes aforesaid, made, produced, purchased, kept, imported, exported, conveyed, publicly exhibited or in any manner put into circulation, or
    (d) advertises or makes known by any means whatsoever that any person is engaged or is ready to engage in any act which is an offence under this section, or that any such obscene object can be procured from or through any person, or
    (e) offers or attempts to do any act which is an offence under this section, shall be punished 1[

~ 189 ~

Section 67[5] of the Information Technology Act 2000 (IT Act). This petition[6] under Section 482[7] of the Code of Criminal Procedure 1973 ('CrPC') also raised questions concerning the criminal liability of directors for the offences attributable to a company, both under the IPC as well as the IT Act, particularly when such company was not arraigned as an accused.

Baazee.com India Private Limited ('BIPL'), a wholly owned subsidary of Ebay Inc. USA, and the owner of the website http://www.baazee.com, was during the relevant period in the process of being acquired by and consequently renamed as Ebay India Private Limited (EIPL). The website baazee.com provided an online platform or market where a seller and a buyer could interact. To be either a seller or buyer a person had to first register himself with baazee.com by filling out an online form giving details including the name, email id, date of birth (the age had to be 18 and above).

A fourth year student of the Indian Institute of Technology (IIT) Kharagpur, was registered as a seller with baazee.com since 21st July 2004. He had

---

on first conviction with imprisonment of either description for a term which may extend to two years, and with fine which may extend to two thousand rupees, and, in the event of a second or subsequent conviction, with imprisonment of either description for a term which may extend to five years, and also with fine which may extend to five thousand rupees]. [Exception- This section does not extend to-
(a) any book, pamphlet, paper, writing, drawing, painting, representation or figure-
(i) the publication of which is proved to be justified as being for the public good on the ground that such book, pamphlet, paper, writing, drawing, painting, representation or figure is in the interest of science, literature, art or learning or other objects of general concern, or
(ii) which is kept or used bona fide for religious purposes;
(b) any representation sculptured, engraved, painted or otherwise represented on or in-
(i) any ancient monument within the meaning of the Ancient Monuments and Archaeological Sites and Remains Act, 1958 (24 of 1958), or
(ii) any temple, or on any car used for the conveyance of idols, or kept or used for any religious purpose.]

5 **Section 67 in The Information Technology Act, 2000**
67. Publishing of information which is obscene in electronic form.- Whoever publishes or transmits or causes to be published in the electronic form, any material which is lascivious or appeals to the prurient interest or if its effect is such as to tend t deprave and corrupt persons who are likely, having regard to all relevant circumstances, to read, see or hear the matter contained or embodied in it, shall be punished on first conviction with imprisonment of either description for a term which may exte d to five years and with fine which may extend to one lakh rupees and in the event of a second or subsequent conviction with imprisonment of either description for a term which may extend to ten years and also with fine which may extend to two lakh rupees.

6 **Meaning of Petition:** A formal message requesting something that is submitted to an authority

7 **Section 482 in The Code Of Criminal Procedure, 1973**
482. Saving of inherent powers of High Court. Nothing in this Code shall be deemed to limit or affect the inherent powers of the High Court to make such orders as may be necessary to give effect to any order under this Code, or to prevent abuse of the process of any Court or otherwise to secure the ends of justice.

already been using the site for listing products for sale. In the evening of Saturday 27th November 2004, he placed on the baazee.com website a listing offering an MMS video clip for sale at Rs. 125 per piece. In order to avoid detection by the filters installed by baazee.com, Ravi Raj included the clip under the category Books and Magazines and sub-category 'e-books'. Although baazee.com did have a filter for some of the words which appear on the website, the listing nevertheless took place. The buyer interested in getting a copy had to click on the 'buy now' option, make a payment through credit card or 'paisa pay' option. The buyer had to pay Rs. 128 per clip which included a commission of Rs.3 that went to BIPL. This was deducted from the amount received from the buyer and the balance of Rs. 125 per clip was remitted to the seller by the HDFC bank. The seller, on receiving confirmation that payment had been made, would send the video clip by an email attachment by a zip file with the description 'dps_rkpuram-sex-scandle.zip'.

On 29th November 2004 baazee.com wrote to Alice Electronics that it had noticed "that the listings put up on site are either obscene or pornographic in nature" and that the Baazee User Agreement prohibits trade in such items. It accordingly informed the seller "we have closed the item as it is against the User Agreement." The video clip was removed on 29th November 2004.

The Crime Branch of Delhi police, on receiving credible information that the said MMS clip was sold for Rs. 125 by a website, registered FIR .

Internet and Pornography:

The regulation of pornography on the internet has posed a serious challenge to governments and legislatures primarily on account of the nature of the medium. The easy availability, even to children, of pornographic material in digital form including video clips, its rapid transmission across the world wide web, and the absence of effective filters to screen out objectionable material from being accessed are factors that compound the challenge. It is said that "controlling pornography on the internet is problematic because we may not know from whom or from where the material originates, how many people are receiving the information, or if the material is crossing international boundaries.[8]

---

8 [See Robyn Forman Pollack, "Creating the Standards of a Global Community: Regulating Pornography on the Internet- an International Concern" 10 Temple International and Comparative Law Journal, (Fall, 1996) 467].

Decision of Metropolitan Magistrate:

The learned Metropolitan Magistrate (MM) by an order dated 14th February 2006 took cognizance of the offences under Sections 292 and 294[9] IPC and Section 67 IT Act. Petition was filed by Avnish Bajaj, the MD of BIPL (EIPL) seeking the quashing of the criminal proceedings on various grounds in High Court

Decision of Delhi High Court:

Court held that the case against the petitioner for the offences under Sections 292 and 294 IPC was quashed[10], prima facie a case is made out against the petitioner for the offence under Section 67 read with Section 85[11] of IT Act.

Court Observation: As this case reveals, the law in our country is not adequate to meet the challenge of regulating the use of the internet to prevent dissemination of pornographic material. It may be useful to look at the legislative response in other common law jurisdictions. In the United

---

9   **Section 294 in The Indian Penal Code, 1860**
    294. [Obscene acts and songs.-- Whoever, to the annoyance of others,
    (a) does any obscene act in any public place, or
    (b) sings, recites or utters any obscene song, ballad or words, in or near any public place, shall be punished with imprisonment of either description for a term which may extend to three months, or with fine, or with both.]

10 **Meaning of Quash:** To annul or set aside. In law, a motion to quash asks the judge for an order setting aside or nullifying an action, such as "quashing" service of a summons when the wrong person was served.

11 **Section 85 of IT Act, 2000**
    85. Offences by companies.
    (1) Where a person committing a contravention of any of the provisions of this Act or of any rule, direction or order made thereunder is a company, every person who, at the time the contravention was committed, was in charge of, and was responsible to, the company for the conduct of business of the company as well as the company, shall be
    guilty of the contravention and shall be liable to be proceeded against and punished accordingly: Provided that nothing contained in this sub-section shall render any such person liable to punishment if he proves that the contravention took place without his knowledge or that he exercised all due diligence to prevent such contravention.
    (2) Notwithstanding anything contained in sub-section (1), where a contravention of any of the provisions of this Act or of any rule, direction or order made thereunder has been committed by a company and it is proved that the contravention has taken place with the consent or connivance of, or is attributable to any neglect on the part of, any director, manager, secretary or other officer of the company, such director, manager, secretary or other officer shall also be deemed to be guilty of the contravention and shall be liable to be proceeded against and punished accordingly.
    Explanation.—For the purposes of this section,—
    (i) "company" means any body corporate and includes a firm or other association of individuals; and
    (ii) "director", in relation to a firm, means a partner in the firm.

States, there have been three legislations that have dealt with censorship of pornographic material on the internet: the Communications Decency Act (CDA), which was enacted as a part of the Telecommunications Act of 1996, the Child Online Protection Act 1998 (COPA) and the Children Internet Protection Act 2003 (CIPA). The CDA sought to prohibit the use of an interactive computer service to send or display in any manner to those under the age of 18, any communication that depicts or displays sexual or excretory activities in a manner that is patently offensive. The CIPA, which casts a duty on public libraries and schools to install software to block obscene or pornographic images, was upheld as constitutionally valid by the U.S. Supreme Court in *United States v. American Library Association*[12].

India may want to develop a different legislative model to regulate the use of the internet with a view to prohibiting its use for disseminating child pornographic materials. Nevertheless, the task deserves the utmost priority.

---

12 (2003) 194 U.S. 539

39

Publishing Sex oriented material in Newspapers and its ill effects on Minors[1]

Ratio Decidendi[2]: *"Fertile imagination of anybody especially of minors should not be a matter that should be agitated in the Court of law."*

"Where sufficient safeguards in terms of various legislations, norms and rules and regulations are available to protect society in general and children in particular, any step to ban publishing of certain news pieces or pictures would fetter independence of free press"

Facts in Nutshell:

Petitioner[3] a lawyer by profession. Respondent No. 1[4] is Union of India, respondent No. 2 is a statutory body, respondent Nos. 3 & 4 are the leading national daily newspapers and respondent No. 5 & 6 are news agencies. The petition[5] involved a substantial question of law and public importance on the fundamental right of the citizens, regarding the freedom of speech and expression as enshrined under Article 19(1)(a)[6] of the Constitution of India. The petitioner's grievance was that the

---

1 Appellants: **Ajay Goswami Vs.** Respondent: **Union of India (UOI) and Ors.**
  AIR2007SC493
  Hon'ble Judges/Coram: Dr. AR. Lakshmanan and Tarun Chatterjee, JJ.

2 **Meaning of Ratio Decidendi:** *Ratio decidendi* is a Latin phrase meaning "the reason" or "the rationale for the decision." The *ratio decidendi* is "the point in a case which determines the judgment" or "the principle which the case establishes."

3 **Meaning of Petitioner:** A person who presents a Petition. (**Meaning of Petition:** A formal message requesting something that is submitted to an authority)

4 **Meaning of Respondent:** A **respondent** is a person who is called upon to issue a response to a communication made by another. In legal usage, this specifically refers to the defendant in a legal proceedingcommenced by a petition, or to an appellee, or the opposing party, in an appeal of a decision by an initial fact-finder.

5 **Meaning of Petition:** A formal message requesting something that is submitted to an authority

6 **Article 19 in The Constitution Of India 1949**
  19. Protection of certain rights regarding freedom of speech etc
  (1) All citizens shall have the right

~ 194 ~

freedom of speech and expression enjoyed by the newspaper industry was not keeping balance with the protection of children from harmful and disturbing materials. Article 19(1)(a) guarantees freedom of speech and expression of individual as well as press. It acknowledges that the press is free to express its ideas but on the same hand, individual also has right to their own space and right not to be exposed against their will to other's expressions of ideas and actions.

By way of petition, the petitioner requested the Court to direct the authorities to strike a reasonable balance between the fundamental right of freedom of speech and expression enjoyed by the press and the duty of the Government, being signatory of United Nations Convention on the Rights of the Child, 1989 and Universal Declaration of Human Rights, to protect the vulnerable minors from abuse, exploitation and harmful effects of such expression.

The Lawyer Petitioner filed petition to seek protection from Court to ensure that minors[7] are not exposed to sexually exploitative materials, whether or not the same is obscene or is within the law. The real objective was that the nature and extent of the material having sexual contents should not be exposed to the minors indiscriminately and without regard to the age of minor. The discretion in this regard should vest with parents, guardians, teachers or experts on Sex education. No attempt has been made till date to define any yardstick for the minors whose tender minds are open for being polluted and are like plain state on which any painting can be drawn.

Is the material in newspaper really harmful for the minors?

In Times of India dated 1.8.2005 an article titled "Porn in potter VI" was published. The author tried to read and suggest sexual messages in these lines. Children who were reading the book might not have any such inclination. However, after reading newspaper their mind would certainly wander to an area which the author might not have even conceived.

No doubt, we are not living an era of Gandhari[8] but certainly we

---

(a) to freedom of speech and expression

7   **Meaning of Minor:** Someone under legal age, which is generally 18, except for certain purposes such as drinking alcoholic beverages.

8   **Gandhari** is a character in the Hindu epic, the Mahābhārata. In the epic, she was an incarnation of Mati, as the daughter of Subala, the king of Gandhara, or the modern Kandahar, a region spanning northwestern Pakistan and eastern Afghanistan, from which her name is derived. Gandhari's marriage was arranged to Dhritarashtra, the eldest prince of the Kuru kingdom, a

have culture and respect for elders and some decorum and decency towards children. Undoubtedly, such kind of stuff is available freely on internet, movies; televisions etc. but are the families and the community environment really ready to accept it in toto[9] or are they passive receiver of the same without any control or check. Are these articles really making our children morally healthy? Moral values should not be allowed to be sacrificed in the guise of social change or cultural assimilation.

Proposals by Petitioner Lawyer:

i) Guidelines in detail may be issued to all the newspapers regarding the matter which may not be suitable for the reading of minors or which may require parents or teachers discretion.

ii) Newspapers should have self regulatory system to access the publication in view of those guidelines.

iii) In case the newspapers publishes any material which is categorized in the guidelines the newspaper be packed in some different form and should convey in bold in front of newspapers of the existence of such material.

iv) This would give discretion to the parents to instruct the news vendor whether to deliver such newspaper or not.

OR

In the alternative, suggested a Committee be appointed to suggest ways and means for regulating the access of minors to adult oriented sexual, titillating or prurient material.

Indecent Representation of Women Act, 1986

Publishing as well as circulating of obscene and nude/semi-nude photographs of women constitutes a penal offence under the provisions of the Indecent Representation of Women (Prohibition) Act, 1986, administered by the Department of Women & Child Development,

---

region inDelhi and Haryana region.

9 **Meaning of Toto:** In the whole; wholly; completely

Ministry of Human Resources Development. Relevant Sections 3[10] & 4[11] of the Indecent Representation of Women (Prohibition) Act, 1986 are reproduced hereunder for ready reference:

3. Prohibition of advertisements containing indecent representation of woman:- No person shall publish, or cause to be published or arrange or take part in the publication or exhibition or, any advertisement which contains indecent representation of women in any form.

4. Prohibition of publication or sending by post of books, pamphlets etc. containing indecent representation of women - No person shall produce or cause to be produced, sell, let to hire, distribute or circulate or send by post any book, pamphlet, paper, slide, film, writing drawing, painting, photographs, representation or figure of women in any form, provided that nothing in this section shall apply to:

(a) any book, pamphlet, paper, slide, film, writing, drawing, painting, photograph, representation or figure:

(i) the publication of which is proved to be justified as being for the public good on the ground that such book, pamphlet, paper, slide, film, writing, drawing, painting, photograph, representation or figure is in the interest

10 **Section 3 of the Indecent Representation of Women Act, 1986:**
3.Prohibition of advertisements containing indecent representation of Women.- No person shall publish, or cause to be published, or arrange or take part in the publication or exhibition of, any advertisement which contains indecent representation of women in any form.

11 **Section 4 of the Indecent Representation of Women Act, 1986:**
4.Prohibition of publication or sending by post of books, pamphlets, etc; containing indecent representation of women.- No person shall produce or cause to be produced, sell , let to hire, distribute, circulate or send by post any book, pamphlet, paper, slide, film, writing, drawing, painting, photograph , representation or figure which contains indecent representation of women in any form:
Provided that noting in this section shall apply to-
(a) any book, pamphlet, paper, slide, film, writing, drawing, painting, photograph, representation or figure –
(i) the publication of which is proved to be justified as justified as being for the public good on the ground that such book, pamphlet, paper, slide , film, writing, drawing, painting, photography, representation or figure is in the interest of science, literature, art, or learning , art, or learning or other objects of general concern; or
(ii) which is kept or used bona fide for religious purpose;
any representation sculptured, engraved, painted or otherwise represented on or in –
(i) any ancient monument within the meaning of the Ancient Monument and Archaeological Sites and Remains Act, 1958 (24 of 1958); or
(ii) any temple, or on any car used or the conveyance of idols, or kept or used for any religious purpose;
any film in respect of which the provisions of Part II of the Cinematograph Act, 1952 (37 of 1952), will be applicable.

of science, literature, art or learning or other object of general concern; or

(ii) which is kept or used bona fide for religious purposes;

(b) any representation sculptured, engraved, painted or otherwise represented on or in -

(i) any ancient monument within the meaning of the Ancient Monument and Archaeological Sites and Remains Act, 1958 (24 of 1958)

(ii) any temple, or on any car used for the conveyance of idols, or kept or used for any religious purposes;

(c) any film in respect of which the provisions of Part II of the Cinematograph Act, 1952 (37 of 1952), will be applicable.

Section 6 of the Indecent Representation of Women (Prohibition) Act, 1986 provides the penalty for committing such offences in contravention of Sections 3 & 4 of the said Act. Section 6 reads as follows:

6. Penalty- Any person who contravenes the provisions of Sections 3 & 4 shall be punishable on first conviction with imprisonment of either description for a term which may extend to two years, and with fine which may extend to two thousand rupees, and in the event of a second or subsequent conviction with imprisonment for a term of not less than six months but which may extend to five years and also with a fine not less than ten thousand rupees but which may extend to one lac rupees.

Sale, letting, hiring, distributing, exhibiting, circulating of obscene books and objects of young persons under the age of twenty years also constitutes a penal offence under Sections 292[12] and 293[13] of the Indian Penal Code and is punishable on first conviction with imprisonment of either description for a term which may extend to two thousand rupees and in the event of a second or subsequent conviction, with imprisonment of either description for a term which may extend to seven years, and also with fine which may extend to five thousand rupees.

---

12 **Section 292 in The Indian Penal Code, 1860**

292. [Sale, etc., of obscene books, etc.-- [(1) For the purposes of sub- section (2), a book, pamphlet, paper, writing, drawing, painting representation, figure or any other object, shall be deemed to be obscene if it is lascivious or appeals to the prurient interest or if its effect, or (where it comprises two or more distinct items) the effect of any one of its items, is, if taken as a whole, such as to tend to deprave and corrupt persons who are likely, having regard to all relevant circumstances, to read, see or hear the matter contained or embodied in it.]

(2) 3[ ] Whoever-

(a) sells, lets to hire, distributes, publicly exhibits or in any manner puts into circulation, or for purposes of sale, hire, distribution, public exhibition or circulation, makes, reduces or has in his possession any obscene book, pamphlet, paper, drawing, painting, representation or figure or any other obscene object whatsoever, or

(b) imports, exports or conveys any obscene object for any of the purposes aforesaid, or knowing or having reason to believe that such object will be sold, let to hire, distributed or publicly exhibited or in any manner put into circulation, or

(c) takes part in or receives profits from any business in the course of which he knows or has reason to believe that any such obscene objects are, for any of the purposes aforesaid, made, produced, purchased, kept, imported, exported, conveyed, publicly exhibited or in any manner put into circulation, or

(d) advertises or makes known by any means whatsoever that any person is engaged or is ready to engage in any act which is an offence under this section, or that any such obscene object can be procured from or through any person, or

(e) offers or attempts to do any act which is an offence under this section, shall be punished 1[on first conviction with imprisonment of either description for a term which may extend to two years, and with fine which may extend to two thousand rupees, and, in the event of a second or subsequent conviction, with imprisonment of either description for a term which may extend to five years, and also with fine which may extend to five thousand rupees]. [Exception- This section does not extend to-

(a) any book, pamphlet, paper, writing, drawing, painting, representation or figure-

(i) the publication of which is proved to be justified as being for the public good on the ground that such book, pamphlet, paper, writing, drawing, painting, representation or figure is in the interest of science, literature, art or learning or other objects of general concern, or

(ii) which is kept or used bona fide for religious purposes;

(b) any representation sculptured, engraved, painted or otherwise represented on or in-

(i) any ancient monument within the meaning of the Ancient Monuments and Archaeological Sites and Remains Act, 1958 (24 of 1958), or

(ii) any temple, or on any car used for the conveyance of idols, or kept or used for any religious purpose.]

13 **Section 293 in The Indian Penal Code, 1860**

293. [Sale, etc., of obscene objects to young person.-- Whoever sells, lets to hire, distributes, exhibits or circulates to any person under the age of twenty years any such obscene object as is referred to in the last preceding section, or offers or attempts so to do, shall be punished 1[on first conviction with imprisonment of either description for a term which may extend to three years, and with fine which may extend to two thousand rupees, and, in the event of a second or subsequent conviction, with imprisonment of either description for a term which may extend to seven years, and also with fine which may extend to five thousand rupees]

Obscenity:

In *Director General, Directorate General of Doordarshan and Ors. v. Anand Patwardhan and Anr.*[14] it was observed that the basic test for obscenity would be:

(a) whether the average person applying contemporary community standards would find that the work, taken as a whole appeal to the prurient interest....

(b) whether the work depicts or describes, in a patently offensive way, sexual conduct specifically, defined by the applicable state law,

(c) whether the work taken as a whole, lacks serious literary, artistic, political or scientific value.

In *Shri Chandrakant Kalyandas Kakodkar v. The State of Maharashtra and Ors.*[15], Court observed that:

The concept of obscenity would differ from country to country depending on the standards of morals of contemporary society. What is considered as a piece of literature in France may be obscene in England and what is considered in both countries as not harmful to public order and morals may be obscene in our country. But to insist that the standard should always be for the writer to see that the adolescent ought not to be brought into contact with sex or that if they read any references to sex in what is written whether that is the dominant theme or not they would be affected, would be to require authors to write books only for the adolescent and not for the adults.

In the case of *Samaresh Bose and Anr. v. Amal Mitra and Anr. :*[16], Court observed that:

The decision of the Court must necessarily be on an objective assessment of the book or story or article as a whole and with particular reference to the passages complained of in the book, story or article. The Court must take an overall view of the matter complained of as obscene in the setting of the whole work, but the matter charged as obscene must also be considered by itself and separately to find out whether it is so gross and its obscenity so pronounced that it is likely to deprave and corrupt those

14 (C.A. No. 613 of 2005), Decided On: 25.08.2006

15 1970 AIR 1390

16 1986CriLJ24

whose minds are open to influence of this sort and into whose hands the book is likely to fall.

Legislations against Obscenity:

Section 13 of the Press Council Act, 1978 specifies the objects and functions of the council.

Section 13(2)(c) states:

to ensure on the part of newspapers, news agencies and journalists, the maintenance of high standards of public taste and foster a due sense of both the rights and responsibilities of citizenship;

Section 14(1) states:

Where, on receipt of a complaint made to it or otherwise, the Council has reason to believe that a newspaper or news agency has offended against the standards of journalistic ethics or public taste or that an editor or working journalist has committed any professional misconduct, the Council may, after giving the newspaper, or news agency, the editor or journalist concerned an opportunity of being heard, hold an inquiry in such manner as may be provided by regulations made under this Act and, if it is satisfied that it is necessary so to do, it may, for reasons to be recorded in writing, warn, admonish or censure the newspaper, the news agency, the editor or the journalist or disapprove the conduct of the editor or the journalist, as the case may be:

Provided that the Council may not take cognizance of a complaint if in the opinion of the Chairman, there is no sufficient ground for holding an inquiry.

Section 14(2) states:

If the Council is of the opinion that it is necessary or expedient in public interest so to do, it may require any newspaper to publish therein in such manner as the Council thinks fit, any particulars relating to any inquiry under this section against a newspaper or news agency, an editor or a journalist working therein, including the name of such newspaper, news agency, editor or journalist.

Section 292 of the Indian Penal Code reads:

Sale, etc., of obscene books, etc. (1) For the purposes of Sub-section

(2), a book, pamphlet, paper, writing, drawing, painting, representation, figure or any other object, shall be deemed to be obscene if it is lascivious or appeals to the prurient interest or if its effect, or (where it comprises two or more distinct items) the effect of any one of its items, is, if taken as a whole, such as to tend to deprave and corrupt person, who are likely, having regard to all relevant circumstances, to read, see or hear the matter contained or embodied in it].

[(2)] Whoever-

(a) sells, lets to hire, distributes, publicly exhibits or in any manner puts into circulation, or for purposes of sale, hire, distribution, public exhibition or circulation, makes, produces or has in his possession any obscene book, pamphlet, paper, drawing, painting, representation or figure or any other obscene object whatsoever, or

(b) imports, exports or conveys any obscene object for any of the purposes aforesaid, or knowing or having reason to believe that such object will be sold, let to hire, distributed or publicly exhibited or in any manner put into circulation, or

(c) takes part in or receives profits from any business in the course of which he knows or has reason to believe that any such obscene objects are for any of the purposes aforesaid, made, produced, purchased, kept, imported, exported, conveyed, publicly exhibited or in any manner put into circulation, or

(d) advertises or makes known by any means whatsoever that any person is engaged or is ready to engage in any act which is an offence under this section, or that any such obscene object can be procured from or through any person, or

(e) offers or attempts to do any act which is an offence under this section,

shall be punished on first conviction with imprisonment of either description for a term which may extend to two years, and with fine which may extend to two thousand rupees, and, in the event of a second or subsequent conviction, with imprisonment of either description for a term which may extend to five years, and also with fine which may extend to five thousand rupees.

[Exception- This section does not extend to- (a) any book, pamphlet, paper, writing, drawing, painting, representation or figure-

(i) the publication of which is proved to be justified as being for the public good on the ground that such book, pamphlet, paper, writing, drawing, painting, representation or figure is in the interest of science, literature, art of learning or other objects of general concern, or

(ii) which is kept or used bona fide for religious purposes;

(b) any representation sculptured, engraved, painted or otherwise represented on or in-

(i) any ancient monument within the meaning of the Ancient Monuments and Archaeological Sites and Remains Act, 1958 (24 of 1958), or

(ii) any temple, or on any car used for the conveyance of idols, or kept or used for any religious purpose.]

Sections 4 and 6 of the Indecent Representation of Women Act, 1986 are also in existence.

Decision of Supreme Court:

In view of the availability of sufficient safeguards in terms of various legislations, norms and rules and regulations to protect the society in general and children, in particular, from obscene and prurient contents, Court was of the opinion that the writ[17] at the instance of the petitioner was not maintainable.

Court held that any steps to impose a blanket ban on publishing of photographs would amount to prejudging the matter as has been held in the matter of *Fraser v. Evans[18]* .

The definition of obscenity differs from culture to culture, between communities within a single culture, and also between individuals within those communities. Many cultures have produced laws to define what is considered to be obscene, and censorship is often used to try to suppress or control materials that are obscene under these definitions. The term obscenity is most often used in a legal context to describe expressions (words, images, actions) that offend the prevalent sexual morality. On the other hand the Constitution of India guarantees the right of freedom to speech and expression to every citizen. This right will encompass an

---

17 **Meaning of Writ:** A written order issued by a court, commanding the party to whom it is addressed to perform or cease performing a specified act.

18 1969 (1) QB 549

individuals take on any issue. However, this right is not absolute, if such speech and expression is immensely gross and will badly violate the standards of morality of a society. Therefore, any expression is subject to reasonable restriction. Freedom of expression has contributed much to the development and well-being of our free society. This right conferred by the Constitution has triggered various issues. One of the most controversial issues is balancing the need to protect society against the potential harm that may flow from obscene material, and the need to ensure respect for freedom of expression and to preserve a free flow of information and idea.

Court was of the view that a culture of 'responsible reading' should be inculcated among the readers of any news article. No news item should be viewed or read in isolation. It is necessary that publication must be judged as a whole and news items, advertisements or passages should not be read without the accompanying message that is purported to be conveyed to the public. Also the members of the public and readers should not look for meanings in a picture or written article, which is not conceived to be conveyed through the picture or the news item.

Therefore fertile imagination of anybody especially of minors should not be a matter that should be agitated in the court of law.

40

Abuse and Trafficking[1]

Ratio Decidendi[2]: *No child shall be deprived of his fundamental rights guaranteed under Constitution of India and bring to child traffic and abuse*

Facts in Nutshell:

Petition[3] was filed in public interest under Article 32[4] of the Constitution in the wake of serious violations and abuse of children who are forcefully detained in circuses, in many instances, without any access to their families under extreme inhuman conditions. There are instances of sexual abuse on a daily basis, physical abuse as well as emotional abuse. The children are deprived of basic human needs of food and water. It was stated in the petition that the Petitioner[5] has filed petition following a series of incidents where the Petitioner came in contact with many children who were trafficked[6] into performing in circuses. The Petitioner found that circus is one of the ancient forms of indigenous entertainment in the

---

1   Appellants: **Bachpan Bachao Andolan Vs.** Respondent: **Union of India (UOI) and Ors.** AIR2011SC3361
    Hon'ble Judges/Coram: Dalveer Bhandari and A. K. Patnaik, JJ.

2   **Meaning of Ration Decidendi:** *Ratio decidendi* is a Latin phrase meaning "the reason" or "the rationale for the decision." The *ratio decidendi* is "the point in a case which determines the judgment" or "the principle which the case establishes."

3   **Meaning of Petition:** A formal message requesting something that is submitted to an authority

4   **Article 32 in The Constitution Of India 1949**
    32. Remedies for enforcement of rights conferred by this Part
    (1) The right to move the Supreme Court by appropriate proceedings for the enforcement of the rights conferred by this Part is guaranteed
    (2) The Supreme Court shall have power to issue directions or orders or writs, including writs in the nature of habeas corpus, mandamus, prohibition, quo warranto and certiorari, whichever may be appropriate, for the enforcement of any of the rights conferred by this Part
    (3) Without prejudice to the powers conferred on the Supreme Court by clause (1) and (2), Parliament may by law empower any other court to exercise within the local limits of its jurisdiction all or any of the powers exercisable by the Supreme Court under clause (2)
    (4) The right guaranteed by this article shall not be suspended except as otherwise provided for by this Constitution

5   **Meaning of Petitioner:** A person who presents a Petition. (**Meaning of Petition:** A formal message requesting something that is submitted to an authority)

6   **Meaning of Trafficking: Human trafficking** is the trade in humans, most commonly for the purpose of sexual slavery, forced labor or for the extraction of organs or tissues, including surrogacy and ova removal

world, with humans having a major role to play. However, the activities that are undertaken in these circuses deprive the artists especially children of their basic fundamental rights. Most of them are trafficked from some poverty-stricken areas of Nepal as well as from backward districts of India. The outside world has no meaning for them. There is no life beyond the circus campus. Once they enter into the circuses, they are confined to the circus arena, with no freedom of mobility and choice. They are entrapped into the world of circuses for the rest of their lives, leading a vagrant tunneled existence away from the hub of society, which is tiresome, claustrophobic and dependent on vicissitudes.

It was submitted that for the first time the Petitioner came to know about the plight of children in Indian circuses way back in 1996. At that time, the Petitioner had rescued 18 girls from a circus performing in Vidisha District of Madhya Pradesh. This was possible after a complaint made by a 12 year old girl, who managed to escape from the circus premises. Her complaint was that she and several other Nepalese girls had been trafficked and forced to stay and perform in the circus where they were being **sexually abused and were kept in most inhuman conditions.**

There are no labour or any welfare laws, which protect the rights of these children. Children are frequently physically, emotionally and sexually abused in these places. The most appalling aspect is that there is no direct legislation, which is vested with powers to deal with the problems of the children who are trafficked into these circuses. The Police, Labour Department or any other State Agency is not prepared to deal with the issue of trafficking of girls from Nepal holding them in bondage and unlawful confinement. There is perpetual **sexual harassment**, violation of the Juvenile Justice Act and all International treaties and Conventions related to Human Rights and Child Rights where India is a signatory. The Petitioner submitted that Supreme Court in the case of *N.R. Nair and Ors. v. Union of India and Ors.*[7] upheld the rights of animals who are being made to perform in these circuses after understanding their plight. The situation of children in circuses is no different if not worse.

Problem of children trafficking:

1. Trafficking in human beings is not a new phenomenon. Women, children and men have been captured, bought and sold in market places for centuries. Human trafficking is one of the most lucrative criminal

---

7 (2001) 6 SCC 84

activities. Estimates of the United Nations state that 1 to 4 million people are trafficked worldwide each year. Trafficking in women and children is an operation which is worth more than $ 10 billion annually. The NHRC Committee on Missing Children has the following statistics to offer:

a. 12.6 million (Governmental sources) to 100 million (unofficial sources) stated to be child labour;

b. 44,000 children are reported missing annually, of which 11,000 get traced;

c. About 200 girls and women enter prostitution daily, of which 20% are below 15 years of age.

2. International conventions exist to punish and suppress trafficking especially women and children. (Refer: UN Protocol to Prevent, Suppress and Punish Trafficking in Persons also referred as the PALERMO Protocol on Trafficking). Trafficking is now defined as an organized crime and a crime against humanity. The convention being an international convention is limited to cross border trafficking but does not address trafficking within the country. The definition of trafficking is significant:

...The recruitment, transportation, transfer, harboring or receipt of persons by means of threat or use of force or other forms of coercion, of abduction, of fraud, of deception, of the abuse of power or of a position of vulnerability or of the giving or receiving of payments or benefits to achieve the consent of a person having control over another person, for the purpose of exploitation....

3. Exploitation shall include at a minimum, the exploitation of the prostitutes of others or other forms of sexual exploitation, forced labour or service, slavery or practices similar to slavery, servitude or the removal of organs.

4. Children under 18 years of age cannot give valid consent. Any recruitment, transportation, transfer, harbouring or receipt of children for the purpose of exploitation is a form of trafficking regardless of the means used. Three significant elements constitute trafficking:

a. The action involving recruitment and transportation;

b. The means employed such as force, coercion, fraud or deception including abuse of power and bribes; and

c.   The purpose being exploitation including prostitution.

5. Internationally, there is a working definition of child trafficking. The working definition is clear because it incorporates the above three elements. In June 2001, India has adopted the PALERMO Protocol to evolve its working definition of child trafficking.

6. The forms and purposes of child trafficking may be:

a.   Bonded labour;

b.   Domestic work;

c.   Agricultural labour;

d.   Employment in construction activity;

e.   Carpet industry;

f.   Garment industry g. Fish/Shrimp Export;

h.   Other sites of work in the formal and informal economy.

7. Trafficking can also be for illegal activities such as:

a.   Begging;

b.   Organ trade;

c.   Drug peddling and smuggling;

8. Trafficking can be for sexual exploitation, i.e.

a.   Forced prostitution;

b.   Socially and religiously sanctified forms of prostitution;

c.   Sex tourism;

d.   Pornography;

9. Child trafficking can be to aid entertainment in sports:

a.   Circus/dance troupes;

b.   Camel jockeying;

10. Trafficking can be for and through marriage. Trafficking can be for and through adoption. It is submitted that intervention is possible in cases of child trafficking only if fundamental principles are kept in mind. The fundamental principles are the following:

    a. The child has to perform to the best of his ability. The growth of a child to its potential fulfillment is the fundamental guarantee of civilization;

    b. Empathy for troubled children by adopting non-discriminatory and attitudes free of bias;

    c. Children must be protected in terms of well-being under all circumstances;

    d. Right to freedom from all forms of exploitation is a fundamental right;

    e. Confidentiality of the child in respect of the child's privacy must be maintained;

    f. Trafficking is an organized crime which could have multiple partners including syndicates.

Articles 23[8], 39[9], 14[10] and 21[11] of the Constitution of India guarantee every child to be freed from exploitation of any form. Article 23 prohibits traffic in human beings, 'beggar' and other forms of forced labour.

Goa Children's Act, 2003 must be viewed as a model legislation. It define child trafficking but also seeks to provide punishment for abuse and assault of children through child trafficking for different purposes such as labour, sale of body parts, organs, adoption, sexual offences of pedophilia, child prostitution, child pornography and child sex tourism. All state authorities such as airport authorities, border police, railway police, traffic police, hotel owners are made responsible under the law for protection of children and for reporting offences against children.

Trafficking in women and children has become an increasingly lucrative business especially since the risk of being prosecuted is very low. Women and children do not usually come to the brothels on their own will, but are brought through highly systematic, organized and illegal trafficking networks run by experienced individuals who buy, transport and sell

8 **Article 23 in The Constitution Of India 1949**
23. Prohibition of traffic in human beings and forced labour
(1) Traffic in human beings and begar and other similar forms of forced labour are prohibited and any contravention of this provision shall be an offence punishable in accordance with law
(2) Nothing in this article shall prevent the State from imposing compulsory service for public purpose, and in imposing such service the State shall not make any discrimination on grounds only of religion, race, caste or class or any of them

9 **Article 39 in The Constitution Of India 1949**
39. Certain principles of policy to be followed by the State: The State shall, in particular, direct its policy towards securing
(a) that the citizens, men and women equally, have the right to an adequate means to livelihood;
(b) that the ownership and control of the material resources of the community are so distributed as best to subserve the common good;
(c) that the operation of the economic system does not result in the concentration of wealth and means of production to the common detriment;
(d) that there is equal pay for equal work for both men and women;
(e) that the health and strength of workers, men and women, and the tender age of children are not abused and that citizens are not forced by economic necessity to enter avocations unsuited to their age or strength;
(f) that children are given opportunities and facilities to develop in a healthy manner and in conditions of freedom and dignity and that childhood and youth are protected against exploitation and against moral and material abandonment

10 **Article 14 in The Constitution Of India 1949**
14. Equality before law The State shall not deny to any person equality before the law or the equal protection of the laws within the territory of India Prohibition of discrimination on grounds of religion, race, caste, sex or place of birth

11 **Article 21 in The Constitution Of India 1949**
21. Protection of life and personal liberty No person shall be deprived of his life or personal liberty except according to procedure established by law

children into prostitution. Traffickers tend to work in groups and children being trafficked often change hands to ensure that neither the trafficker nor the child gets caught during transit. Different groups of traffickers include gang members, police, pimps and even politicians, all working as a nexus. Trafficking networks are well organized and have linkages both within the country and in the neighbouring countries. Most traffickers are men. The role of women in this business is restricted to recruitment at the brothels. The typical profile of a trafficker is a man in his twenties or thirties or a woman in her thirties or forties who have travelled the route to the city several times and know the hotels to stay in and the brokers to contact. They frequently work in groups of two or more. Male and female traffickers are sometimes referred to as dalals and dalalis (commission agents) respectively and are either employed by a brothel owner directly or operate independently. Often collusion of family members forms an integral part of trafficking with uncles, cousins and stepfathers acting as trafficking agents.

Decision of the Court:

Court held that in order to implement the fundamental right of the children under Article 21A[12] it is imperative that the Central Government must issue suitable notifications prohibiting the employment of children in circuses.

---

12 **Article 21A of Constitution**
   Right to education
   "21A. The State shall provide free and compulsory education to all children of the age of six to fourteen years in such manner as the State may, by law, determine."

41

DNA Test to Determine Paternity[1]

Facts in Nutshell:

The case relates to refusal by a party to the litigation to comply with the court direction made in accordance with law to furnish a blood sample for DNA testing which would enable authoritative adjudication on the real issue in the matter. The Plaintiff[2] filed the suit seeking declaration that the Plaintiff is the naturally born son of the Defendants[3] and that the Defendant No. 1 is the father of the Plaintiff. It is asserted that, though he was born to Smt. Ujjwala Sharma, Defendant No. 1 whilst her marriage to Sh. B.P. Sharma subsisted, the Plaintiff was not born from their wedlock. Reliance in this behalf has been placed on the report of blood samples drawn from Shri B.P. Sharma and DNA profiling which have been compared with the DNA profiling of the Plaintiff's blood sample which report reflects that Sh. B.P. Sharma cannot be his (the Plaintiff's) biological father. The Plaintiff has categorically asserted that he was born from an extramarital relationship between the Defendants. In this regard, he places reliance on the proximity between the parties in the plaint and relies on photographs which according to the Plaintiff manifest that the Defendants as well as the Plaintiff shared an intimate relationship.

The Defendant No. 1 does not dispute that the Plaintiff is the biological son of the Defendant No. 2, but denies relationship or intimacy with her as well as the Plaintiff. During the pendency of the suit, the Plaintiff filed IA No. 4720/2008 on 11th April, 2008 seeking a direction to the Defendant No. 1 to submit to DNA testing.

Short Summary of Case:

It is the case of the Plaintiff and Defendant No. 2 that the Plaintiff was born outside of marriage. He was born from a relationship between the

---

1 Appellants: **Rohit Shekhar Vs.** Respondent: **Shri Narayan Dutt Tiwari and Anr.**
  2011(4)RCR(Civil)459
  Hon'ble Judges: Gita Mittal, J.

2 **Meaning of Plaintiff:**
  The party who initiates a lawsuit by filing a complaint with the clerk of the court against the defendant(s) demanding damages, performance and/or court determination of rights.

3 **Meaning of Defendant:** A person against whom an action or claim is brought in a court of law

Defendant Nos. 1 and 2. The Defendant No. 2 has stated that though she was married to Sh. B.P. Sharma from which marriage they were blessed with one son Siddharth on 30th October, 1968; that the Defendant No. 2 and her ex-husband did not have marital relationship or co-habitation since 1970; that the Defendant No. 1 became close to the Defendant No. 2 from 1968 and they entered into an intimate relationship in 1977 which resulted in the birth of Rohit Shekhar, the present Plaintiff on 15th February, 1979.

Decision by High Court:

The parties or their counsel were directed to appear before the Joint Registrar on 8th February, 2011. The Joint Registrar obtained particulars and details to facilitate the DNA testing of the first Defendant; the said Defendant was directed to furnish such sample on a date and time to be designated by the Joint Registrar, by taking or drawing appropriate samples after ascertaining the details from the concerned accredited agency i.e. Centre for Cellular & Molecular Biology (Constituent Laboratory of the Council of Scientific Industrial Research, Government of India, Habsiguda Uppal Road, Hyderabad -500 007, Andhra Pradesh, India. The said institution shall furnish the report to this Court within six weeks of receiving the samples.

Defendant challenged the order of the court by way of special leave petition[4] in Supreme Court of India.

The Defendant No. 1 put forth the following reasons for the application:

(i) no useful purpose would be served to subject Defendant No. 1 to the test

(ii) final relief cannot be granted to the Plaintiff because of Section 112of the Evidence Act[5]

---

4 **Article 136 in The Constitution Of India**
136. Special leave to appeal by the Supreme Court (1) Notwithstanding anything in this Chapter, the Supreme Court may, in its discretion, grant special leave to appeal from any judgment, decree, determination, sentence or order in any cause or matter passed or made by any court or tribunal in the territory of India
(2) Nothing in clause (1) shall apply to any judgment, determination, sentence or order passed or made by any court or tribunal constituted by or under any law relating to the Armed Forces

5 **Birth during marriage, conclusive proof of legitimacy**
The fact that any person was born during the continuance of a valid marriage between his mother and any man, or within two hundred and eighty days after its dissolution, the mother remaining unmarried, shall be conclusive proof that he is the legitimate son of that man, unless it can be shown that the parties to the marriage had no access to each other at any time when he could

(iii) no sample can be obtained from the Defendant No. 1 per force without his express consent or else it would violate fundamental rights of the Defendant No. 1 protected under Article 21 of the Constitution[6].

(iv) for the above reasons, not to pressurise, coerce or force the Defendant No. 1 to provide blood and/or tissue sample for DNA testing

Question before the Court:

The application therefore raises the question as to whether a person can be physically compelled to give a blood sample for DNA profiling in compliance with a civil court order in a paternity action? If it were held that the same was permissible, how is the court to mould its order and what would be the modalities for drawing the involuntary sample?

Submission by Plaintiff Counsel:

The Plaintiff submits that the Court has power under Section 75(e)[7] of the Code of Civil Procedure (CPC) read with Order-XXVI, Rule-10 (A) to issue a direction for holding a scientific technical or expert investigation.

Another question before the court was if a third party (to a marriage, like the first Defendant here) may be compelled to undergo scientific tests of the nature of giving blood samples for the purpose of DNA testing. In the case of *Goutam Kundu v. State of West Bengal and Anr.*[8] court held that

1. A matrimonial court has the power to order a person to undergo medical test.

2. Passing of such an order by the court would not be in violation of the right to personal liberty under Article 21of the Indian Constitution.

3. However, the Court should exercise such a power if the applicant has a strong prima facie case and there is sufficient material before the Court. If despite the order of the court, the Respondent refuses to submit himself to medical examination, the court will be entitled to draw an adverse

---

have been begotten.

6 **Article 21 in The Constitution Of India**
   Protection of life and personal liberty No person shall be deprived of his life or personal liberty except according to procedure established by law

7 Section 75(e) of CPC: Power of the Court to issue Commissions
   (e) to hold a scientific, technical, or expert investigation;

8 MANU/SC/0345/1993 : (1993) 3 SCC 418

inference against him.

In *Goutam Kundu v. State of West Bengal and Anr.*[9] , it has been laid down that courts in India cannot order blood test as a matter of course and such prayers cannot be granted to have roving inquiry; there must be strong prima facie case and court must carefully examine as to what would be the consequence of ordering the blood test.

Submissions by Defendant No.1 Counsel:

Learned Counsel cited *Selvi v. State of Karnataka*[10] and placed observations of the Supreme Court in para 264 of the judgment:

264. In light of these conclusions, we hold that no individual should be forcibly subjected to any of the techniques in question, whether in the context of investigation in criminal cases or otherwise. Doing so would amount to an unwarranted intrusion into personal liberty. However, we do leave room for the voluntary administration of the impugned techniques in the context of criminal justice provided that certain safeguards are in place. Even when the subject has given consent to undergo any of these tests, the test results by themselves cannot be admitted as evidence because the subject does not exercise conscious control over the responses during the administration of the test. However, any information or material that is subsequently discovered with the help of voluntary administered test results can be admitted in accordance with Section 27[11] of the Evidence Act, 1872.

Miss. Swati Lodha v. State of Rajasthan and Anr.[12] In this case the court was concerned with the refusal to submit to a blood test by a person accused of the offence of rape in which a child had been born to the victim. In para 16 of the pronouncement, the court considered the value to be attached to the test also and held as follows:

16. A review of the above law, would go to show the following propositions are well-settled:

---

9   MANU/SC/0345/1993 : (1993) 3 SCC 418

10 MANU/SC/0325/2010 : (2010) 7 SCC 263

11 **Section 27 of the Evidence Act:** How much of information received from accused may be proved.- Provided that, when any fact is deposed to as discovered in consequence of information received from a person accused of any offence, in the custody of a police- officer, so much of such information, whether it amounts to a confession or not, as relates distinctly to the fact thereby discovered, may be proved.

12 MANU/RH/0088/1990 : 1991 Cri.L.J. 939

(1) Report of a blood-test is capable of amounting to corroboration of the statement of the complainant. It amounts to corroboration even under the common law. The nature of the corroboration would necessarily vary according to the particular circumstances of the offence charged. The test applicable to determine the nature and extent of the corroboration is the same whether the case falls within the rule of common law or within that class of offences for which corroboration is required by statute. A Criminal Court can make a direction for a blood-test to be taken by taking blood-sample of the complainant, accused and of the child. In certain cases, where it is contrary to the interest of a minor, the Court may not make a blood-test direction.

(2) The Court cannot order an adult to submit to blood test. A blood-test which involves insertion of a needle in the veins of a person, is an assault, unless consented to. It would need express statutory authority to require an adult to submit to it. This is based on the fundamental that human body is inviolable and no one can prick it.

(3) Where a Court makes a direction for a blood-test, and the accused fails or refuses to comply with the blood-test direction, the Court can in the circumstances of the case, use the refusal or failure of the accused to submit to blood test as a corroborative evidence against him. If a party refuses to submit to blood-test, the Court may infer that some impediment existed which pointed out towards the implication of the accused.

Decision by Court:

Court held that refusal by the Defendant No. 1 to submit the blood sample is wilful, malafide, unreasonable and unjustified. It held that ordering a test upon a person to determine biological relationships between him and the Plaintiff would not attract the sanction of Article 21 of the Constitution of India. Hence the prayer of Defendant No.1 for not doing DNA testing was rejected by court.

Miscellaneous (Surrogacy, Illegitimate Child, Divorce, Maternity Leave, Dowry Death, Abortion)

Woman:

A woman both in the eye of law and the society is not merely a person either in the gender or the existence. She has an inherent personality since birth called 'womanhood'. A woman is the mother first before having any other status. The age factor is not determinative of the status or the existence of womanhood. A woman is defined in Section 10[1] of the Indian Penal Code denoting female gender of any age. A woman is possessed of a great born virtue called 'modesty', to mean 'womanly propriety of behaviour, scrupulous chastity of thought, speech and conduct (in men or women) reserve or sense of shame proceeding from instinctive aversion to impure or coarse suggestions."

Dignity of Women:

Unfortunately, a woman, in our country, belongs to a class or group of society who are in a disadvantaged position on account of several social barriers and impediments and have, therefore, been the victim of tyranny at the hands of men with whom they, fortunately, under the Constitution enjoy equal status. Women also have the right to life and liberty; they also have the right to be respected and treated as equal citizens. Their honour and dignity cannot be touched or violated. They also have the right to lead an honourable and peaceful life. Women, in them, have many personalities combined. They are Mother, Daughter, Sister and Wife and not play things for center spreads in various magazines, periodicals or newspapers nor can they be exploited for obscene purposes. They must have the liberty, the freedom and, of course, independence to live the roles assigned to them by Nature so that the society may flourish as they alone have the talents and capacity to shape the destiny and character of men anywhere and in every part of the world. Rape is thus not only a crime against the person of a woman (victim), it is a crime against the

---

1 **Section 10 in The Indian Penal Code, 1860**
   10. " Man"." Woman".-- The word" man" denotes a male human being of any age; the word" woman" denotes a female human being of any age.

~ 217 ~

entire society. It destroys the entire psychology of a woman and pushes her into deep emotional crises. It is only by her sheer will power that she rehabilitates herself in the society which, on coming to know of the rape, looks down upon her in derision and contempt. Rape is, therefore, the most hated crime. It is a crime against basic human rights and is also violative of the victim's most cherished of the Fundamental Rights, namely, the Right to Life contained in Article 21[2]. To many feminists and psychiatrists, rape is less a sexual offence than an act of aggression aimed at degrading and humiliating women. The rape laws do not, unforunately, take care of the social aspect of the matter and are inept in many respects. In *Women's Forum v.Union of India*[3], in which Court observed as under: It is rather unfortunate that in recent times, there has been an increase in violence against women causing serious concern. Rape does indeed pose a series of problems for the criminal justice system. There are cries for harshest penalties, but often times such crimes eclipse the real plight of the victim. Rape is an experience which shakes the foundations of the lives of the victims. For many, its effect is a long-term one, impairing their capacity for personal relationships, altering their behavior values and generating and less fears. In addition to the trauma of the rape itself, victims have had to suffer further agony during legal proceedings.

Court further observed as under: The defects in the present system are : Firstly, complaints are handled roughly and are not even such attention as is warranted. The victims, more often than not, are humiliated by the police. The victims have invariably found rape trials a traumatic experience. The experience of giving evidence in court has been negative and destructive. The victims often say, they considered the ordeal to be even worse than the rape itself. Undoubtedly, the court proceedings added to and prolonged the psychological stress they had had to suffer as a result of the rape itself.

Marriage:

Marriage is the very foundation of the civilised society. The relation once formed, the law steps in and binds the parties to various obligations and liabilities there under. Marriage is an institution in the maintenance of which the public at large is deeply interested. It is the foundation of the

---

2 **Article 21 in The Constitution Of India 1949**
   21. Protection of life and personal liberty No person shall be deprived of his life or personal liberty except according to procedure established by law

3 (1995)1SCC14

family and in turn of the society without which no civilisation can exist. Till the time we achieve the goal - uniform civil code for all the citizens of India - there is an open inducement to a Hindu husband, who wants to enter into second marriage while the first marriage is subsisting, to become a Muslim. Since monogamy[4] is the law for Hindus and the Muslim law permits as many as four wives in India, errand Hindu husband embraces Islam to circumvent the provisions of the Hindu law and to escape from penal consequences.

The doctrine of indissolubility of marriage, under the traditional Hindu law, did not recognise that conversion would have the effect of dissolving a Hindu marriage. Conversion to another religion by one or both the Hindu spouses did not dissolve the marriage. It would be useful to have a look at some of the old cases on the subject. In Re Ram Kumari[5] where a Hindu wife became convert to the Muslim faith and then married a Mohammedan, it was held that her earlier marriage with a Hindu husband was not dissolved by her conversion. She was charged and convicted of bigamy under Section 494 of the IPC. It was held that there was no authority under Hindu law for the proposition that an apostate is absolved from all civil obligations and that so far as the matrimonial bond was concerned, such view was contrary to the spirit of the Hindu law. In *Gul Mohammed v. Emperor*[6] a Hindu wife was fraudulently taken away by the accused[7] a Mohammedan who married her according to Muslim law after converting her to Islam. It was held that the conversion of the Hindu wife to Mohammedan faith did not ipso facto[8] dissolve the marriage and she could not during the life time of her former husband enter into a valid contract of marriage. Accordingly the accused was convicted for adultery under Section 497[9] of the IPC.

---

4 **Meaning of Monogamy:**
   Monogamy is a form of marriage in which an individual has only one spouse during their lifetime or at any one time (serial monogamy), as compared to polygamy or polyamory. In current usage, monogamy often refers to having one sexual partner irrespective of marriage or reproduction.

5 1891 Cal 246

6 MANU/NA/0076/1946

7 **Meaning of Accused:** A person charged with a criminal offense, or the state of being so charged

8 **Meaning of Ipso Facto:**
   Ipso facto is a Latin phrase, directly translated as "by the fact itself," which means that a certain phenomenon is a *direct* consequence, a resultant *effect*, of the action in question, instead of being brought about by a previous action. It is a term of art used in philosophy, law, and science.

9 **Section 497 in The Indian Penal Code, 1860**
   497. Adultery.-- Whoever has sexual intercourse with a person who is and whom he knows or has reason to believe to be the wife of another man, without the consent or connivance of that man, such sexual intercourse not amounting to the offence of rape, is guilty of the offence of adultery,

In *Nandi @ Zainab v. The Crown[10]*, Nandi, the wife of the complainant, changed her religion and became a Mussalman and thereafter married a Mussalman named Rukan Din. She was charged with an offence under Section 494 of the Indian Penal Code. It was held that the mere fact of her conversion to Islam did not dissolve the marriage which could only be dissolved by a decree[11] of court. *Emperor v. Mt. Ruri[12]*, was a case of Christian wife. The Christian wife renounced Christianity and embraced Islam and then married a Mahomedan. It was held that according to the Christian marriage law, which was the law applicable to the case, the first marriage was not dissolved and therefore the subsequent marriage was bigamous.

In India there has never been a matrimonial law of general application. Apart from statute law a marriage was governed by the personal law of the parties. A marriage solemnised under a particular statute and according to personal law could not be dissolved according to another personal law, simply because one of the parties had changed his or her religion.

Adultery under I.P.C, 1860

Section 497 I.P.C, 1860 is one of the six sections is Chapter XX of the Penal Code, which is entitled 'Of Offences Relating to Marriage'. Section 497 reads thus ;

Whoever has sexual intercourse with a person who is and whom he knows or has reason to believe to be the wife of another man, without the consent or connivance of that man, such sexual intercourse not amounting to the offence of rape, is guilty of the offence of adultery, and shall be punished with imprisonment of either description for a term which may extend to five years, or with fine, or with both. In such case the wife shall not be punishable as an abettor. Section 498 I.P.C, 1860[13]

---

and shall be punished with imprisonment of either description for a term which may extend to five years, or with fine, or with both. In such case the wife shall not be punishable as an abettor.

10 ILR (1920) Lah 440

11 **Meaning of Decree:**
 1. An authoritative order having the force of law.
 2. The judgment of a court of equity, admiralty, probate, or divorce.

12 AIR (1919) Lah 389

13 **Section 498 in The Indian Penal Code, 1860**
 498. Enticing or taking away or detaining with criminal intent a married woman.-- Whoever takes or entices away any woman who is and whom he knows or has reason to believe to be the wife of any other man, from that man, or from any person having the care of her on behalf of that man,

prescribes punishment for enticing or taking away or detaining a married woman with criminal intent.

Law Commission 42nd Report, 1971

The offence of adultery, by its very definition, can be committed by a man and not by a woman : "Whoever has sexual intercourse with a person who is and whom he knows or has reason to believe to be the wife of another man ... is guilty of the offence of adultery." The argument really comes to this that the definition should be recast by extending the ambit of the offence of adultery so that, both the man and the woman should be punishable for the offence of adultery. The Law Commission of India in its 42nd Report, 1971, recommended the retention of Section 497 in its present form with the modification that, even the wife, who has sexual relations with a person other than her husband, should be made punishable for adultery. The suggested modification was not accepted by the legislature. Mrs. Anna Chandi, who was in the minority, voted for the deletion of Section 497 on the ground that "it is the right time to consider the question whether the offence of adultery as envisaged in Section 497 is in tune with our present day notions of woman's status in marriage'". The repot of the Law Commission show that there can be two opinions on the desirability of retaining a provision like the one contained in Section 497 on the statute book. But, we cannot strike down that section on the ground that it is desirable to delete it.

The offence of adultery as defined in that section can only be committed by a man, not by a woman. Indeed, the section provides expressly that the wife shall not be punishable even as an abettor. No grievance can then be made that the section does not allow the wife to prosecute the husband for adultery. The contemplation of the law, evidently, is that the wife, who is involved in an illicit relationship with another man, is a victim and not the author of the crime. The offence of adultery, as defined in Section 497, is considered by the Legislature as an offence against the sanctity of the matrimonial home, an act which is committed by a man, as it generally is. Therefore, those men who defile that sanctity are brought within the net of the law. Law does not confer freedom upon husbands to be licentious by gallivanting with unmarried woman. It only makes a

---

with intent that she may have illicit intercourse with any person, or conceals or detains with that intent any such woman, shall be punished with imprisonment of either description for a term which may extend to two years, or with fine, or with both.

specific kind of extra-marital relationship an offence, the relationship between a man and a married woman, the man alone being the offender. An unfaithful husband risks or, perhaps, invites a civil action by the wife for separation.

Legitimate and Illegitimate Children:

The word 'legitimate' when used with reference to a child, means lawfully begotten, born in a wedlock. In a number of decisions, legitimate is termed as lawful, real or genuine. In common law, the legal significance of the word 'children' if used in a will[14] is legal children and it will not include illegitimate children unless the testator[15] intends to include them. Under the marriage laws where a marriage has been declared void ab initio[16], the child of such marriage is for all purposes a legitimate child of the parents.

Advanced Law Lexicon, Vol. II, defines legitimate child as one born in lawful wedlock or born before the marriage of its parties, who afterwards marry and which receives the recognition of its father and one of such children is just as legitimate before the law as the other.

Illegitimacy is defined as being that which is contrary to law and it is said that the term usually is applied to children born out of lawful wedlock. Black's Law Dictionary, 4th Edn., defines illegitimate child as that which is contrary to law; it is usually applied to children born outside lawful wedlock.

In India the personal law of succession of Hindus, Christians and Muslims does not recognise children born outside wedlock as legitimate children. Among Christians and Hindus, a husband or wife cannot marry for a second time during the subsistence of the first marriage. For Muslims, their personal law permits polygamy[17]. It simply means that personal

---

14 **Meaning of Will:** A document in which a person specifies the method to be applied in the management and distribution of his estate after his death.

15 **Meaning of Testator:** A **testator** is a person who has written and executed a last will and testament that is in effect at the time of his/her death. It is any "person who makes a will.

16 **Meaning of Void-ab-Initio:** The term **void** *ab initio*, which means "to be treated as invalid from the outset.

17 **Meaning of Polygamy: Polygamy** is a marriage which includes more than two partners. When a man is married to more than one wife at a time, the relationship is called polygyny, and there is no marriage bond between the wives; and when a woman is married to more than one husband at a time, it is called polyandry, and there is no marriage bond between the husbands. If a marriage

laws of the religions in this country recognises only children begotten in wedlock as legitimate children and they alone are entitled to succeed to the estate of their deceased father. Children born out of wedlock are always considered as illegitimate. It is relevant to refer to some of the provisions in the Divorce Act, 1869 and the Hindu Marriage Act, 1955. Section 21 of Divorce Act reads as follows:

21. Children of annulled marriage.- Where a marriage is annulled on the ground that a former husband or wife was living, and it is adjudged that the subsequent marriage was contracted in good faith and with full belief of the parties that the former husband or wife was dead, or when a marriage is annulled on the ground of insanity, children begotten before the decree is made, shall be specified in the decree, and shall be entitled to succeed, in the same manner as legitimate children, to the estate of the parent who at the time of the marriage was competent to contract.

Section 18[18] read with Section 19[19] of the Divorce Act confer jurisdiction upon the court to declare a marriage null and void for the reasons stated therein. Section 21 of the Divorce Act extracted above confer status of legitimacy only to a limited class of children stated therein who are begotten before the decree is made in an annulled marriage and shall be entitled to succeed to the estate of the parent who at the time of marriage was competent to contract, as legitimate children. Thus Section 21 does not confer such status even on all children begotten in all marriages subsequently declared null and void.

Section 16[20] of the Hindu Marriage Act confers status on a limited class

---

includes multiple husbands and wives, it can be called group marriage.

18 **Section 18 in The Indian Divorce Act, 1869**
  18. Petition for decree of nullity.- Any husband or wife may present a petition to the District Court or to the High Court, praying that his or her marriage may be declared null and void.

19 **Section 19 in The Indian Divorce Act, 1869**
  19. Grounds of decree.- Such decree may be made on any of the following grounds:-
  (1) that the respondent was impotent at the time of the marriage and at the time of the institution of the suit;
  (2) that the parties are within the prohibited degrees of consanguinity (whether natural or legal) or affinity;
  (3) that either party was a lunatic or idiot at the time of the marriage;
  (4) that the former husband or wife of either party was living at the time of the marriage, and the marriage with such former husband or wife was then in force. Nothing in this section shall affect the jurisdiction of the High Court to make decrees of nullity of marriage on the ground that the consent of either party was obtained by force or fraud.

20 **Section 16 in The Hindu Marriage Act, 1955**

of children as legitimate and they are entitled to succeed to the estate of the deceased along with the children born in the wedlock. Under Hindu Law an illegitimate child has never been considered as nullius filius[21]. In some cases, he has been considered to be a member of the family. More appropriately, it can be said that in Hindu Law the illegitimate child and putative father and natural mother have never been considered strangers to each other. From the texts and the judicial pronouncements, one thing is manifestly clear that an illegitimate son is recognised but with many riders and his rights are discriminatory in nature. A son born out of wedlock is also accepted and not totally thrown out but he had been given an inferior status and thus compassion along with discrimination exists. The Apex Court in Gaurav Jain v. Union of India[22], while dealing with writ petition[23] under Article 32[24] of the Constitution of India pertaining to

---

(1) Legitimacy of children of void and voidable marriages. Notwithstanding that a marriage is null and void under section 11, any child of such marriage who would have been legitimate if the marriage had been valid, shall be legitimate, whether such child is born before or after the commencement of the Marriage Laws.

Amendment Act, 1976 , (68 of 1976 .) and whether or not a decree of nullity is granted in respect of that marriage under this Act and whether or not the marriage is held to be void otherwise than on a petition under this Act.

(2) Where a decree of nullity is granted in respect of a voidable marriage under section 12, any child begotten or conceived before the decree is made, who would have been the legitimate child of the parties to the marriage if at the date of the decree it had been dissolved instead of being annulled, shall be deemed to be their legitimate child notwithstanding the decree of nullity.

(3) Nothing contained in sub- section (1) or sub- section (2) shall be construed as conferring upon any child of a marriage which is null and void or which Is annulled by a decree of nullity under section 12, any rights in or to the property of any person, other than the parents, in any case where, but for the passing of this Act, such child would have been incapable of possessing or acquiring any such rights by reason of his not being the legitimate child of his parents.]

21 **Meaning of Nullius Filius:** *An illegitimate child who had few legal rights under the* Law

22 AIR 1997 SC 3021

23 **Meaning of Writ Petition:**
Under the Indian legal system, jurisdiction to issue 'prerogative writs' is given to the Supreme Court, and to the High Courts of Judicature of all Indian states. Parts of the law relating to writs are set forth in the Constitution of India. The Supreme Court, the highest in the country, may issue writs under Article 32 of the Constitution for enforcement of Fundamental Rights and under Articles 139 for enforcement of rights other than Fundamental Rights, while High Courts, the superior courts of the States, may issue writs under Articles 226. 'Writ' is eminently designed by the makers of the Constitution, and in the same way it is developed very widely and efficiently by the courts in India. The Constitution broadly provides for five kinds of "prerogative" writs, namely, Habeas Corpus, Certiorari, Mandamus, Quo Warranto and Prohibition.

24 **Article 32 in The Constitution Of India 1949**
32. Remedies for enforcement of rights conferred by this Part
(1) The right to move the Supreme Court by appropriate proceedings for the enforcement of the rights conferred by this Part is guaranteed
(2) The Supreme Court shall have power to issue directions or orders or writs, including writs in the nature of habeas corpus, mandamus, prohibition, quo warranto and certiorari, whichever may be

the plight of prostitutes/ fallen women and their progeny, spoke about the preamble of the Constitution and stated that it is an integral part of the Constitution and that pledges to secure socio-economic justice to all its citizens with stated liberties, equality of status and of opportunity, assuring fraternity and dignity of the individual in a united and integrated Bharat and illegitimate children too are part of citizenry.

Surrogacy:

The question of becoming parents through surrogacy came to be considered by the Supreme Court in a judgment in *Baby Manji Yamada v. Union of India*[25]. Though in that case, there was a dispute between biological parents and host, the matter was directed to be taken to the Commission for Protection of Child Rights Act, 2005. But, however various forms of surrogacy was discussed in the said judgment from paragraph 8 to 16 and it was stated as follows:

8. Surrogacy is a well-known method of reproduction whereby a woman agrees to become pregnant for the purpose of gestating and giving birth to a child she will not raise but hand over to a contracted party. She may be the child's genetic mother (the more traditional form for surrogacy) or she may be, as a gestational carrier, carry the pregnancy to delivery after having been implanted with an embryo. In some cases surrogacy is the only available option for parents who wish to have a child that is biologically related to them.

9. The word surrogate, from Latin subrogate, means appointed to act in the place of. The intended parent(s) is the individual or couple who intends to rear the child after its birth.

10. In traditional surrogacy (also known as the Straight method) the surrogate is pregnant with her own biological child, but this child was conceived with the intention of relinquishing the child to be raised by others; by the biological father and possibly his spouse or partner, either male or female. The child may be conceived via home artificial insemination using fresh or frozen sperm or impregnated

---

appropriate, for the enforcement of any of the rights conferred by this Part

(3) Without prejudice to the powers conferred on the Supreme Court by clause (1) and (2), Parliament may by law empower any other court to exercise within the local limits of its jurisdiction all or any of the powers exercisable by the Supreme Court under clause (2)

(4) The right guaranteed by this article shall not be suspended except as otherwise provided for by this Constitution

25 (2008) 13 SCC 518

via IUI (intrauterine insemination), or ICI (intracervical insemination) which is performed at a fertility clinic.

11. In gestational surrogacy (also known as the Host method) the surrogate becomes pregnant via embryo transfer with a child of which she is not the biological mother. She may have made an arrangement to relinquish it to the biological mother or father to raise, or to a parent who is themselves unrelated to the child (e.g. because the child was conceived using egg donation, germ donation or is the result of a donated embryo). The surrogate mother may be called the gestational carrier.

12. Altruistic surrogacy is a situation where the surrogate receives no financial reward for her pregnancy or the relinquishment of the child (although usually all expenses related to the pregnancy and birth are paid by the intended parents such as medical expenses, maternity clothing, and other related expenses).

13. Commercial surrogacy is a form of surrogacy in which a gestational carrier is paid to carry a child to maturity in her womb and is usually resorted to by well-off infertile couples who can afford the cost involved or people who save and borrow in order to complete their dream of being parents. This medical procedure is legal in several countries including in India where due to excellent medical infrastructure, high international demand and ready availability of poor surrogates it is reaching industry proportions. Commercial surrogacy is sometimes referred to by the emotionally charged and potentially offensive terms wombs for rent, out sourced pregnancies or baby farms.

14. Intended parents may arrange a surrogate pregnancy because a woman who intends to parent is infertile in such a way that she cannot carry a pregnancy to term. Examples include a woman who has had a hysterectomy, has a uterine malformation, has had recurrent pregnancy loss or has a health condition that makes it dangerous for her to be pregnant. A female intending parent may also be fertile and healthy, but unwilling to undergo pregnancy.

15. Alternatively, the intended parent may be a single male or a male homosexual couple.

16. Surrogates may be relatives, friends, or previous strangers. Many

surrogate arrangements are made through agencies that help match up intended parents with women who want to be surrogates for a fee. The agencies often help manage the complex medical and legal aspects involved. Surrogacy arrangements can also be made independently. In compensated surrogacies the amount a surrogate receives varies widely from almost nothing above expenses to over $30,000. Careful screening is needed to assure their health as the gestational carrier incurs potential obstetrical risks.

42

Is Surrogate Mother entitled to Maternity Benefits?[1]

Question before the Court:

The short question that arises for consideration in writ petition[2] was whether a woman employee working in the Chennai Port Trust was entitled to avail maternity leave[3] even in case where she gets the child through arrangement by Surrogate[4] parents?

Facts in Nutshell:

The petitioner[5] was working as an Assistant Superintendent in the Traffic department of the Chennai Port Trust. She had put in 24 years of service. She was married. Her son (ShyamSundar) aged 20 years died the to road accident. After his birth, the petitioner has removed her uterus due to some problem. Therefore, she in order to have a child had entered into an arrangement with Prashanth Multi Speciality hospital, Chennai to have a baby through surrogate procedure. Finally with the consent of her husband and his cooperation, a female baby was born through a host mother. She had incurred substantial expenditure towards treatment. In order to look after the newly born baby, she had applied for maternity leave. But she was informed that she was not entitled for maternity leave

---

1 Appellants: **K. Kalaiselvi Vs.** Respondent: **Chennai Port Trust**
  MANU/TN/0157/2013
  Hon'ble Judges/Coram: K. Chandru, J.

2 **Meaning of Writ Petition:**
  Under the Indian legal system, jurisdiction to issue 'prerogative writs' is given to the Supreme Court, and to the High Courts of Judicature of all Indian states. Parts of the law relating to writs are set forth in the Constitution of India. The Supreme Court, the highest in the country, may issue writs under Article 32 of the Constitution for enforcement of Fundamental Rights and under Articles 139 for enforcement of rights other than Fundamental Rights, while High Courts, the superior courts of the States, may issue writs under Articles 226. 'Writ' is eminently designed by the makers of the Constitution, and in the same way it is developed very widely and efficiently by the courts in India. The Constitution broadly provides for five kinds of "prerogative" writs, namely, Habeas Corpus, Certiorari, Mandamus, Quo Warranto and Prohibition.

3 **Meaning of Maternity Leave:** A period of paid absence from work

4 **Meaning of Surrogate:** One that takes the place of another; a substitute.

5 **Meaning of Petitioner:** A person who presents a Petition. (**Meaning of Petition:** A formal message requesting something that is submitted to an authority)

(post delivery) for having a child through surrogate procedure though such a rejection was not possible in case of a person adopting a child. The petitioner, therefore, requested for sanction of maternity leave to look after the newly born girl child and reimburse the medical expenses and also to issue the FMI Card incorporating the newly born child through her representation.

The petitioner produced before the respondent[6] (Port Trust) all documents relating to surrogate arrangement, hospital expenditures incurred by her as well as the birth certificate evidencing that the female child was born. Writ petition was filed for a consequential direction to the Chennai Port Trust to grant leave to the petitioner on equal footing in terms of Rule 3-A[7] of the Madras Port Trust (Leave) Regulations, 1987.

Surrogacy:

The question of becoming parents through surrogacy came to be considered by the Supreme Court in a judgment in *Baby Manji Yamada v. Union of India*[8]. Though in that case, there was a dispute between biological parents and host, the matter was directed to be taken to the Commission for Protection of Child Rights Act, 2005. But, however various forms of surrogacy was discussed in the said judgment from paragraph 8 to 16 and it was stated as follows:

8. Surrogacy is a well-known method of reproduction whereby a woman agrees to become pregnant for the purpose of gestating and giving birth to a child she will not raise but hand over to a contracted party. She may be the child's genetic mother (the more traditional form for surrogacy)

---

6 **Meaning of Respondent:** A **respondent** is a person who is called upon to issue a response to a communication made by another. In legal usage, this specifically refers to the defendant in a legal proceedingcommenced by a petition, or to an appellee, or the opposing party, in an appeal of a decision by an initial fact-finder.

7 **Rule 3A, which reads as follows:**
3-A. Leave to female employees on adoption of a child:
A female employee on her adoption a child may be granted leave of the kind and admissible (including commuted leave without production of medical certificate for a period not exceeding 60 days and leave not due) upto one year subject to the following conditions:
(i) the facility will not be available to an adoptive mother already having two living children at the time of adoption;
(ii) the maximum admissible period of leave of the kind due and admissible will be regulated as under:
(a) If the age of the adopted child is less than one month, leave upto one year may be allowed.
(b) If the age of the child is six months or more, leave upto six months may be allowed.
(c) If the age of the child is nine months or more leave upto three months may be allowed.

8 (2008) 13 SCC 518

or she may be, as a gestational carrier, carry the pregnancy to delivery after having been implanted with an embryo. In some cases surrogacy is the only available option for parents who wish to have a child that is biologically related to them.

9. The word surrogate, from Latin subrogate, means appointed to act in the place of. The intended parent(s) is the individual or couple who intends to rear the child after its birth.

10. In traditional surrogacy (also known as the Straight method) the surrogate is pregnant with her own biological child, but this child was conceived with the intention of relinquishing the child to be raised by others; by the biological father and possibly his spouse or partner, either male or female. The child may be conceived via home artificial insemination using fresh or frozen sperm or impregnated via IUI (intrauterine insemination), or ICI (intracervical insemination) which is performed at a fertility clinic.

11. In gestational surrogacy (also known as the Host method) the surrogate becomes pregnant via embryo transfer with a child of which she is not the biological mother. She may have made an arrangement to relinquish it to the biological mother or father to raise, or to a parent who is themselves unrelated to the child (e.g. because the child was conceived using egg donation, germ donation or is the result of a donated embryo). The surrogate mother may be called the gestational carrier.

12. Altruistic surrogacy is a situation where the surrogate receives no financial reward for her pregnancy or the relinquishment of the child (although usually all expenses related to the pregnancy and birth are paid by the intended parents such as medical expenses, maternity clothing, and other related expenses).

13. Commercial surrogacy is a form of surrogacy in which a gestational carrier is paid to carry a child to maturity in her womb and is usually resorted to by well-off infertile couples who can afford the cost involved or people who save and borrow in order to complete their dream of being parents. This medical procedure is legal in several countries including in India where due to excellent medical infrastructure, high international demand and ready availability of poor surrogates it is reaching industry proportions. Commercial surrogacy is sometimes referred to by the emotionally charged and potentially offensive terms wombs for rent, outsourced pregnancies or baby farms.

14. Intended parents may arrange a surrogate pregnancy because a woman who intends to parent is infertile in such a way that she cannot carry a pregnancy to term. Examples include a woman who has had a hysterectomy, has a uterine malformation, has had recurrent pregnancy loss or has a health condition that makes it dangerous for her to be pregnant. A female intending parent may also be fertile and healthy, but unwilling to undergo pregnancy.

15. Alternatively, the intended parent may be a single male or a male homosexual couple.

16. Surrogates may be relatives, friends, or previous strangers. Many surrogate arrangements are made through agencies that help match up intended parents with women who want to be surrogates for a fee. The agencies often help manage the complex medical and legal aspects involved. Surrogacy arrangements can also be made independently. In compensated surrogacies the amount a surrogate receives varies widely from almost nothing above expenses to over $30,000. Careful screening is needed to assure their health as the gestational carrier incurs potential obstetrical risks.

International Conventions on Women and Children: UDHR, 1948

Universal Declaration of Human Rights evolved by the United Nations and adopted by the General Assembly on 10.12.1948. He placed reliance upon Article 25(2) which reads as follows:

(2) Motherhood and childhood are entitled to special care and assistance. All children whether born in or out of wedlock, shall enjoy the same social protection.

Beijing Declaration and Platform for Action Fourth World Conference on Women, dated 15.09.1995, wherein the right of all women to control all aspects of their health, in particular their own fertility is basic to their empowerment was reaffirmed. Articles 17 and 33 reads as follows:

17. The explicit recognition and reaffirmation of the right of all women to control all aspects of their health, in particular their own fertility, is basic "to their empowerment;

33. Ensure respect for "international law, including humanitarian law, in order to protect women and girls in particular;

Convention on the Rights of the Child by United Nations General Assembly by a resolution on 20.11.1989, wherein Article 6 reads as follows:

Article 6.

1. States Parties recognize that every child has the inherent right to life. 2 States Parties shall ensure to the maximum extent possible the survival and development of the child.

Decision of the High Court:

Court do not find anything immoral and unethical about the petitioner having obtained a child through surrogate arrangement. For all practical purpose, the petitioner is the mother of the girl child and her husband is the father of the said child. When once it is admitted that the said minor child is the daughter of the petitioner and at the time of the application, she was only one day old, she is entitled for leave akin to persons who are granted leave in terms of Rule 3-A of the Leave Regulations. The purpose of the said rule is for proper bonding between the child and parents. Even in the case of adoption, the adoptive mother does not give birth to the child, but yet the necessity of bonding of the mother with the adoptive child has been recognised by the Central Government. Therefore, the petitioner is entitled for leave in terms of Rule 3-A. The respondent Chennai Port Trust was directed to grant leave to the petitioner in terms of Rule 3-A recognising the child obtained surrogate procedure. Further a direction was issued to the respondent to include the name of the child , as a member of the petitioner's family and also include her name in the FMI card forthwith.

43

Illegitimate Children Right to Succession in Property[1]

Question before the Court:

Right of succession[2] of illegitimate children[3] born to Christian parents is the bone of contention cropped up for consideration in this case. While considering this, following issues arise for consideration:

(i) Whether the requirement of a central legislation recognising the right of illegitimate children of all classes irrespective of their religion to inherit the property of their parents is the need of the hour?

(ii) Whether illegitimate children born to Christian father and mother are entitled to inherit the property of their father under the Indian Succession Act?

(iii) Whether children born to parents living as husband and wife during the subsistence of the father's first marriage are legitimate or illegitimate in the eyes of law?

Facts in Nutshell:

The case of the appellants[4] in brief is as follows:

The deceased[5] Dr. Antony was a 36-year old doctor who died in a motor accident while studying for M.S. course in the Medical College Hospital, Kottayam. The motorbike in which the deceased was travelling as pillion

---

1 Appellants: **Jane Antony and Ors.** Vs. Respondent: **V.M. Siyath and Ors.**
  2009ACJ2272
  Hon'ble Judges/Coram: C.N. Ramachandran Nair and Harun-Ul-Rashid, JJ.

2 **Meaning of Right of Succession:** The statutory rules of inheritance of a dead person's estate when the property is not given by the terms of a will, also called laws of "descent and distribution.

3 **Meaning of Illegitimate Children:** Illegitimate children are those born out of wedlock and without the legal namesake and legal responsibility of their fathers.

4 **Meaning of Appellant:** A person who, dissatisfied with the judgment rendered in a lawsuit decided in a lower court or the findings from a proceeding before an Administrative Agency, asks a superior court to review the decision.

5 **Meaning of Deceased:** A dead person.

rider along with his relative was knocked down by a Tempo van. The deceased sustained injuries and was admitted in the Medical College Hospital, Kottayam where he later died. The appellant No. 1, who was also a doctor by profession, the widow of the deceased, appellant Nos. 2 and 3 are her children born to the deceased and appellant Nos. 4 and 5 are the parents of the deceased. In the claim petition[6] filed by the appellants before the Tribunal, respondent Nos. 4 and 5 who were the children of the deceased and one Mary Antony got impleaded as additional respondents. Even though Mary Antony, claimed to be married to the deceased and respondent Nos. 4 and 5 are the children born in that wedlock, Tribunal held that since the first marriage was subsisting there could not be another valid marriage by deceased with Mary Antony. However, respondent Nos. 4 and 5, the children born to the deceased through Mary Antony, were granted compensation along with the appellants. Out of the total compensation awarded, Rs. 50,000 each was given to the parents of the deceased who were appellant Nos. 4 and 5 and the balance was apportioned among appellant Nos. 1 to 3 and respondent Nos. 4 and 5 equally. It was against the Tribunal award, appeal[7] was filed for enhancement of compensation and also for cancelling the award passed in favour of respondent Nos. 4 and 5 (Children).

Legitimate and Illegitimate Children:

The word 'legitimate' when used with reference to a child, means lawfully begotten, born in a wedlock. In a number of decisions, legitimate is termed as lawful, real or genuine. In common law, the legal significance of the word 'children' if used in a will[8] is legal children and it will not include illegitimate children unless the testator[9] intends to include them. Under the marriage laws where a marriage has been declared void ab

---

6 **Meaning of Petition:** A formal message requesting something that is submitted to an authority

7 **Meaning of Appeal:** In law, an **appeal** is a process for requesting a formal change to an official decision. Very broadly speaking there are appeals on the record and *de novo* appeals. In *de novo* appeals, a new decision maker re-hears the case without any reference to the prior decision maker. In appeals on the record, the decision of the prior decision maker is challenged by arguing that he or she misapplied the law, came to an incorrect factual finding, acted in excess of his jurisdiction, abused his powers, was biased, considered evidence which he should not have considered or failed to consider evidence that he should have considered.

8 **Meaning of Will:** A document in which a person specifies the method to be applied in the management and distribution of his estate after his death.

9 **Meaning of Testator:** A **testator** is a person who has written and executed a last will and testament that is in effect at the time of his/her death. It is any "person who makes a will.

initio[10], the child of such marriage is for all purposes a legitimate child of the parents.

Advanced Law Lexicon, Vol. II, defines legitimate child as one born in lawful wedlock or born before the marriage of its parties, who afterwards marry and which receives the recognition of its father and one of such children is just as legitimate before the law as the other.

Illegitimacy is defined as being that which is contrary to law and it is said that the term usually is applied to children born out of lawful wedlock. Black's Law Dictionary, 4th Edn., defines illegitimate child as that which is contrary to law; it is usually applied to children born outside lawful wedlock.

In India the personal law of succession of Hindus, Christians and Muslims does not recognise children born outside wedlock as legitimate children. Among Christians and Hindus, a husband or wife cannot marry for a second time during the subsistence of the first marriage. For Muslims, their personal law permits polygamy[11]. It simply means that personal laws of the religions in this country recognises only children begotten in wedlock as legitimate children and they alone are entitled to succeed to the estate of their deceased father. Children born out of wedlock are always considered as illegitimate. It is relevant to refer to some of the provisions in the Divorce Act, 1869 and the Hindu Marriage Act, 1955. Section 21 of Divorce Act reads as follows:

21. Children of annulled marriage.- Where a marriage is annulled on the ground that a former husband or wife was living, and it is adjudged that the subsequent marriage was contracted in good faith and with full belief of the parties that the former husband or wife was dead, or when a marriage is annulled on the ground of insanity, children begotten before the decree is made, shall be specified in the decree, and shall be entitled to succeed, in the same manner as legitimate children, to the estate of the parent who at the time of the marriage was competent to contract.

---

10 **Meaning of Void-ab-Initio:** The term **void *ab initio***, which means "to be treated as invalid from the outset.

11 **Meaning of Polygamy: Polygamy** is a marriage which includes more than two partners. When a man is married to more than one wife at a time, the relationship is called polygyny, and there is no marriage bond between the wives; and when a woman is married to more than one husband at a time, it is called polyandry, and there is no marriage bond between the husbands. If a marriage includes multiple husbands and wives, it can be called group marriage.

Section 18[12] read with Section 19[13] of the Divorce Act confer jurisdiction upon the court to declare a marriage null and void for the reasons stated therein. Section 21 of the Divorce Act extracted above confer status of legitimacy only to a limited class of children stated therein who are begotten before the decree is made in an annulled marriage and shall be entitled to succeed to the estate of the parent who at the time of marriage was competent to contract, as legitimate children. Thus Section 21 does not confer such status even on all children begotten in all marriages subsequently declared null and void.

Section 16[14] of the Hindu Marriage Act confers status on a limited class of children as legitimate and they are entitled to succeed to the estate of the deceased along with the children born in the wedlock. Under Hindu Law an illegitimate child has never been considered as nullius filius[15]. In some cases, he has been considered to be a member of the family. More appropriately, it can be said that in Hindu Law the illegitimate child and

---

12 **Section 18 in The Indian Divorce Act, 1869**
18. Petition for decree of nullity.- Any husband or wife may present a petition to the District Court or to the High Court, praying that his or her marriage may be declared null and void.

13 **Section 19 in The Indian Divorce Act, 1869**
 19. Grounds of decree.- Such decree may be made on any of the following grounds:-
(1) that the respondent was impotent at the time of the marriage and at the time of the institution of the suit;
(2) that the parties are within the prohibited degrees of consanguinity (whether natural or legal) or affinity;
(3) that either party was a lunatic or idiot at the time of the marriage;
(4) that the former husband or wife of either party was living at the time of the marriage, and the marriage with such former husband or wife was then in force. Nothing in this section shall affect the jurisdiction of the High Court to make decrees of nullity of marriage on the ground that the consent of either party was obtained by force or fraud.

14 **Section 16 in The Hindu Marriage Act, 1955**
(1) Legitimacy of children of void and voidable marriages. Notwithstanding that a marriage is null and void under section 11, any child of such marriage who would have been legitimate if the marriage had been valid, shall be legitimate, whether such child is born before or after the commencement of the Marriage Laws.
Amendment Act, 1976 , (68 of 1976 .) and whether or not a decree of nullity is granted in respect of that marriage under this Act and whether or not the marriage is held to be void otherwise than on a petition under this Act.
(2) Where a decree of nullity is granted in respect of a voidable marriage under section 12, any child begotten or conceived before the decree is made, who would have been the legitimate child of the parties to the marriage if at the date of the decree it had been dissolved instead of being annulled, shall be deemed to be their legitimate child notwithstanding the decree of nullity.
(3) Nothing contained in sub- section (1) or sub- section (2) shall be construed as conferring upon any child of a marriage which is null and void or which Is annulled by a decree of nullity under section 12, any rights in or to the property of any person, other than the parents, in any case where, but for the passing of this Act, such child would have been incapable of possessing or acquiring any such rights by reason of his not being the legitimate child of his parents.]

15 **Meaning of Nullius Filius:** *An illegitimate child who had few legal rights under the* Law

putative father and natural mother have never been considered strangers to each other. From the texts and the judicial pronouncements, one thing is manifestly clear that an illegitimate son is recognised but with many riders and his rights are discriminatory in nature. A son born out of wedlock is also accepted and not totally thrown out but he had been given an inferior status and thus compassion along with discrimination exists. The Apex Court in Gaurav Jain v. Union of India[16], while dealing with writ petition[17] under Article 32[18] of the Constitution of India pertaining to the plight of prostitutes/ fallen women and their progeny, spoke about the preamble of the Constitution and stated that it is an integral part of the Constitution and that pledges to secure socio-economic justice to all its citizens with stated liberties, equality of status and of opportunity, assuring fraternity and dignity of the individual in a united and integrated Bharat and illegitimate children too are part of citizenry.

---

16 AIR 1997 SC 3021

17 **Meaning of Writ Petition:**
Under the Indian legal system, jurisdiction to issue 'prerogative writs' is given to the Supreme Court, and to the High Courts of Judicature of all Indian states. Parts of the law relating to writs are set forth in the Constitution of India. The Supreme Court, the highest in the country, may issue writs under Article 32 of the Constitution for enforcement of Fundamental Rights and under Articles 139 for enforcement of rights other than Fundamental Rights, while High Courts, the superior courts of the States, may issue writs under Articles 226. 'Writ' is eminently designed by the makers of the Constitution, and in the same way it is developed very widely and efficiently by the courts in India. The Constitution broadly provides for five kinds of "prerogative" writs, namely, Habeas Corpus, Certiorari, Mandamus, Quo Warranto and Prohibition.

18 **Article 32 in The Constitution Of India 1949**
32. Remedies for enforcement of rights conferred by this Part
(1) The right to move the Supreme Court by appropriate proceedings for the enforcement of the rights conferred by this Part is guaranteed
(2) The Supreme Court shall have power to issue directions or orders or writs, including writs in the nature of habeas corpus, mandamus, prohibition, quo warranto and certiorari, whichever may be appropriate, for the enforcement of any of the rights conferred by this Part
(3) Without prejudice to the powers conferred on the Supreme Court by clause (1) and (2), Parliament may by law empower any other court to exercise within the local limits of its jurisdiction all or any of the powers exercisable by the Supreme Court under clause (2)
(4) The right guaranteed by this article shall not be suspended except as otherwise provided for by this Constitution

Non-Discrimination provisions for Children:

Universal Declaration of Human Rights, Article 25(2):

Motherhood and childhood are entitled to special care and assistance. All children whether born in or out of wedlock, shall enjoy the same social protection.

Article 1. All human beings are born free and equal in dignity and rights. They are endowed with reason and conscience and should act towards one another in a spirit of brotherhood.

Muslim Law prohibits inheritance to property of the deceased by illegitimate children. One of the reasons for permitting polygamy is that under no circumstances the child born to them shall be illegitimate. The system of monogamy prevails in Hindu and Christian religions and members of such communities are expected to cohabit with their lawful spouses only. Polygamy is permitted among Muslims to prevent birth of illegitimate children as one of its pious objects. At present in our society a large number of illegal relationship prevail and the number of illegitimate children are increasing in alarming proportions in all communities. Several men and women live together without marrying and the society is not attributing immorality to them. The only exception is the life of prostitutes (unchaste women) and children born to them, who cannot claim father for them.

Section 125(1)[19], Criminal Procedure Code gives statutory recognition for right of maintenance of children both legitimate and illegitimate from their father. Since children have no role in their birth, illegitimate children

---

19 **Section 125 in The Code Of Criminal Procedure, 1973**
   125. Order for maintenance of wives, children and parents.
   (1) If any person having sufficient means neglects or refuses to maintain-
   (a) his wife, unable to maintain herself, or
   (b) his legitimate or illegitimate minor child, whether married or not, unable to maintain itself, or
   (c) his legitimate or illegitimate child (not being a married daughter) who has attained majority, where such child is, by reason of any physical or mental abnormality or injury unable to maintain itself, or
   (d) his father or mother, unable to maintain himself or herself, a Magistrate of the first class may, upon proof of such neglect or refusal, order such person to make a monthly allowance for the maintenance of his wife or such child, father or mother, at such monthly rate not exceeding five hundred rupees in the whole, as such Magistrate thinks fit, and to pay the same to such person as the Magistrate may from time to time direct: Provided that the Magistrate may order the father of a minor female child referred to in clause (b) to make such allowance, until she attains her majority, if the Magistrate is satisfied that the husband of such minor female child, if married, is not possessed of sufficient means.

are like any other children born to their parents. It is unfortunate that there is no law in this country to protect the interest of the illegitimate children. Their right to succeed to the estate of their deceased father or mother is not recognised by the administrators or government, as the case may be by enacting legislation. The legitimate status of the children which depend very much upon the marriage between their parents being valid or void, thus turned on the act of parents over which the innocent child had no hold or control. But, for no fault of it, the innocent baby has to suffer a permanent setback in life and in the eyes of the society by being treated as illegitimate. In other words, for the act of the parent, the innocent children should not be made to suffer. There are several cases in our country where man and woman live together as husband and wife, children are begotten to them and are taken care of by them. When the question arises as to whether such children can succeed to the estate of their deceased parents, there is no statute in this country enabling them to inherit the property of their parents.

An illegitimate child not only suffers from a social stigma in every legal order but he is also put to an unfortunate position as regards his rights of inheritance and support are concerned. Its suffering or deprivations are based on the maxim, pater est quern nuptiae demonstrant[20].

European convention for the Protection of Human Rights and Fundamental Freedoms, 1950, Article 14:

The enjoyment of rights and freedoms set forth in this convention shall be secured without discrimination on any ground such as sex, colour, language, religion, political or other opinion, national or social origin, association with a national minority, property, birth or other status.

Declaration of the Rights of the Child-Principle I:

The child shall enjoy all the rights set forth in this declaration. Every child without any exception whatsoever shall be entitled to these rights, without distinction or discrimination on account of race, colour, sex, language, religion, political or other opinion, national or social origin, property, birth or other status, whether of himself or of his family.

International Covenant on Economic, Social and Cultural Rights, 1966:

---

20 **Meaning of Pater Est Quern Nuptiae Demonstrant:** The father is he whom the marriage points out.

Article 2 (2) states that the parties to the present covenant undertake to guarantee that the rights enunciated in the present covenant will be exercised without discrimination of any kind as to race, colour, sex, language, religion, political or other opinion, national or social origin, property, birth or other status.

International Covenant on Civil and Political Rights:

Article 24 (1). Every child shall have, without any discrimination as to race, colour, sex, language, religion, national or social origin, property, or birth, the right to such measures of protection as required by his status as a minor, on the part of his family, society and the State.

Convention on the Rights of the Child:

Article 2 (2) states that parties shall take all appropriate measures to ensure that the child is protected against all forms of discrimination or punishment on the basis of the status, activities, expressed opinions...

Legitimacy is a status. It is the condition of belonging to a class in society the members of which are regarded as having been begotten in lawful matrimony by the men whom the law regards as their fathers. The status of legitimacy gives the child certain rights both against the man whom the law regards as his father and generally in society. An illegitimate child in the eyes of law is nullius filius. So, a relation means a relation flowing from lawful wedlock. The rule under law of succession is that children means legitimate children. *So the statutory provisions and judicial decisions are so clear that under Christian Law in India a child does not include illegitimate child and, therefore, such child is not entitled to a share in the property of the deceased parents.*

The provisions of Section 125 of Criminal Procedure Code which is secular in nature is applicable to persons of all communities in India independent of their personal law. Right of the child legitimate or illegitimate under the Code of Criminal Procedure is an individual right of the child independent of the mother. While deciding the question of right of a child for maintenance, paternity and not legitimacy has to be taken into account. The provision aims at securing enforcement of duty imposed upon a person by law. The courts in India recognised the presumption of valid marriage from long cohabitation. Several cases have come to our notice where a man and woman living together as husband and wife without undergoing the formalities of marriage and children born in such relationship are not treated as legitimate under law. No child is born in the world without a father and a mother. The child has no role to play in his/her birth. Many such illegitimate children may not know who their progenitors are. The children born to unchaste women belong to that class. The mother of such children also may not know who is the father of the child. But the fact remains that all children both legitimate and illegitimate are born to their father and mother. In the present world by scientific means or tests, identity of the father of any child can be established. Children born to a mother and father who cohabited for a considerable period of time as husband and wife and being regarded by their neighbours and friends as husband and wife and their parents also acknowledged them as their children and so described in documents like ration card, voters' list and school register, there is a strong presumption that the children are legitimate children. Parliament recognised all the children both legitimate and illegitimate to be maintained by their father under the Code of Criminal Procedure.

Decision of the High Court:

If all the children both legitimate and illegitimate are held entitled to the maintenance, there is no reason or logic in denying them their right of inheritance to succeed to the properties of their parents in cases of intestacy. Court suggested to the Central Government to enact a legislation to confer right of succession on all illegitimate children irrespective of their religion in tune with Section 125 of the Code of Criminal Procedure which is for all purposes a secular legislation. Court also suggested to enact separate laws for members of different religions or a single statute like Section 125 of the Code of Criminal Procedure enabling illegitimate children to succeed to the estate of their deceased father and mother. Court awarded equal compensation to respondents number 4-5 (Children's)

44

Identity of Children born from Surrogate Mother[1]

Question before the Court:

The question whether a child born in India to a surrogate mother, an Indian national, whose biological father was a foreign national, would get citizenship in India, by birth, was a momentous question which has no precedent in this country.

Facts in Nutshell:

Petitioner[2] was a German national and was a biological father of two babies given birth by a surrogate mother a citizen of India. Petitioner's wife a German national. Due to biological reasons, the wife of the petitioner was not in a position to conceive a child. Desiring to have a child of their own, they opted for In Vitro Fertilization (IVF). Assisted Reproductive Technology Infertility Clinic at Anand came to their help. Investigation revealed that wife of the petitioner would not be in a position to reproduce ova (eggs) as a result of which it would not be possible to conceive a child even with the help of a surrogate mother by using the sperm of the petitioner. An Indian citizen keeping anonymity volunteered to donate ova, and through a scientific process the petitioner's sperm was fertilized with the donor's ova and the fertilized embryo was implanted to the uterus of the surrogate mother. Petitioner and his wife had entered into a surrogacy agreement with the surrogate mother. She (Surrogate Mother) had also agreed to hand over the child to the petitioner and his wife on delivery. Further surrogate mother had also agreed that she would not take any responsibility about the well being of the child and the biological parents would have legal obligation to accept their child and that surrogate mother would deliver and the child would have all

---

1   Appellants: **Jan Balaz Vs.** Respondent: **Anand Municipality and 6 Ors.**
    AIR2010Guj21
    Hon'ble Judges/Coram: K.S. Radhakrishnan, C.J. and Anant S. Dave, J.

2   **Meaning of Petitioner:** A person who presents a Petition. (**Meaning of Petition:** A formal message requesting something that is submitted to an authority)

inheritance facts of a child of biological parents as per the prevailing law.

Surrogate mother gave birth to two baby boys on 4.1.2008. Petitioner then applied for registration of the birth of the children in the prescribed form to Anand Nagar Palika. Anand Nagar Palika issued a certificate of birth to the children as per the provisions of Registration of Birth and Deaths Act, 1969. Earlier date of birth was shown as 14.1.2008, which was later corrected as 4.1.2008 and the name of the petitioner's wife who was shown as the mother of the babies, was replaced with the name of Surrogate Mother.

Petitioner and his wife, though German nationals, are working in United Kingdom, stated that they are desirous of settling down in U.K. and for the said purpose they have to obtain VISA from the Consulate of the United Kingdom in India. Since babies were born in India and are Indian citizens, petitioner applied for their Passport in India showing their names as "Balaz Nikolas" and "Balaz Leonard". Petitioner's name was shown as the father and surrogate mother's name was shown as the mother. Applications were entertained by the Passport Authorities and Passport No. G-8229646 and Passport No. G-8229647 respectively were issued in the name of above mentioned babies. Later, petitioner received an intimation-cum-notice issued by the Government of India, Ministry of External Affairs, Regional Passport Office that since the matter was pending in Hon'ble High Court of Gujarat and this is the citizenship related issue you are hereby informed to surrender both the passport to this office immediately, it will be returned to you after the final decision received from Hon'ble High Court.

Petitioner surrendered both the Passports before the Passport Authority at Ahmedabad. Petitioner seeks direction to the Regional Passport Officer to return those Passports so that he can take the babies to Germany and then make an application in Germany so as to acquire German Citizenship. Petitioner submitted that surrogacy was not recognized in Germany. Petitioner submitted that since babies are born in India and are citizens of India, Germany would not recognize them as its citizens. Denial of Passports, according to the petitioner, was illegal and violative of Article 21[3] of the Constitution of India.

---

3   **Article 21 in The Constitution Of India 1949**
   21. Protection of life and personal liberty No person shall be deprived of his life or personal liberty except according to procedure established by law

Citizenship and Passport:

As per Passport Act, 1967, only Indian citizens can apply for Indian Passport and as per Section 6(2)(a)[4] of the Act, Passport cannot be issued to non-citizens.

Surrogacy:

Commercial surrogacy is never considered to be illegal in India and few of the countries like Ukrain, California in the United States. Law Commission of India in it's 220th Report on "Need for Legislation to regulate Assisted Reproductive Technology Clinics as well as rights and obligations of parents to a "surrogacy" has opined that surrogacy agreement will continue to be governed by contract among parties, which will contain all terms requiring consent of surrogate mother to bear the child, agreement of a husband and other family members for the same, medical procedures of artificial insemination, reimbursement of all reasonable expenses for carrying the child to full term, willingness to hand over a child to a commissioning parents etc. Law Commission has also recommended that legislation itself should recognize a surrogate child to be the legitimate child of the commissioning parents without there being any need for adoption or even declaration of guardian. Further it was also suggested that birth certificate of surrogate child should contain names of the commissioning parents only and that the right to privacy of the donor as well as surrogate mother should be protected. Exploitation of women through surrogacy was also a worrying factor, which is to be taken care of through legislation. Law Commission has expressed its desire that Assisted Reproductive Technology Bill with all safeguards would be passed in the near future.

In Baby Manje's case[5] decided by the apex Court of India where the Japanese Embassy in India refused to grant the child, born to surrogate

---

4   **Section 6(2) in The Passports Act, 1967**
    (2) Subject to the other provisions of this Act, the passport authority shall refuse to issue a passport or travel document for visiting any foreign country under clause (c) of sub- section (2) of section 5 on any one or more of the following grounds, and on no other ground, namely:--
    (a) that the applicant is not a citizen of India;
    (b) that the applicant may, or is likely to, engage outside India in activities prejudicial to the sovereignty and integrity of India;
    (c) that the departure of the applicant from India may, or is likely to, be detrimental to the security of India;
    (d) that the presence of the applicant outside India may, or is likely to, prejudice the friendly relations of India with any foreign country

5   (2008) 13 SCC 518.

Indian mother, VISA or Passport on the ground that the Japanese Civil Code recognizes a mother only to be a woman who gives birth to a baby. Attempts made to adopt Manji also did not fructify since Guardian Wards Act, 1890 did not allow single man to adopt those babies. Efforts were made to obtain Indian Passport, which also required a birth certificate. Question arose as to who was the real mother whether it was anonymous egg donor or the surrogate mother. Birth certificate was then issued by the local Municipality, by showing the father's name. Later the Regional Passport Office, Rajasthan issued a certificate of identity as part of a transit document and not the Passport. Certificate did not contain nationality, mother's name or religion of the baby.

Decision of the Court:

Court held that even if the children are described as illegitimate children, even then they are born in this country(India) to an Indian national and hence, they are entitled to get Citizenship by birth as per Section 3(1)(c)(ii)[6] of the Citizenship Act, 1955, since one of their parent is an Indian citizen.

Section 3 uses the expression "every person born" and the emphasis is on the expressions 'person' and 'born'. 'Person' means a natural person. Both the babies in this case are persons born in India, indisputedly one of their parents is an Indian citizen, a surrogate mother. The two babies have therefore satisfied the ingredients of Section 3(1)(c)(ii) and hence they are Indian citizens by birth. Passport to travel abroad therefore, cannot be denied to those babies, who are Indian citizens, which would otherwise be violative of Article 21 of the Constitution of India. Section 6 of the Passport Act refers to the grounds for refusal of Passport. Section 6(2)(a) says that Passport can be denied if the applicant is not a citizen of India. In the instant case it was already found that two babies born to the surrogate mother are Indian citizens by birth and hence entitled to get Passports.

---

6   Relevant portion of Section 3
    3. Citizenship by birth - (1) Except as provided in sub-section (2), every person born in India, --
    (a) ...
    (b) ...
    (c) on or after the commencement of the Citizenship (Amendment) Act, 2003, where --
    (i) ......
    (ii) one of whose parents is a citizen of India and the other is not an illegal migrant at the time of his birth, shall be a citizen of India by birth.

45

Guidelines for assisting the Victims of Rape[1]

Facts in Nutshell:

Subhra Chakraborty (alias - Kalpana) who was student of the Baptist College, Kohima where the opposite party, Shri Bodhisattwa Gautam was a lecturer, filed a complaint in the Court of the Judicial Magistrate, 1st Class, Kohima, Nagaland, alleging, inter alia, as under:

That, complainant[2] begs to state that in April 1989 the accused[3] person entered into Baptist College, Kohima as a Lecturer thereof and the complainant was a student of the said College at that relevant period. That, the accused person was in said Service in Kohima from April 1989 till he resigned the Service and was residing in a rented house.

That, on the 10th June, 1989 for the 1st time the accused visited the complainant's residence in Kohima and thereafter often he used to visit complainant's residence, as a teacher he was respected by the complainant as well as all the members including her parents. In course of such visits the accused voluntarily told complainant that he was already in her love. Thus there developed a love affair between themselves. The accused gave false assurance of marriage to the innocent complainant and thereby the accused dishonestly procured sexual intercourse with the complainant. The accused often use to induce the complainant to have biological contact with him, but whenever he was approached by the complainant to complete the marriage ceremony, the accused very tactfully used to defer the marriage sometimes saying that he was waiting for his parents formal consent and sometimes saying to cooperate him till he got a Govt. Service. In course of continuation of the affairs between the complainant and the accused, the complainant got pregnant twice.

---

1 Appellants: **Shri Bodhisattwa Gautam Vs.** Respondent: **Miss Subhra Chakraborty**
   AIR1996SC922
   Hon'ble Judges: and S. Saghir Ahmad, JJ.

2 **Meaning of Complainant:** A party that makes a complaint or files a formal charge, as in a court of law; a plaintiff.

3 **Meaning of Accused:** A person charged with a criminal offense, or the state of being so charged

The complainant being pregnant was placed in a very awkward position, as such, agreed said secret marriage, accordingly the accused on the 20th September, 1993, married the complainant in front of the God he Worships in his residence in Kenozou Valley, Kohima by putting Vermilion (sindur) on the complainant's forehead and accepted the complainant as his lawful wife and thus the complainant was consorted and consoled. But the complainant faced further corporal punishment[4], as the accused kept on insisting the complainant to be refrained from giving birth to the baby and was pressurising her to undergo operation/abortion despite her refusal for the same. The accused with fraudulent intention to deceive the complainant proposed the said abortion on the plea that birth of the baby would be a barrier to convince his parents to accept the complainant as their daughter-in-law and such event would lead the complainant to a path of unhappiness. The complainant being an innocent lady failed to understand the accused's wicked and mischievous plan whereby the accused succeeded and dishonestly motivated the complainant for abortion and compelled the complainant to undergo operation in the Putonou Clinic, and aborted October '93.

The complainant was forced to undergo abortion even second time with the pretext that if the complainant gave birth to any child before the accused could convince his parents she would never be accepted by Bodhisatta's parents and relatives further their marriage being a secret one, the developed stage of the complainant would hamper the dignity of her own parents and other paternal relations irreparably and thus taking the privilege of complainant innocence the accused has exploited the complainant in a very pre-planned way. The accused was so wicked that he even furnished a false name in the said Nursing Home and signed the consent Register/Paper as BIKASH GAUTAM concealing his real name BODHISATTA GAUTAM.

Registration of Complaint:

This complaint was registered as Criminal Case Under

---

4   **Meaning of Corporal Punishment:** Punishment of a physical nature, such as caning, flogging, or beating

Sections 312[5]/420[6]/493[7]/496[8]/498-A[9], Indian Penal Code and Bodhisattwa Gautam was summoned but he, in the meantime, filed a petition in the Gauhati High Court under Section 482[10] of the CrPC for quashing of the complaint and the proceedings initiated on its basis, on the ground that the allegations, taken at their face-value, do not make out any case against him. But the High Court by its judgment and order dismissed the petition compelling Bodhisattwa Gautam to approach Supreme Court by way of

---

5 **Section 312 in The Indian Penal Code, 1860**
312. Causing miscarraige.-- Whoever voluntarily causes a woman with child to miscarry, shall if such miscarriage be not caused in good faith for the purpose of saving the life of the woman, be punished with imprisonment of either description for a term which may extend to three years, or with fine, or with both; and, if the woman be quick with child, shall be punished with imprisonment of either description for a term which may extend to seven years, and shall also be liable to fine. Explanation.- A woman who causes herself to miscarry, is within the meaning of this section.

6 **Section 420 in The Indian Penal Code, 1860**
420. Cheating and dishonestly inducing delivery of property.-- Whoever cheats and thereby dishonestly induces the person deceived to deliver any property to any person, or to make, alter or destroy the whole or any part of a valuable security, or anything which is signed or sealed, and which is capable of being converted into a valuable security, shall be punished with imprisonment of either description for a term which may extend to seven years, and shall also be liable to fine. Of fraudulent deeds and dispositions of property

7 **Section 493 in The Indian Penal Code, 1860**
493. Cohabitation caused by a man deceitfully inducing a belief of lawful marriage.-- Every man who by deceit causes any woman who is not lawfully married to him to believe that she is lawfully married to him and to cohabit or have sexual intercourse with him in that belief, shall be punished with imprisonment of either description for a term which may extend to ten years, and shall also be liable to fine.

8 **Section 496 in The Indian Penal Code, 1860**
496. Marriage ceremony fraudulently gone through without lawful marriage.-- Whoever, dishonestly or with a fraudulent intention, goes through the ceremony of being married, knowing that he is not thereby lawfully married, shall be punished with imprisonment of either description for a term which may extend to seven years, and shall also be liable to fine.

9 **Section 498A in The Indian Penal Code, 1860**
498A. Husband or relative of husband of a woman subjecting her to cruelty.-- Whoever, being the husband or the relative of the husband of a woman, subjects such woman to cruelty shall be punished with imprisonment for a term which may extend to three years and shall also be liable to fine.
Explanation.- For the purposes of this section," cruelty" means-
(a) any wilful conduct which is of such a nature as is likely to drive the woman to commit suicide or to cause grave injury or danger to life, limb or health (whether mental or physical) of the woman; or
(b) harassment of the woman where such harassment is with a view to coercing her or any person related to her to meet any unlawful demand for any property or valuable security or is on account of failure by her or any person related to her to meet such demand.] CHAPTER XXI OF DEFAMATION CHAPTER XXI OF DEFAMATION

10 **Section 482 in The Code Of Criminal Procedure, 1973**
482. Saving of inherent powers of High Court. Nothing in this Code shall be deemed to limit or affect the inherent powers of the High Court to make such orders as may be necessary to give effect to any order under this Code, or to prevent abuse of the process of any Court or otherwise to secure the ends of justice.

Special Leave Petition[11].

Dignity of Women and Rape:

Unfortunately, a woman, in our country, belongs to a class or group of society who are in a disadvantaged position on account of several social barriers and impediments and have, therefore, been the victim of tyranny at the hands of men with whom they, fortunately, under the Constitution enjoy equal status. Women also have the right to life and liberty; they also have the right to be respected and treated as equal citizens. Their honour and dignity cannot be touched or violated. They also have the right to lead an honourable and peaceful life. Women, in them, have many personalities combined. They are Mother, Daughter, Sister and Wife and not play things for center spreads in various magazines, periodicals or newspapers nor can they be exploited for obscene purposes. They must have the liberty, the freedom and, of course, independence to live the roles assigned to them by Nature so that the society may flourish as they alone have the talents and capacity to shape the destiny and character of men anywhere and in every part of the world. Rape is thus not only a crime against the person of a woman (victim), it is a crime against the entire society. It destroys the entire psychology of a woman and pushes her into deep emotional crises. It is only by her sheer will power that she rehabilitates herself in the society which, on coming to know of the rape, looks down upon her in derision and contempt. Rape is, therefore, the most hated crime. It is a crime against basic human rights and is also violative of the victim's most cherished of the Fundamental Rights, namely, the Right to Life contained in Article 21[12]. To many feminists and psychiatrists, rape is less a sexual offence than an act of aggression aimed at degrading and humiliating women. The rape laws do not, unfortunately, take care of the social aspect of the matter and are inept in many respects.

---

11 Article 136 in The Constitution Of India 1949
   136. Special leave to appeal by the Supreme Court
   (1) Notwithstanding anything in this Chapter, the Supreme Court may, in its discretion, grant special leave to appeal from any judgment, decree, determination, sentence or order in any cause or matter passed or made by any court or tribunal in the territory of India
   (2) Nothing in clause (1) shall apply to any judgment, determination, sentence or order passed or made by any court or tribunal constituted by or under any law relating to the Armed Forces

12 Article 21 in The Constitution Of India 1949
   21. Protection of life and personal liberty No person shall be deprived of his life or personal liberty except according to procedure established by law

In *Women's Forum v.Union of India*[13], in which Court observed as under:

It is rather unfortunate that in recent times, there has been an increase in violence against women causing serious concern. Rape does indeed pose a series of problems for the criminal justice system. There are cries for harshest penalties, but often times such crimes eclipse the real plight of the victim. Rape is an experience which shakes the foundations of the lives of the victims. For many, its effect is a long-term one, impairing their capacity for personal relationships, altering their behavior values and generating and less fears. In addition to the trauma of the rape itselfs, victims have had to suffer further agony during legal proceedings.

This Court further observed as under:

The defects in the present system are : Firstly, complaints are handled roughly and are not even such attention as is warranted. The victims, more often than not, are humiliated by the police. The victims have invariably found rape trials a traumatic experience. The experience of giving evidence in court has been negative and destructive. The victims often say, they considered the ordeal to be even worse than the rape itself. Undoubtedly, the court proceedings added to and prolonged the psychological stress they had had to suffer as a result of the rape itself.

Directions of Supreme Court for assisting the Victims of Rape:

(1) The complainants of sexual assault cases should be provided with legal representation. It is important to have some one who is well-acquainted with the criminal justice system. The role of the victim's advocate would not only be to explain to the victim the nature of the proceedings, to prepare her for the case and to assist her in the police station and in court but to provide her with guidance as to how she might obtain help of a different nature from other agencies, for example, mind counselling or medical assistance. It is important to secure continuity of assistance by ensuring that the same person who looked after the complainant's interests in the police station represnet her till the end of the case.

(2) Legal assistance will have to be provided at the police station since the victim of sexual assault might very well be in a distressed state upon arrival at the police station, the guidance and support of a lawyer at this stage and whilst she was being questioned would be of great assistance to her.

13 (1995)1SCC14

(3) The police should be under a duty to inform the victim of her right to representation before any questions were asked of her and that the police report should state that the victim was so informed.

(4) A list of advocates willing to act in these cases should be kept at the police station for victims who did not have a particular lawyer in mind or whose own lawyer was unavailable.

(5) The advocate shall be appointed by the court, upon application by the police at the earliest convenient movement, but in order to ensure that victims were questioned without undue delay, advocates would be authorised to act at the police station before leave of the court was sought or obtained.

(6) In all rape trials anonymity of the victims must be maintained, as far as necessary.

(7) It is necessary, having regard to the Directive Principles contained under Article 38(1)[14] of the Constitution of India to set up Criminal Injuries Compensation Board. Rape victims frequently incur substantial financial loss. Some, for example, are too traumatized to continue in employment.

(8) Compensation for victims shall be awarded by the court on conviction of the offender and by the Criminal Injuries Compensation Board whether or not a conviction has taken place. The Board will take into account pain, suffering and shock as well as loss of earnings due to pregnancy and the expenses of the child but if this occurred as a result of the rape.

Decision of the Supreme Court:

Court held that Bodhisattwa Gautam had married Subhra Chakraborty before the God he worshiped by putting Vermilion on her forehead and accepting her as his wife and also having impregnated her twice resulting in abortion on both the occasions. Court being prima-facie satisfied, dispose of matter by providing that Bodhisattwa Gautam shall pay to Subhra Chakraborty a sum of Rs. 1,000 every month as interim compensation during the pendency of Criminal Case in the court of Judicial Magistrate, 1st Class, Kohima, Nagaland.

---

14 **Article 38(1) in The Constitution Of India 1949**
   (1) The State shall strive to promote the welfare of the people by securing and protecting as effectively as it may a social order in which justice, social, economic and political, shall inform all the institutions of the national life

46

Privately viewing obscene film constitutes no offence[1]

Facts in Nutshell:

The petitioners[2]/accused were the students of Acharya Polytechnic Engineering College, Bangalore. The accused[3] No. 1, and 2 were tenants[4]. On information, sub-inspector of Peenya police raided the residence of the petitioners on and found the accused were watching obscene film in the computer of Accused No 1. The Police seized the computer and 3-C. Ds. After investigation, the investigating officer laid charge sheet against the petitioners/accused for the offence punishable under Section 292[5] of

---

1   Appellants: **Sri DeepankarChowdariand Ors. Vs.** Respondent: **The State of Karnataka**
     2008CriLJ3408
     Hon'ble Judges/Coram: K. Bhakthavatsala, J.

2   **Meaning of Petitioner:** A person who presents a Petition. (**Meaning of Petition:** A formal message requesting something that is submitted to an authority)

3   **Meaning of Accused:** A person charged with a criminal offense, or the state of being so charged

4   **Meaning of Tenant:** Someone who pays rent to use land or a building or a car that is owned by someone else; "the landlord can evict a tenant who doesn't pay the rent"

5   **Section 292 in The Indian Penal Code, 1860**
     292. [Sale, etc., of obscene books, etc.-- [(1) For the purposes of sub- section (2), a book, pamphlet, paper, writing, drawing, painting representation, figure or any other object, shall be deemed to be obscene if it is lascivious or appeals to the prurient interest or if its effect, or (where it comprises two or more distinct items) the effect of any one of its items, is, if taken as a whole, such as to tend to deprave and corrupt persons who are likely, having regard to all relevant circumstances, to read, see or hear the matter contained or embodied in it.]
     (2) 3[ ] Whoever-
     (a) sells, lets to hire, distributes, publicly exhibits or in any manner puts into circulation, or for purposes of sale, hire, distribution, public exhibition or circulation, makes, reduces or has in his possession any obscene book, pamphlet, paper, drawing, painting, representation or figure or any other obscene object whatsoever, or
     (b) imports, exports or conveys any obscene object for any of the purposes aforesaid, or knowing or having reason to believe that such object will be sold, let to hire, distributed or publicly exhibited or in any manner put into circulation, or
     (c) takes part in or receives profits from any business in the course of which he knows or has reason to believe that any such obscene objects are, for any of the purposes aforesaid, made, produced, purchased, kept, imported, exported, conveyed, publicly exhibited or in any manner put into circulation, or
     (d) advertises or makes known by any means whatsoever that any person is engaged or is ready to engage in any act which is an offence under this section, or that any such obscene object can be procured from or through any person, or
     (e) offers or attempts to do any act which is an offence under this section, shall be punished 1[

~ 252 ~

I.P.C. It was the case of the petitioners that they have not committed the offence alleged against them and they have prayed for quashing the proceedings.

Question before the Court:

Whether privately viewing obscene film constitutes an offence punishable under Section 292 of IPC?

Obscenity:

In *JagdishChavla and Ors. v. State of Rajasthan*[6] on the point that possession of the obscene object is punishable under Section 292 of IPC, if the possession is for the purpose of sale, hire, distribution, public exhibition or circulation. If the obscene object is kept in a house and is not for sale, hire, public exhibition or circulation, the accused cannot be charged under Section 292 of IPC.

Madras High Court in v. Sundarrajan v. State (un reported) has held that if a blue film is found in the possession of the accused, he cannot be convicted[7] simply on the ground of possession unless it is further proved that the purpose of keeping the same was selling or letting for hire.

Decision of the High Court:

Court held that the act of the accused privately viewing obscene film does not constitute an offence under Section 292 of Indian penal code.

---

on first conviction with imprisonment of either description for a term which may extend to two years, and with fine which may extend to two thousand rupees, and, in the event of a second or subsequent conviction, with imprisonment of either description for a term which may extend to five years, and also with fine which may extend to five thousand rupees]. [Exception- This section does not extend to-

(a) any book, pamphlet, paper, writing, drawing, painting, representation or figure-

(i) the publication of which is proved to be justified as being for the public good on the ground that such book, pamphlet, paper, writing, drawing, painting, representation or figure is in the interest of science, literature, art or learning or other objects of general concern, or

(ii) which is kept or used bona fide for religious purposes;

(b) any representation sculptured, engraved, painted or otherwise represented on or in-

(i) any ancient monument within the meaning of the Ancient Monuments and Archaeological Sites and Remains Act, 1958 (24 of 1958), or

(ii) any temple, or on any car used for the conveyance of idols, or kept or used for any religious purpose.]

6   MANU/RH/0366/1999

7   **Meaning of Convicted: S**omeone guilty of an offense or crime, especially by the verdict of a court

47

Picture of Woman in the Nude is not per se Obscene[1]

Facts in Nutshell:

M/s. Debonair Publications Private Limited, Bombay (for short "the Company"), publishes a monthly magazine entitled "Debonair" in English from Bombay. At the relevant time, namely June and July 1977, Sada Nand, petitioner[2] No. 1, was employed with the Company and was working as printer and publisher of the magazine "Debonair". The second petitioner Vinod Mehta was editor of the said magazine while Mahinder Pal and Jasbir Singh, petitioners 3 & 4, were partners of a firm called Mis. News Centre situated at Delhi which was doing the business of selling the newspapers and magazines including "Debonair". On 28th June 1977, Sadar Bazar Police seized a copy of the magazine "Debonair", June 1977 issue, from the shop of one Chiranji Lal at Chowk Baratooti on the ground that the said magazine contained obscene matter viz. photos of naked women and a case under Section 292[3], Indian Penal Code (for short 'IPC')

---

1 Appellants: **Sada Nand and Ors. Vs.** Respondent: **State (Delhi Administration)**
(1986)ILR Delhi81
Hon'ble Judges/Coram: J.D. Jain, J.

2 **Meaning of Petitioner:** A person who presents a Petition. (**Meaning of Petition:** A formal message requesting something that is submitted to an authority)

3 **Section 292 in The Indian Penal Code, 1860**
292. [Sale, etc., of obscene books, etc.-- [(1) For the purposes of sub- section (2), a book, pamphlet, paper, writing, drawing, painting representation, figure or any other object, shall be deemed to be obscene if it is lascivious or appeals to the prurient interest or if its effect, or (where it comprises two or more distinct items) the effect of any one of its items, is, if taken as a whole, such as to tend to deprave and corrupt persons who are likely, having regard to all relevant circumstances, to read, see or hear the matter contained or embodied in it.]
(2) 3[ ] Whoever-
(a) sells, lets to hire, distributes, publicly exhibits or in any manner puts into circulation, or for purposes of sale, hire, distribution, public exhibition or circulation, makes, reduces or has in his possession any obscene book, pamphlet, paper, drawing, painting, representation or figure or any other obscene object whatsoever, or
(b) imports, exports or conveys any obscene object for any of the purposes aforesaid, or knowing or having reason to believe that such object will be sold, let to hire, distributed or publicly exhibited or in any manner put into circulation, or

was registered against the petitioners on its basis. Subsequently, the police put in challans against the petitioners and the petitioners were summoned[4] by the court of concerned Metropolitan Magistrate. Hence, they filed petitions for quashing and setting aside the police reports as also their prosecution[5] for the said offence in High Court.

Submissions of Learned Counsel for Petitioners:

The submission of the learned counsel for the petitioners was that the magazine "Debonair" primarily caters to the needs of educated and supplicated readers in the society and as such it has acquired a reputation as a magazine of high standard. It publishes articles, views, reviews, features and photographs of high quality on various subjects like politics, economies, business management, cinema, sports. etc. together with some light leading material. It also publishes a large number of photographs in its every issue which are of topical as well as artistic value. It contains a centrally spread page and one or two other photographs of semi-nude and nude female forms in surroundings of natural beauty.

(c) takes part in or receives profits from any business in the course of which he knows or has reason to believe that any such obscene objects are, for any of the purposes aforesaid, made, produced, purchased, kept, imported, exported, conveyed, publicly exhibited or in any manner put into circulation, or

(d) advertises or makes known by any means whatsoever that any person is engaged or is ready to engage in any act which is an offence under this section, or that any such obscene object can be procured from or through any person, or

(e) offers or attempts to do any act which is an offence under this section, shall be punished 1[on first conviction with imprisonment of either description for a term which may extend to two years, and with fine which may extend to two thousand rupees, and, in the event of a second or subsequent conviction, with imprisonment of either description for a term which may extend to five years, and also with fine which may extend to five thousand rupees]. [Exception- This section does not extend to-

(a) any book, pamphlet, paper, writing, drawing, painting, representation or figure-

(i) the publication of which is proved to be justified as being for the public good on the ground that such book, pamphlet, paper, writing, drawing, painting, representation or figure is in the interest of science, literature, art or learning or other objects of general concern, or

(ii) which is kept or used bona fide for religious purposes;

(b) any representation sculptured, engraved, painted or otherwise represented on or in-

(i) any ancient monument within the meaning of the Ancient Monuments and Archaeological Sites and Remains Act, 1958 (24 of 1958), or

(ii) any temple, or on any car used for the conveyance of idols, or kept or used for any religious purpose.]

4   **Meaning of Summoned:**To order to appear in court by the issuance of a summons.

5   **Meaning of Prosecution:**
    a. the institution and carrying on of legal proceedings against a person.
    b. the officials who institute and conduct such proceedings.

The photographs are works of eminent and highly skilled photographers and are of high artistic value. The photographs exhibit the creativity of the artist and are of great aesthetic value. Further they are designed to promotes art of photography. So, the mere fact that the photographs are of nude men nude women would not render them obscene or pornographic. Photographic features when examined would show that the emphasis is not on the nudeness of the female but is rather on beauty as conceived and unfolded by the artist. In short, their submission was that the photographs of nude women which were alleged to obscene were not so and petitioners prosecution for offence under Section 292 Indian Penal Code was totally misconceived and not warranted by law.

Test of Obscenity:

Test of obscenity which was formulated by Cockburn, C.J. in *Queen v. Hicklin*[6]

> ".... I think the test of obscenity is this, whether the tendency of the matter charged as obscenity is to deprave and corrupt those whose minds are open to such immoral influences, and into whose hands a publication of this sort may fall.......it is quite certain that it would suggest to the minds of the young of either sex, or even to persons of more advanced years, thoughts of a most impure and libidinous character."

In *Ranjit D. Udeshi v. The State of Maharashtra,*[7] the Supreme Court had an occasion to consider whether the famous book of Lady Chatterley's Lover unexpurgated edition written by D. H. Lawrence contained obscene and pornographic matter or not. Hidayatullah, J. (AS his Lordship then was) considered the above test and also the test laid down in certain other American cases. Said his Lordship:

> "NONE has so far attempted a definition of obscenity because the meaning can be laid bare without attempting a definition by describing what must be looked for. It may, however, be said at once that treating with sex and nudity in art and literature cannot

---

6   1868 Lr 3 Qb 360 : (1)

7   1965CriLJ8

be regarded as evidence of obscenity without something more. It is not necessary that the angels and saints of Michael Angelo should be made to wear breeches before they can be viewed. If the rigid test of treating with sex as the minimum ingredient were accepted hardly any writer of fiction today would escape the fate Lawrence had in his days. Half the book-shop would close and the other half would deal in nothing but moral and religious books which Lord Campbell boasted was the effect of his Act."

In *Chandrakant Kalyandas Kakodkar v. The State of Maharashtra and others*[8] The Supreme Court emphasised that:

"THE concept of obscenity would differ from country to country depending on the standards of morals of contemporary society. What is considered as a piece of literature in France may be obscene in England and what is considered in both countries as not harmful to public order and morals may be obscene in our country......... The standards of contemporary society in India are also fast changing. The adults and adolescents have available to them a large number of classics, novels, stories and pieces of literature which have a content of sex. love and romance. As observed in Udeshi's case(supra) , if a reference to sex by itself is considered obscene, no books can be sold except those which are purely religious. In the field of art and cinema also the adolescent is shown situations which even a quarter of a century ago would be considered derogatory to public morality, but having regard to changed conditions are more taken for granted without in anyway tending to debase or debauch the mind. What we have to see is that whether a class, not an isolated case, into whose hands the book, article or story falls suffer in their moral outlook or become depraved by leading ft or might have impure and lecherous thoughts aroused in their minds. The charge of obscenity must, therefore, be judged from this aspect"

Observation of the High Court:

Court observed that it is well recognized principle that the concept of obscenity is moulded to a very great extent by the social outlook of the

---

8   1970CriLJ1273

people who are generally expected to read the book or article. Keeping these guidelines in view, Courte carefully glanced through both the June and July 1977 issues of the magazine "Debonair". There were pictures of nude or seminude women at pages 8, 9, 18, 39. 58 & 68 of June 1977 issue of the magazine'. Likewise there were pictures of nude/semi-nude women at pages 40, 64 & 66 of July 1977 issue of the said magazine. *Generally speaking pictures of a nude/semi-nude women cannot per se be called obscene unless the same are suggestive of deprave mind and are designed to excite sexual passion in ties persons who are likely to look at them or see them.* This will naturally depend on the particular posture and the background in which a nude semi-nude women is shown. In *Sreeram Saksena v. Emperor*[9], some postcards of women in the nude were said to be obscene. These pictures had been reproduced from some of the photographs contained in the picture books named "Sun Bothers", "Eve in the Sunlight", "Perfect Womanhood", and "Health and Efficiency" which were being sold in the market. It was held by their Lordships that :

"A picture of a woman in the nude is not per se obscene. Unless there is something in it which would shock or offend the taste of any ordinary or decent-minded person. When there is nothing in it to offend an ordinary decent person it is impossible to say that it is obscene. Unless the pictures of nude female forms are incentive to sensuality and excite impure thoughts in the minds of ordinary persons of normal temperament who may happen to look at them, they cannot be regarded as obscene within the meaning of Section 292, IPC. For the purpose of deciding whether a picture is obscene or not one has to consider to a great extent the surrounding circumstances, the pose, the posture, the suggestive element in the picture, the person into whose hands it is likely to fall, etc."

Likewise, was held by a Division Bench of Allahabad High Court in *State v. Thakur Prasad and others.*[10] , that :

"A picture of a woman in the nude is not per se obscene. For the purpose of deciding whether a picture is obscene or not one has to consider to a great extent the surrounding circumstances, the pose,

---

9   Air 1940 Calcutta 290

10 AIR1959All49

the posture, the suggestive element in -the picture, and the person or persons in whose hands it is likely to fall."

Decision of the High Court:

Court held that no prima facie case for prosecution[11] of the petitioners for an offence under Section 292 Indian Penal Code was made out.

---

11 **Meaning of Prosecution:**
  a. the institution and carrying on of legal proceedings against a person.
  b. the officials who institute and conduct such proceedings.

48

Showing Blue Films to Young Men will constitute Obscenity[1]

Facts in Nutshell:

The prosecution[2] case was that on 07.12.2001 on the basis of secret information the patrolling party raided the premises and found that the Appellants[3] were showing blue film to young men and about 15 viewers were there in the hall. It was alleged that CD of blue film, namely "Size Matter" was displayed by the Appellants to the viewers on Videocon TV Sony C.D. player, one CD namely "Size Matter", two C. Ds. of "JawaniKaKhel", remote, ticket book, T.V. and poster were taken into possession in the presence of the witnesses. The Appellants were charged

---

1 Appellants: **Gita Ram and Anr. Vs.** Respondent: **State of H.P.**
   2013(2)SCALE165
   Hon'ble Judges/Coram: T.S. Thakur and M.Y. Eqbal, JJ.

2 **Meaning of Prosecution:**
   a. the institution and carrying on of legal proceedings against a person.
   b. the officials who institute and conduct such proceedings.

3 **Meaning of Appellant:** A person who, dissatisfied with the judgment rendered in a lawsuit decided in a lower court or the findings from a proceeding before an Administrative Agency, asks a superior court to review the decision.

for offences punishable under Section 292[4] read with Section 34[5] Indian Penal Code and Section 7[6] of Cinematograph Act.

---

4   **Section 292 in The Indian Penal Code, 1860**

292. [Sale, etc., of obscene books, etc.-- [(1) For the purposes of sub- section (2), a book, pamphlet, paper, writing, drawing, painting representation, figure or any other object, shall be deemed to be obscene if it is lascivious or appeals to the prurient interest or if its effect, or (where it comprises two or more distinct items) the effect of any one of its items, is, if taken as a whole, such as to tend to deprave and corrupt persons who are likely, having regard to all relevant circumstances, to read, see or hear the matter contained or embodied in it.]

(2) 3[ ] Whoever-

(a) sells, lets to hire, distributes, publicly exhibits or in any manner puts into circulation, or for purposes of sale, hire, distribution, public exhibition or circulation, makes, reduces or has in his possession any obscene book, pamphlet, paper, drawing, painting, representation or figure or any other obscene object whatsoever, or

(b) imports, exports or conveys any obscene object for any of the purposes aforesaid, or knowing or having reason to believe that such object will be sold, let to hire, distributed or publicly exhibited or in any manner put into circulation, or

(c) takes part in or receives profits from any business in the course of which he knows or has reason to believe that any such obscene objects are, for any of the purposes aforesaid, made, produced, purchased, kept, imported, exported, conveyed, publicly exhibited or in any manner put into circulation, or

(d) advertises or makes known by any means whatsoever that any person is engaged or is ready to engage in any act which is an offence under this section, or that any such obscene object can be procured from or through any person, or

(e) offers or attempts to do any act which is an offence under this section, shall be punished 1[on first conviction with imprisonment of either description for a term which may extend to two years, and with fine which may extend to two thousand rupees, and, in the event of a second or subsequent conviction, with imprisonment of either description for a term which may extend to five years, and also with fine which may extend to five thousand rupees]. [Exception- This section does not extend to-

(a) any book, pamphlet, paper, writing, drawing, painting, representation or figure-

(i) the publication of which is proved to be justified as being for the public good on the ground that such book, pamphlet, paper, writing, drawing, painting, representation or figure is in the interest of science, literature, art or learning or other objects of general concern, or

(ii) which is kept or used bona fide for religious purposes;

(b) any representation sculptured, engraved, painted or otherwise represented on or in-

(i) any ancient monument within the meaning of the Ancient Monuments and Archaeological Sites and Remains Act, 1958 (24 of 1958), or

(ii) any temple, or on any car used for the conveyance of idols, or kept or used for any religious purpose.]

5   **Section 34 in The Indian Penal Code, 1860**

34. [Acts done by several persons in futherance of common intention.-- When a criminal act is done by several persons in furtherance of the common intention of all, each of such persons is liable for that act in the same manner as if it were done by him alone.]

6   **Section 7 in The Cinematograph Act, 1952**

7. Penalties for contraventions of this Part. [(1) If any person--

(a) exhibits or permits to be exhibited to be exhibited in any place--

(i) any film other than a film which has been certified by the Board as suitable for unrestricted public exhibition or for public exhibition restricted to adults 3[or to members of any profession or any class of persons] and which, when exhibited, displays the prescribed mark of the Board and has not been altered or tampered with in any way since such mark was affixed thereto,

(ii) any film, which has been certified by the Board as suitable for public exhibition restricted to adults, to any person who is not an adult,

Decision of the Trail Court:

Sub Divisional Judicial Magistrate convicted and sentenced the Appellants to undergo simple imprisonment for 6 months under Section 292 of the Indian Penal Code and fine of Rs. 1,000/- under Section 7 of Cinematograph Act. On appeal filed by the Appellants, the Additional Sessions Judge Fast Track Court, Solan affirmed the judgment passed by the Trial Court. However, the Appellants being first offenders Sessions Judge showed some leniency in sentence of imprisonment and instead of imprisonment of 6 months the Appellants were sentenced to simple imprisonment for one month each. The sentence awarded by the Trial Court was modified to that extent. The imposition of fine of Rs. 1,000/- by the trial court for the offence under Section 292 Indian Penal Code and further fine of Rs. 1000/- was imposed on them for offence under Section 7 of the Cinematograph Act, were maintained. The Appellants then preferred revision before the High Court of Himachal Pradesh. The High Court examined all the materials available on record as also the

---

(iia) [any film which has been certified by the Board as suitable for public exhibition restricted to any profession or class of persons, to a person who is not a member of such profession or who is not a member of such class, or]

(b) without lawful authority (the burden of proving which shall be on him), alters or tampers with in any way any film after it has been certified, or

(c) fails to comply with the provision contained in section 6A or with any order made by the Central Government or by the Board in the exercise of any of the powers or functions conferred on it by this Act or the rules made thereunder, [he shall be punishable with imprisonment for a term which may extend to three years, or with fine which may extend to one lakh rupees, or with both, and in the case of a continuing offence with a further fine which may extend to twenty thousand rupees for each day during which the offence continues: Provided that a person who exhibits or permits to be exhibited in any place a video film in contravention of the provisions of sub- clause (i) of clause (a) shall be punishable with imprisonment for a term which shall not be less than three months, but which may extend to three years and with fine which shall not be less than twenty thousand rupees, but which may extend to one lakh rupees, and in the case of a continuing offence with a further fine which may extend to twenty thousand rupees for each day during which the offence continues: Provided further that a court may, for adequate and special reasons to be mentioned in the judgment, impose a sentence of imprisonment for a term of less than three months, or a fine of less than twenty thousand rupees:"; [Provided further that] notwithstanding anything contained in section 29 of the Code of Criminal Procedure, 1973 (2 of 1974), it shall be lawful for any Metropolitan Magistrate, or any Judicial Magistrate of the first class specially empowered by the State Government in this behalf, to pass a sentence of fine exceeding five thousand rupees on any person convicted of any offence punishable under this Part: [Provided also] that no distributor or exhibitor or owner or employee of a cinema house shall be liable to punishment for contravention of any condition of endorsement of caution on a film certified as" UA" under this Part.]

(2) If any person is convicted of an offence punishable under this section committed by him in respect of any film, the convicting court may further direct that the film shall be forfeited to the Government.

(3) The exhibition of a film, in respect of which an" A" certificate 1[or a" S" certificate or a" UA" certificate] has been granted, to children below the age of three years accompanying their parents or guardians shall not be deemed to be an offence within the meaning of this section.

evidence, both oral and documentary and finally came to the conclusion that there is no perversity in the impugned judgment. Accordingly, the revision was dismissed. They approach Supreme Court by Special Leave Petition[7].

Obscenity:

Punjab and Haryana High Court in the case of *Bharat Bhushan v. State of Punjab*[8] held that:

Exhibiting blue film in which man and woman were shown in the act of sexual intercourse to young boys would definitely deprave and corrupt their morals. Their minds are impressionable. On their impressionable minds anything can be imprinted. Things would have been different if that blue film had been exhibited to mature minds. Showing a man and a woman in the act of sexual intercourse tends to appealing to the carnal side of the human nature.

Decision of the Supreme Court:

Court held that nature of the activities and the offence committed by the Appellants does not need any leniency.

---

7   Article 136 in The Constitution Of India 1949
    136. Special leave to appeal by the Supreme Court
    (1) Notwithstanding anything in this Chapter, the Supreme Court may, in its discretion, grant special leave to appeal from any judgment, decree, determination, sentence or order in any cause or matter passed or made by any court or tribunal in the territory of India
    (2) Nothing in clause (1) shall apply to any judgment, determination, sentence or order passed or made by any court or tribunal constituted by or under any law relating to the Armed Forces

8   1999 (2) RCR (Criminal) 148

49

Vulgar language used in book would not be deemed to be obscene[1]

Facts in Nutshell:

Complainant[2] purchased a book titled 'the Indian Call Girls' from Bhatia Novels & Stationers, 3 , New Delhi and on reading the said book he found that the book contained matters offensive to chastity, decency and the book tends to deprave and corrupt the minds of the persons who are likely to read this book. No particulars were mentioned in the complaint as to what portions of the book were obscene. Even in his statement the complainant did not mention any such particular except generally deposing that the book contains filthy and foul language and reading the book provokes lustful feelings in the mind of the reader and thus, the same was obscene.

Decision of the Learned Magistrate:

The learned Magistrate after going through the book pointed out in his order that certain passages appearing at pages 34, 39 & 40 of the book were obscene.

Meaning of Obscene:

Webster's Third New International Dictionary at page 1557 defines 'obscene' as what is repulsive by reason of malignance, hypocrisy, cynicism, irresponsibility, gross disregard of moral or ethical principals. In *Ranjit D. Udeshi v. State of Maharashtra[3]*, it was laid down that in a prosecution under Section 292 IPC the question whether the book was obscene or not does not altogether depend on oral evidence of a writer and art critic because the offending novel and the portions which are

---

1 Appellants: **Dr. Promilla Kapur Vs.** Respondent: **Yash Pal Bhasin and others**
  MANU/DE/0030/1989
  Hon'ble Judges/Coram: P.K. Bahri, J.

2 **Meaning of Complainant:** A party that makes a complaint or files a formal charge, as in a court of law; a plaintiff.

3 1965CriLJ8

the subject of the charge must be judged of by the court. It was held that the word 'obscene' means what is offensive to modesty or decency which gives rise to emotions of lewdness, filthiness and repulsiveness. It was also held that there is some difference between the obscenity and pornography as the latter denotes writings, pictures etc. only intended to arouse sexual desire while the former may include writing etc. not intended to do so but which have that tendency and both, of course, offend against public decency and morals but pornography is obscenity in a more aggravated form. It was observed that merely treating with sex and nudity in art and literature cannot be regarded as evidence of obscenity without something more. It was further held that the test of obscenity, as applied in India, is this : whether the tendency of the matter charged as obscenity is to deprave and corrupt those whose minds are open to such immoral influences and into whose hands a publication of this sort may fall. If it is quite certain that the book would suggest to the minds of the young of either sex, or even to persons of more advanced years, thoughts of a most impure and libidinous character, the book would be treated as obscene. It was also emphasized that an overall view of the obscene matter in the setting of the whole work would, of course, be necessary but the obscene matter also must be considered by itself and separately to find out whether it is so gross and its obscenity so decided that it is likely to deprave and corrupt those whose minds are open to influences of this sort and into whose hands the book is likely to fall.

In *Samaresh Bose v. Amal Mitra*[4]. In this judgment it was held that in judging the question of obscenity the Judge in the first place should try to place himself in the position of the author and from the view point of the author the Judge should try to understand what is it that the author seeks to convey and what the author conveys has any literary and artistic value and thereafter the Judge should place himself in the position of a reader of every age group in whose hands the book is likely to fall and should try to appreciate what kind of possible influence the book is likely to have on the minds of the readers. It was also held in this very judgment that a novel written by a well known writer of novels and stories, by which the author intends to expose various evils and ills pervading the society and to oppose with particular emphasis the problems which ail and afflict the society in spheres, cannot be said to be obscene merely because slang

---

4   1986CriLJ24

and unconventional words have been used in the book in which there have been emphasis on sex and discretion of female bodies and there are the narrations of feelings, thoughts and actions in vulgar language. It was also observed that some portions of the books may appear to be vulgar and readers of cultured and refined taste may feel shocked and disgusted and equally in some portions, the words used and description given may not appear to be in proper taste and in some places there may have been an exhibition of bad taste leaving it to the readers of experience but certainly not sufficient to bring home to the adolescents any suggestion which is depraving or lascivious.

Decision of the High Court:

Court held that it is true that prostitution has been always looked down upon with hatred throughout the ages by the society, and particularly 'sex' has been considered an ugly word and any talk about sex in our conservative society was considered a taboo not many years ago but with this country progressing materially and with the spread of education and coming of western culture, the society has become more open. It is indeed obvious that the phenomenon of call girls has peaked in our country amongst the affluent section of the society. The society is changing vastly with spiritual thinking taking a back seat and there is nothing wrong if a research on the subjects of call girls in order to know the reasons as to why and how the young girls fall in this profession of call girls and what society could do in order to eradicate or at least minimise the possibility of young budding girls joining this flesh trade. Mere fact that some sort of vulgar language has been used in some portions of the book in describing the sexual intercourse would not in court opinion, in the overall setting of the book, be deemed to be obscene. If some portions of the book are taken in isolation, those portions may have the effect of given lustful thoughts to some young adolescent minds but for that reason alone it would not be in the interests of justice to declare the book as obscene.

50

Divorce must be for a reasonable cause[1]

Facts in Nutshell:

Petitioner[2] alleged that she was the legally wedded wife of the respondent[3]. Both are Muslims by religion and their marriage was solemnized in accordance with Mohammedan Law. For a period of two years she lived happily with her husband. Thereafter, it was the case of the petitioner that the respondent started ill-treating, harassing and abusing her. During the year 1984 the respondent drove her away from his house. On account of the intervention of the elders, the respondent took the petitioner with him. Again he continued to ill-treat her. The respondent later married another woman at Gulbarga. The petitioner was not employed anywhere and she has no income of her own. She cannot maintain herself. She requires at least a sum of Rs. 500/- per month towards her maintenance. Therefore, she filed the petition under Section 125 of the Cr. P.C.[4], before

---

1 Appellants: **Zulekha Begum alias Rahmathunnisa Begum Vs.** Respondent: **Abdul Raheem**
   ILR 2000 KARNATAKA 743
   Hon'ble Judges/Coram: K.H.N. Kuranga, J.

2 **Meaning of Petitioner:** A person who presents a Petition. (**Meaning of Petition:** A formal message requesting something that is submitted to an authority)

3 **Meaning of Respondent:** A respondent is a person who is called upon to issue a response to a communication made by another. In legal usage, this specifically refers to the defendant in a legal proceedingcommenced by a petition, or to an appellee, or the opposing party, in an appeal of a decision by an initial fact-finder.

4 **Section 125, CrPc, 1973:**
   125. Order for maintenance of wives, children and parents,
   (1) If any person having sufficient means neglects or refuses to maintain—
   (a) his wife, unable to maintain herself, or
   (b) his legitimate or illegitimate minor child, whether married or not, unable to maintain itself, or
   (c) his legitimate or illegitimate child (not being a married daughter) who has attained majority, where such child is, by reason of any physical or mental abnormality or injury unable to maintain itself, or
   (d) his father or mother, unable to maintain himself or herself, a Magistrate of the first class may, upon proof of such neglect or refusal, order such person to make a monthly allowance for the maintenance of his wife or such child, father or mother, at such monthly rate not exceeding five hundred rupees in the whole, as such magistrate thinks fit, and to pay the same to such person as the Magistrate may from time to time direct: Provided that the Magistrate may order the father of a minor female child referred to in clause (b) to make such allowance, until she attains her majority, if the Magistrate is satisfied that the husband of such minor female child, if married, is not possessed of sufficient means
   Explanation—For the purposes of this Chapter—
   (a) "minor" means a person who, under the provisions of the Indian Majority Act, 1875 (9 of 1875)

the Family Court for grant of maintenance of Rs. 500/- per month.

Question before the Court:

1. Whether the petitioner proves that she continues to be the legally wedded wife of the respondent and that there was no divorce given by her husband?

2. Whether the right given to the Mohammedan husband under the Muslim Personal Law to divorce his wife by giving a talaq is an absolute right and whether he can exercise that right at his whim or caprice?

Divorce under Mohammedan Law:

His Lordship Justice V.R. Krishna Iyer of Kerala High Court (as he then was) in the decision in *A. Yousuf Rawther v Sowramma*, has held thus:

"It is a popular fallacy that a Muslim mate enjoys, under the Quaranic Law, unbridled authority to liquidate the marriage. The whole Quaranic expressly forbids a man to seek pretexts for divorcing his wife, so long as she remains faithful and obedient to him. "If they (namely women) obey you, then do not seek a way against them". (Quaranic IV 34). The Islamic Law gives to the man primarily the faculty of dissolving the marriage, if the wife, by her infidelity or her bad character, renders the married life unhappy but, in the absence of serious reasons, no man can justify

is deemed not to have attained his majority;
(b) "wife" includes a woman who has been divorced by, or has obtained a divorce from, her husband and has not remarried
(2) Such allowance shall be payable from the date of the order, or, if so ordered, from the date of the application for maintenance
(3) If any person so ordered fails without sufficient cause to comply with the order, any such Magistrate may, for every breach of the order, issue a warrant for levying the amount due in the manner provided for levying fines, and may sentence such person, for the whole, or any port of each month's allowance remaining unpaid after the execution of the warrant, to imprisonment for a term which may extend to one month or until payment if sooner made:
Provided that no warrant shall be issued for the recovery of any amount due under this section unless application be made to the Court to levy such amount within a period of one year from the date on which it became due:
Provided further that if such person offers to maintain his wife on condition of her living with him, and she refuses to live with him, such Magistrate may consider any grounds of refusal stated by her, and may make an order under this section notwithstanding such offer, if he is satisfied that there is just ground for so doing
(4) No wife shall be entitled to receive an allowance from her husband under this section if she is living in adultery, or if, without any sufficient reason, she refuses to live with her, husband, or if they are living separately by mutual consent
(5) On proof that any wife in whose favour an order has been made under this section is living in adultery, or that without sufficient reason she refuses to live with her husband, or that they are living separately by mutual consent, the Magistrate shall cancel the order

a divorce either in the eye of religion or the law. If he abandons his wife or puts her away in simple caprice, he draws upon himself the divine anger, for the curse of god, said the Prophet, rests on him who repudiated his wife capriciously. . . After quoting from the Quran and the Prophet Dr. Galwash concludes that divorce is permissible in Islam only in cases of extreme emergency. When all efforts for effecting a reconciliation have failed, the parties may proceed to a dissolution of the marriage by 'Talaq' or by 'Khola'. When the proposal of divorce proceeds from the husband, it is called 'talaq', and when it takes effect at the instance of the wife it is called 'Khola'. .. ".

Similar view was also expressed by a Single Judge of Calcutta High Court in the case of *Motiur Rahaman v Sabina Khatun*, wherein he has stated as follows:

"Though under the aforesaid Section 308 of the Mohammedan Law by the author Mulla, the husband is not required to assign any cause for the divorce, but there must be a reasonable cause for the same, which should be preceded by a pre-divorce conference so as to make an endeavour for reconciliation between the parties, if possible.

It follows from the above decisions that under the Quran the marital status is to be maintained as far as possible and there should be conciliation before divorce and therefore the Quran discourages divorce and it permits only after pre-divorce conference.

Decision of the High Court:

Court held that, a Mohammedan husband cannot divorce his wife at his whim or caprice, i.e., divorce must be for a reasonable cause, and it must be preceded by a pre-divorce conference to arrive at a settlement. Even if there is any reasonable cause for the divorce, yet there must be evidence to show that there was an attempt for a settlement prior to the divorce and when there was no such attempt prior to divorce to arrive at a settlement by mediators, then there cannot be a valid divorce under Mohammedan Law.

Court held that the talaq or divorce given by the respondent to the petitioner was not valid in law.

51

Irretrievable Breakdown of Marriage[1]

Facts in Nutshell:

The brief facts of the case are that parties were married according to Arya Samaj rites and ceremonies at Delhi. The marriage was also registered. Out of the wedlock, two sons were born. After solemnization of the marriage between the parties, the appellant (wife) has treated the respondent (husband) with cruelty as under:

The appellant on the smallest pretext would pick up a fight with the respondent and would humiliate, insult and abuse the respondent in front of the children and also in front of the relatives of the respondent. The appellant even refused to do the normal household chores. On smallest pretext, the appellant would pack up respondent's clothes and ask him to leave as the residence was on her name since sometimes the residence was allotted to the appellant.

To defame, humiliate and harass the respondent, the appellant went to the office of the respondent and met his senior, who was the Secretary to the Government of India. To him the appellant narrated a false and frivolous story that the respondent is bad husband, he does not take care of his children, he wants to keep a mistress and he beats her up. This has greatly lowered the respect of the respondent in the office and has caused great mental torture to him.

---

1   Appellants: **Smt. Vimla Mehra W/o Sh. K.S. Mehra D/o Sh. T.C. Sohal Vs.** Respondent: **Shri K.S. Mehra S/o Sh. M.R. Mehra**
    158(2009)DLT136
    Hon'ble Judges/Coram: V.B. Gupta, J.

Decision of the Trail Court:

Appeal[2] was filed by the appellant[3] (wife) under Section 28[4] of Hindu Marriage Act, 1955 (for short as 'Act') against the judgment and decree[5] passed by Addl. District Sessions Judge, Delhi. The trial court has decreed the petition under Section 13(1)(i-a)[6] of the Act for divorce filed

---

2   **Meaning of Appeal:** In law, an **appeal** is a process for requesting a formal change to an official decision. Very broadly speaking there are appeals on the record and *de novo* appeals. In *de novo* appeals, a new decision maker re-hears the case without any reference to the prior decision maker. In appeals on the record, the decision of the prior decision maker is challenged by arguing that he or she misapplied the law, came to an incorrect factual finding, acted in excess of his jurisdiction, abused his powers, was biased, considered evidence which he should not have considered or failed to consider evidence that he should have considered.

3   **Meaning of Appellant:** A person who, dissatisfied with the judgment rendered in a lawsuit decided in a lower court or the findings from a proceeding before an Administrative Agency, asks a superior court to review the decision.

4   **Section 28 in The Hindu Marriage Act, 1955**
28. [Appeals from decrees and orders.
(1) All decrees made by the court in any proceeding under this Act shall, subject to the provisions of sub- section (3), be appealable as decrees of the court made in the exercise of its original civil jurisdiction, and every such appeal shall lie to the court to which appeals ordinarily lie from the decisions of the court given in the exercise of its original civil jurisdiction.
(2) Orders made by the court in any proceeding under this Act under section 25 or section 26 shall, subject to the provisions of sub- section (3), be appealable if they are not interim orders, and every such appeal shall lie to the court to which appeals ordinarily lie from the decisions of the court given in exercise of its original civil jurisdiction.
(3) There shall be no appeal under this section on the subject of costs only.
(4) Every- appeal under this section shall be preferred within a period of thirty days from the date of the decree or order.

5   **Meaning of Decree:**
1. An authoritative order having the force of law.
2. The judgment of a court of equity, admiralty, probate, or divorce.

6   **Section 13 in The Hindu Marriage Act, 1955**
13. Divorce.
(1) Any marriage solemnized, whether before or after the commencement of this Act, may, on a petition presented by either the husband or the wife, be dissolved by a decree of divorce on the ground that the other party-
(i) [has, after the solemnization of the marriage, had voluntary, sexual intercourse with any person other than his or her spouse; or
(ia) has, after the solemnization of the marriage, treated the petitioner with cruelty; or
(ib) has deserted the petitioner for a continuous period of not less than two years immediately preceding the presentation of the petition; or]
(ii) has ceased to be a Hindu by conversion to another religion; or
(ii) has ceased to be a Hindu by conversion to another religion; or
(iii) [has been incurably of unsound mind, or has been suffering continuously or intermittently from mental disorder of such a kind and to such an extent that the petitioner cannot reasonably be expected to live with the respondent. Explanation.- In this clause,-
(a) the expression" mental disorder" means mental illness, arrested or incomplete development of mind, psychopathic disorder or any other disorder or disability of mind and includes schizophrenia;
(b) the expression" psychopathic disorder" means a persistent disorder or disability of mind (whether or not including sub- normality of intelligence) which results in abnormally aggressive or

on behalf of the respondent[7](husband).

Cruelty:

The cruelty is a ground for divorce under Section 13 of the Hindu Marriage Act. The word 'cruelty' has not been defined in the Hindu Marriage Act. D. Tolstoy in his celebrated book "The Law and Practice of Divorce and Matrimonial Causes" (Sixth Edition, p. 61) defined cruelty in these words:

Cruelty which is a ground for dissolution of marriage may be defined as willful and unjustifiable conduct of such a character as to cause danger to life, limb or health, bodily or mental, or as to give rise to a reasonable apprehension of such a danger.

The Shorter Oxford Dictionary defines "cruelty" as "the quality of being cruel; disposition of inflicting suffering; delight in or indifference to another's pain; mercilessness; hard-heartedness". The term "mental cruelty" has been defined in Black's Law Dictionary [8th Edition, 2004] as under:

Mental Cruelty - As a ground for divorce, one spouse's course of conduct (not involving actual violence) that creates such anguish that it endangers the life, physical health, or mental health of the other spouse. The concept of cruelty has been summarized in Halsbury's Laws of England [Vol.13, 4th Edition, Para 1269] as under:

The general rule in all cases of cruelty is that the entire matrimonial relationship must be considered, and that rule is of special value when the cruelty consists not of violent acts but of injurious reproaches, complaints, accusations or taunts. In cases where no violence is averred, it is undesirable to consider judicial pronouncements with a view to creating certain categories of acts or conduct as having or lacking the nature or quality which renders them capable or incapable in all circumstances

---

seriously irresponsible conduct on the part of the other party, and whether or not it require or is susceptible to medical treatment; or]

(iv) has [been suffering from a virulent and incurable from of leprosy; or

(v) has [been suffering from venereal disease in a communicable from; or

(vi) has renounced the world by entering any religious order; or

(vii) has not been heard of as being alive for a period of seven years or more by those persons who would naturally have heard of it, had that party been alive.

7   **Meaning of Respondent:** A **respondent** is a person who is called upon to issue a response to a communication made by another. In legal usage, this specifically refers to the defendant in a legal proceeding commenced by a petition, or to an appellee, or the opposing party, in an appeal of a decision by an initial fact-finder.

of amounting to cruelty; for it is the effect of the conduct rather than its nature which is of paramount importance in assessing a complaint of cruelty. Whether one spouse has been guilty of cruelty to the other is essentially a question of fact and previously decided cases have little, if any, value. The court should bear in mind the physical and mental condition of the parties as well as their social status, and should consider the impact of the personality and conduct of one spouse on the mind of the other, weighing all incidents and quarrels between the spouses from that point of view; further, the conduct alleged must be examined in the light of the complainant's capacity for endurance and the extent to which that capacity is known to the other spouse. Malevolent intention is not essential to cruelty but it is an important element where it exits.

In 24 American Jurisprudence 2d, the term "mental cruelty" has been defined as under:

Mental Cruelty as a course of unprovoked conduct toward one's spouse which causes embarrassment, humiliation, and anguish so as to render the spouse's life miserable and unendurable. The plaintiff must show a course of conduct on the part of the defendant which so endangers the physical or mental health of the plaintiff as to render continued cohabitation unsafe or improper, although the plaintiff need not establish actual instances of physical abuse.

In the case of *Shobha Rani v. Madhukar Reddi*[8] , the Apex Court has observed as under;

Section 13(1)(ia) uses the word "treated the petitioner with cruelty". The word "cruelty" has not been defined. Indeed it could not have been defined. It has been used in relation to human conduct or human behavior. It is the conduct in relation to or in respect of matrimonial duties and obligations. It is a course of conduct of one which is adversely affecting the other. The cruelty may be mental or physical, intentional or unintentional. If it is physical the Court will have no problem to determine it. It is a question of fact and degree. If it is mental the problem presents difficulty. First, the enquiry must begin as to the nature of the cruel treatment. Second, the impact of such treatment in the mind of the spouse. Whether it caused reasonable apprehension that it would be harmful or injurious to live with the other. Ultimately, it is a matter of inference to be drawn by taking into account the nature of the conduct and its effect on the complaining

---

8 [1988]1SCR1010

spouse. There may, however, be cases where the conduct complained of itself is bad enough and per se unlawful or illegal. Then the impact or the injurious effect on the other spouse need not be enquired into or considered. In such cases, the cruelty will be established if the conduct itself is proved or admitted.

In *Savitri Pandey v. Prem Chandra Pandey*[9], the Apex Court has observed as under;

Mental cruelty is the conduct of other spouse which causes mental suffering or fear to the matrimonial life of the other. "Cruelty", therefore, postulates a treatment of the petitioner with such cruelty as to cause a reasonable apprehension in his or her mind that it would be harmful or injurious for the petitioner to live with the other party. Cruelty, however, has to be distinguished from the ordinary wear and tear of family life. It cannot be decided on the basis of the sensitivity of the petitioner and has to be adjudged on the basis of the course of conduct which would, in general, be dangerous for a spouse to live with the other.

In the case of *Ashok Hurra v. Rupa Bipin Zaveri etc.*[10] , Court while dealing with a matrimonial matter quoted few excerpts from the Seventy-first Report of the Law Commission of India on the Hindu Marriage Act, 1955 - "Irretrievable Breakdown of Marriage". Irretrievable breakdown of marriage is now considered, in the laws of a number of countries, a good ground of dissolving the marriage by granting a decree of divorce.

Proof of such a breakdown would be that the husband and wife have separated and have been living apart for, say, a period of five or ten years and it has become impossible to resurrect the marriage or to reunite the parties. It is stated that once it is known that there are no prospects of the success of the marriage, to drag the legal tie acts as a cruelty to the spouse and gives rise to crime and even abuse of religion to obtain annulment of marriage.

The theoretical basis for introducing irretrievable breakdown as a ground of divorce is one with which, by now, lawyers and others have become familiar. Restricting the ground of divorce to a particular offence or matrimonial disability, it is urged, causes injustice in those cases where the situation is such that although none of the parties is at fault, or the fault is of such a nature that the parties to the marriage do not want to

---

9 [2002]1SCR50

10 [1997]2SCR875

divulge it, yet there has arisen a situation in which the marriage cannot be worked. The marriage has all the external appearances of marriage, but none of the reality. As is often put pithily, the marriage is merely a shell out of which the substance is gone. In such circumstances, it is stated, there is hardly any utility in maintaining the marriage as a facade, when the emotional and other bounds which are of the essence of marriage have disappeared. After the marriage has ceased to exist in substance and in reality, there is no reason for denying divorce. The parties alone can decide whether their mutual relationship provides the fulfilment which they seek. Divorce should be seen as a solution and an escape route out of a difficult situation. Such divore is unconcerned with the wrongs of the past, but is concerned with bringing the parties and the children to terms with the new situation and developments by working out the most satisfactory basis upon which they may regulate their relationship in the changed circumstances.

Moreover, the essence of marriage is a sharing of common life, a sharing of all the happiness that life has to offer and all the misery that has to be faced in life, an experience of the joy that comes from enjoying, in common, things of the matter and of the spirit and from showering love and affection on one's offspring. Living together is a symbol of such sharing in all its aspects. Living apart is a symbol indicating the negation of such sharing. It is indicative of a disruption of the essence of marriage --"breakdown"- and if it continues for a fairly long period, it would indicate destruction of the essence of marriage - "irretrievable breakdown".

In *Naveen Kohli v. Neelu Kohli*[11], the Apex Court has observed as under:

Irretrievable breakdown of marriage is not a ground for divorce under the Hindu Marriage Act, 1955. Because of the change of circumstances and for covering a large number of cases where the marriages are virtually dead and unless this concept is pressed into services, the divorce cannot be granted. Ultimately, it is for the Legislature whether to include irretrievable breakdown of marriage as a ground of divorce or not but in court considered opinion the Legislature must consider irretrievable breakdown of marriage as a ground for grant of divorce under the Hindu Marriage Act, 1955.

Decision of the High Court:

Court held that the marriage between the parties was performed in the

---

11 *Naveen Kohli v. Neelu Kohli 128 (2006) DLT 360 (SC)*

year 1978 and since 1998 there has been no cohabitation[12] between the parties. There is complete loss of trust and faith between the parties and there is no love between the parties. There is a complete break down of the marriage and the marriage between the parties have broke down irretrievably and it cannot be said to be alive. Since marriage between the parties has broken down and there is no chance of it being retrieved, the continuance of such marriage, would itself amounts to cruelty and as such the respondent(husband) is entitled to a decree of divorce on the ground of cruelty as per Section 13(1)(ia) of the Act.

12 **Meaning of Cohabitation:** To live together in a sexual relationship, especially when not legally married.

52

Sting Operations to Defame Someone[1]

Ratio Decidendi[2]: *"Court should not punish an individual for an alleged offence which is the outcome of any staged activity to induce the person to commit a crime"*

Facts in Nutshell:

In today's age and world, the impact of media is far reaching. Electronic media as compared to print media has an added advantage because visuals have greater ramification and impact as it directly and immediately influences the mind of the viewer. With the growth of the number of News Channels and increasing popularity of "breaking news", electronic media has come to play a major role in stirring public opinion and consciousness. It is this potency to reach the public that entails that all the channels understand and realise the heavy responsibility that is thrust on them and that there is no case for possible misuse. Keeping in mind the role a responsible media can play in disseminating information and creating awareness among masses without crossing the limits that a civilised society would expect.

Court came across a news item reported in the daily edition of Hindustan Times dated 7th September, 2007 in respect of a sting operation relating to one Ms. Uma Khurana. Prior to the said date, 'Live India' a Television News Channel aired a programme on 30th August, 2007 regarding the above-said sting operation conducted by them showing Ms. Uma Khurana, a teacher with a Delhi Government school, purportedly forcing a girl student into **Prostitution**. Subsequent to the said telecast, aghast at the said act of the teacher, a crowd gathered at the school gate and started raising slogans demanding handing over of Ms. Uma Khurana

---

1   Appellants: **Court on its Own Motion Vs.** Respondent: **State**
    2008(100)DRJ144
    Hon'ble Judges/Coram: Mukundakam Sharma, C.J. and Sanjiv Khanna, J.

2   **Meaning of Ration Decidendi:** *Ratio decidendi* is a Latin phrase meaning "the reason" or "the rationale for the decision." The *ratio decidendi* is "the point in a case which determines the judgment" or "the principle which the case establishes."

to them. In the commotion and mayhem that followed some persons physically attacked Ms. Uma Khurana and even tore her clothes. Shocked by the aforesaid incident and consequent to public outcry the Directorate of Education, Government of Delhi first suspended Ms. Khurana and later dismissed her from service, in exercise of special powers vested in the Government. Police also sprung into action and started investigation. Later the aforementioned news item was published in the Hindustan Times which indicated that there was something more to the whole string operation than what met the eyes. In the aforesaid news item it was stated that the girl who had been shown as a student who was allegedly being forced into prostitution by Ms. Uma Khurana was neither a school girl nor a prostitute but a *budding journalist eager to make a name in the media world.*

After taking suo moto notice[3], court issued notices to the Government of NCT of Delhi and the Delhi Police. After investigation position was clearly established that an innocent person was being induced to commit a very heinous crime. Her reputation has been damaged in the eyes of the public and even her modesty was outraged in the sense that she was manhandled and her clothes were torn by some people. The sting operation has become a stinking experience for Ms. Uma Khurana as she has not only lost her reputation but also her job.

Question before the Court:

The question was how the recurrence of such incident could be stopped and minimised so that an innocent person cannot be victimised and not made to lose reputation.

Cable Television Act, 1995:

Section 5 of the Cable Television Networks (Regulation) Act, 1995 read with provisions of Cable Television Networks Rules, 1994, no programme can be transmitted/re-transmitted on any cable service which contains anything obscene, defamatory, deliberate, false and suggestive innuendos and half truths. Rule 6 of the Cable Television Network Rules, 1994 prescribes a

---

3   **Meaning of Suo-Moto Notice:** Suo motu, meaning "on its own motion," is a Latin legal term, approximately equivalent to the English term sua sponte. It is used, for example, where a government agency acts on its own cognizance, as in "the Commission took suo motu control over the matter."

programme code that should be followed by any person responsible for transmission/re-transmission of any programme. The programme code is fairly exhaustive and stipulates that no programme which encourages and incites violence, maligns and slanders any individual and person, contain any false and half truths etc, should be carried and broadcast in a cable service. Section 20 of the said Act empowers the government to prohibit operation of any cable television network if it thinks it is necessary and expedient in public interest to do so, by a notification in the official gazette. Further, the Central Government can by an order regulate or prohibit transmission or re-transmission of any programme which is not in conformity with the programme code. Additionally, power has been given to the Central Government to regulate and prohibit transmission or re-transmission by any channel of a programme if it is not in the interest of integrity and sovereignty of India, security of India, friendly relations of India with any foreign State or public order, decency or morality.

Duty of the Press:

The duty of the press as the fourth pillar of democracy is immense. It has great power and with it comes increasing amounts of responsibility. No doubt the media is well within its rightful domain when it seeks to use tools of investigative journalism to bring us face to face with the ugly underbelly of the society. However, it is not permissible for the media to entice and try to actively induce an individual into committing an offence which otherwise he is not known and likely to commit. In such cases there is no predisposition. If one were to look into our mythology even a sage like Vishwamitra succumbed to the enchantment of "Maneka". It would be stating the obvious that the Media is not to test individuals by putting them through what one might call the "inducement test" and portray it as a scoop that has uncovered a hidden or concealed truth. In such cases the individual may as well claim that the person offering inducement is equally guilty and a party to the crime, that he/she is being accused of. This would infringe upon the individual's right to privacy. All TV channels/ Media shall take steps and prohibit its reporters from producing or airing any programme which is based on entrapment and which are fabricated, intrusive and sensitive. Responsible and senior TV journalists/reporters and editors who are involved in production and airing of programmes through electronic media should take steps for drawing up a self-regulatory code of conduct. The Press Council of India should also examine and can take initiative in this regard.

Guidelines for Media regarding sting operation telecast:

1. A channel proposing to telecast a sting operation shall obtain a certificate from the person who recorded or produced the same certifying that the operation is genuine to his knowledge.

2. There must be concurrent record in writing of the various stages of the sting operation.

3. Permission for telecasting a sting operation be obtained from a committee appointed by the Ministry of Information and Broadcasting. The said committee will be headed by a retired High Court Judge to be appointed by the Government in consultation with the High Court & two members, one of which should be a person not below the rank of Additional Secretary and the second one being the Additional Commissioner of Police. Permission to telecast sting operation will be granted by the committee after satisfying itself that it is in public interest to telecast the same. This safeguard is necessary since those who mount a sting operation themselves commit the offences of impersonation, criminal trespass under false pretence and making a person commit an offence.

4. While the transcript of the recordings may be edited, the films and tapes themselves should not be edited. Both edited and unedited tapes be produced before the committee.

5. Sting operation shown on TV or published in print media should be scheduled with an awareness of the likely audience/reader in mind. Great care and sensitivity should be exercised to avoid shocking or offending the audience.

6. All television channels must ensure compliance with the Certification Rules prescribed under the Cable Television Network (Regulation) Act 1995 and the Rules made there under.

7. The Chief Editor of the channel shall be made responsible for self regulation and ensure that the programmes are consistent with the Rules and comply with all other legal and administrative

requirements under various statutes in respect of content broadcast on the channel.

8. The subject matter of reports or current events shall not:

    (a) Deliberately present as true any unverified or inaccurate facts so as to avoid trial by media since a "man is innocent till proven guilty by law";

    (b) Present facts and views in such a manner as is likely to mislead the public about their factual inaccuracy or veracity;

    (c) Mislead the public by mixing facts and fiction in such a manner that the public are unlikely to be able to distinguish between the two;

    (d) Present a distorted picture of reality by over-emphasizing or under-playing certain aspects that may trivialize or sensationalize the content;

    (e) Make public any activities or material relating to an individual's personal or private affairs or which invades an individual's privacy unless there is an identifiable large public interest;

    (f) Create public panic or unnecessary alarm which is likely to encourage or incite the public to crime or lead to disorder or be offensive to public or religious feeling.

9. Broadcasters/Media shall observe general community standards of decency and civility in news content, taking particular care to protect the interest and sensitivities of children and general family viewing.

10. News should be reported with due accuracy. Accuracy requires the verification (to the fullest extent possible) and presentation of all facts that are necessary to understand a particular event or issue.

11. Infringement of privacy in a news based/related programme is a sensitive issue. Therefore, greater degree of responsibility should be exercised by the channels while telecasting any such

programmes, as may be breaching privacy of individuals.

12. Channels must not use material relating to persons' personal or private affairs or which invades an individual's privacy unless there is identifiable larger public interest reason for the material to be broadcast or published.

53

Female student could not be deprived from her student status because of her pregnancy[1]

Ratio Decidendi[2]: *"No student can be deemed to have pursued a course of study who does not comply with various requirements prescribed under Act, Statute, Ordinances or Rules."*

Facts in Nutshell:

'Our Colleges of law do not hold a place of high esteem either at home or abroad, nor has law become an area of profound scholarship or enlightened research' observed Dr. Sarvepalli Radhakrishnan some decades ago. But today we have travelled a long distance since then, altering the landscape of legal education in our country. We are just marginally away from the profound scholarship and enlightened research and we must proudly admit that Dr. Radhakrishnan's powerful and poignant words are amenable to radical restatement today. Petitioners[3] were detained from appearing in the semester examinations on account of shortfall of their attendance. Petitioners seek relaxation in the shortfall of the attendance in all those lectures during which period they could not attend classes being at the advance stage of **pregnancy.**

---

1   Appellants: **Vandana Kandari Vs.** Respondent: **University of Delhi**
    170(2010)DLT755
    Hon'ble Judges/Coram: Kailash Gambhir, J.

2   **Meaning of Ration Decidendi:** *Ratio decidendi* is a Latin phrase meaning "the reason" or "the rationale for the decision." The *ratio decidendi* is "the point in a case which determines the judgment" or "the principle which the case establishes."

3   **Meaning of Petitioner:** A person who presents a Petition. (**Meaning of Petition:** A formal message requesting something that is submitted to an authority)

Article 42[4] of the Constitution of India:

Article 42 of the Constitution of India by virtue of the Directive Principles of State Policy[5], a duty has been cast upon the State to make adequate provisions for securing just and humane conditions of work and for *maternity relief.*

Bar Council Rules regarding Attendance:

BCI Rules made under the provisions of the Advocates Act, 1961. Reference was made to Rule 4 thereof which reads as under:

4. The student shall be required to put in minimum attendance of 66% of the lectures on each of the subjects as also at the moot courts and practical training courses:

Provided that in exceptional cases for reasons to be recorded and communicated to the Bar Council of India, the Dean of the Faculty of Law or the Principals of Law Colleges may condone attendance short of those required by this rule, if the student had attended 66% of the lectures in the aggregate of the semester or examination as the case may be.

Setalvad Commission on Legal Education:

In 1954 the Setalvad Commission in its report (XIVth report of the Law Commission) while making scathing remarks on the status of legal education, gave suggestions for the reforms in legal education. Two scores and nine years ago it was lamented in Setalvad Commission's Report that:

There are already plethora of LLBs, half baked lawyers who do not know even the elements of law and who are let loose upon the society as drones and parasites in different parts of the country. Several of them did not even know what subjects were prescribed in the LL.B. programme, did not know the names of the prescribed books....

4   Article 42 in The Constitution Of India 1949
    42. Provision for just and humane conditions of work and maternity relief: The State shall make provision for securing just and humane conditions of work and for maternity relief

5   **Meaning of Directive Principles of State Policy:**   The **Directive Principles of State Policy** are guidelines to the central and state governments of India, to be kept in mind while framing laws and policies. These provisions, contained in Part IV of the Constitution of India, are not enforceable by any court, but the principles laid down therein are considered fundamental in the governance of the country, making it the duty of the State to apply these principles in making laws to establish a just society in the country. The principles have been inspired by the Directive Principles given in the Constitution of Ireland and also by the principles of Gandhism; and relate to social justice, economic welfare, foreign policy, and legal and administrative matters.

Women and Maternity Leave:

Article 15(3)[6] empowers the State to make special provisions for women. Women constitute 50% of the country's population and without making education a reality for them, fundamental rights shall remain beyond the reach of a large majority of population of this country which is illiterate. The Supreme Court in a catena of judgments has held that right to education is implicit in right to life and personal liberty guaranteed by Article 21[7] and now with the Right to Education Act in force, education cannot be kept outside the reach of any citizen. Education is the greatest leveler of all inequalities and only if women are given equal opportunity for education they can stand on an equal footing with men. Of all the rights of women, to be a mother is the greatest. Long ago, the Universal Declaration of Human Rights, by Article 25 had declared that everyone has the right to a standard of living adequate for the health and well-being of himself and of his family, including food, clothing, housing and medical care and necessary social services, and the right to security in the event of unemployment, sickness, disability, widowhood, old age or other lack of livelihood in circumstances beyond his control. Article 25(2) provides that:

2) Motherhood and childhood are entitled to special care and assistance. All children, whether born in or out of wedlock, shall enjoy the same social protection.

The Preamble of CEDAW reiterates that discrimination against women, violates the principles of equality of rights and respect for human dignity; is an obstacle to the participation on equal terms with men in the political, social, economic and cultural life of their country; hampers the growth of the personality from society and family and makes it more difficult for

---

6 **Article 15 in The Constitution Of India 1949**
   15. Prohibition of discrimination on grounds of religion, race, caste, sex or place of birth
   (1) The State shall not discriminate against any citizen on grounds only of religion, race, caste, sex, place of birth or any of them
   (2) No citizen shall, on grounds only of religion, race, caste, sex, place of birth or any of them, be subject to any disability, liability, restriction or condition with regard to
   (a) access to shops, public restaurants, hotels and palaces of public entertainment; or
   (b) the use of wells, tanks, bathing ghats, roads and places of public resort maintained wholly or partly out of State funds or dedicated to the use of the general public
   (3) Nothing in this article shall prevent the State from making any special provision for women and children

7 **Article 21 in The Constitution Of India 1949**
   21. Protection of life and personal liberty No person shall be deprived of his life or personal liberty except according to procedure established by law

the full development of potentialities of women in the service of their countries and of humanity. It would be pertinent to quote the relevant provisions here:

11(2). In order to prevent discrimination against women on the ground of marriage or **maternity** and to ensure their effective right to work, states parties shall take appropriate measures;

(a) To prohibit, subject to the imposition of sanctions, dismissal on the grounds of pregnancy or of maternity leave and discrimination in dismissals on the basis of martial status;

(b) To introduce maternity leave with pay or with comparable social benefits without loss of former employment, seniority or social allowances;

In *Air India v. Nergesh Mirza*[8] where the Apex Court was confronted with the constitutional validity of Regulation 46(i) (c) of Air India Employees' Services Regulations which provided that the services of the Air Hostesses would stand terminated on first pregnancy. It would be pertinent to quote the relevant para of the said judgment here:

Having taken the Air Hostess in service and after having utilised her services for four years, to terminate her service by the Management if she becomes pregnant amounts to compelling the poor Air Hostess not to have any children and thus interfere with and divert the ordinary course of human nature. Court held that the termination of the services of an Air Hostess under such circumstances is not only a callous and cruel act but an open insult to Indian womanhood the most sacrosanct and cherised institution. Court observed that such a course of action is extremely detestable and adhorrent to the notions of a civilised society. Apart from being grossly unethical, it smacks of a deep rooted sense of utter selfishness at the cost of all human values. Such a provision, therefore, is not only manifestly unreasonable and arbitrary but contains the quality of unfairness and exhibits naked despotism and is, therefore, clearly violative of Article 14[9] of the Constitution.

---

8 (1981) 4 SCC 335

9 **Article 14 in The Constitution Of India 1949**
   14. Equality before law The State shall not deny to any person equality before the law or the equal protection of the laws within the territory of India Prohibition of discrimination on grounds of religion, race, caste, sex or place of birth

Decision of the Court:

Court held that if any female candidate is deprived or detained in any of the semester just on the ground that she could not attend classes being in the advanced stage of pregnancy or due to the delivery of the child, then such an act on the part of any of the university or college would not only be completely in negation of the conscience of the Constitution of India but also of the women rights and gender equality this nation has long been striving for. It is a saying that 'Motherhood is priced of God, at price no man may dare to lessen or misunderstand'. By not granting students relaxation, we will be making motherhood a crime which no civilized democracy in the history of mankind has ever done or will ever do. We cannot make them pay the price for the glory that is motherhood.

In *S. Khushboo v. Kanniamal and Anr.*[10] where court has given liberty to the live-in relationship from the shackles of being an offence and also in the latter case where it has held that premarital sex is not an offence. The society today is changing at a rapid pace and we must be in tune with the realities and not hold on to archaic social mores. Once such a right, however unpopular, is recognized then it cannot be ruled out that there can be more cases of girl students proceeding on *maternity leave* when while they are still in college. Law should be an instrument of social change and not a defender of it. Motherhood is not a medical condition but a promise. We all know to our mothers to whom we owe our existence and to punish a woman for becoming a mother would surely be the mother of all ironies. Hence, a female student cannot be deprived from her student status or can be detained in any semester on account of the fact that she could not attend the classes because of her pregnancy. Court also observed college is a time when students are able to grow and mature before going into the real world. At omega, it would be in the right earnest to hope that the students understand that attending college is important in the context of their future plans and goals, not just in terms of grades and academic success. Nevertheless, law colleges would still remain places where pebbles are polished and not where diamonds are dimmed and law students not bottles to be filled but candles to be lit.

---

10 MANU/SC/0310/2010

54

Mother is Natural Guardian of Minor[1]

Facts in Nutshell:

Petitioner[2] and Dr. Mohan Ram were married at Bangalore and in July 1984, a son named Rishab Bailey was born to them. In December, 1984 the petitioner applied to the Reserve Bank of India for 9% Relief Bond to be held in the name of their minor son Rishab along with an intimation that the petitioner No. 1 being the mother, would act as the **natural guardian** for the purposes of investments. The application however was sent back to the petitioner by the RBI Authority advising her to produce the application signed by the father and in the alternative the Bank informed that a certificate of guardianship from a Competent Authority in her favour, ought to be forwarded to the Bank forthwith so as to enable the Bank to issue Bonds as requested and it was this communication from the RBI authorities, which was stated to be arbitrary and opposed to the basic concept of justice in petition[3] under Article 32[4] of the Constitution challenging the validity of Section 6[5] of the Hindu Minority

---

1   Appellants:**Ms. Githa Hariharan & Anr. Vs.** Respondent: **Reserve Bank of India & Anr.**
    AIR1999SC1149
    Hon'ble Judges/Coram: Dr. A. S. Anand, CJI., M. Srinivasan and U. C. Banerjee, JJ.

2   **Meaning of Petitioner:** A person who presents a Petition. (**Meaning of Petition:** A formal message requesting something that is submitted to an authority)

3   **Meaning of Petition:** A formal message requesting something that is submitted to an authority

4   **Article 32 in The Constitution Of India 1949**
    32. Remedies for enforcement of rights conferred by this Part
    (1) The right to move the Supreme Court by appropriate proceedings for the enforcement of the rights conferred by this Part is guaranteed
    (2) The Supreme Court shall have power to issue directions or orders or writs, including writs in the nature of habeas corpus, mandamus, prohibition, quo warranto and certiorari, whichever may be appropriate, for the enforcement of any of the rights conferred by this Part
    (3) Without prejudice to the powers conferred on the Supreme Court by clause (1) and (2), Parliament may by law empower any other court to exercise within the local limits of its jurisdiction all or any of the powers exercisable by the Supreme Court under clause (2)
    (4) The right guaranteed by this article shall not be suspended except as otherwise provided for by this Constitution

5   Section 6(a) of the HMG Act the father of a Hindu minor is the only natural guardian.
    . Section 6 of the HMG Act reads as follows:
    The natural guardians of a Hindu minor, in respect of the minor's person as well as in respect of the minor's property (excluding his or her undivided interest in joint family property), are-
    (a) in the case of a boy or an unmarried girl - the father, and after him, the mother provided that

and Guardianship Act, 1956.

Guardian:

The term 'guardian' is defined in Section 4(b)[6] of HMG Act as a person having the care of the person of a minor or of his property or of both, his person and property, and includes a natural guardian among others. Whenever a dispute concerning the guardianship of a minor, between the father and mother of the minor is raised in a Court of law, the Court is primarily concerned with the best interests of the minor and his welfare in the widest sense while determining the question as regards custody and guardianship of the minor. The question, however, assumes importance only when the mother acts as guardian of the minor during the life time of the father, without the matter going to Court, and the validity of such an action is challenged on the ground that she is not the legal guardian of the minor in view of Section 6(a)[7] (HMG act).

As regards the concept of guardianship both the parents under the Hindu law were treated as natural guardians, of the persons and the separate property of their minor children, male or female except however that the

---

the custody of a minor who has not completed the age of five years shall ordinarily be with the mother;

(b) in the case of an illegitimate boy or an illegitimate unmarried girl - the mother, and after her, the father;

(c) in the case of a married girl - the husband;

Provided that no person shall be entitled to act as the natural guardian of a minor under the provisions of this section-

(a) if he has ceased to be a Hindu, or (b) if he has completely and finally renounced the world becoming a hermit (vanaprastha) or an ascetic (yati or sanyasi).

Explanation-1 n this section, the expression "father" and "mother" do not include a step-father and a step-mother".

6   Section 4(b) of Hindu Minority and Guardianship Act, 1956
    4 . Definitions.- In this Act,-
    (a) "minor" means a person who has not completed the age of eighteen years;
    (b) "major" means a person having the care of the person of a minor or of his property or of both his person and property, and includes-
    (i) a natural guardian,
    (ii) a guardian appointed by the will of the minor's father or mother,
    (iii) a guardian appointed or declared by a court, and
    (iv) a person empowered to act as such by or under any enactment relating to any court of wards

7   Section 6(a) of Hindu Minority and Guardianship Act, 1956
    6 . Natural guardians of a Hindu minor.- The natural guardians of a Hindu, minor, in respect of the minor's person as well as in respect of the minor's property (excluding his or her undivided interest in joint family property), are-
    (a) in the case of a boy or an unmarried girl-the father, and after him, the mother: provided that the custody of a minor who has not completed the age of five years shall ordinarily be with the mother

husband is the natural guardian of his wife howsoever young she might be and the adopted father being the natural guardian of the adopted son. The law however provided that upon the death of the father and in the event of there being no testamentary guardian appointed by the father, the mother succeeds to the natural guardianship of the person and separate property of their minor children. Conceptually, this guardianship however is in the nature of a sacred trust and the guardian cannot therefore, during his lifetime substitute another person to be the guardian in his place though however entrustment of the custody of the child for education or purposes allying may be effected temporarily with a power to revoke at the option of the guardian.

Prior to the enactment, the law recognised both de facto and de jure guardian of a minor: A guardian-de-facto implying thereby one who has taken- upon himself the guardianship of a minor-whereas the guardian de jure is a legal guardian who has a legal right to guardianship of a person or the property or both as the case may be. This concept of legal guardian includes a natural guardian: a testamentary guardian or a guardian of a Hindu minor appointed or declared by Court of law under the general law of British India.

In the case of *J. V. Gajre v. Pathankhan and Ors.*[8] in which Supreme Court in paragraph 11 of the report observed:

The father and mother of the appellant[9] had fallen out and that the mother was living separately for over 20years. It was the mother who was actually managing the affairs of her minor daughter, who was under her care and protection. From 1951 on wards the mother in the usual course of management had been leasing out the properties of the appellant to the tenant. Though from 1951 to 1956 the leases were oral, for the year 1956-57 a written lease was executed by the tenant in favour of the appellant represented by her mother. It is no doubt true that the father was alive but he was not taking any interest in the affairs of the minor and it was as good as if he was non-existent so far as the minor appellant was concerned. ***Court held that in the particular circumstances, the mother can be considered to be the natural guardian of her minor daughter.***

---

8   [1971]2SCR1

9   **Meaning of Appellant:** A person who, dissatisfied with the judgment rendered in a lawsuit decided in a lower court or the findings from a proceeding before an Administrative Agency, asks a superior court to review the decision.

Decision of the Supreme Court:

While both the parents are duty bound to take care of the person and property of their minor child and act in the best interest of his welfare, Court hold that in all situations where the father is not in actual charge of the affairs of the minor either because of his indifference or because of an agreement between him and the mother of the minor (oral or written) and the minor is in the exclusive care and custody of the mother or the father for any other reason is unable to take care of the minor because of his physical and/or mental incapacity, the mother, can act as natural guardian of the minor and all her actions would be valid even during the life time of the father, who would be deemed to be 'absent' for the purposes of Section 6(a) of HMG Act and Section 19(b)[10] of Guardians Wards Act. Hence, the Reserve Bank of India was not right in insisting upon an application signed by the father to open a deposit account in the name of the minor particularly when there was already a letter jointly written by both petitioners evidencing their mutual agreement. The Reserve Bank, now ought to accept the application filed by the mother.

---

10 **Section 19 in The Guardians And Wards Act, 1890**
 19. Guardian not to be appointed by the Court in certain cases.- Nothing in this Chapter shall authorize the Court to appoint or declare a guardian of the property of a minor whose property is under the superintendence of a Court of Wards, or to appoint or declare a guardian of the person--
 (a) of a minor who is a married female and whose husband is not, in the opinion of the Court, unfit to be guardian of her person, or
 (b) of a minor whose father is living and is not, in the opinion of the Court, unfit to be guardian of the person of the minor

55

Domestic Violence against Women[1]

Question before the Court:

(i) Whether continued deprivation of economic or financial resources and continued prohibition or denial of access to shared household is a Domestic Violence

(ii) Whether the protection under the Domestic Violence Act will be available to the Petitioner[2] (wife), who was driven out from her husband's shared house hold prior to coming into effect of the Domestic Violence Act, if such denial of residence continued even after the Domestic Violence Act came into force.

Facts in Nutshell:

Petitioner (wife) filed a case against her husband seeking protection under Domestic Violence Act, in the Court of the Learned Chief Judicial Magistrate, Dibrugarh praying for urgent relief of accommodation for the Petitioner in the shared household and other such relief. The learned Chief Judicial Magistrate thereafter transferred the case to the Court of learned Additional Chief Judicial Magistrate, Dibrugarh for disposal.

The Petitioner and the Respondent[3] got married by performing Nam-Kirtan (as per Hindu Rites and Customs). After getting married, they started living together as husband and wife and accordingly two children were born out of the wedlock. Thereafter, the Respondent (Husband) started falsely accusing the Petitioner for living an adulterous[4] life and

---

1 Appellants: **Rina Devi Bora Vs.** Respondent: **Dwijen Ch. Bora and Anr.**
   2009(4)GLT432
   Hon'ble Judges/Coram: Arun Chandra Upadhyay, J.

2 **Meaning of Petitioner:** A person who presents a Petition. (**Meaning of Petition:** A formal message requesting something that is submitted to an authority)

3 **Meaning of Respondent:** A **respondent** is a person who is called upon to issue a response to a communication made by another. In legal usage, this specifically refers to the defendant in a legal proceeding commenced by a petition, or to an appellee, or the opposing party, in an appeal of a decision by an initial fact-finder.

4 **Meaning of Adultery: Adultery** (also called **philandery**, anglicised from Latin *adulterium*) is sexual intercourse between a married person and someone other than their spouse or spouses.

started to torment her without any rhyme or reason. On 6th August, 2006, the Respondents took up a quarrel over transfer of two kathas of land which was refused by the Petitioner and on such refusal the Petitioner was allegedly assaulted by the Respondent and, accordingly, she was compelled to leave the house of the Respondent.

Domestic Violence:

On close analysis of the provisions of Section 3[5] of the Domestic Violence Act, it appears that domestic violence has been defined to include any omission, commission or conduct of the Respondent(husband)

---

5   Section 3 in The Protection Of Women From Domestic Violence Act, 2005
   3. Definition of domestic violence.- For the purposes of this Act, any act, omission or commission or conduct of the respondent shall constitute domestic violence in case it-
   (a) harms or injures or endangers the health, safety, life, limb or well- being, whether mental or physical, of the aggrieved person or tends to do so and includes causing physical abuse, sexual abuse, verbal and emotional abuse and economic abuse; or
   (b) harasses, harms, injures or endangers the aggrieved person with a view to coerce her or any other person related to her to meet any unlawful demand for any dowry or other property or valuable security; or
   (c) has the effect of threatening the aggrieved person or any person related to her by any conduct mentioned in clause (a) or clause (b); or
   (d) otherwise injures or causes harm, whether physical or mental, to the aggrieved person. Explanation I.- For the purposes of this section,-
   (i) " physical abuse" means any act or conduct which is of such a nature as to cause bodily pain, harm, or danger to life, limb, or health or impair the health or development of the aggrieved person and includes assault, criminal intimidation and criminal force;
   (ii) " sexual abuse" includes any conduct of a sexual nature that abuses, humiliates, degrades or otherwise violates the dignity of woman;
   (iii) " verbal and emotional abuse" includes-
   (a) insults, ridicule, humiliation, name calling and insults or ridicule specially with regard to not having a child or a male child; and
   (b) repeated threats to cause physical pain to any person in whom the aggrieved person is interested.
   (iv) " economic abuse" includes-
   (a) deprivation of all or any economic or financial resources to which the aggrieved person is entitled under any law or custom whether payable under an order of a court or otherwise or which the aggrieved person requires out of necessity including, but not limited to, household necessities for the aggrieved person and her children, if any, stridhan, property, jointly or separately owned by the aggrieved person, payment of rental related to the shared household and maintenance;
   (b) disposal of household effects, any alienation of assets whether movable or immovable, valuables, shares, securities, bonds and the like or other property in which the aggrieved person has an interest or is entitled to use by virtue of the domestic relationship or which may be reasonably required by the aggrieved person or her children or her stridhan or any other property jointly or separately held by the aggrieved person; and
   (c) prohibition or restriction to continued access to resources or facilities which the aggrieved person is entitled to use or enjoy by virtue of the domestic relationship including access to the shared household. Explanation II.- For the purpose of determining whether any act, omission, commission or conduct of the respondent constitutes" domestic violence" under this section, the overall facts and circumstances of the case shall be taken into consideration.

which harms or injuries and/or causes economic abuses to the Petitioner (wife). The definition of economic abuses in Section 3(iv) clearly reflects deprivation of all or any economic or financial resources to which the aggrieved person is entitled under any law or custom including use or enjoyment of access to shared household. It will be pertinent to portray the provision of Section 3 of the Domestic Violence Act, which runs as follows:

3. Definition of domestic Violence -- For the purpose of this Act, any act, omission or commission or conduct of the Respondent shall constitute domestic Violence in case it --

(a) harms or injures or endangers the health, safety, life, limb or well-being, whether mental or physical, of the aggrieved person or tends to do so and includes causing physical abuse, sexual abuse, verbal and emotional abuse and economic abuse; or

(b) harasses, harms, injures or endangers the aggrieved person with a view to coerce her or any other person related to her to meet any unlawful demand for any dowry or other property or valuable security; or

(c) has the effect of threatening the aggrieved person or any person related to her by any conduct mentioned in Clause (a) or Clause (b); or

(d) otherwise injures or causes harm, whether physical or mental to the aggrieved person.

Explanation- I -- For the purpose of this section--

(i) "physical abuse" means an act or conduct which is of such a nature as to cause bodily pain, harm, or danger to life, limb, or health or impair the health or development of the aggrieved person and includes assault, criminal intimidation and criminal force;

(ii) "sexual abuse" includes any conduct of a sexual nature that abuses, humiliates, degrades or otherwise violates the dignity of woman;

(iii) "verbal and emotional abuse" includes--

(a) insults, ridicule, humiliation, name calling and insults or ridicule specially with regard to not having a child or a male child; and

(b) repeated threats to cause physical pain to any person in whom the aggrieved person is interested.

(iv) "economic abuse" includes --

(a) deprivation of all or any economic or financial resources to which the aggrieved person is entitled under any law or custom whether payable under an order of a court or otherwise or which the aggrieved person requires out of necessity including, but not limited to, household necessities for the aggrieved person and her children, if any, stridhan, property, jointly or separately owned by the aggrieved person, payment of rental related to the shared household and maintenance;

(b) disposal of household effects, any alienation of assets whether movable or immovable, valuables, shares, securities, bonds and the like or other property in which the aggrieved person has an interest or is entitled to use by virtue of the domestic relationship or which may be reasonably required by the aggrieved person or her children or her stridhan or any other property jointly or separately held by the aggrieved person; and

(c) prohibition or restriction to continued access to resources or facilities which the aggrieved person is entitled to use or enjoy by virtue of the domestic relationship including access to the shared household."

Deprivation of an aggrieved woman from maintenance and denial of access to shared household itself is a domestic violence as envisaged under Section 3 of the Domestic Violence Act. As a matter of fact, any continued deprivation of economic or financial resources or prohibition of access to shared household would be a domestic violence. The definition of domestic violence itself clearly spells out that it is not necessary that the aggrieved person has to be ill treated and assaulted by the Respondent to constitute domestic violence, any continuous deprivation and prohibition as defined under Section 3 of the Domestic Violence Act, comes within the purview of the domestic violence.

Preamble of the Domestic Violence Act clearly specifies that this Act has been enacted chiefly to provide protection to women who are the victims of domestic violence and to prevent the occurrence of domestic violence in the society or matters connected therewith. The Hon'ble Supreme Court in *Vimlaben Ajitbhai Patel v. Vatslaben Ashokbhi Patel*[6], held that the Domestic Violence Act provides for a higher right in favour of the wife. She not only acquires a right to be maintained but also there under acquires a right of residence which is a higher right. The said right, as per the legislation, extends only to joint properties in which husband

6 (2008) 4 SCC 649

has a share.

Decision of the High Court:

Court held that the continued deprivation of economic or financial resources and continued prohibition or denial of access to shared household to the aggrieved person is a domestic violence and the protection under the Domestic Violence Act will be available to the Petitioner (wife), who was driven out from her husband's shared household.

56

Dowry Death[1]

Facts in Nutshell:

Smt. Urmila, a youthful wife of 20 years of appellant[2] Raju, residing with her parents in village Bhadwa, district Fatehpur, married in 1983, was brought to the district hospital Fatehpur on 11-10-1986 by Raju's cousin Vijai Bahadur Singh with extensive burn injuries. She was admitted and medically examined by Dr. Harish Chandra wherein she died. An inquest[3] (Panchnama) was done on the dead body of Urmila by Sub-Inspector. From the evidence it was proved that the appellant Raju was married to the deceased Smt. Urmila in December, 1983 and her death under unnatural circumstances had occurred on 11-10-1986. This will be within about three years of the date of marriage.

Decision of Trial Judge

The Trial Judge acquitted[4] Km. Aruna but convicted and sentenced the other appellants as under:--1. Raja appellant both under Section 302[5], I.P.C. -- Death sentence 2. Smt. Gulhari Devi. both under Section 304B[6],

---

1   Appellants: **Bhoora Singh** Vs. Respondent: **State**
    1993CriLJ2636
    Hon'ble Judges/Coram: Palok Basu, B.L. Yadav and J.N. Dubey, JJ.

2   **Meaning of Appellant:** A person who, dissatisfied with the judgment rendered in a lawsuit decided in a lower court or the findings from a proceeding before an <u>Administrative Agency</u>, asks a superior court to review the decision.

3   **Meaning of Inquest:**
    a. A judicial inquiry into a matter usually held before a jury, especially an inquiry into the cause of a death.
    b. A jury making such an inquiry.

4   **Meaning of Acquittal:** In the common law tradition, an **acquittal** formally certifies that the accused is free from the charge of an offense, as far as the criminal law is concerned.

5   **Section 302 IPC , 1860: Punishment for murder.**
    302. Punishment for murder.--Whoever commits murder shall be punished with death, or [imprisonment for life], and shall also be liable to fine.

6   **Section 304B in The Indian Penal Code, 1860**
    304B. Dowry death.--
    (1) Where the death of a woman is caused by any burns or bodily injury or occurs otherwise than under normal circumstances within seven years of her marriage and it is shown that soon before her death she was subjected to cruelty or harassment by her husband or any relative of her husband for, or in connection with, any demand for dowry, such death shall be called" dowry

I.P.C. -- 7 years' Rigorous Imprisonment both under Section 498A[7], I.P.C. -- 3 years' Rigorous Imprisonment both under Section 4[8] Dowry -- 6 months' R.I. plus Prohibition Act Rs. 500/- fine. 3. Appellant Bhoora under Section 498A -- 3 years' R.I. & Singh Rs. 500/- fine. under Section 4 Dowry -- 6 months' R.I. plus Prohibition Act, Rs. 500/- as fine.

Against those convictions[9] and sentences two criminal appeals have been preferred and the usual Reference has been sent up by the Sessions Judge because of death sentence having been awarded to Raju and Smt. Gulhari.

Section 304 B, IPC, 1860

Section 304B, IPC and Section 113B[10] of the Indian Evidence Act were added on 19-11-1986 by Dowry Prohibition (Amendment) Act 1986. The new offence 'dowry death' created under Section 304B, IPC is punishable with a minimum sentence of 7 years which may extend to imprisonment for life. Therefore, this section is creating a substantive offence and is not merely a provision effecting a change in the procedure for trial of a preexisting substantive offence.

---

death", and such husband or relative shall be deemed to have caused her death. Explanation.- For the purposes of this sub- section," dowry" shall have the same meaning as in section 2 of the Dowry Prohibition Act, 1961 (28 of 1961).
(2) Whoever commits dowry death shall be punished with imprisonment for a term which shall not be less than seven years but which may extend to imprisonment for life.]

7 **Section 498A, IPC, 1860**
Husband or relative of husband of a woman subjecting her to cruelty.
Whoever, being the husband or the relative of the husband of a woman, subjects such woman to cruelty shall be punished with imprisonment for a term which may extend to three years and shall also be liable to fine.

8 **Section 4 in The Dowry Prohibition Act 1961**
4. Penalty for demanding dowry. If any person, after the commencement of this Act, demands, directly or indirectly, from the parents or guardian of a bride or bridegroom, as the case may be, any dowry, he shall be punishable with imprisonment which may extend to six months, or with fine which may extend to five thousand rupees, or with both: Provided that no court shall take cognizance of any offence under this section except with the previous sanction of the State Government or of such officer as the State Government may, by general or special order, specify in this behalf.

9 **Meaning of Convicted: S**omeone guilty of an offense or crime, especially by the verdict of a court.

10 **Section 113B in The Indian Evidence Act, 1872**
113B. [Presumption as to dowry death.- When the question is whether a person has committed the dowry death of a woman and it is shown that soon before her death such woman had been subjected by such person to cruelty or harassment for, or in connection with, any demand for dowry, the court shall presume that such person had caused the dowry death. Explanation.-- For the purposes of this section," dowry death" shall have the same meaning as in section 304B of the Indian Penal Code.]

The gist of the two offences punishable under Section 302, IPC and Section 304B, IPC is the extinction of life under unnatural circumstances and there is nothing in the two sections to either explicitly or impliedly exclude either of the two if one is applicable. For charging an accused under Section 302, IPC the prosecution has, in fact, to prove by evidence that the accused by his acts has caused the death of the deceased with the intention of causing death. But for the exceptions carved out in Section 300, IPC which may amount to culpable homicide not amounting to murder, all other instances of culpable homicide would be punishable as murder under Section 302, IPC because it shall come within the definition of murder as delineated under Section 300, IPC. But Section 304B, IPC reads as under :--

304-B. Dowry death-- (1) where the death of a woman is caused by any burns or bodily injury or occurs otherwise than in normal circumstances, within 7 years of her marriage and it is shown that soon before her death she was subjected to cruelty or harassment by her husband or any relative of her husband for, or in connection with, any demand for dowry such death shall be called "dowry death" and such husband or relative shall be deemed to have caused her death.

Explanation : For the purposes of this sub-section, "dowry", shall have the same meaning as in Section 2[11] of the Dowry Prohibition Act, 1961.

(2) Whoever commits dowry death shall he punished with imprisonment for a term which shall not be less than 7 years but which may extend to imprisonment for life.

Section 113B of the Evidence Act should be quoted below :

113-B. When the question is whether a person has committed the dowry death of a woman and it is shown that soon before her death such woman had been subjected by such person to cruelty or harassment for, or in

---

11 **Section 2 in The Dowry Prohibition Act 1961**2. Definition of" dowry". In this Act," dowry" means any property or valuable security given or agreed to be given either directly or indirectly-
(a) by one party to a marriage to the other party to the marriage; or
(b) by the parents of either party to a marriage or by a other person, to either party to the marriage or to any other person; at or before or after the marriage us consideration for the marriage of the said parties, but does not include dower or mahr in the case of persons to whom the Muslim Personal Law (Shariat) applies. Explanation I.- For the removal of doubts, it is hereby declare that any presents made at the time of a marriage to either party to the marriage in the form of cash, ornaments, clothes or other articles, shall not be deemed to be dowry within the meaning of this section, unless they are made as consideration for the marriage of the said parties.

connection with, any demand for dowry, the court shall presume that such person had caused the dowry death.

Explanation : For the purposes of this section, "dowry death" shall have the same meaning as in Section 304B of the Indian Penal Code (45 of 1860) .

The applicability of the Section 113B is limited to cases 'when the question is whether a person has committed dowry death of a woman.... ' That too requires proof of two further facts. Firstly, it is shown that soon before her death such a woman had been subjected by such person to 'cruelty' or 'harassment' and, secondly, that the cruelty of her husband was 'for or in connection with any demand for dowry'. If these two facts are established by evidence the presumption under Section 113B as to the commission of the offence under Section 304B, IPC. would be attracted straightway.

In *State of Punjab v. Iqbal Singh*[12] the Supreme Court has dealt with the legislative intent behind the enactment of Sections 304B, 498A, IPC. and Section 113A[13] and 113B of the Indian Evidence Act. The accused in the said case was charged Under Section 306[14], IPC as his wife Mohinder Kaur had set herself and her three children ablaze on 7-6-1983 at the residence of her husband Iqbal Singh. The Trial Judge had convicted the accused and had brought in Section 113A of the Indian Penal Code to his aid. The High Court had, however, acquitted Iqbal Singh. The State of Punjab took up the matter in appeal to the Supreme Court which was allowed and the trial court's judgment in so far as Iqbal Singh was concerned was restored.

Decision of the High Court

Court dismissed the appeal field by Bhoora Singh. His conviction under Section 498A, I.P.C. and the sentence of three years' R.I. and a fine of Rs.

---

12 MANU/SC/0354/1991

13 **Section 113A, Evidence, Act , 1872**
Presumption as to abetment of suicide by a married woman.
When the question is whether the commission of suicide by a woman had been abetted by her husband or any relative of her husband and it is shown that she had committed suicide within a period of seven years from the date of her marriage and that her husband or such relative of her husband had subjected her to cruelty, the court may presume, having regard to all the other circumstances of the case, that such suicide had been abetted by her husband or by such relative of her husband. Explanation.--For the purposes of this section, "cruelty" shall have the same meaning as in section 498A of the Indian Penal Code (45 of 1860).]

14 **Section 306 in The Indian Penal Code, 1860**
306. Abetment of suicide.-- If any person commits suicide, whoever abets the commission of such suicide, shall be punished with imprisonment of either description for a term which may extend to ten years, and shall also be liable to fine.

500/- was upheld. His conviction under Section 4 of the Dowry Prohibition Act and the sentence of six months' R.I. and a fine of Rs. 500/- was also upheld. The conviction of Raju alias Raghuvendra Pratap Singh and Smt. Gulhari alias Champa Devi under Section 302, I.P.C. and the sentence of death awarded to them thereunder were set aside. They were acquitted of the charges punishable Under Section 304B, I.P.C. Their conviction under Section 498A, I.P.C. and the sentence of three years' R.I. and a fine of Rs. 500/- each were upheld. Their conviction under Section 4 of the Dowry Prohibition Act and the sentence of six months' R.I. and a fine of Rs. 500/- thereunder were also upheld.

57

Punishment for Adultery[1]

Ratio Decidendi[2]: *"Breaking a matrimonial home is serious offence of crime."*

Facts in Nutshell:

Petition[3] under Article 32 of the Constitution[4] where the petitioner (wife) challenged the validity of Section 497 of the Penal Code[5] which defines the offence of adultery and prescribes punishment for it. The petitioner filed a petition for divorce against her husband on the ground of desertion[6]. The trial court dismissed that petition, holding that the petitioner herself had deserted the husband and not the other way about. Thereafter, the husband filed a petition for divorce against the petitioner

---

1 Appellants: **Sowmithri Vishnu Vs.**Respondent: **Union of India (UOI) and Anr.**
   AIR1985SC1618
   Hon'ble Judges/Coram: Y. V. Chandrachud, C.J., R. S. Pathak and A. N. Sen, JJ.

2 **Meaning of Ration Decidendi:** *Ratio decidendi* is a Latin phrase meaning "the reason" or "the rationale for the decision." The *ratio decidendi* is "the point in a case which determines the judgment" or "the principle which the case establishes."

3 **Meaning of Petition:** A formal message requesting something that is submitted to an authority

4 **Article 32 of the Constitution, 1950:**
   32. Remedies for enforcement of rights conferred by this Part
   (1) The right to move the Supreme Court by appropriate proceedings for the enforcement of the rights conferred by this Part is guaranteed
   (2) The Supreme Court shall have power to issue directions or orders or writs, including writs in the nature of habeas corpus, mandamus, prohibition, quo warranto and certiorari, whichever may be appropriate, for the enforcement of any of the rights conferred by this Part
   (3) Without prejudice to the powers conferred on the Supreme Court by clause (1) and (2), Parliament may by law empower any other court to exercise within the local limits of its jurisdiction all or any of the powers exercisable by the Supreme Court under clause (2)
   (4) The right guaranteed by this article shall not be suspended except as otherwise provided for by this Constitution

5 **Section 497 of Indian Penal Code, 1860:**
   Section 497 in The Indian Penal Code, 1860
   497. Adultery.-- Whoever has sexual intercourse with a person who is and whom he knows or has reason to believe to be the wife of another man, without the consent or connivance of that man, such sexual intercourse not amounting to the offence of rape, is guilty of the offence of adultery, and shall be punished with imprisonment of either description for a term which may extend to five years, or with fine, or with both. In such case the wife shall not be punishable as an abettor.

6 **Meaning of Desertion:**
   Wilful abandonment, especially of one's spouse without consent, in violation of legal or moral obligations.

on two "grounds :

Firstly, that she had deserted him

Secondly, that she was living in adultery with a person called Dharma Ebenezer.

Decision of Trial Court & High Court:

Husband contended before the trail court that petitioner (wife) was living in Adultery and hat contention was accepted by Trial court but, in a revision application filed by the petitioner (wife), the High Court accepted her plea and held that since, the finding recorded in the earlier petition was binding on the parties, a decree for divorce hid to be passed in favour of the husband on the ground of desertion and that, it was unnecessary to inquire into the question of adultery.

Adultery under I.P.C, 1860

Section 497 I.P.C, 1860 is one of the six sections is Chapter XX of the Penal Code, which is entitled 'Of Offences Relating to Marriage'. Section 497 reads thus ;

Whoever has sexual intercourse with a person who is and whom he knows or has reason to believe to be the wife of another man, without the consent or connivance of that man, such sexual intercourse not amounting to the offence of rape, is guilty of the offence of adultery, and shall be punished with imprisonment of either description for a term which may extend to five years, or with fine, or with both. In such case the wife shall not be punishable as an abettor. Section 498 I.P.C, 1860[7] prescribes punishment for enticing or taking away or detaining a married woman with criminal intent.

Submissions on behalf of the Lawyer:

Lawyer who appeared on behalf of the petitioner (wife), contended that

---

7 **Section 498 in The Indian Penal Code, 1860**
   498. Enticing or taking away or detaining with criminal intent a married woman.-- Whoever takes or entices away any woman who is and whom he knows or has reason to believe to be the wife of any other man, from that man, or from any person having the care of her on behalf of that man, with intent that she may have illicit intercourse with any person, or conceals or detains with that intent any such woman, shall be punished with imprisonment of either description for a term which may extend to two years, or with fine, or with both.

Section 497 of the Penal Cede is violative of Article 14 of the Constitution[8] because, by making an irrational classification between man and women, it unjustifiably denies to women the right which is given to men. This argument rests on the following three grounds : (1) Section 497 confers upon the husband the right to prosecute the adulterer but, it does not confer any right upon the wife to prosecute the woman with whom her husband has committed adultery; (2) Section 497 does not confer any right on the wife to prosecute the husband who has committed adultery with another woman; and, (3) Section 497 does not take in cases where the husband has sexual relations with an unmarried woman, with the result that husbands have, as it were, a free licence under the law to have extra-marital relationship with unmarried women. The learned Counsel complained that Section 497 is flagrant instance of 'gender discrimination', 'legislative despotism' and 'male chauvinism'. It was urged that the section may, at first blush, appear as if it is a beneficial legislation intended to serve the interests of women but, on closer examination, it would be found that the provision contained in the section is a kind of 'Romantic Paternalism', which stems from the assumption that women, like chattels, are the property of men.

Law Commission 42nd Report, 1971

The offence of adultery, by its very definition, can be committed by a man and not by a woman : "Whoever has sexual intercourse with a person who is and whom he knows or has reason to believe to be the wife of another man ... is guilty of the offence of adultery." The argument really comes to this that the definition should be recast by extending the ambit of the offence of adultery so that, both the man and the woman should be punishable for the offence of adultery. The Law Commission of India in its 42nd Report, 1971, recommended the retention of Section 497 in its present form with the modification that, even the wife, who has sexual relations with a person other than her husband, should be made punishable for adultery. The suggested modification was not accepted by the legislature. Mrs. Anna Chandi, who was in the minority, voted for the deletion of Section 497 on the ground that "it is the right time to consider the question whether the offence of adultery as envisaged in Section 497 is in tune with our present day notions of woman's status in

---

8 Article 14 of the Constitution, 1950
   14. Equality before law The State shall not deny to any person equality before the law or the equal protection of the laws within the territory of India Prohibition of discrimination on grounds of religion, race, caste, sex or place of birth

marriage'". The repot of the Law Commission show that there can be two opinions on the desirability of retaining a provision like the one contained in Section 497 on the statute book. But, we cannot strike down that section on the ground that it is desirable to delete it.

The offence of adultery as defined in that section can only be committed by a man, not by a woman. Indeed, the section provides expressly that the wife shall not be punishable even as an abettor. No grievance can then be made that the section does not allow the wife to prosecute the husband for adultery. The contemplation of the law, evidently, is that the wife, who is involved in an illicit relationship with another man, is a victim and not the author of the crime. The offence of adultery, as defined in Section 497, is considered by the Legislature as an offence against the sanctity of the matrimonial home, an act which is committed by a man, as it generally is. Therefore, those men who defile that sanctity are brought within the net of the law. Law does not confer freedom upon husbands to be licentious by gallivanting with unmarried woman. It only makes a specific kind of extra-marital relationship an offence, the relationship between a man and a married woman, the man alone being the offender. An unfaithful husband risks or, perhaps, invites a civil action by the wife for separation.

Grievance of Petitioner[9]

The demand of the petitioner that sexual relationship of a husband with an unmarried women should also be comprehended with in the definition of 'adultery' is a crusade by a woman against a woman. If the paramour of a married woman can be guilty of adultery, why can an unmarried girl who has sexual relations with a married man not be guilty of adultery? That was the grievance of the petitioner.

Section 497 I.P.C is in violation of Article 21 of the Constitution[10]

Petitioner challenged the validity of Section 497 on yet another ground, namely, that it violates Article 21 of the Constitution. Relying upon the decisions of Court in *Francis Coralie v. Union Territory* [11] and *Board of*

---

9 **Meaning of Petitioner:** A person who presents a Petition. (**Meaning of Petition:** A formal message requesting something that is submitted to an authority)

10 **Article 21 in The Constitution Of India 1949**
   21. Protection of life and personal liberty No person shall be deprived of his life or personal liberty except according to procedure established by law.

11 AIR 1981 SC 746

Trustees, fort of Bombay v. Nadkarni [12] counsel argued that the right to life includes the right to reputation and, therefore, if the outcome of a trial is likely to affect the reputation of a person adversely, he or she night to be entitled to appear and be heard in that trial. A law which docs not confer upon such a person the right of being heard is violative of Article 21.

Court in *Yusuf Abdul Aziz v. The State of Bombay* [13] held that Section 497 of the Penal Code does not offend Articles 14 and 15 of the Constitution.

Decision of the Supreme Court:

Court held that since Petitioner's (Wife) husband already obtained divorce against her on the ground of desertion, no useful purpose will be served by inquiring into the allegation whether she had adulterous relationship with Dharma Ebenezer, against whom the husband has lodged a complaint under Section 497 of the Penal Code. Writ Petition [14] was dismissed by the Court.

---

12 (1983)ILLJ1SC

13 [1954]1SCR930

14 **Meaning of Writ Petition:**
Under the Indian legal system, jurisdiction to issue 'prerogative writs' is given to the Supreme Court, and to the High Courts of Judicature of all Indian states. Parts of the law relating to writs are set forth in the Constitution of India. The Supreme Court, the highest in the country, may issue writs under Article 32 of the Constitution for enforcement of Fundamental Rights and under Articles 139 for enforcement of rights other than Fundamental Rights, while High Courts, the superior courts of the States, may issue writs under Articles 226. 'Writ' is eminently designed by the makers of the Constitution, and in the same way it is developed very widely and efficiently by the courts in India. The Constitution broadly provides for five kinds of "prerogative" writs, namely, Habeas Corpus, Certiorari, Mandamus, Quo Warranto and Prohibition.

58

Compulsory Registration for Marriage[1]

Marriage:

The origin of marriage amongst Aryans in India, as noted in Mayne's Hindu Law and Usage, as amongst other ancient peoples is a matter for the Science of anthropology. From the very commencement of the Rigvedic age, marriage was a well- established institution, and the Aryans ideal of marriage was very high. The Convention on the Elimination of All Forms of Discrimination Against Women (in short 'CEDAW') was adopted in 1979 by the United Nations General Assembly. India was a signatory to the Convention on 30th July, 1980 and ratified on 9th July, 1993 with two Declaratory Statements and one Reservation. Article 16(2) of the Convention says "though India agreed on principle that compulsory registration of marriages is highly desirable, it was said as follows:

It is not practical in a vast country like India with its variety of customs, religions and level of literacy' and has expressed reservation to this very clause to make registration of marriage compulsory.

Compulsory Registration of Marriages:

Compulsory registration of marriages would be a step in the right direction for the prevention of child marriages still prevalent in many parts of the country. In the Constitution of India, 1950 (in short the 'Constitution') List III (the Concurrent List) of the Seventh Schedule provides in **Entries 5 and 30 as follows:**

5. Marriage and divorce; infants and minors; adoption; wills, intestacy and succession; joint family and partition; all matters in respect of which parties in judicial proceedings were immediately before the commencement of this Constitution subject to their personal law.

30. Vital statistics including registration of births and deaths.

It is to be noted that vital statistics including registration of deaths and

1   Appellants: **Smt. Seema Vs.** Respondent: **Ashwani Kumar**
    AIR2006SC1158
    Hon'ble Judges: Dr. Arijit Pasayat and S. H. Kapadia , JJ.

births is covered by Entry 30. The registration of marriages would come within the ambit of the expression 'vital statistics'.

There are four Statutes which provide for compulsory registration of marriages. They are: (1) The Bombay Registration of Marriages Act, 1953 (applicable to Maharashtra and Gujarat), (2) The Karnataka Marriages (Registration and Miscellaneous Provisions) Act, 1976, (3) The Himachal Pradesh Registration of Marriages Act, 1996, and (4) The Andhra Pradesh Compulsory Registration of Marriages Act, 2002.

Under the Special Marriage Act, 1954 which applies to Indian citizens irrespective of religion each marriage is registered by the Marriage Officer specially appointed for the purpose. The registration of marriage is compulsory under the Indian Christian Marriage Act, 1872. Under the said Act, entries are made in the marriage register of the concerned Church soon after the marriage ceremony along with the signatures of bride and bridegroom, the officiating priest and the witnesses. The Parsi Marriage and Divorce Act, 1936 makes registration of marriages compulsory. Under Section 8[2] of the Hindu Marriage Act, 1955 (in short the 'Hindu Act') certain provisions exist for registration of marriages. However, it is left to the discretion of the contracting parties to either solemnize the marriage before the Sub-Registrar or register it after performing the marriage ceremony in conformity with the customary beliefs. However, the Act makes it clear that the validity of the marriage in no way will be affected by omission to make the entry in the register.

---

2 **Section 8 in The Hindu Marriage Act, 1955**
8. Registration of Hindu marriages.
(1) For the purpose of facilitating the proof of Hindu marriages, the State Government may make rules providing that the parties to any of such marriage may have the particulars relating to their marriage entered in such manner and subject to such conditions as may be prescribed in a Hindu Marriage Register kept for the purpose.
(2) Notwithstanding any thing contained in sub- section (1), the State Government may, if it is of opinion that it is necessary or expedient so to do, provide that the entering of the particulars referred to in sub- section (1) shall be compulsory in the State or in any part thereof, whether in all cases or in such cases as may be specified, and where any such direction has been issued, any person contravening any rule made in this behalf shall be punishable with fine which may extend to twenty- five rupees.
(3) All rules made under this section shall be laid before the State Legislature, as soon as may be, after they are made.
(4) The Hindu Marriage Register shall at all reasonable times be open for inspection, and shall be admissible as evidence of the statements therein contained and certified extracts therefrom shall, on application, be given by the Registrar on payment to him of the prescribed fee.
(5) Notwithstanding anything contained In this section, the validity of any Hindu marriage shall in no way be affected by the omission to Make the entry, RESTITUTION OF CONJUGAL RIGHTS AND JUDICIAL SEPARATION

If the marriage is registered it also provides evidence of the marriage having taken place and would provide a rebuttable presumption of the marriage having taken place. Though, the registration itself cannot be a proof of valid marriage per se, and would not be the determinative factor regarding validity of a marriage, yet it has a great evidentiary value in the matters of custody of children, right of children born from the wedlock of the two persons whose marriage is registered and the age of parties to the marriage. That being so, it would be in the interest of the society if marriages are made compulsorily registrable. The legislative intent in enacting Section 8 of the Hindu Act is apparent from the use of the expression for the purpose of facilitating the proof of Hindu Marriages. As a natural consequence, the effect of non registration would be that the presumption which is available from registration of marriages would be denied to a person whose marriage is not registered.

Decision of the Court:

Court held that marriages of all persons who are citizens of India belonging to various religions should be made compulsorily registrable in their respective States, where the marriage is solemnized.

59

Right to Marriage and Right to Privacy[1]

Facts in Nutshell:

The appellant[2] after obtaining the Degree of MBBS from Jawaharlal institute of Post Graduate Medical Education and Research, Chandigarh, completed his internship and junior residence at the same college. In June, 1990 he joined as Assistant Surgeon Grade-I. The appellant joined the further Course of Diploma in Ophthalmology which he completed in April, 1993. In August, 1993 he resumed his duties in the Nagaland State Health Service as Assistant Surgeon Grade-I. One Itokhu Yepthomi who was ailing from a disease which was provisionally diagnosed as Aortic Anuerism was advised to go to the Apollo Hospital at Madras and the appellant was directed by the Government of Nagaland to accompany the said patient to Madras for treatment. For the treatment of the above disease, Itokhu Yepthomi was posted for surgery which however, was cancelled due to shortage of blood. On June 1, 1995 the appellant was asked to donate blood. Their blood samples were taken and the result showed that the appellant's blood group was A(+ve).

In August, 1995 the appellant proposed marriage to one Ms. Akali which was accepted and the marriage was proposed to be held on December 12, 1995. But the marriage was called off on the ground of blood test conducted at the respondent's[3] hospital in which the appellant was found to be HIV(+). The appellant went again to the respondents' hospital at Madras where several tests were conducted and he was found to be

---

1 Appellants: **Mr 'X' Vs. Respondent: Hospital 'Z'**
   AIR1999SC495
   Hon'ble Judges: S. Saghir Ahmad and B.N. Kirpal, JJ.

2 **Meaning of Appellant:** A person who, dissatisfied with the judgment rendered in a lawsuit decided in a lower court or the findings from a proceeding before an Administrative Agency, asks a superior court to review the decision.

3 **Meaning of Respondent:** A **respondent** is a person who is called upon to issue a response to a communication made by another. In legal usage, this specifically refers to the defendant in a legal proceeding commenced by a petition, or to an appellee, or the opposing party, in an appeal of a decision by an initial fact-finder.

HIV(+). Since the marriage had been settled but was subsequently called off, several people including members of the appellant's family and persons belonging to his community became aware of the appellant's HIV(+) status

The appellant then approached the National Consumer Disputes Redressal Commission for damages against the respondents, on the ground that the information which was required to be kept secret under Medical ethics was disclosed illegally and, therefore, the respondents were liable to pay damages. The Commission dismissed the Petition on the ground that the appellant may seek his remedy in the civil court.

International Code of Medical Ethics laid down as under :

"A physician shall preserve absolute confidentiality on all he knows about his patient even after his patient has died." It is under these provisions that the Code of Medical Ethics has been made by the Indian Medical Council which provides as under :

"Do not disclose the secrets of a patient that have been learnt in the exercise of your profession. Those may be disclosed only in a Court of Law under orders of the presiding judge."

It is true that in the doctor-patient relationship, the most important aspect is the doctor's duty of maintaining secrecy. A doctor cannot disclose to a person any information regarding his patient which he has gathered in the course of treatment nor can the doctor disclose to anyone else the mode of treatment or the advice given by him to the patient.

Reference may be made to Article 8 of the European Convention on Human Rights which defines this right as follows :

"(1) Every one has the right to respect for his private and family life, his home and his correspondence. (2) There shall be no interference by a public authority with the exercise of this right except such as is in accordance with the law and is necessary in democratic society in the interests of national security, public safety or the economic well being of the country, for the prevention of disorder or crime, for the protection of health or morals or for the protection of the rights and freedoms of others."

Right to Privacy:

Right to privacy has been culled out of the provisions of Article 21[4] and other provisions of the Constitution relating to Fundamental Rights read with Directive Principles of State Policy. It was in this context that it was held by this Court in *Kharak Singh vs . State of Uttar Pradesh*[5] that police surveillance of a person by domiciliary visits would be violative of Article 21 of the Constitution. In another classic judgment rendered by Jeevan Reddy, J., in *R. Rajagopal @ RR Gopal & Anr. vs . State of Tamil Nadu & Ors.*[6] , the right of privacy vis-a-vis the right of the Press under Article 19[7]

---

4 **Article 21 in The Constitution Of India 1949**
   21. Protection of life and personal liberty No person shall be deprived of his life or personal liberty except according to procedure established by law

5 1963CriLJ329

6 AIR1995SC264

7 **Article 19 in The Constitution Of India 1949**
   19. Protection of certain rights regarding freedom of speech etc
   (1) All citizens shall have the right
   (a) to freedom of speech and expression;
   (b) to assemble peaceably and without arms;
   (c) to form associations or unions;
   (d) to move freely throughout the territory of India;
   (e) to reside and settle in any part of the territory of India; and
   (f) omitted
   (g) to practise any profession, or to carry on any occupation, trade or business
   (2) Nothing in sub clause (a) of clause (1) shall affect the operation of any existing law, or prevent the State from making any law, in so far as such law imposes reasonable restrictions on the exercise of the right conferred by the said sub clause in the interests of the sovereignty and integrity of India, the security of the State, friendly relations with foreign States, public order, decency or morality or in relation to contempt of court, defamation or incitement to an offence
   (3) Nothing in sub clause (b) of the said clause shall affect the operation of any existing law in so far as it imposes, or prevent the State from making any law imposing, in the interests of the sovereignty and integrity of India or public order, reasonable restrictions on the exercise of the right conferred by the said sub clause
   (4) Nothing in sub clause (c) of the said clause shall affect the operation of any existing law in so far as it imposes, or prevent the State from making any law imposing, in the interests of the sovereignty and integrity of India or public order or morality, reasonable restrictions on the exercise of the right conferred by the said sub clause
   (5) Nothing in sub clauses (d) and (e) of the said clause shall affect the operation of any existing law in so far as it imposes, or prevent the State from making any law imposing, reasonable restrictions on the exercise of any of the rights conferred by the said sub clauses either in the interests of the general public or for the protection of the interests of any Scheduled Tribe
   (6) Nothing in sub clause (g) of the said clause shall affect the operation of any existing law in so far as it imposes, or prevent the State from making any law imposing, in the interests of the general public, reasonable restrictions on the exercise of the right conferred by the said sub clause, and, in particular, nothing in the said sub clause shall affect the operation of any existing law in so far as it relates to, or prevent the State from making any law relating to,
   (i) the professional or technical qualifications necessary for practising any profession or carrying on any occupation, trade or business, or
   (ii) the carrying on by the State, or by a corporation owned or controlled by the State, of any

of the Constitution were considered and it was laid down as under :

"The right to privacy is implicit in the right to life and liberty guaranteed to the citizens of this country by Article 21. It is a "right to be let alone." A citizen has a right to safeguard the privacy of his own, his family, marriage, procreation, motherhood, child-bearing and education among other matters. None can publish anything concerning the above matters without his consent -- whether truthful or otherwise and whether laudatory or critical. If he does so, he would be violating the right to privacy of the person concerned and would be liable in an action for damages. Position may, however, be different, if a person voluntarily thrusts himself into controversy or voluntarily invites or raises a controversy.'

Negligent/Malignant act likely to spread infection of disease dangerous to life

Sections 269 and 270 of the Indian Penal Code provide as under :

"269. Negligent act likely to spread infection of disease dangerous to life -Whoever unlawfully or negligently does any act which is, and which he knows or has reason to believe to be, likely to spread the infection of any disease dangerous to life, shall be punished with imprisonment of either description for a term which may extend to six months, or with fine, or with both.

270. Malignant act likely to spread infection of disease dangerous to life -Whoever malignantly does any act which is, and which he knows or has reason to believe to be, likely to spread the infection of any disease dangerous to life, shall be punished with imprisonment of either description for a term which may extend to two years, or with fine, or with both."

These two Sections spell out two separate and distinct offences by providing that if a person, negligently or unlawfully, does an act which he knew was likely to spread the infection of a disease, dangerous to life, to another person, then, the former would be guilty of an offence, punishable with imprisonment for the term indicated therein. Therefore, if a person suffering from the dreadful disease "AIDS", knowingly marries a woman and thereby transmits infection to that woman, he would be

---

trade, business, industry or service, whether to the exclusion, complete or partial, of citizens or otherwise

guilty of offences indicated in Sections 269 and 270 of the Indian Penal Code. The above statutory provisions thus impose a duty upon the person not to marry as the marriage would have the effect of spreading the infection of his own disease, which obviously is dangerous to life, to the woman whom he marries apart from being an offence.

Decision of Supreme Court:

Court held that Ms. Akali, with whom the marriage of the appellant was settled, was saved in time by the disclosure of the vital information that the appellant was HIV(+). The disease which is communicable would have been positively communicated to her immediately on the consummation of marriage. As a human being, Ms. Akali must also enjoy, as she, obviously, is entitled to, all the Human Rights available to any other human being. This is apart from, and, in addition to, the Fundamental Rights available to her under Article 21 of Constitution, which guarantees "Right to Life" to every citizen of this country. Since "Right to Life" includes right to lead a healthy life so as to enjoy all faculties of the human body in their prime condition, the respondents (hospital), by their disclosure that the appellant was HIV(+), cannot be said to have, in any way, either violated the rule of confidentiality or the right of privacy.

60

De-criminalization of consensual - same - sex acts [1]

Facts in Nutshell:

Writ petition[2] were preferred by Naz Foundation, a Non Governmental Organisation (NGO) as a Public Interest Litigation[3] to challenge the constitutional validity of Section 377 of the Indian Penal Code, 1860 (IPC)[4], which criminally penalizes what is described as "unnatural offences", to the extent the said provision criminalises consensual sexual acts between adults in private. The challenge is founded on the plea that Section 377 IPC, on account of it covering sexual acts between consenting adults in private infringes the fundamental rights guaranteed

---

1   Appellants: **Naz Foundation** vs. Respondent: **Government of NCT and Ors.**
    2010CriLJ94
    Hon'ble Judges: Ajit Prakash Shah, C.J. and S. Muralidhar, J.

2   **Meaning of Writ Petition:** Under the Indian legal system, jurisdiction to issue 'prerogative writs' is given to the Supreme Court, and to the High Courts of Judicature of all Indian states. Parts of the law relating to writs are set forth in the Constitution of India. The Supreme Court, the highest in the country, may issue writs under Article 32 of the Constitution for enforcement of Fundamental Rights and under Articles 139 for enforcement of rights other than Fundamental Rights, while High Courts, the superior courts of the States, may issue writs under Articles 226. 'Writ' is eminently designed by the makers of the Constitution, and in the same way it is developed very widely and efficiently by the courts in India. The Constitution broadly provides for five kinds of "prerogative" writs, namely, Habeas Corpus, Certiorari, Mandamus, Quo Warranto and Prohibition.

3   **Meaning of Public Interest Litigation:** In Indian law,Article 32 of the indian constitution contains a tool which directy joints the public with judiciary **public-interest litigation** is litigation for the protection of the public interest. PIL may be introduced in a court of law by the court itself (*suo motu*), rather than the aggrieved party or another third party. For the exercise of the court's jurisdiction, it is unnecessary for the victim of the violation of his or her rights to personally approach the court. In PIL, the right to file suit is given to a member of the public by the courts through judicial activism. The member of the public may be a non-governmental organization (NGO), an institution or an individual.

4   **Section 377 IPC Unnatural Offences -** Whoever voluntarily has carnal intercourse against the order of nature with any man, woman or animal, shall be punished with imprisonment for life, or with imprisonment of either description for a term which may extend to ten years, and shall also be liable to fine.
    Explanation - Penetration is sufficient to constitute the carnal intercourse necessary to the offence described in this section.

under Articles 14,[5] 15[6], 19[7] & 21[8] of the Constitution of India. Limiting their plea, the petitioners submit that Section 377 IPC should apply only to non-consensual penile non-vaginal sex and penile non- vaginal sex involving minors. The Union of India is impleaded as respondent No. 5 through Ministry of Home Affairs and Ministry of Health & Family Welfare. Respondent No. 4 is the National Aids Control Organisation (hereinafter referred to as "NACO") a body formed under the aegis of Ministry of Health & Family Welfare, Government of India. NACO is charged with formulating and implementing policies for the prevention of HIV/ AIDS in India. Respondent No. 3 is the Delhi State Aids Control Society. Respondent No. 2 is the Commissioner of Police, Delhi. Respondents No. 6 to 8 are individuals and NGOs, who were permitted to intervene on their request. The writ petition was dismissed by Court in 2004 on the ground that there is no cause of action in favour of the petitioner and that such a petition cannot be entertained to examine the academic challenge to the constitutionality of the legislation. The Supreme Court vide order

---

5   **Article 14 in The Constitution Of India 1949**
    14. Equality before law The State shall not deny to any person equality before the law or the equal protection of the laws within the territory of India Prohibition of discrimination on grounds of religion, race, caste, sex or place of birth

6   **Article 15 in The Constitution Of India 1949**
    15. Prohibition of discrimination on grounds of religion, race, caste, sex or place of birth
    (1) The State shall not discriminate against any citizen on grounds only of religion, race, caste, sex, place of birth or any of them
    (2) No citizen shall, on grounds only of religion, race, caste, sex, place of birth or any of them, be subject to any disability, liability, restriction or condition with regard to
    (a) access to shops, public restaurants, hotels and palaces of public entertainment; or
    (b) the use of wells, tanks, bathing ghats, roads and places of public resort maintained wholly or partly out of State funds or dedicated to the use of the general public
    (3) Nothing in this article shall prevent the State from making any special provision for women and children
    (4) Nothing in this article or in clause (2) of Article 29 shall prevent the State from making any special provision for the advancement of any socially and educationally backward classes of citizens or for the Scheduled Castes and the Scheduled Tribes

7   19. Protection of certain rights regarding freedom of speech etc
    (1) All citizens shall have the right
    (a) to freedom of speech and expression;
    (b) to assemble peaceably and without arms;
    (c) to form associations or unions;
    (d) to move freely throughout the territory of India;
    (e) to reside and settle in any part of the territory of India; and
    (f) omitted
    (g) to practise any profession, or to carry on any occupation, trade or business

8   **Article 21 in The Constitution Of India 1949**
    21. Protection of life and personal liberty No person shall be deprived of his life or personal liberty except according to procedure established by law

dated 03.02.2006 in Civil Appeal No. 952/2006 set aside the said order of the Court observing that the matter does require consideration and is not of a nature which could have been dismissed on the aforesaid ground. The matter was remitted to the Court for fresh decision.

History of the Legislation

The legislative history of the subject indicates that the first records of sodomy as a crime at Common Law in England were chronicled in the Fleta, 1290, and later in the Britton, 1300. Both texts prescribed that sodomites should be burnt alive. Acts of sodomy later became penalized by hanging under the Buggery Act of 1533 which was re-enacted in 1563 by Queen Elizabeth I, after which it became the charter for the subsequent criminalisation of sodomy in the British Colonies. Oral- genital sexual acts were later removed from the definition of buggery in 1817. And in 1861, the death penalty for buggery was formally abolished in England and Wales. However, sodomy or buggery remained as a crime "not to be mentioned by Christians."

Indian Penal Code was drafted by Lord Macaulay and introduced in 1861 in British India. Section 377 IPC is contained in Chapter XVI of the IPC titled "Of Offences Affecting the Human Body". Within this Chapter Section 377 IPC is categorised under the sub-chapter titled "Of Unnatural Offences" and reads as follows:

377. Unnatural Offences - Whoever voluntarily has carnal intercourse against the order of nature with any man, woman or animal, shall be punished with imprisonment for life, or with imprisonment of either description for a term which may extend to ten years, and shall also be liable to fine.

Explanation - Penetration is sufficient to constitute the carnal intercourse necessary to the offence described in this section.

Judicial Interpretation

The marginal note refers to the acts proscribed as "unnatural offences". This expression, however, is not used in the text of Section 377 IPC. The expression "carnal intercourse" is used in Section 377 IPC as distinct from the expression "sexual intercourse", which appears in Sections 375 and 497 IPC. According to the Concise Oxford Dictionary (ninth edition, 1995), the term "carnal" means "of the body or flesh;

worldly" and "sensual, sexual". Consent is no defence to an offence under Section 377 IPC and no distinction regarding age is made in the section. In *Khanu v. Emperor*[8], Kennedy A.J.C. held that "section 377 IPC punishes certain persons who have carnal intercourse against the order of nature with inter alia human beings.... [if the oral sex committed in this case is carnal intercourse], it is clearly against the order of nature, because the natural object of carnal intercourse is that there should be the possibility of conception of human beings, which in the case of coitus per os is impossible."[page 286] . In *Lohana Vasantlal Devchand v. State*,[9] the issue was whether oral sex amounted to an offence under Section 377IPC. It was held that the "orifice of the mouth is not, according to nature, meant for sexual or carnal intercourse." In *Calvin Francis v. Orissa*[10] relying on Lohana, it was held that oral sex fell within the ambit of Section 377 IPC. The Court used the references to the Corpus Juris Secundum relating to sexual perversity and abnormal sexual satisfaction as the guiding criteria. In *Fazal Rab Choudhary v. State of Bihar*[11] , it was observed that Section 377 IPC implied "sexual perversity". It is evident that the tests for attracting the penal provisions have changed from the non-procreative to imitative to sexual perversity.

The Challenge

The petitioner NGO has been working in the field of HIV/AIDS Intervention and prevention. This necessarily involves interaction with such sections of society as are vulnerable to contracting HIV/AIDS and which include gay community or individuals described as "men who have sex with men" (MSM). For sake of convenient reference, they would hereinafter be referred to as "homosexuals" or "gay" persons or gay community. Homosexuals, according to the petitioner, represent a population segment that is extremely vulnerable to HIV/AIDS infection. The petitioner claims to have been impelled to bring this litigation in public interest on the ground that HIV/AIDS prevention efforts were found to be severely impaired by discriminatory attitudes exhibited by state agencies towards gay community, MSM or trans-gendered individuals, under the cover of enforcement of Section 377 IPC, as a result of which basic fundamental human rights of such individuals/groups (in minority) stood denied and they were subjected to abuse, harassment, assault from public and public authorities.

---

9   AIR 1968 Guj 252

10 1992 (2) Crimes 455

11 1983CriLJ632

Submission on Behalf of Petitioner

According to the petitioner, Section 377 IPC is based upon traditional Judeo-Christian moral and ethical standards, which conceive of sex in purely functional terms, i.e., for the purpose of procreation only. Any non-procreative sexual activity is thus viewed as being "against the order of nature". The submission is that the legislation criminalising consensual oral and anal sex is outdated and has no place in modern society. In fact, studies of Section 377IPC jurisprudence reveal that lately it has generally been employed in cases of child sexual assault and abuse. By criminalising private, consensual same-sex conduct, Section 377 IPC serves as the weapon for police abuse; detaining and questioning, extortion, harassment, forced sex, payment of hush money; and perpetuates negative and discriminatory beliefs towards same-sex relations and sexuality minorities; which consequently drive the activities of gay men and MSM, as well as sexuality minorities underground thereby crippling HIV/AIDS prevention efforts. Section 377 IPC thus creates a class of vulnerable people that is continually victimised and directly affected by the provision. It has been submitted that the fields of psychiatry and psychology no longer treat homosexuality as a disease and regard sexual orientation to be a deeply held, core part of the identities of individuals.

The petitioner also submitted that while right to privacy is implicit in the right to life and liberty and guaranteed to the citizens, in order to be meaningful, the pursuit of happiness encompassed within the concepts of privacy, human dignity, individual autonomy and the human need for an intimate personal sphere require that privacy - dignity claim concerning private, consensual, sexual relations are also afforded protection within the ambit of the said fundamental right to life and liberty given under Article 21. It is averred that no aspect of one's life may be said to be more private or intimate than that of sexual relations, and since private, consensual, sexual relations or sexual preferences figure prominently within an individual's personality and lie easily at the core of the "private space", they are an inalienable component of the right of life. Based on this line of reasoning, a case has been made to the effect that the prohibition of certain private, consensual sexual relations (homosexual) provided by Section 377 IPC unreasonably abridges the right of privacy and dignity within the ambit of right to life and liberty under Article 21. The petitioner argues that fundamental right to privacy under Article 21 can be abridged only for a compelling state interest which, in its submission, is amiss here. Also based on the fundamental right to life under Article 21 is the further submission that Section 377 IPC has a damaging impact upon the lives of homosexuals inasmuch as it not only perpetuates social stigma and police/public abuse but also drives homosexual activity underground thereby jeopardizing HIV/AIDS prevention efforts and, thus, rendering gay men and MSM increasingly vulnerable to contracting HIV/AIDS.

Further, it has been submitted on behalf of the petitioner that Section 377 IPC's legislative objective of penalizing "unnatural sexual acts" has no rational nexus to the classification created between procreative and non- procreative sexual acts, and is thus violative of Article 14 of the Constitution of India. Section 377's legislative objective is based upon stereotypes and misunderstanding that are outmoded and enjoys no historical or logical rationale which render it arbitrary and unreasonable. It is further the case of the petitioner that the expression "sex" as used in Article 15 cannot be read restrictive to "gender" but includes "sexual orientation" and, thus read, equality on the basis of sexual orientation is implied in the said fundamental right against discrimination. The petitioner argues that criminalization of predominantly homosexual activity through Section 377 IPC is discriminatory on the basis of sexual orientation and, therefore, violative of Article 15. It is further the case of the petitioner that the prohibition against homosexuality in Section 377IPC curtails or infringes the basic freedoms guaranteed under Article 19(1)(a)(b)(c) & (d); in that, an individual's ability to make personal statement about one's sexual preferences, right of association/assembly and right to move freely so as to engage in homosexual conduct are restricted and curtailed.

Reply by Union of India- Contradictory stands of Ministry of Home Affairs and Ministry of Health & Family Welfare

A rather peculiar feature of the case is that completely contradictory affidavits[12] have been filed by two wings of Union of India. The Ministry of Home Affairs (MHA) sought to justify the retention of Section 377 IPC, whereas the Ministry of Health & Family Welfare insisted that continuance of Section 377IPC has hampered the HIV/AIDS prevention efforts.

The Director (Judicial) in the Ministry of Home Affairs, Government of India, in his affidavit, justify the retention of Section 377 IPC on the statute book broadly on the reason that it has been generally invoked in cases of allegation of child sexual abuse and for complementing lacunae

---

12 **Meaning of Affidavits:** A written declaration made under oath before a notary public or other authorized officer.

in the rape laws and not mere homosexuality. This penal clause has been used particularly in cases of assault where bodily harm is intended and/or caused. It has been submitted that the impugned provision is necessary since the deletion thereof would well open flood gates of delinquent behaviour and can possibly be misconstrued as providing unfettered licence for homosexuality.

Reference has been made to 42nd report of the Commission wherein it was observed that Indian society by and large disapproved of homosexuality, which disapproval was strong enough to justify it being treated as a criminal offence even where the adults indulge in it in private. Union of India submitted that law cannot run separately from the society since it only reflects the perception of the society. It claims that at the time of initial enactment, Section 377 IPC was responding to the values and morals of the time in the Indian society. It has been submitted that in fact in any parliamentary secular democracy, the legal conception of crime depends upon political as well as moral considerations notwithstanding considerable overlap existing between legal and safety conception of crime i.e. moral factors.

Affidavit of Narco/Ministry of Health & Family Welfare

In the reply affidavit filed on behalf of NACO, it has been submitted that the report of the Expert Group on Size Estimation of Population with High Risk Behaviour for NACPIII Planning, January 2006 estimated that there are about 25 lakh MSM (Men having sex with men). The National Sentinel Surveillance Data 2005 shows that more than 8% of the population of MSM is infected by HIV while the HIV prevalence among the general population is estimated to be lesser than 1%. Given the high vulnerability of MSM to HIV infection, NACO has developed programmes for undertaking targeted interventions among them. These projects are implemented by NGOs with financial support from NACO. Presently 1,46,397 MSM (6%) are being covered through 30 targeted interventions. Under the targeted intervention projects, the objectives are to:

a. reduce number of partners and by bringing about a change in their behaviour;

b. reduce their level of risk by informing them about and providing access to condoms;

c. providing access to STD services.

According to the submissions of NACO, those in the High Risk Group are mostly reluctant to reveal same sex behaviour due to the fear of law enforcement agencies, keeping a large section invisible and unreachable and thereby pushing the cases of infection underground making it very difficult for the public health workers to even access them. It illustrates this point by referring to the data reflected in the National Baseline Behaviour Surveillance Survey (NBBSS of 2002) which indicates that while 68.6% MSM population is aware about the methods of preventing infection, only 36% of them actually use condoms.

NACO has further submitted that enforcement of Section 377 IPC against homosexual groups renders risky sexual practices to go unnoticed and unaddressed inasmuch as the fear of harassment by law enforcement agencies leads to sex being hurried, particularly because these groups lack 'safe place', utilise public places for their indulgence and do not have the option to consider or negotiate safer sex practices. It is stated that the very hidden nature of such groups constantly inhibits/impedes interventions under the National AIDS Control Programme aimed at prevention. Thus NACO reinforces the plea raised by the petitioner for the need to have an enabling environment where the people involved in risky behaviour are encouraged not to conceal information so that they can be provided total access to the services of such preventive efforts.

Response of Other Respondents[13]

'Voices against Section 377 IPC' (hereinafter referred to as "respondent No. 8") is a coalition of 12 organisations that represent child rights, women's rights, human rights, health concerns as well as the rights of same sex desiring people including those who identify as Lesbian, Gay, Bisexual, Transgenders, Hijra and Kothi persons (which are referred to in the affidavit as "LGBT"). It has been submitted on its behalf that organisations that constitute respondent No. 8 are involved in diverse areas of public and social importance and that in the course of their work they have repeatedly come across gross violation of basic human rights of "LGBT" persons, both as a direct and indirect consequence of the enforcement of Section 377 IPC.

Respondent No. 8 supports the cause espoused by the petitioner in this

---

13 **Meaning of Respondent:** A **respondent** is a person who is called upon to issue a response to a communication made by another. In legal usage, this specifically refers to the defendant in a legal proceeding commenced by a petition, or to an appellee, or the opposing party, in an appeal of a decision by an initial fact-finder.

PIL and avers that Section 377 IPC, which criminalises 'carnal intercourse against the order of the nature', is an unconstitutional and arbitrary law based on archaic moral and religious notions of sex only for procreation. It asserts that criminalisation of adult consensual sex under Section 377 IPC does not serve any beneficial public purpose or legitimate state interest. On the contrary, according to respondent No. 8, Section 377 IPC by criminalising the aforementioned kinds of sexual acts has created an association of criminality towards people with same sex desires. It pleads that the continued existence of this provision on the statute book creates and fosters a climate of fundamental rights violations of the gay community, to the extent of bolstering their extreme social ostracism.

Reference was made to a judgment of the High Court of Madras reported as *Jayalakshmi v. The State of Tamil Nadu*[14], in which an eunuch had committed suicide due to the harassment and torture at the hands of the police officers after he had been picked up on the allegation of involvement in a case of theft. There was evidence indicating that during police custody he was subjected to torture by a wooden stick being inserted into his anus and some police personnel forcing him to have oral sex. The person in question immolated himself inside the police station on 12.6.2006 and later succumbed to burn injuries on 29.6.2006. The compensation of Rs. 5,00,000/- was awarded to the family of the victim.

Submission by Additional Solicitor General of India

Learned ASG submitted that there is no fundamental right to engage in the same sex activities. In our country, homosexuality is abhorrent and can be criminalised by imposing proportional limits on the citizens' right to privacy and equality. Learned ASG submitted that right to privacy is not absolute and can be restricted for compelling state interest. Article19(2)[15] expressly permits imposition of restrictions in the interest of decency and morality. Social and sexual mores in foreign countries cannot justify de-criminalisation of homosexuality in India. According to him, in the western societies the morality standards are not as high as in India. Learned ASG further submitted that Section 377 IPC is not

---

14 (2007)4MLJ849

15 **Article 19(2) in The Constitution Of India 1949**
   (2) Nothing in sub clause (a) of clause (1) shall affect the operation of any existing law, or prevent the State from making any law, in so far as such law imposes reasonable restrictions on the exercise of the right conferred by the said sub clause in the interests of the sovereignty and integrity of India, the security of the State, friendly relations with foreign States, public order, decency or morality or in relation to contempt of court, defamation or incitement to an offence

discriminatory as it is gender neutral. If Section 377 IPC is struck down there will be no way the State can prosecute any crime of nonconsensual carnal intercourse against the order of nature or gross male indecency.

Article 21, The Right to Life and Protection of a Person's Dignity, Autonomy and Privacy

Dignity

In *Francis Coralie Mullin v. Administrator, Union Territory of Delhi and Ors.*[16], Justice P.N. Bhagwati explained the concept of right to dignity in the following terms:

...We think that the right to life includes the right to live with human dignity and all that goes along with it, namely, the bare necessaries of life such as adequate nutrition, clothing and shelter and facilities for reading, writing and expressing oneself in diverse forms, freely moving about and mixing and commingling with fellow human beings. Every act which offends against or impairs human dignity would constitute deprivation pro tanto of this right to live and it would have to be in accordance with reasonable, fair and just procedure established by law which stands the test of other fundamental rights. [para 8 of SCC]

Privacy

Article 12 of the Universal Declaration of Human Rights (1948) refers to privacy and it states:

No one shall be subjected to arbitrary interference with his privacy, family, home or correspondence nor to attacks upon his honour and reputation. Everyone has the right to the protection of the law against such interference or attacks.

Article 17 of the International Covenant of Civil and Political Rights (to which India is a party), refers to privacy and states that:

No one shall be subjected to arbitrary or unlawful interference with his privacy, family, home and correspondence, nor to unlawful attacks on his honour and reputation.

A two-Judge Bench in *R. Rajagopal v. State of T.N.* [17], held the right to

---

16 1981CriLJ306 .

17 AIR1995SC264

privacy to be implicit in the right to life and liberty guaranteed to the citizens of India by Article 21. "It is the right to be left alone". A citizen has a right to safeguard the privacy of his own, his family, marriage, procreation, motherhood, child bearing and education among many other matters.

"Aravanis (hijras) are discriminated by the society and remain isolated" following directions were issued:

In 2006, the State of Tamil Nadu recognising that "aravanis (hijras) are discriminated by the society and remain isolated" issued directions thus:

I. Counseling be given to children who may feel different from other individuals in terms of their gender identity.

II. Family counseling by the teachers with the help of NGOs sensitized in that area should be made mandatory so that such children are not disowned by their families. The C.E.O.s, D.E.O.s, District Social Welfare Officers and Officers of Social Defence are requested to arrange compulsory counseling with the help of teachers and NGOs in the Districts wherever it is required.

III. Admission in School and Colleges should not be denied based on their sex identity. If any report is received of denying admission of aravani's suitable disciplinary action should be taken by the authorities concerned.

Law Commission's 172nd Report

In the 172nd report, the Law Commission has recommended deletion of Section 377 IPC, though in its earlier reports it had recommended the retention of the provision. In the 172nd report, the Law Commission of India, focused on the need to review the sexual offences laws in the light of increased incidents of custodial rape and crime of sexual abuse against youngsters, and inter alia, recommended deleting the Section 377 IPC by effecting the recommended amendments in Sections 375 to 376E of IPC. The Commission discussed various provisions related to sexual offences and was of considered opinion to amend provisions in the Indian Penal Code, 1860; the Code of Criminal Procedure, 1973; and Indian Evidence Act, 1872. In the Indian penal Code, recasting of 375 IPC has been recommended by redefining it under the head of 'Sexual Assault' encompassing all ranges of non consensual sexual offences/assaults, which in particular penalize not only the sexual intercourse with a woman as in accordance with the current 'Rape Laws'; but any non-consensual or non-willing penetration with bodily part or object manipulated by the another person except carried out for proper hygienic or medicinal purposes.

The recommended provision to substitute the existing Section 375 IPC reads thus:

375. Sexual Assault: Sexual assault means -

(a) penetrating the vagina (which term shall include the labia majora),

the anus or urethra of any person with -

i) any part of the body of another person or

ii) an object manipulated by another person

except where such penetration is carried out for proper hygienic or medical purposes;

(b) manipulating any part of the body of another person so as to cause penetration of the vagina (which term shall include the labia majora), the anus or the urethra of the offender by any part of the other person's body;

(c) introducing any part of the penis of a person into the mouth of another person;

(d) engaging in cunnilingus or fellatio; or

(e) continuing sexual assault as defined in clauses (a) to (d) above in circumstances falling under any of the six following descriptions:

First- Against the other person's will.

Secondly- Without the other person's consent.

Thirdly- With the other person's consent when such consent has been obtained by putting such other person or any person in whom such other person is interested, in fear of death or hurt.

Fourthly- Where the other person is a female, with her consent, when the man knows that he is not the husband of such other person and that her consent is given because she believes that the offender is another man to whom she is or believes herself to be lawfully married.

Fifthly- With the consent of the other person, when, at the time of giving such consent, by reason of unsoundness of mind or intoxication or the administration by the offender personally or through another of any stupefying or unwholesome substance, the other person is unable to understand the nature and consequences of that to which such other person gives consent.

Sixthly- With or without the other person's consent, when such other person is under sixteen years of age.

Explanation: Penetration to any extent is penetration for the purposes of this section.

Exception: Sexual intercourse by a man with his own wife, the wife not being under sixteen years of age, is not sexual assault.

Pertinently, the major thrust of the recommendation is on the word 'Person' which makes the sexual offences gender neutral unlike gender specific as under the 'Rape Laws' which is the current position in statute book. Amendments in Section 376A, 376B, 376C, 376D have been recommended on the same lines with enhanced punishments. An added explanation defining sexual intercourse is sought to be introduced governing Section 376B, 376C, 376D. Insertion of new Section 376E has been recommended to penalize non consensual, direct or indirect, intentional unlawful sexual contact with part of body or with an object, any part of body of another person. This section specifically penalizes the person committing unlawful sexual contact who is in a position of trust or authority towards a young person (below the age of sixteen years), thereby protecting children. Conclusively the Section 377 IPC in the opinion of the Commission, deserves to be deleted in the light of recommended amendments. However persons, having carnal intercourse with any animal, were to be left to their just deserts. Though the Law Commission report would not expressly say so, it is implicit in the suggested amendments that elements of "will" and "consent" will become relevant to determine if the sexual contact (homosexual for the purpose at hand) constitute an offence or not.

Whether Section 377 IPC Violates Constitutional Guarantee of Equality Under Article 14 of the Constitution

The scope, content and meaning of Article 14 of the Constitution has been the subject matter of intensive examination by the Supreme Court in a catena of decisions. The decisions lay down that though Article 14 forbids class legislation, it does not forbid reasonable classification for the purpose of legislation. In order, however, to pass the test of permissible classification, two conditions must be fulfilled, namely, (i) that the classification must be founded on an intelligible differentia which distinguishes persons or things that are grouped together from those that are left out of the group; and (ii) that the differentia must have a rational relation to the objective sought to be achieved by the statute in question. The classification may be founded on differential basis according to objects sought to be achieved but what is implicit in it is that there ought to be a nexus, i.e., causal connection between the basis of classification and object of the statute under consideration[18]. In considering reasonableness from the point of view of Article 14, the Court has also to consider the objective for such classification. If the objective be illogical, unfair and unjust, necessarily the classification will have to be held as unreasonable[19].

Section 377 IPC Targets Homosexuals as a Class

Section 377 IPC is facially neutral and it apparently targets not identities but acts, but in its operation it does end up unfairly targeting a particular community. The fact is that these sexual acts which are criminalised are associated more closely with one class of persons, namely, the homosexuals as a class. Section 377 IPC has the effect of viewing all gay men as criminals. When everything associated with homosexuality is treated as bent, queer, repugnant, the whole gay and lesbian community is marked with deviance and perversity. They are subject to extensive prejudice because what they are or what they are perceived to be, not because of what they do. The result is that a significant group of the population is, because of its sexual nonconformity, persecuted, marginalised and turned in on itself[20].

The inevitable conclusion is that the discrimination caused to MSM and gay community is unfair and unreasonable and, therefore, in breach of Article14 of the Constitution of India.

---

18 *Budhan Choudhry v. State of Bihar*, 1955CriLJ374.

19 *Deepak Sibal v. Punjab University* , [1989]1SCR689

20 [Sachs, J. in The National Coalition for Gay and Lesbian Equality v. The Minister of Justice, para 108].

Infringement of Article 15 - Whether 'Sexual Orientation' is a Ground Analogous to 'Sex'

Article 15 is an instance and particular application of the right of equality which is generally stated in Article 14. Article 14 is genus while Article 15along with Article 16[21] are species although all of them occupy same field and the doctrine of "equality" embodied in these Articles has many facets. Article15 prohibits discrimination on several enumerated grounds, which include 'sex'. The argument of the petitioner is that 'sex' in Article 15(1) must be read expansively to include a prohibition of discrimination on the ground of sexual orientation as the prohibited ground of sex- discrimination cannot be read as applying to gender simpliciter. The purpose underlying the fundamental right against sex discrimination is to prevent behaviour that treats people differently for reason of not being in conformity with generalization concerning "normal" or "natural" gender roles. Discrimination on the basis of sexual orientation is itself grounded in stereotypical judgments and generalization about the conduct of either sex. This is stated to be the legal position in International Law and comparative jurisprudence.

Court hold that sexual orientation is a ground analogous to sex and that discrimination on the basis of sexual orientation is not permitted by Article 15. Further, Article 15(2) incorporates the notion of horizontal application of rights. In other words, it even prohibits discrimination of one citizen by another in matters of access to public spaces. In courts view, discrimination on the ground of sexual orientation is impermissible even on the horizontal application of the right enshrined under Article 15."

---

21 **Article 16 in The Constitution Of India 1949**
16. Equality of opportunity in matters of public employment
(1) There shall be equality of opportunity for all citizens in matters relating to employment or appointment to any office under the State
(2) No citizen shall, on grounds only of religion, race, caste, sex, descent, place of birth, residence or any of them, be ineligible for, or discriminated against in respect or, any employment or office under the State
(3) Nothing in this article shall prevent Parliament from making any law prescribing, in regard to a class or classes of employment or appointment to an office under the Government of, or any local or other authority within, a State or Union territory, any requirement as to residence within that State or Union territory prior to such employment or appointment
(4) Nothing in this article shall prevent the State from making any provision for the reservation of appointments or posts in favor of any backward class of citizens which, in the opinion of the State, is not adequately represented in the services under the State
(5) Nothing in this article shall affect the operation of any law which provides that the incumbent of an office in connection with the affairs of any religious or denominational institution or any member of the governing body thereof shall be a person professing a particular religion or belonging to a particular denomination

Supreme Court in *Anuj Garg v. Hotel Association of India*[22] , constitutional validity of Section 30 of the Punjab Excise Act, 1914 prohibiting employment of "any man under the age of 25 years" or "any woman" in any part of such premises in which liquor or intoxicating drug is consumed by the public was challenged before the High Court of Delhi. The High Court declared Section 30 of the Act as ultra vires Articles 19(1) (g)[23], 14and 15 of the Constitution of India to the extent it prohibits employment of any woman in any part of such premises, in which liquor or intoxicating drugs are consumed by the public. National Capital Territory of Delhi accepted the said judgment but an appeal was filed by few citizens of Delhi. The appeal was ultimately dismissed by the Supreme Court, but the principles laid down by the Court relating to the scope of the right to equality enunciated in Articles 14and 15 are material for the purpose of the present case. At the outset, the Court observed that the Act in question is a pre- constitutional legislation and although it is saved in terms of Article 372 of the Constitution[24], challenge to its validity on the touchstone of Articles 14, 15 and 19 of the Constitution of India, is permissible in law. There is thus no presumption of constitutionality of a colonial legislation. Therefore, though the statute could have been held to be a valid piece of legislation keeping in view the societal condition of those times, but with the changes occurring therein both in the domestic as also international arena, such a law can also be declared invalid.

In Anuj Garg, the Court, however, clarified that the heightened review standard does not make sex a proscribed classification, "... sex classifications" may be used to compensate women "for particular economic disabilities (they have) suffered", "to promote equal employment opportunity", to advance full development of the talent and capacities of our nation's people. Such classifications may not be used, as they once were, to create or perpetuate the legal, social, and economic

---

22 AIR2008SC663

23 **Article 19(1)(g) in The Constitution Of India 1949**
(g) to practise any profession, or to carry on any occupation, trade or business

24 **Article 352 in The Constitution Of India 1949**
352. Proclamation of Emergency
(1) If the President is satisfied that a grave emergency exists whereby the security of India or of any part of the territory thereof is threatened, whether by war or external aggression or armed rebellion, he may, by Proclamation, made a declaration to that effect in respect of the whole of India or of such part of the territory thereof as may be specified in the Proclamation Explanation A Proclamation of Emergency declaring that the security of India or any part of the territory thereof is threatened by war or by external aggression or by armed rebellion may be made before the actual occurrence of war or of any such aggression or rebellion, if the President is satisfied that there is imminent danger thereof

inferiority of women."

As held in Anuj Garg, if a law discriminates on any of the prohibited grounds, it needs to be tested not merely against "reasonableness" under Article14 but be subject to "strict scrutiny". The impugned provision in Section 377 IPC criminalises the acts of sexual minorities particularly men who have sex with men and gay men. It disproportionately impacts them solely on the basis of their sexual orientation. The provision runs counter to the constitutional values and the notion of human dignity which is considered to be the cornerstone of our Constitution. Section 377 IPC in its application to sexual acts of consenting adults in privacy discriminates a section of people solely on the ground of their sexual orientation which is analogous to prohibited ground of sex. A provision of law branding one section of people as criminal based wholly on the State's moral disapproval of that class goes counter to the equality guaranteed under Articles 14 and 15 under any standard of review.

Grounds on which Act of the legislature can be held to invalid

There is one and only one ground for declaring an Act of the legislature (or a provision in the Act) to be invalid, and that is if it clearly violates some provision of the Constitution in so evident a manner as to leave no manner of doubt. This violation can, of course, be in different ways, e.g. if a State legislature makes a law which only the Parliamnet can make under List I to the Seventh Schedule, in which case it will violate Article 246(1) of the Constitution[25], or the law violates some specific provision of the Constitution (other than the directive principles). But before declaring the statute to be unconstitutional, the Court must be absolutely sure that there can be no manner of doubt that it violates a provision of the Constitution. If two views are possible, one making the statute constitutional and the other making it unconstitutional, the former view must always be preferred. Also, the Court must make every effort to uphold the constitutional validity of a statute, even if that requries giving a strained construction or narrowing down its scope [26] Also, it is none of the concern of the Court whether the legislation in its opinion is wise or unwise.

---

25 **Article 246(1) in The Constitution Of India 1949**
  (1) Notwithstanding anything in clauses (2) and (3), Parliament has exclusive power to make laws with respect to any of the matters enumerated in List I in the Seventh Schedule (in this Constitution referred to as the Union List)

26 *Mark Netto v. State of Kerala and Ors.* [1979]1SCR609

Decision of the Court

Court declared that Section 377 IPC, insofar it criminalizes consensual sexual acts of adults in private, is violative of Articles 21, 14 and 15 of the Constitution. The provisions of Section 377 IPC will continue to govern non-consensual penile non-vaginal sex and penile non-vaginal sex involving minors. By 'adult' court mean everyone who is 18 years of age and above. A person below 18 would be presumed not to be able to consent to a sexual act. This clarification will hold till, of course, Parliament chooses to amend the law to effectuate the recommendation of the Law Commission of India in its 172nd Report which court believe removes a great deal of confusion. Secondly, court clarified that there judgment will not result in the re-opening of criminal cases involving Section 377 IPC that have already attained finality.

61

Unnatural Sex[1]

Facts in Nutshell:

Petitioner[2], the Sub-Warden of the Boarding Home attached to St. Mary's Higher Secondary School Tuticorin. During the period from September, 1986 to 16th February, 1987, an impression was gaining momentum in the said School that he voluntarily had carnal intercourse against the orders of nature with the inmates of the Boarding Home.

One M. Mohan was studying in the VIX Standard in the School. He informed his brother about the perverted sexual assaults of the Sub-Warden on the inmates of the Home, inclusive of himself. His brother lodged complaint with Police.

The sexual perversion takes shape in manifold forms going by different names such as,

"SODOMY : Non coital carnal copulation with a member of the same or opposite sex, e.g., per anus or per os (mouth).

BUGGERY : Intercourse per anux by a man with a man or woman; or intercourse per anux or per vaginam by a man or a woman with an animal.

BESTIALITY : Sexual intercourse by a human being with a lower animal.

TRIBADISM : Friction of the external genital organs by one woman on another by mutual bodily contact for the gratification of the sexual desire.

SADISM : A form of sexual perversion in which the infliction of pain and torture act as sexual stimulants.

MASOCHISM : Opposite of sadism and sexual gratification is sought from

---

1 Appellants: **Brother John Antony Vs. Respondent: The State**
   1992CriLJ1352
   Hon'ble Judge: Janarthanam, J.

2 **Meaning of Petitioner:** A person who presents a Petition. (**Meaning of Petition:** A formal message requesting something that is submitted to an authority)

the desire to be beaten, tormented or humiliated by one's sexual partner.

FETICHISM : Experiencing sexual excitement leading to orgasm from some part of the body of a woman or some article belonging to her.

EXHIBITIONISM : Exposure of genital organs in Public."

Question before the Court:

The question that arises for consideration was as to whether Section 377[3], I.P.C. describing 'UNNATURAL OFFENCES' would take, in its fold and sweep and amplitude all the sexual perverse acts as catelogued above.

Section 377, IPC the Explanation appended to it consists of the following ingredients:-

"(1) A person accused of this offence had carnal intercourse with man, woman or animal;

(2) Such intercourse was against the order of nature; and

(3) Such act by the person accused of the offence was done voluntarily."

The meaning of the two words in the phraseology 'carnal intercourse' may be understood by reference to certain Dictionaries. Butterworths Medical Dictionary, Section Edition furnishes the meaning of the words, intercourse' 'coitus' and 'carnal knowledge' at pages 896, 386 and 302 respectively thus :

INTERCOURSE : Coitus, Carnal Intercourse, Sexual Intercourse, Coitus (L. Intercourse's interposition). COITUS : Sexual union Coitus, Incompletus Coitus, Interruptus Coitus in which the male organ is withdrawn from the vagina before ejaculation takes place. : Coitus Reservatus, Sexual intercourse in which the male withholds his orgasm until the female climax or as a means of contraception, or sometimes as a morbid condition associated with inability to ejaculate.

CARNAL KNOWLEDGE : Sexual connection or partial sexual connection

---

3 **Section 377 in The Indian Penal Code, 1860**

377. Unnatural offences.-- Whoever voluntarily has carnal intercourse against the order of nature with any man, woman or animal, shall be punished with 1[imprisonment for life], or with imprisonment of either description for a term which may extend to ten years, and shall also be liable to fine. Explanation.- Penetration is sufficient to constitute the carnal intercourse necessary to the offence described in this section.

with some degree of penetration."

In understanding the phraseology, 'carnal intercourse', the Explanation appended to the section assumes signal importance. According to the Explanation, penetration is sufficient to constitute the carnal intercourse necessary to the offence described in the section.

The Shorter Oxford English Dictionary, Volume IX, Third Edition at page 1464, the meaning for the words 'penetrate' and 'penetration' are given thus:

"PENETRATE: To make its (or one's) way into or through something, or to some point or place implying remoteness or difficulty of access)

In *State of Kerala v. K. Govindan* [4] the question that came up for consideration was as to whether the act of committing intercourse between the things is carnal intercourse against the order of nature. A learned Judge of Kerala High Court, who decided the case, held that committing intercourse by inserting the male organ between the thighs of another is an unnatural offence under section 377 of the Indian Penal Code. The reasoning given therein by learned Judge was that when the male organ was inserted between the thighs kept together and tight, there was penetration to constitute the unnatural offence.

In *Khandu v. Emperor* [5] Sexual intercourse per nose with a bullock is an unnatural offence within the meaning of Section 377, IPC.

If a person accused of this offence (Section 377 Unnatural Offences), voluntarily had carnal intercourse with any man, woman or animal with a little bit of penetration against the order of nature such an act would fall within the clutches of the section in committing the unnatural offence liable to be punished there under. Except the sexual perversions of sodomy, buggery and bestiality, all other sexual perversions, as catalogued above, would not fall within the sweep of this section.

Decision of the High Court:

The alleged over acts attributed to the petitioner would fall under two categories, namely, -

(1) insertion of the penis of the petitioner into the mouth of the victim boy

4   1969 CrLJ 818
5   AIR 1934 Lah 261 : (1934 (Cri LJ 1096)

and doing the act of incarnal intercourse up to the point of ejaculation of semen into the mouth; and (2) manipulation and movement of the penis of the petitioner whilst being held by the victim boys in such a way as to create an orifice like thing for making the manipulated movements of insertion and withdrawal up to the point of ejaculation of semen.

As regards the alleged act of the petitioner falling under the first category, prima facie there can be no manner of doubt whatever as to such an alleged act of his falling within the ambit of Section 377, I.P.C.

62

Second marriage during subsistence of first marriage is void[1]

Facts in Nutshell:

According to the Petitioner[2] three children (two sons and a daughter) were born out of the wed-lock. In early 1988, the petitioner was shocked to learn that her husband had solemnised second marriage. The marriage was solemnised after they converted themselves to **Islam** and adopted Muslim religion. According to the petitioner, conversion of her husband to Islam was only for the purpose of marrying other woman and circumventing the provisions of Section 494[3], IPC.

Question before the Court:

The questions for consideration was whether a Hindu husband, married under Hindu law, by embracing Islam, can solemnised second marriage? Whether such a marriage without having the first marriage dissolved under law, would be a valid marriage qua the first wife who continue to be Hindu? Whether the apostate husband would be guilty of the offence under Section 494 of the Indian Penal Code (IPC)?

---

1 Appellants: **Smt. Sarla Mudgal, President, Kalyani and others Vs.** Respondent: **Union of India and others**
   AIR1995SC1531
   Hon'ble Judges: Kuldip Singh and R.M. Sahai, JJ.

2 **Meaning of Petitioner:** A person who presents a Petition. (**Meaning of Petition:** A formal message requesting something that is submitted to an authority)

3 **Section 494 in The Indian Penal Code, 1860**
   494. Marrying again during lifetime of husband or wife.-- Whoever, having a husband or wife living, marries in any case in which such marriage is void by reason of its taking place during the life of such husband or wife, shall be punished with imprisonment of either description for a term which may extend to seven years, and shall also be liable to fine. Exception.- This section does not extend to any person whose marriage with such husband or wife has been declared void by a Court of competent jurisdiction, nor to any person who contracts a marriage during the life of a former husband or wife, if such husband or wife, at the time of the subsequent marriage, shall have been continually absent from such person for the space of seven years, and shall not have been heard of by such person as being alive within that time provided the person contracting such subsequent marriage shall, before such marriage takes place, inform the person with whom such marriage is contracted of the real state of facts so far as the same are within his or her knowledge.

Marriage:

Marriage is the very foundation of the civilised society. The relation once formed, the law steps in and binds the parties to various obligations and liabilities there under. Marriage is an institution in the maintenance of which the public at large is deeply interested. It is the foundation of the family and in turn of the society without which no civilisation can exist. Till the time we achieve the goal - uniform civil code for all the citizens of India - there is an open inducement to a Hindu husband, who wants to enter into second marriage while the first marriage is subsisting, to become a Muslim. Since monogamy[4] is the law for Hindus and the Muslim law permits as many as four wives in India, errand Hindu husband embraces Islam to circumvent the provisions of the Hindu law and to escape from penal consequences.

The doctrine of indissolubility of marriage, under the traditional Hindu law, did not recognise that conversion would have the effect of dissolving a Hindu marriage. Conversion to another religion by one or both the Hindu spouses did not dissolve the marriage. It would be useful to have a look at some of the old cases on the subject. In Re Ram Kumari[5] where a Hindu wife became convert to the Muslim faith and then married a Mohammedan, it was held that her earlier marriage with a Hindu husband was not dissolved by her conversion. She was charged and convicted of bigamy under Section 494 of the IPC. It was held that there was no authority under Hindu law for the proposition that an apostate is absolved from all civil obligations and that so far as the matrimonial bond was concerned, such view was contrary to the spirit of the Hindu law. In *Gul Mohammed v. Emperor*[6] a Hindu wife was fraudulently taken away by the accused[7] a Mohammedan who married her according to Muslim law after converting her to Islam. It was held that the conversion of the Hindu wife to Mohammedan faith did not ipso facto[8] dissolve the

---

4 **Meaning of Monogamy:**
   Monogamy is a form of marriage in which an individual has only one spouse during their lifetime or at any one time (serial monogamy), as compared to polygamy or polyamory. In current usage, monogamy often refers to having one sexual partner irrespective of marriage or reproduction.

5 1891 Cal 246

6 MANU/NA/0076/1946

7 **Meaning of Accused:** A person charged with a criminal offense, or the state of being so charged

8 **Meaning of Ipso Facto:**
   Ipso facto is a Latin phrase, directly translated as "by the fact itself," which means that a certain phenomenon is a *direct* consequence, a resultant *effect*, of the action in question, instead of being brought about by a previous action. It is a term of art used in philosophy, law, and science.

marriage and she could not during the life time of her former husband enter into a valid contract of marriage. Accordingly the accused was convicted for adultery under Section 497[9] of the IPC.

In *Nandi @ Zainab v. The Crown*[10], Nandi, the wife of the complainant, changed her religion and became a Mussalman and thereafter married a Mussalman named Rukan Din. She was charged with an offence under Section 494 of the Indian Penal Code. It was held that the mere fact of her conversion to Islam did not dissolve the marriage which could only be dissolved by a decree[11] of court. *Emperor v. Mt. Ruri*[12], was a case of Christian wife. The Christian wife renounced Christianity and embraced Islam and then married a Mahomedan. It was held that according to the Christian marriage law, which was the law applicable to the case, the first marriage was not dissolved and therefore the subsequent marriage was bigamous.

In India there has never been a matrimonial law of general application. Apart from statute law a marriage was governed by the personal law of the parties. A marriage solemnised under a particular statute and according to personal law could not be dissolved according to another personal law, simply because one of the parties had changed his or her religion.

Hindu Marriage Act, 1955

Where a marriage take place under Hindu Law the parties acquire a status and certain rights by the marriage itself under the law governing the Hindu Marriage and if one of the parties is allowed to dissolve the marriage by adopting and enforcing a new personal law, it would tantamount to destroying the existing rights of the other spouse who continues to be Hindu. Under the Hindu Personal Law as it existed prior to its codification in 1955, a Hindu marriage continued to subsist even after one of the spouses converted to Islam. There was no automatic

---

9 **Section 497 in The Indian Penal Code, 1860**
   497. Adultery.-- Whoever has sexual intercourse with a person who is and whom he knows or has reason to believe to be the wife of another man, without the consent or connivance of that man, such sexual intercourse not amounting to the offence of rape, is guilty of the offence of adultery, and shall be punished with imprisonment of either description for a term which may extend to five years, or with fine, or with both. In such case the wife shall not be punishable as an abettor.

10 ILR (1920) Lah 440

11 **Meaning of Decree:**
   1. An authoritative order having the force of law.
   2. The judgment of a court of equity, admiralty, probate, or divorce.

12 AIR (1919) Lah 389

dissolution of the marriage. The position has not changed after coming into force of the Hindu Marriage Act, 1955 (the Act) rather it has become worse for the apostate. The Act applies to Hindus by religion in any of its forms or developments. It also applied to Buddhists, Jains and Sikhs. It has no application to Muslims, Christians and Parsees.

A marriage solemnised, whether before or after the commencement of the Act, can only be dissolved by a decree of divorce on any of the grounds enumerated in Section 13[13] of the Act. One of the grounds under Section 13(1)(ii) is that "the other party has ceased to be a Hindu by conversion to another religion". A marriage performed under the Act cannot be dissolved except on the grounds available under Section 13 of the Act. In that situation parties who have solemnised the marriage under the Act remain married even when the husband embraces Islam in pursuit of other wife. A second marriage by an apostate[14] under the shelter of conversion to Islam would nevertheless be a marriage in violation of the provisions of the Act by which he would be continuing to be governed so far as his first marriage under the Act is concerned despite his conversion to Islam. The second marriage of an apostate would, therefore, be illegal marriage qua his wife who married him under the Act and continues to

---

13 **Section 13 in The Hindu Marriage Act, 1955**
   13. Divorce.
   (1) Any marriage solemnized, whether before or after the commencement of this Act, may, on a petition presented by either the
   husband or the wife, be dissolved by a decree of divorce on the ground that the other party-
   (i) [has, after the solemnization of the marriage, had voluntary, sexual intercourse with any person other than his or her spouse; or
   (ia) has, after the solemnization of the marriage, treated the petitioner with cruelty; or
   (ib) has deserted the petitioner for a continuous period of not less than two years immediately preceding the presentation of the petition; or]
   (ii) has ceased to be a Hindu by conversion to another religion; or
   (iii) [has been incurably of unsound mind, or has been suffering continuously or intermittently from mental disorder of such a kind and to such an extent that the petitioner cannot reasonably be expected to live with the respondent. Explanation.- In this clause,-
   (a) the expression" mental disorder" means mental illness, arrested or incomplete development of mind, psychopathic disorder or any other disorder or disability of mind and includes schizophrenia;
   (b) the expression" psychopathic disorder" means a persistent disorder or disability of mind (whether or not including sub- normality of intelligence) which results in abnormally aggressive or seriously irresponsible conduct on the part of the other party, and whether or not it require or is susceptible to medical treatment; or]
   (iv) has [been suffering from a virulent and incurable from of leprosy; or
   (v) has [been suffering from venereal disease in a communicable from; or
   (vi) has renounced the world by entering any religious order; or
   (vii) has not been heard of as being alive for a period of seven years or more by those persons who would naturally have heard of it, had that party been alive.

14 **Meaning of Apostate:** One who has abandoned one's religious faith, a political party, one's principles, or a cause.

be Hindu. Between the apostate and his Hindu wife the second marriage is in violation of the provisions of the Act and as such would be nonest.

Bigamy:

Section 494 Indian Penal Code is as under :-

Marrying again during lifetime of husband or wife. Whoever, having a husband or wife living, marries in any case in which such marriage is void by reason of its taking place during the life of such husband or wife, shall be punished with imprisonment of either description for a term which may extend to seven years, and shall also be liable to fine.

Decision of the Supreme Court:

Court held that the second marriage of a Hindu husband after his conversion to islam is a void[15] marriage in terms of Section 494 IPC. Second marriage of a Hindu-husband after conversion to Islam, without having his first marriage dissolved under law, would be invalid. The second marriage would be void in terms of the provisions of Section 494 IPC and the apostate-husband would be guilty of the offence under Section 494 IPC.

---

15 **Meaning of Void:** Not legally binding

63

Beauty contests not obscene under any law[1]

Facts in Nutshell:

A women Organisation called Prerana Woman's Welfare Organisation, Hyderabad proposed to hold a beauty contest called 'Miss Andhra Personality Contest' (in short, beauty contest) at Bharathi Vidya Bhavan, Hyderabad which was opposed by the other organisations by sending petitions[2] to the Hon'ble the Chief Justice of High Court, based upon which public interest litigation (PIL)[3] was registered as a taken up matter and the organisations were treated as the petitioners[4] whereas the Respondent[5] No. 1, the Commissioner of Police, Hyderabad, Respondent No.2, the Government of Andhra Pradesh and Respondent No.3 Prerana Women s Organisation, Hyderabad were called upon to answer the petitioners.

Contentions of Petitioners against Beauty Contests:

1. Beauty contests are unconstitutional as it offends Article 51A(e)[6], Article

---

1   Appellants: **Chandra Rajakumari and Anr. Vs.** Respondent: **Commissioner of Police, Hyderabad and Ors.**
    AIR1998AP302
    Hon'ble Judge: B.K. Somasekhara, J.

2   **Meaning of Petition:** A formal message requesting something that is submitted to an authority

3   **Meaning of PIL:** In Indian law,Article 32 of the indian constitution contains a tool which directy joints the public with judiciary **public-interest litigation** is litigation for the protection of the public interest. PIL may be introduced in a court of law by the court itself (*suo motu*), rather than the aggrieved party or another third party. For the exercise of the court's jurisdiction, it is unnecessary for the victim of the violation of his or her rights to personally approach the court. In PIL, the right to file suit is given to a member of the public by the courts through judicial activism. The member of the public may be a non-governmental organization (NGO), an institution or an individual.

4   **Meaning of Petitioner:** A person who presents a Petition. (**Meaning of Petition:** A formal message requesting something that is submitted to an authority)

5   **Meaning of Respondent:** A **respondent** is a person who is called upon to issue a response to a communication made by another. In legal usage, this specifically refers to the defendant in a legal proceeding commenced by a petition, or to an appellee, or the opposing party, in an appeal of a decision by an initial fact-finder.

6   **Article 51A(e) in The Constitution Of India 1949**
    51A. Fundamental duties It shall be the duty of every citizen of India (e) to promote harmony and the spirit of common brotherhood amongst all the people of India transcending religious, linguistic and regional or sectional diversities; to renounce practices derogatory to the dignity of women

21[7] and Article 14[8] of the Constitution of India in as much as repugnant to International Conventions and Covenants and the resolutions of the United Nations and Conferences on Women.

2. They are opposed to the decency, public morality and dignity of women in general and women of Indian society in particular and repugnant to Indian culture, traditions, and the social values.

3. The beauty contests are intended to exploit women for commercialisation by capitalists and the business world for enriching themselves at the cost of indecent representation of women in all forms and by all methods as they are transformed into marketable commodity.

4. They are also intended to divert the youth and the spirit of the youth in the country from their real problems of socio and economic survival and development by developed countries as against the developing countries like India

5. They are injurious to the body, the mind and the social existence of the entire womanhood and the society at large.

6. The beauty contests are discriminatory in choosing women only by vested interests in the society for personal gain and exploitation

7. The beauty contests are the means to achieve the lecherous and lustful desire of the erratic and sexual maniacs.

8. The beauty contests in any form amounts to indecent representation of women within the meaning of Section 2(c)[9] of the Indecent Representation of Women (Prohibition) Act, 1986 prohibited under

---

7　Article 21 in The Constitution Of India 1949
21. Protection of life and personal liberty No person shall be deprived of his life or personal liberty except according to procedure established by law

8　Article 14 in The Constitution Of India 1949
14. Equality before law The State shall not deny to any person equality before the law or the equal protection of the laws within the territory of India Prohibition of discrimination on grounds of religion, race, caste, sex or place of birth

9　Section 2(c) of the Indecent Representation of Women (Prohibition) Act, 1986:
'(c) "indecent representation of women" means—
(i) publication or distribution in any manner, of any material depicting women as a sexual object or which is lascivious or appeals to the prurient interests; or
(ii) depiction, publication or distribution in any manner, of the figure of a woman, her form or body or any part thereof in such a way as to have the effect of being indecent or derogatory to or denigrating women or which is likely to deprave, corrupt or injure the public morality or morals

Sections of the said Act and all its materials prohibited under Section 4[10] of the Act are illegal under the Act, they being indecent or derogatory or denigrating women or is likely to deprave, corrupt or injure the public morality or morals and as they are punishable under Section 6[11] of the said Act rigorously.

9. The beauty contests in any form outrages the modesty of a woman and amounts to an assault punishable under Section 364[12] of IPC and therefore must be taken to be prohibited in law.

10. The beauty contests in all forms called by any name violates the human rights enshrined in the Constitution of India in various forms which includes the right of a woman to live happily with dignity and decency.

---

10 **Section 4 - Prohibition of publication or sending by post of books, pamphlets, etc., containing indecent representation of women**
No person shall produce or cause to be produced, sell, letto hire, distribute, circulate or send by post any book, pamphlet, paper, slide, film, writing, drawing, painting, photograph, representation or figure which contains indecent representation of women in any form:
Provided that nothing in this section shall apply to--
(a) any book, pamphlet, paper, slide, film, writing, drawing, painting, photograph, representation or figure--
(i) the publication of which is proved to be justified as being for the public good on the ground that such book, pamphlet, paper, slide, film, writing, drawing, painting, photograph, representation or figure is in the interest of science, literature, art, or learning or other objects of general concern; or
(ii) which is kept or used bona fide for religious purposes;
(b) any representation sculptured, engraved, painted or otherwise represented on or in--
(i) any ancient monument within the meaning of the Ancient Monument and Archaeological Sites and Remains Act, 1958 (24 of 1958); or
(ii) any temple, or on any car used for the conveyance of idols, or kept or used for any religious purpose.
(c) any film in respect of which the provisions of Part II of the Cinematograph Act, 1952 (37 of 1952), will be applicable

11 **Section 6 of the Indecent Representation of Women (Prohibition) Act, 1986:**
Section 6 - Penalty
Any person who contravenes the provisions of section 3 or section 4 shall be punishable on first conviction with imprisonment of either description for a term which may extend to two years, and with fine which may extend to two thousand rupees, and in the event of a second or subsequent conviction with imprisonment for a term of not less than six months but which may extend to five years and also with a fine not less than ten thousand rupees but which may extend to one lakh rupees

12 **Section 364 in The Indian Penal Code, 1860**
364. Kidnapping or abducting in order to murder.-- Whoever kidnaps or abducts any person in order that such person may be murdered or may be so disposed of as to be put in danger of being murdered, shall be punished with 1[imprisonment for life] or rigorous imprisonment for a term which may extend to ten years, and shall also be liable to fine. Illustrations
(a) A kidnaps Z from 2[India], intending or knowing it to be likely that Z may be sacrificed to an idol. A has committed the offence defined in this section.
(b) A forcibly carries or entices B away from his home in order that B may be murdered. A has committed the offence defined in this section.

Beauty:

That beauty is part of the whole universal expression as understood by one and all. That beauty is the sense or the essence of human comprehension and pleasure is beyond doubt. It is the joy for ever in the acclaimed poetic declaration in literature. That beauty is the best dimension of nature or divine is also a concluded theological postulation The Indian or even Sanatana or ancient Dharmic or religious thinking also mounts beauty into one of the three forms of God viz., (Sathyam (truth), Shivam (good) and Sundaram (beauty). Possibly, no section of human society should be opposed to beauty nor it is opposed. Beauty means "a combination of qualities such as shape, colour etc., that pleases the aesthetic senses especially site, a combination of qualities that pleases the intellect of moral sense (the beauty of the argument), an excellent specimen, an attractive feature, an advantage a beautiful woman"[13] and "combination of qualities that give pleasure to the senses (especially eye, ear or to the mind)", "quality that is pleasing to the eye"[14], and "the qualities in a person or thing that give pleasure to the senses or pleasurably exhaled the mind or spirit, loveliness, a beautiful person or thing, especially a beautiful woman, excellent quality[15].

Woman:

A woman both in the eye of law and the society is not merely a person either in the gender or the existence. She has an inherent personality since birth called 'womanhood'. A woman is the mother first before having any other status. The age factor is not determinative of the status or the existence of womanhood. A woman is defined in Section 10[16] of the Indian Penal Code denoting female gender of any age. A woman is possessed of a great born virtue called 'modesty', to mean 'womanly propriety of behaviour, scrupulous chastity of thought, speech and conduct (in men or women) reserve or sense of shame proceeding from instinctive aversion to impure or coarse suggestions."

---

13 (P.96 L.C. of the Concise Oxford Dictionary New Edition)

14 (P.32, RC. Webster's Dictionary-New Revised and expanded Edition)

15 (P.42, L.C., the Penguin English Dictionary Reprint 1992).

16 **Section 10 in The Indian Penal Code, 1860**
10. " Man"." Woman".-- The word" man" denotes a male human being of any age; the word" woman" denotes a female human being of any age.

Obscenity:

In *Ranjit D. Udeshi v. State of Maharashtra,*[17] the meaning of obscenity was described as follows :

"..... that where obscenity and art are mixed, art must so preponderate as to throw the obscenity into a shadow or the obscenity so trivial and insignificant that it can have no effect and may be overlooked. In other words, treating with sex in a manner offensive to public decency and morality (and these are the words of our Fundamental Law), judged of by our national standards and considered likely to pander to lascivious, prurient or sexually precocious minds, must determine the result. We need not attempt to bowdlerise all literate and thus rob speech and expression of freedom. A balance should be maintained between freedom of speech and expression and public decency and morality but when the latter is substantially transgressed the former must give way."

The test of obscenity is adopted from the expressions of Cockburn, C.J., in Hicklin's case as-

"I think the test of obscenity is thus, whether the tendency of the matter charged as obscenity is to deprave and corrupt those whose minds are open to such immoral influences and into whose hands publication of this sort may fall. It is quite certain that it would suggest to the minds of the young of either sex, or even to persons of more advanced years, thought of most impure and libidinous character."

The Indecent Representation of Women (Prohibition) Act, 1986

Indecent representation of women is defined in Section 2(c) of the Act to be repeated herein:

"2. (c) ' 'indecent representation of women'' means the depiction in any manner of the figure of a woman, her form or body or any part thereof in such a way as to have the effect of being indecent, or derogatory to, or denigrating, women, or is likely to deprave, corrupt or injure the public morality or morals."

If beauty contests depicts a woman in figure, body or part so as to have the effect of being indecent etc., as above, they should amount to indecent representation of women.

---

17 1965CriLJ8

Decision of the High Court:

Court held that the beauty contest in any form in its true sense of the term can be neither obscene nor prohibited under any law as long as it is intended for the welfare of women in all respects and it is intended only as a form of art and entertainment and in a way a sport to select the winners on comparative merit, but if it indecently represents any woman by depicting in any manner the figure of a woman, form, body or any part thereof in such a way so as to have the effect of being indecent, or derogatory to or denigrating women or is likely to deprave, corrupt or injure the public morality or morals within the meaning of Section 2(c) of the Indecent Representation of Women (Prohibition) Act, 1986. It offends Article 14, 21 and 51A of the Constitution of India and the international covenants accepted by the UNO in addition to violation of human rights as is understood both under the Constitution and any law relating to protection of human rights and punishable as per law in such cases. It also amounts to public immorality and repugnant and to public opinion offending the dignity of woman and womanhood as a whole and depraves the woman society in particular so as to exploit either for commercialisation or for lust. It is also obscene in its true sense of the term as long as it does not conform to the decencies and the moralities as is understood in the Indian society.

64

Pregnancies and Abortion[1]

Facts in Nutshell:

Petitioner[2] in High Court prayed for issue of a direction to the Superintendent, Government Kasthuri Bhai Gandhi Hospital, Triplicane Madras, to terminate the pregnancy of his daughter . Thus, he prays for a direction to put an end to a life in the womb of his daughter on the ground that she was still in her teens and teenage pregnancy will lead to many complications physically, physiologically, mentally and socially. The petitioner's daughter left the house stating that she was going to the temple, but did not return home. On enquiries, the petitioner came to know that the first respondent[3] had kidnapped her for the purpose of marrying her and gave a complaint in Police Station under Section 366-A[4] of the Indian Penal Code. When the petitioner went to the first respondent's house, he was prevented from seeing his daughter. Hence, he was obliged to move the Court for issue of a habeas corpus[5].

Decision of Division bench of High Court:

The Division Bench of the High Court passed an order that Sasikala (Daughter of Petitioner) is a minor, her date of birth being 20.11.1977

---

1   Appellants: **V. Krishnan Vs.** Respondent: **G. Rajan alias Madipu Rajan and The Inspector of Police (Law and Order)**
   1994WritLR91
   Hon'ble Judges: Srinivasan and Abdul Hadi, JJ.

2   **Meaning of Petitioner:** A person who presents a Petition. (**Meaning of Petition:** A formal message requesting something that is submitted to an authority)

3   **Meaning of Respondent:** A **respondent** is a person who is called upon to issue a response to a communication made by another. In legal usage, this specifically refers to the defendant in a legal proceeding commenced by a petition, or to an appellee, or the opposing party, in an appeal of a decision by an initial fact-finder.

4   **SECTION 366A: Procuration of Minor Girl**
   Whoever, by any means whatsoever, induces any minor girl under the age of eighteen years to go from any place or to do any act with intent that such girl may be, or knowing that it is likely that she will be, forced or seduced to illicit intercourse with another person shall be punishable with imprisonment which may extend to ten years, and shall also be liable to fine.

5   **Meaning of Habeas Corpus:** A writ of *habeas corpus* is a writ (legal action) that requires a person under arrest to be brought before a judge or into court. The principle of habeas corpus ensures that a prisoner can be released from unlawful detention—that is, detention lacking sufficient cause or evidence.

and as she is not willing to go with her father, (the petitioner) she should be kept in Avvai Home at Adyar till she attains majority. The petitioner undertook to bear the expenses during her stay at Awai Home. The Bench made it clear that during her stay at Awai Home, the petitioner may be permitted to see his daughter during regular visiting hours; but neither the first respondent nor his parents shall be permitted to see the girl.

During visits to the Home where her daughter was kept Petitioner (Father) was shocked to learn that his daughter has become pregnant. After referring to the provision in Section 3[6] of the Medical Termination of Pregnancy Act, the petitioner stated as follows:-" My daughter is only **16 years** (Minor) and continuance of pregnancy may endanger her life and health because of anticipated complicated of Teenage Pregnancy. She was illegally made pregnant and her delivery of child may lead to many complications physically, physiology mentally and socially. According to medical expert a woman can safely deliver a child only after twenty one years of age. My daughter life would be ruined if the pregnancy is not terminated."

---

6   Section 3 in The Medical Termination Of Pregnancy Act, 1971

3. When pregnancies may be terminated by registered medical practitioners.

(1) Notwithstanding anything contained in the Indian Penal Code, (45 of 1860) a registered medical practitioner shall not be guilty of any offence under that Code or under any other law for the time being in force, if any pregnancy is terminated by him in accordance with the provisions of this Act.

(2) Subject to the provisions of sub- section (4), a pregnancy may be terminated by a registered medical practitioner,-

(a) where the length of the pregnancy does not exceed twelve weeks, if such medical practitioner is, or

(b) where the length of the pregnancy exceeds twelve weeks but does not exceed twenty weeks, if not less than two registerd medical practitioners are of opinion, formed in good faith, that-

(i) the continuance of the pregnancy would involve a risk to the life of the pregnant woman or of grave injury to her physical or mental health; or

(ii) there is a substantial risk that if the child were born, it would suffer from such physical or mental abnormalities as to be seriously handicapped. Explanation I.- Where any pregnancy is alleged by the pregnant woman to have been caused by rape, the angwish caused by such pregnancy shall be presumed to constitute a grave injury to the mental health of the pregnant woman. Explanation II.- Where any pregnancy occurs as a result of failure of any device or method used by any married woman or her husband for the purpose of limiting the number of children, the anguish caused by such unwanted pregnancy may be presumed to constitute a grave injury to the mental health of the pregnant woman.

(3) In determining whether the continuance of a pregnancy would involve such risk of injury to the health as is mentioned in sub- section (2), account may be taken of the pregnant woman' s actual or reasonably foreseeable environment.

(4) (a) No pregnancy of a woman, who has not attained the age of eighteen years, or, who, having attained the age of eighteen years, is a lunatic, shall be terminated except with the consent in writing of her guardian.

(b) Save as otherwise provided in clause (a), no pregnancy shall be terminated except with the consent of the pregnant woman.

Question before the Court:

The question was whether the guardian of a minor girl is entitled to an order from the Court directing the termination of the pregnancy of his ward when the pregnant girl is not agreeable for such termination.

Medical Opinion on Teenage Pregnancies and Abortion:

Teenage pregnancies are generally discouraged in view of the fact that in many a girl the cervix could not have grown fully and properly and deliveries may have to be caused by caesarean operations. But, even to-day, normal deliveries are recorded in the case of several teenage girls. As per the Medical History, the youngest mother in the world delivered a child in Lema, Peru, in May 1939 and her age at that time was 5 years 8 months. But, once a pregnancy has come into existence, the question is whether the same should be terminated because the pregnant girl is in her teens. N. Jeffcoate in "Principles of Gynaecology", 5th Edition, says that "Termination of pregnancy, therapeutic or legal, is always potentially dangerous". (Page 630). It is also the opinion of the Medical Experts that termination of first pregnancy would result in sterility and the woman concerned may not have any pregnancy thereafter.

The Religious Viewpoint

A. Christianity

The Catholic Church has always denounced and opposed abortion. It has consistently defended the right of the unborn to live. The belief is that human life comes from God at the time of conception and that man is only the custodian of his life rather than the owner and abortion represents an act that denies the sanctity of life on the assumption that the woman is the owner of her life and that of her unborn child.

B. Islam

In Syed Abdul A'la Maududi's "Birth Control", the following passage is found at pages 82 and 83:-

"The Holy Qur'an lays down a fundamental principle that effecting change in the scheme of God (Khalq-Allah) is a fiendish act. (Al-Qur-an, 4: 119.) Changing 'God's scheme and creation signifies misuse of a thing, its utilisation for a purpose other than the one for which it was intended, or to use it in a manner that its real purpose is defeated. In the light of this fundamental principle let us see as to what is "God's scheme" in the marital relationship of man and woman, i.e., what is the real natural purpose of this relationship and whether birth control changes it in the other direction. The Qur'an is not silent on this point. It has, on the one hand, forbidden sexual relations outside marriage, and on the other, laid bare the objective which matrimonial relationship between men and women are to serve. These objectives are (a) procreation and (b) fostering of love and affection and promoting culture and civilization. The Qur'an says:

"Your wives are a tilth for you, so go into your tilth as you like and do good beforehand for yourselves."

This verse expounds the first objectives of marriage. The other one is referred to in the following verse: "And one of His signs is that he created mates for you from yourselves that you may find consolation in them and He ordained between you love and compassion."

In the first verse by describing woman as a tilth an important biological fact has been pointed out. Biologically man is tiller and woman a tilth and the foremost purpose of the inter-relationship between the two is the procreation of human race. This is an objective which is common to all human beings, animals, and the world of vegetation. The tiller of the soil cultivates the land not in vain, but for the produce. Take away this purpose, and the entire pursuit becomes meaningless. Through the parable of the tilth this important fact has been stressed by the Qur'an."

At pages 99 and 100, it is said:-

"Medical opinion is almost unanimous in asserting that abortion is highly dangerous for the general health of a woman and her nervous system. Dr. Fredrick J. Taussig who has so succinctly summed up the expert medical opinion on the subject:

"When pregnancy is prematurely interrupted by what we term abortion, the human race suffers loss and damage in 3 ways:

First an infinite number of potential human beings are destroyed before their birth.

Secondly, abortion carries with it a considerable death rate among expectant mothers.

And finally, abortion leaves in its wake a high incidence of pathologic conditions some of which interfere with the further possibility of reproduction."

C. Hinduism

Abortion or killing of foetus has always been considered to be a sin and prohibited as such. The person who causes abortion is described as "Bhrunaha "and the killing of foetus is described as Bhrunahatih. References in Atharvana Vedha show that abortion was known in the Vedic age. Abortion was always considered to be a sin for which, however, expiation ceremonies were prescribed in Taittinyapanishad and also in Arunam. Manu in his Dharma Sastra said that a killer of a priest or destroyer of an embryo casts his guilt on the willing eater of his provisions.[7] Kautilya's Arthasastra provides for the highest punishment for causing abortion by physical assault. It refers to Yajnavalkya and Manu as well as Vishnupurana. Lesser punishments are also provided for inducing miscarriage by drugs.

Indian Law on Abortion:

In India causing abortion has been an offence far ever. The Indian Penal Code uses the expression miscarriage and deals with it in Section 312 to 318. Section 312 reads:

"Whoever voluntarily causes a woman with child to miscarry, shall, if such marriage is not caused in good faith for the purpose of saving the life of the woman, be punished with imprisonment of either description for a term which may extend to three years, or with fine, or with both; and, if the woman be quick with child, shall be punished with imprisonment of either description for a term which may extend to seven years, and shall also be liable to fine.

Explanation: A woman who causes herself to miscarry, is within the meaning of this section."

Thus, the only exception is that caused in good faith for the purpose of saving the life of the woman. Under the section, the consent of the pregnant woman is immaterial as she is also liable to be punished.

---

7 (Chapter VIII Verse 317)

In *Sushil Kumar Verma v. Usha*[8], a single Judge of the Delhi High Court held that the wife's aborting foetus in her first pregnancy without the consent of the husband would amount to cruelty within the meaning of Section 13(1)(ia)[9] of the Hindu Marriage Act (25 of 1955). That is a case in which the Court took the view that the *wife is not entitled to terminate her pregnancy without the consent of her husband.*

Decision of the High Court:

Court dismissed Petitioner (Father) Petition[10] for termination of Pregnancy of her Daughter.

---

8   AIR 1987 Del 86

9   **Section 13 in The Hindu Marriage Act, 1955**
    13. Divorce.
    (1) Any marriage solemnized, whether before or after the commencement of this Act, may, on a petition presented by either the
    husband or the wife, be dissolved by a decree of divorce on the ground that the other party-
    (i) [has, after the solemnization of the marriage, had voluntary, sexual intercourse with any person other than his or her spouse; or
    (ia) has, after the solemnization of the marriage, treated the petitioner with cruelty; or
    (ib) has deserted the petitioner for a continuous period of not less than two years immediately preceding the presentation of the petition; or]
    (ii) has ceased to be a Hindu by conversion to another religion

10 **Meaning of Petition:** A formal message requesting something that is submitted to an authority.

65

Mentally retarded women and Abortion[1]

Facts in Nutshell:

A Division Bench of the High Court of Punjab and Haryana ruled that it was in the best interests of a mentally retarded woman to undergo an abortion. The said woman (name withheld, hereinafter 'victim') had become pregnant as a result of an alleged **rape** that took place while she was an inmate at a government-run welfare institution located in Chandigarh. After the discovery of her pregnancy, the Chandigarh Administration (Respondent), approached the High Court seeking approval for the termination of her pregnancy, keeping in mind that in addition to being mentally retarded she was also an orphan who did not have any parent or guardian to look after her or her prospective child. The High Court directed the termination of the pregnancy in spite of the Expert Body's findings which showed that the victim had expressed her willingness to bear a child. Aggrieved by orders, the appellants[2] moved Supreme Court.

Section 3 of the Medical Termination of Pregnancy Act, 1971 [Hereinafter also referred to as 'MTP Act'] which reads as follows:

Section 3. When pregnancies may be terminated by registered medical practitioners.- (1) Notwithstanding anything contained in the Indian Penal Code [45 of 1860], a registered medical practitioner shall not be guilty of any offence under that Code or under any other law for the time being in force, if any, pregnancy is terminated by him in accordance with the provisions of this Act.

---

1 Appellants: **Suchita Srivastava and Anr. Vs.** Respondent: **Chandigarh Administration** AIR2010SC235
   Hon'ble Judges: K. G. Balakrishnan, C.J., P. Sathasivam and B. S. Chauhan, JJ.

2 **Meaning of Appellant:** A person who, dissatisfied with the judgment rendered in a lawsuit decided in a lower court or the findings from a proceeding before an Administrative Agency, asks a superior court to review the decision.

(2) Subject to the provisions of Sub-section (4), a pregnancy may be terminated by a registered medical practitioner:

(a) where the length of the pregnancy does not exceed twelve weeks, if such medical practitioner is, or

(b) where the length of the pregnancy exceeds twelve weeks but does not exceed twenty weeks, if not less than two registered medical practitioners are, of opinion, formed in good faith, that -

(i)the continuance of the pregnancy would involve a risk to the life of the pregnant woman or of grave injury to her physical or mental health; or

(ii)there is a substantial risk that if the child were born, it would suffer from such physical or mental abnormalities as to be seriously handicapped.

Explanation 1. - Where any pregnancy is alleged by the pregnant woman to have been caused by rape, the anguish caused by such pregnancy shall be presumed to constitute a grave injury to the mental health of the pregnant woman.

Explanation 2. - Where any pregnancy occurs as a result of failure of any device or method used by any married woman or her husband for the purpose of limiting the number of children, the anguish caused by such unwanted pregnancy may be presumed to constitute a grave injury to the mental health of the pregnant woman.

(3) In determining whether the continuance of a pregnancy would involve such risk of injury to the health as is mentioned in Sub-section (2), account may be taken of the pregnant woman's actual or reasonable foreseeable environment.

(4) (a) No pregnancy of a woman who has not attained the age of eighteen years, or, who, having attained the age of eighteen years, is a mentally ill person, shall be terminated except with the consent in writing of her guardian.

(b) Save as otherwise provided in Clause (a), no pregnancy shall be terminated except with the consent of the pregnant woman.

A plain reading of the above-quoted provision makes it clear that Indian law allows for abortion only if the specified conditions are met. When the MTP Act was first enacted in 1971 it was largely modelled on the Abortion

Act of 1967 which had been passed in the United Kingdom. The legislative intent was to provide a qualified 'right to abortion' and the termination of pregnancy has never been recognised as a normal recourse for expecting mothers. There is no doubt that a woman's right to make reproductive choices is also a dimension of 'personal liberty' as understood under Article 21[3] of the Constitution of India. It is important to recognise that reproductive choices can be exercised to procreate as well as to abstain from procreating. The crucial consideration is that a woman's right to privacy, dignity and bodily integrity should be respected. This means that there should be no restriction whatsoever on the exercise of reproductive choices such as a woman's right to refuse participation in sexual activity or alternatively the insistence on use of contraceptive methods. Furthermore, women are also free to choose birth-control methods such as undergoing sterilisation procedures. Taken to their logical conclusion, reproductive rights include a woman's entitlement to carry a pregnancy to its full term, to give birth and to subsequently raise children. However, in the case of pregnant women there is also a 'compelling state interest' in protecting the life of the prospective child. Therefore, the termination of a pregnancy is only permitted when the conditions specified in the applicable statute have been fulfilled. Hence, the provisions of the MTP Act, 1971 can also be viewed as reasonable restrictions that have been placed on the exercise of reproductive choices.

A perusal of the above mentioned provision makes it clear that ordinarily a pregnancy can be terminated only when a medical practitioner is satisfied that a 'continuance of the pregnancy would involve a risk to the life of the pregnant woman or of grave injury to her physical or mental health' [as per Section 3(2)(i)] or when 'there is a substantial risk that if the child were born, it would suffer from such physical or mental abnormalities as to be seriously handicapped' [as per Section 3(2)(ii)]. While the satisfaction of one medical practitioner is required for terminating a pregnancy within twelve weeks of the gestation period, two medical practitioners must be satisfied about either of these grounds in order to terminate a pregnancy between twelve to twenty weeks of the gestation period. The explanations to this provision have also contemplated the termination of pregnancy when the same is the result of a rape or a failure of birth-control methods since both of these eventualities have been equated with a 'grave injury to the mental health' of a woman. In all such circumstances, the consent

---

3   Article 21 in The Constitution Of India 1949
    21. Protection of life and personal liberty No person shall be deprived of his life or personal liberty
    except according to procedure established by law

of the pregnant woman is an essential requirement for proceeding with the termination of pregnancy. This position has been unambiguously stated in Section 3(4)(b) of the MTP Act, 1971. The exceptions to this rule of consent have been laid down in Section 3(4)(a) of the Act. Section 3(4)(a) lays down that when the pregnant woman is below eighteen years of age or is a 'mentally ill' person, the pregnancy can be terminated if the guardian of the pregnant woman gives consent for the same. The only other exception is found in Section 5(1) of the MTP Act which permits a registered medical practitioner to proceed with a termination of pregnancy when he/she is of an opinion formed in good faith that the same is 'immediately necessary to save the life of the pregnant woman'.

Principles contained in the *United Nations Declaration on the Rights of Mentally Retarded Persons, 1971*[4] which have been reproduced below:

1. The mentally retarded person has, to the maximum degree of feasibility, the same rights as other human beings.

2. The mentally retarded person has a right to proper medical care and physical therapy and to such education, training, rehabilitation and guidance as will enable him to develop his ability and maximum potential.

3. The mentally retarded person has a right to economic security and to a decent standard of living. He has a right to perform productive work or to engage in any other meaningful occupation to the fullest possible extent of his capabilities.

4. Whenever possible, the mentally retarded person should live with his own family or with foster parents and participate in different forms of community life. The family with which he lives should receive assistance. If care in an institution becomes necessary, it should be provided in surroundings and other circumstances as close as possible to those of normal life.

5. The mentally retarded person has a right to a qualified guardian when this is required to protect his personal well-being and interests.

6. The mentally retarded person has a right to protection from exploitation, abuse and degrading treatment. If prosecuted for any offence, he shall have a right to due process of law with full recognition being given to his degree of mental responsibility.

---

4   [G.A. Res. 2856 (XXVI) of 20 December, 1971]

7. Whenever mentally retarded persons are unable, because of the severity of their handicap, to exercise all their rights in a meaningful way or it should become necessary to restrict or deny some or all of these rights, the procedure used for that restriction or denial of rights must contain proper legal safeguards against every form of abuse. This procedure must be based on an evaluation of the social capability of the mentally retarded person by qualified experts and must be subject to periodic review and to the right of appeal to higher authorities.

Decision of the Supreme Court:

Court held that the victim's pregnancy cannot be terminated without her consent. The language of the MTP Act clearly respects the personal autonomy of mentally retarded persons who are above the age of majority. Proceeding with an abortion at such a late stage (19-20 weeks of gestation period) poses significant risks to the physical health of the victim.

66

Medical Examination and Right to Privacy[1]

Ratio Decidendi[2]: *"Wife to undergo medical examination, at the time of Divorce will not be in violation of the right to privacy and personal liberty."*

Facts in Nutshell:

The wife filed Petition[3] in Senior Civil Judges Court praying for dissolution of marriage on the grounds of husband being of unsound mind and sexually impotent and also made several elaborate allegations. The husband, who was the respondent[4] denied those allegations. A specific stand was taken by husband in counter that she (wife) had some trouble in connection with her uterus even before the marriage and in the said context, she cannot conceive and beget children and she was treated in England and finally various attempts to use the sperm of respondent proved futile in view of the condition of her uterus.

Decision of the Senior Civil Judge:

The learned Judge ultimately dismissed the said application filed by Wife for divorce. Aggrieved by the same, the civil revision petition was preferred in High Court.

Dispute between Husband and Wife: Potency

In *G. Venkatanarayana v. Kurupati Laxmi Devi*[5] , the learned Judge of High Court, Justice Rama Rao, observed at Para 6 as hereunder:

---

1   Appellants: **Padala Kaniki Reddy Vs.** Respondent: **Padala Sridevi**
    2006(5)ALD322
    Hon'ble Judges: P.S. Narayana, J.

2   **Meaning of Ration Decidendi:** *Ratio decidendi* is a Latin phrase meaning "the reason" or "the rationale for the decision." The *ratio decidendi* is "the point in a case which determines the judgment" or "the principle which the case establishes."

3   **Meaning of Petition:** A formal message requesting something that is submitted to an authority

4   **Meaning of Respondent:** A **respondent** is a person who is called upon to issue a response to a communication made by another. In legal usage, this specifically refers to the defendant in a legal proceeding commenced by a petition, or to an appellee, or the opposing party, in an appeal of a decision by an initial fact-finder.

5   AIR1985AP1

The human body is the most ancient apparatus and defied probe and vulnerability to diagnosis and treatment of ailments for long time. The human intellect generated by the human body unraveled the mysteries and complications in the human body and the process of experimentation for several years, dissection of anatomy scientific analysis and modern scientific approach contributed to discovery of diverse methods of diagnosis of deficiencies and aliments and treatment of the same. There is a gradual change over from oral diagnosis and treatment to discovery of deficiencies precisely by scientific data and effective and expeditious treatment by prescription of medicines and surgery. The transplantation of heart and other parts of the body, scanning the body to detect deficiencies and malfunctioning, invasive diagnosis and treatment yielded dividends of minimizing wear and tear of the body and thereby improving the longevity and quality of life though the avoidance of final exist is not in sight. The close affinity between law and medicine is demonstrated by medical jurisprudence. The physician as an expert witness has become a common and welcome feature in Courts ranging from opinions on nature and degree of injuries to the proximate cause of death in criminal cases, assessment of insanity and several other situations.

When there is a dispute between the wife and husband about the potency of either of them their evidence reflected by truth constitutes the cream of evidence and the marshalling of adventitious or extraneous circumstances afford a poor substitute. In the event of diametrically opposite and rival versions of the parties the recourse to medical test resolves the riddle and the medical opinion assumes the acceptable piece of evidence. In the present atmosphere of looking forward to progeny of artificial insemination, scientific probe by virginity tests and the knowledge of pre-delivery sex the depreciation of the importance of determination of potency by medical test does not bear the impress of realistic approach.

In *Revamma v. Santhappa*[6], while dealing with an application for issuance of a direction to the wife to be examined by the doctor in relation to impotency, it was held by the learned Judge Justice Datar as hereunder:

In a case where a party alleges that a person is impotent or suffering from other such incurable disease, it is for the person making such an allegation to prove the same. A party cannot be compelled to undergo medical examination.

---

6   AIR 1972 Mys. 157 : 1972 (1) MP LJ 136

In *Smt. Ningamma v. Chikkaiah*[7] , Justice Hari Nath Tilhari, observed that to compel a person to undergo or to submit himself or herself to medical examination of his or her blood test or the like without his consent or against his wish tantamount to interference with his fundamental right of life or liberty particularly even where there is no provision either in the Code of Civil Procedure or the Evidence Act or any other law which may be said to authorize the Court to compel a person to undergo such a medical test as blood group test or the like against his wish, and to create doubt about the chastity of a woman or create doubt about the man's paternity will amount to nothing but interference with the right of personal liberty.

In three Judge Bench of the Apex Court in *Sharda v. Dharmpal*[8], Justice S.B. Sinha speaking for the Court while summing up observed at Para 81 as hereunder:

1. A matrimonial Court has the power to order a person to undergo medical test.

2. Passing of such an order by the Court would not be in violation of the right to personal liberty under Article 21[9] of the Indian Constitution.

3. However, the Court should exercise such a power if the applicant has a strong prima facie case and there is sufficient material before the Court. If despite the order of the Court, the respondent refuses to submit himself to medical examination, the Court will be entitled to draw an adverse inference against him.

Decision of the High Court:

Court directed wife to submit to the medical examination as she filed for divorce petition in court and alleged that her husband was impotent . The wife had prayed in the Court by filing Petition for dissolution of marriage on certain grounds (Sexual impotency). However, for some reasons, the wife had not chosen to file any application (to undergo a medical test for potency), but the husband had chosen to do so. Therefore, court directed wife to undergo medical examination.

---

7 AIR2000Kant50

8 [2003]3SCR106

9 **Article 21 in The Constitution Of India 1949**
   21. Protection of life and personal liberty No person shall be deprived of his life or personal liberty except according to procedure established by law

67

Two-finger test violates victim's privacy and dignity[1]

Facts in Nutshell:

Criminal appeal[2] was preferred against the judgment passed by the High Court of Punjab & Haryana at Chandigarh by way of which the High Court has affirmed the judgment by the Additional Sessions Judge, Jind by way of which the Appellant[3] No. 1 was convicted[4] Under Section 376[5] of the Indian Penal Code, 1860 (hereinafter referred to as

---

1   Appellants: **Lillu @ Rajesh and Anr. Vs.** Respondent: **State of Haryana**
    2013(6)SCALE17
    Hon'ble Judges/Coram: B.S. Chauhan and Fakkir Mohamed Ibrahim Kalifulla, JJ.

2   **Meaning of Appeal:** In law, an **appeal** is a process for requesting a formal change to an official decision. Very broadly speaking there are appeals on the record and *de novo* appeals. In *de novo* appeals, a new decision maker re-hears the case without any reference to the prior decision maker. In appeals on the record, the decision of the prior decision maker is challenged by arguing that he or she misapplied the law, came to an incorrect factual finding, acted in excess of his jurisdiction, abused his powers, was biased, considered evidence which he should not have considered or failed to consider evidence that he should have considered.

3   **Meaning of Appellant:** A person who, dissatisfied with the judgment rendered in a lawsuit decided in a lower court or the findings from a proceeding before an Administrative Agency, asks a superior court to review the decision.

4   **Meaning of Convicted:** Someone guilty of an offense or crime, especially by the verdict of a court

5   **Section 376 in The Indian Penal Code, 1860**
    376. Punishment for rape.--
    (1) Whoever, except in the cases provided for by sub- section (2), commits rape shall be punished with imprisonment of either description for a term which shall not be less than seven years but which may be for life or for a term which may extend to ten years and shall also be liable to fine unless the woman raped is his own wife and is not under twelve years of age, in which case, he shall be punished with imprisonment of either description for a term which may extend to two years or with fine or with both:
    Provided that the court may, for adequate and special reasons to be mentioned in the judgment, impose a sentence of imprisonment for a term of less than seven years.
    (2) Whoever,-
    (a) being a police officer commits rape-
    (i) within the limits of the police station to which he is appointed; or
    (ii) in the premises of any station house whether or not situated in the police station to which he is appointed; or
    (iii) on a woman in his custody or in the custody of a police officer subordinate to him; or
    (b) being a public servant, takes advantage of his official position and commits rape on a woman

'Indian Penal Code') and awarded the sentence of seven years rigorous imprisonment with a fine of Rs. 5,000/- and in default of making payment, to further undergo imprisonment for two years. Further he has been convicted Under Section 506[6] Indian Penal Code and awarded the sentence of two years rigorous imprisonment. Both the sentences have been directed to run concurrently. The other co-accused[7], namely, Manoj, Satish @ Sitta and Kuldeep have been convicted separately Under Sections 376, 506, 366[8] and 363[9] Indian Penal Code. Kuldeep Singh alone

---

in his custody as such public servant or in the custody of a public servant subordinate to him; or
(c) being on the management or on the staff of a jail, remand home or other place of custody established by or under any law for the time being in force or of a women' s or children' s institution takes advantage of his official position and commits rape on any inmate of such jail, remand home, place or institution; or
(d) being on the management or on the staff of a hospital, takes advantage of his official position and commits rape on a woman in that hospital; or
(e) commits rape on a woman knowing her to be pregnant; or
(f) commits rape on a woman when she is under twelve years of age; or
(g) commits gang rape, shall be punished with rigorous imprisonment for a term which shall not be less than ten years but which may be for life and shall also be liable to fine: Provided that the court may, for adequate and special reasons to be mentioned in the judgment, impose a sentence of imprisonment of either description for a term of less than ten years. Explanation 1.- Where a women' s is raped by one or more in a group of persons acting in furtherance of their common intention, each of the persons shall be deemed to have committed gang rape within the meaning of this sub- section. Explanation 2.-" women' s or children' s institution" means an institution, whether called and orphanage or a home for neglected women or children or a widows' home or by any other name, which is established and maintained for the reception and care of women or children. Explanation 3.-" hospital" means the precincts of the hospital and includes the precincts of any institution for the reception and treatment of persons during convalescence or of persons requiring medical attention or rehabilitation.

6 **Section 506 in The Indian Penal Code, 1860**
506. Punishment for criminal intimidation.-- Whoever commits the offence of criminal intimidation shall be punished with imprisonment of either description for a term which may extend to two years, or with fine, or with both; If threat be to cause death or grievous hurt, etc. If threat be to cause death or grievous hurt, etc.-- and if the threat be to cause death or grievous hurt, or to cause the destruction of any property by fire, or to cause an offence punishable with death or 3[imprisonment for life], of with imprisonment for a term which may extend to seven years, or to impute unchastity to a woman, shall be punished with imprisonment of either description for a term which may extend to seven years, or with fine, or with both.

7 **Meaning of Accused:** A person charged with a criminal offense, or the state of being so charged

8 **SECTION 366: Kidnapping Abducting or Inducing Woman to Compel her Marriage, etc**
Whoever kidnaps or abducts any woman with intent that she may be compelled, or knowing it to be likely that she will be compelled, to marry any person against her will, or in order that she may be forced or seduced to illicit intercourse, or knowing it to be likely that she will be forced or seduced to illicit intercourse, shall be punished with
imprisonment of either description for a term which may extend to ten years, shall also be liable to fine and whoever, by means of criminal intimidation as defined in this Code or of abuse of authority or any method of compulsion, induces any woman to go from any place with intent that she may be, or knowing that it is likely that she will be , forced or seduced illicit intercourse with another person shall be punishable as aforesaid.

9 **Section 363 in The Indian Penal Code, 1860**

has been found guilty Under Section 376(2)(g)[10] Indian Penal Code, and has been awarded sentence of life imprisonment. Out of these four convicts, Kuldeep Singh and Manoj did not prefer any appeal against the High Court's judgment, while Appellant Nos. 1 i.e. Lillu @ Rajesh preferred the appeal.

Contentions of Learned Counsel for Appellant:

Learned Counsel for the Appellant, submitted that the prosecution[11] failed to prove the date of birth of the prosecutrix[12] and that she was about 17-18 years of age on the date of incident. Thus, it was a clear cut case of *consent.* The possibility of prosecutrix being habitual to sexual intercourse could not be ruled out accord.

Two Finger Test (Case Laws Referred):

In *Narayanamma (Kum) v. State of Karnataka and Ors.*[13] , Court held that fact of admission of two fingers and the hymen rupture does not give a clear indication that prosecutrix is habitual to sexual intercourse. The doctor has to opine as to whether the hymen stood ruptured much earlier or carried an old tear. The factum of admission of two fingers could not be held adverse to the prosecutrix, as it would also depend upon the size of the fingers inserted. The doctor must give his clear opinion as to whether it was painful and bleeding on touch, for the reason that such

---

363. Punishment for kidnapping.-- Whoever kidnaps any person from 1[India] or from lawful guardianship, shall be punished with imprisonment of either description for a term which may extend to seven years, and shall also be liable to fine.

10 **Section 376 in The Indian Penal Code, 1860**
376. Punishment for rape.--
(g) commits gang rape, shall be punished with rigorous imprisonment for a term which shall not be less than ten years but which may be for life and shall also be liable to fine: Provided that the court may, for adequate and special reasons to be mentioned in the judgment, impose a sentence of imprisonment of either description for a term of less than ten years. Explanation 1.- Where a women' s is raped by one or more in a group of persons acting in furtherance of their common intention, each of the persons shall be deemed to have committed gang rape within the meaning of this sub- section. Explanation 2.-" women' s or children' s institution" means an institution, whether called and orphanage or a home for neglected women or children or a widows' home or by any other name, which is established and maintained for the reception and care of women or children. Explanation 3.-" hospital" means the precincts of the hospital and includes the precincts of any institution for the reception and treatment of persons during convalescence or of persons requiring medical attention or rehabilitation.

11 **Meaning of Prosecution:**
a. the institution and carrying on of legal proceedings against a person.
b. the officials who institute and conduct such proceedings.

12 **Meaning of Prosecutrix:** A female prosecutor.

13 (1994) 5 SCC 728

conditions obviously relate to the hymen.

Court while dealing with the issue in *State of Uttar Pradesh v. Munshi[14]*, has expressed its anguish and held that even if the victim of rape was previously accustomed to sexual intercourse, it cannot be the determinative question. On the contrary, the question still remains as to whether the accused committed rape on the victim on the occasion complained of. *Even if the victim had lost her virginity earlier, it can certainly not give a licence to any person to rape her.* It is the accused who was on trial and not the victim. So as to whether the victim is of a promiscuous character is totally an irrelevant issue altogether in a case of rape. Even a woman of easy virtue has a right to refuse to submit herself to sexual intercourse to anyone and everyone, because she is not a vulnerable object or prey for being sexually assaulted by anyone and everyone. A prosecutrix stands on a higher pedestal than an injured witness for the reason that an injured witness gets the injury on the physical form, while the prosecutrix suffers psychologically and emotionally.

In *Narender Kumar v. State (NCT of Delhi)[15]* , Court dealt with a case where the allegation was that the victim of rape herself was an unchaste woman, and a woman of easy virtue. The court held that so far as the prosecutrix is concerned, mere statement of prosecutrix herself is enough to record a conviction[16], when her evidence is read in its totality and found to be worth reliance. The incident in itself causes a great distress and humiliation to the victim though, undoubtedly a false allegation of rape can cause equal distress, humiliation and damage to the accused as well.

Rape is a Crime against Human Rights:

In *State of Punjab v. Ramdev Singh[17]* , Court held that rape is violative of victim's fundamental right under Article 21[18] of the Constitution. So, the courts should deal with such cases sternly and severely. Sexual violence, apart from being a dehumanizing act, is an unlawful intrusion on the right

14 AIR 2009 SC 370

15 AIR 2012 SC 2281

16 **Meaning of Conviction:** In law, a **conviction** is the verdict that results when a court of law finds a defendant guilty of a crime.

17 AIR 2004 SC 1290

18 **Article 21 in The Constitution Of India 1949**
21. Protection of life and personal liberty No person shall be deprived of his life or personal liberty except according to procedure established by law

of privacy and sanctity of a woman. It is a serious blow to her supreme honour and offends her self-esteem and dignity as well. It degrades and humiliates the victim and where the victim is a helpless innocent child or a minor, it leaves behind a traumatic experience. A rapist not only causes physical injuries, but leaves behind a scar on the most cherished position of a woman, i.e. her dignity, honour, reputation and chastity. Rape is not only an offence against the person of a woman, rather a crime against the entire society. It is a crime against basic human rights and also violates the most cherished fundamental right guaranteed under Article 21 of the Constitution.

Right of Rape Survivors

In view of International Covenant on Economic, Social, and Cultural Rights 1966; United Nations Declaration of Basic Principles of Justice for Victims of Crime and Abuse of Power 1985, rape survivors are entitled to legal recourse that does not retraumatize them or violate their physical or mental integrity and dignity. They are also entitled to medical procedures conducted in a manner that respects their right to consent. *Medical procedures should not be carried out in a manner that constitutes cruel, inhuman, or degrading treatment and health should be of paramount consideration while dealing with gender-based violence.* The State is under an obligation to make such services available to survivors of sexual violence. Proper measures should be taken to ensure their safety and there should be no arbitrary or unlawful interference with his privacy.

Decision of the Supreme Court:

Court held that undoubtedly the two finger test and its interpretation violates the right of rape survivors to privacy, physical and mental integrity and dignity. Thus two finger test even if the report is affirmative, cannot ipso facto[19] be given rise to presumption of consent. Court dismissed the appeal.

---

19 **Meaning of Ipso Facto:** By the fact itself; by that very fact

Glossary of Common Legal Terms

Advocate

A person authorized to appear in a litigation on behalf of a party. An advocate possesses a law degree and is enrolled with a Bar Council, as prescribed by the Advocates Act, 1961. Advocates are the only class of persons legally entitled to practise law. They provide legal advice. After being authorized to appear in a case by a client who has signed a vakalat, advocates prepare cases and argue them in Court. In the Bombay and Calcutta High Courts there is a separate class of legal practitioners, known as solicitors, who prepare the case, but do not argue in Court. When appearing in a courtroom, an advocate usually dresses in black and white, and wears a band and gown. Any complaint against an advocate is made to the Bar Council of India. See junior advocate, advocate-on-record, senior advocate, amicus curiae, vakalath.

Advocate-on-record (AOR)

An advocate who has passed a qualifying examination conducted by the Supreme Court. The examination is taken by an advocate who has been enrolled with a Bar Council for at least five years and has completed one year''s training with an AOR of not less than five years standing. Only an AOR can file a vakalath, a petition, an affidavit or any other application on behalf of a party in the Supreme Court. All the procedural aspects of a case are dealt with by the AOR, with the assistance of a registered clerk. It is the AOR''s name that appears on the cause list. The AOR is held accountable, by the Court, for the conduct of the case. Any notices and correspondence from the Court are sent to the AOR, and not to the party.

Advocate's fees

There are no standardized fees charged for the various tasks performed by an advocate. Some advocates charge a lump sum amount for dealing with an entire case, others charge separate fees for each task - e.g., drafting, filing, legal advice, arguing. Senior advocates generally charge a separate fee for every hearing. In the majority of PIL cases, these fees have been waived by the advocates. When appearing on behalf of a legal aid committee, an advocate receives expenses and nominal fees, at no cost to the party. In some PIL cases the Court has awarded costs to the party.

Affidavit

This is a sworn statement made by a party, in writing, made in the presence of an oath commissioner or a notary public which is used either in support of applications to the Court or as evidence in court proceedings. In writ jurisdiction, cases are generally disposed of on the basis of affidavits. An affidavit in reply to a petition, filed by a respondent, is called a counter affidavit. The petitioner's response to this counter, is called a rejoinder affidavit. All affidavits are verified as to the truth of their contents.

Amicus curiae

Translated from the Latin as 'friend of the Court'. An advocate appears in this capacity when asked to help with the case by the Court or on volunteering services to the Court.

Appeal

The correctness of the decision of a lower court or tribunal is questioned by way of an appeal in a higher court.

Cognizable offence

An offence in which arrest can be made without a warrant.

Commission

A commission is appointed by a court to ascertain or investigate facts needed to decide a case. A commission is usually given specific terms of reference. Members of a commission have been chosen from amongst experts, academics, social activists/workers, advocates, judges and others. Costs of the commission are usually borne by the State. Such commissions have often been appointed in PILs.

Court Fees

These are mandatory charges payable by affixing judicial stamps on petitions, applications and various kinds of documents before they are filed in a court. It is only in legal aid matters that the petitioners are exempt from paying these fees.

Court Master

An officer of the court who occupies a seat just below the judges' dias and assists in the conduct of proceedings.

Decree

The formal expression of an adjudication which, so far as regards the Court expressing it, conclusively determines the rights of the parties with regard to all or any of the matters in controversy in the suit and may be either preliminary or final.

Decree –holder

A person in whose favour a decree has been passed or an order capable of execution has been made.

High Court

Article 214 of the Constitution provides that each state shall have a High Court. This is the highest court in a state and is subordinate only to the Supreme Court of India. The powers of the High Court are broadly categorized as judicial and administrative. In its judicial function the High Court can be approached directly (eg. writ petitions), or in appeals or revisions—both civil and criminal. In its administrative function the High Court supervises the functioning of the lower judiciary in the State. In the civil side, in an ascending order of hierarchy, is the Civil Judge (Junior Division), Civil Judge (Senior Division), the Additional District Judge and the District Judge; the criminal side includes Metropolitan Magistrates, Chief Metropolitan Magistrates, Additional Sessions Judges and the Sessions Judge. The powers of a High Court do not extend beyond the territory of the State. While every decision of the Supreme Court is binding on the High Courts, the decisions of one High Court is not binding on the other. The High Court is a court of record.

Judgment

The final order of a court in a case which, while giving reasons, conclusively decides the rights of parties in the case, resolves the dispute and grants reliefs. See bench, order.

Judgment-debtor

Any person against whom a decree has been passed or an order capable of execution has been made.

Judicial Review

A term that describes the function of the judiciary being able to examine and correct the actions of all the organs of State—the executive, the legislature and the judiciary itself. Judicial review is part of the basic structure of the Indian Constitution.

Junior Advocate

Any advocate who wants to practise law, enrols with a Bar Council and generally begins work in the office of a practising advocate.

Jurisdiction

This indicates the scope and extent of a court's powers. For instance, a court only has territorial jurisdiction within the territory over which its powers extend. Jurisdiction is also used to describe the nature of the proceedings in the Court, for example: civil original jurisdiction, criminal appellate jurisdiction. A court's decision can always be challenged on the ground that while deciding a case it has exceeded its jurisdiction, i.e. powers, or that it has exercised a jurisdiction it does not possess.

Legal Aid

A system by which legal services are rendered at government cost to those in financial need and who cannot afford the cost of litigation. This is mandated by Article 39A of the Constitution. In Delhi, the Delhi High Court Legal Services Committee (DHCLSC) and the Delhi Legal Services Authority (DLSA) provide legal aid on behalf of the State.

Legal Representative

A person who in law represents the estate of a deceased person, and includes any person who intermeddles with the estate of the deceased and where a party sues or is sued in a representative character the person on whom the estate devolves on the death of the party so suing or sued

Locus Standi

Translated from Latin as 'place of standing', locus standi gives the right to pursue a litigation. Under this rule, only a person or group of persons affected by the issue may petition the Court. A petition may be dismissed on the preliminary ground that the petitioner lacks locus standi. However, in PIL, the locus standi of public spirited persons to petition on behalf of others has been recognized. This relaxation of the rule of standing is an important feature of PIL—for instance, journalists, lawyers, politicians, social activists, students, or any 'concerned individual' not acting for personal interest or gain, and not as a 'busy body', have been given standing.

Mesne-profits

Those profits which the person in wrongful possession of such property actually received or might with ordinary diligence have received therefrom, together with interest on such profits, but shall not include profits due to improvements made by the person in wrongful possession.

Notification

Notice, information or announcement published in the official gazette notifying, for instance, the coming into effect of a changed law.

Obiter dicta

Remarks of a judge, which are said by the way and are not directly relevant to the case at hand.

Ratio decidendi

The reason behind or crux of a judicial decision.

Res Judicata

A legal principle which prevents a party to a case which has been finally decided from bringing an action on the same issue. For example, a case is barred by res judicata if an earlier case between the same parties has decided upon the same points. This is embodied in Section 11 of the Code of Civil Procedure, 1908.

Respondent

A party against whom a petition is filed. A proforma respondent is a party against whom no relief is sought.

Review

A court has the power to review its orders on specified grounds, as provided by law. Generally the same court which passed the order or judgement in a case reviews its decision. There is, however, no inherent power in a court to review its decisions. The power has to be given by statute or be found in the Constitution.

Revision

Orders that cannot be appealed against can be revised by the High Court on specific grounds, as provided in S 115 of the Code of Civil Procedure, 1908 and Ss. 397 and 401 of the Code of Criminal Procedure, 1973.

Supreme Court

The highest court in the country constituted under Article 124 of the Constitution. Its decisions are law under Article 141 and are binding on all lower courts. It has unlimited powers to do complete justice. It exercises original as well as appellate jurisdiction. Under Article 143 the President of India can ask the Supreme Court for an opinion on questions of law or fact. States can file suits against each other or against the Union of India under Article 131. The Supreme Court can transfer cases to itself from the High Courts or from one High Court to another under Article 139A of the Constitution. It can also transfer civil cases from one Court to another under S 25 of the Code of Civil Procedure, 1908, and likewise criminal cases under S 406 of the Code of Criminal Procedure, 1973. Apart from special leave petitions, in certain instances, appeals can be filed directly against the judgments of lower courts and tribunals. Petitions challenging the election of the President or Vice-President of India are also filed directly in the Supreme Court. The chairperson of a public service commission may be removed only after an inquiry by the Supreme Court. The Supreme Court has a sanctioned strength of 31 judges, headed by the Chief Justice of India. The seat of the Supreme Court is New Delhi and its language is English.

Void

One that law regards as never having taken place.

Writ

A writ is a direction that the Court issues, which is to be obeyed by the authority/person to whom it is issued.

Writ Petition

A petition seeking issuance of a writ is a writ petition. Pits in the first instance in the High Courts and the Supreme Court are writ petitions. A writ of habeas corpus is issued to an authority or person to produce in court a person who is either missing or kept in illegal custody. Where the detention is found to be without authority of law, the Court may order compensation to the person illegally detained. A writ of mandamus is a direction to an authority to either do or refrain from doing a particular act. For instance, a writ to the Pollution Control Board to strictly enforce the Pollution Control Acts. For a mandamus to be issued, it must be shown:

a) That the authority was under obligation, statutory or otherwise to act in a particular manner;

b) that the said authority failed in performing such obligation;

c) that such failure has resulted in some specific violation of a fundamental right of either the petitioner or an indeterminate class of persons.

A writ of certiorari is a direction to an authority to produce before the Court the records on the basis of which a decision under challenge in the writ petition has been taken. By looking into those records, the Court will examine whether the authority applied its mind to the relevant materials before it took the decision. If the Court finds that no reasonable person could come to the decision in question, it will set aside (quash) that decision and give a further direction to the authority to consider the matter afresh. For instance, the permission given by an authority to operate a distillery next to a school can be challenged by filing a petition asking for a writ of certiorari.

A writ of prohibition issues to prevent a judicial authority subordinate to the High Court from exercising jurisdiction over a matter pending before it. This could be on the ground that the authority lacks jurisdiction and further that prejudice would be caused if the authority proceeds to decide the matter. Where the authority is found to be biased and refuses to rescue, a writ of prohibition may issue.

A petition seeking a writ of quo warranto questions the legal basis and authority of a person appointed to public office. For instance, the appointment of a member of a Public Service Commission not qualified to hold the post can be questioned by a writ of quo warranto and appointment nullified if found to be illegal.

A writ of declaration issues to declare an executive, legislative or quasi- judicial act to be invalid in law. For instance, a court could declare S. 81 of the Mental Health Act, 1987 that permits use of mentally ill patients for experimentation to be violative of the fundamental rights of the mentally ill and therefore illegal and void. A petition seeking such declaratory relief must also necessarily seek certain consequential reliefs. For instance, immediate discontinuance of the illegal practice and appropriate remedial compensation.

These apart, a writ petition could seek other writs, orders and directions which the Court may fashion in response to the facts placed before it.

You cannot strengthen the weak
by weakening the strong.

You cannot help small men
by tearing down big men.

You cannot help the poor
by destroying the rich.

You cannot lift the wage earner
by pulling down the wage-payer.

You cannot keep out of trouble
by spending more than your income.

You cannot further the brotherhood
of man by inciting class hatreds.

You cannot build character and
courage by taking away a man's
initiative and independence.

You cannot help men permanently
by doing for them what they could
and should do for themselves.

- **Abraham Lincoln**

www.ingramcontent.com/pod-product-compliance
Lightning Source LLC
Chambersburg PA
CBHW021356210326
41599CB00011B/895